Value Management

To Jacqui and Jing

Value Management

Translating Aspirations into Performance

ROGER H. DAVIES

and

ADAM J. DAVIES

GOWER

© Impact Dynamics Limited 2011

Published by
Gower Publishing Limited
Wey Court East
Union Road
Farnham
Surrey
GU9 7PT
England

Gower Publishing Company
Suite 420
101 Cherry Street
Burlington
VT 05401-4405
USA

www.gowerpublishing.com

British Library Cataloguing in Publication Data
Davies, Roger.
  Value management : translating aspirations into performance.
  1. Value analysis (Cost control) 2. Industrial management.
  I. Title II. Davies, Adam J.
  658.1'552–dc22

Library of Congress Cataloging-in-Publication Data
Davies, Roger H.
  Value management : translating aspirations into performance / Roger H. Davies and Adam J. Davies.
       p. cm.
  Includes bibliographical references and index.
  ISBN 978-1-4094-0955-7 (hbk. : alk. paper) – ISBN 978-1-4094-0956-4 (ebook)
  1. Management – Great Britain. 2. Organizational change – Great Britain. 3. Value.
4. Human services – Great Britain. 5. Public-private sector cooperation – Great Britain.
I. Davies, Adam J. II. Title.

  HD70.G7D38 2011
  658–dc22
                                                                                      2011016174
9781409409557 (hbk)
9781409409564 (ebk)

Printed and bound in Great Britain by the
MPG Books Group, UK

Contents

PART III   PROCESS

APPENDICES: PRECISION – ADVANCED TECHNIQUES AND TOOLS

List of Figures

List of Tables

About the Authors

Roger H. Davies is a Chartered Engineer who began his career in manufacturing, initially working on robotic automation for Lesney and product design at ESSO before joining Plessey, where he took a leading role in applying three, at that time, revolutionary advances, Activity-Based Costing, IDEF0 process modelling and computer simulation. Subsequently, Roger grew the concept of Value Management into a key proposition within an international Management Consultancy, and in 2002, he founded Impact Dynamics Limited, which is dedicated to business performance transformation.

Adam J. Davies has worked for Impact Dynamics over seven years, training in Value Management while following a Degree in Business Management and American Studies at Winchester University, in which he graduated with first class honours. During this time, Adam developed his interest in value creation through self-learning and specialist training in stock trading, subsequently moving to Melbourne Australia in order to complete a Masters in Applied Finance at the Monash University Business School. Adam also worked on developing Impact Dynamics' suite of Value Management toolsets.

Reviews for Value Management

'Before applying the Value Management *approach, we had tried measuring performance indicators but we didn't run our business by them because we weren't convinced we had the key ones. Conversely, the causal approach, in particular dynamics modeling, enabled us to define the most critical drivers of value against which we are now confident we are measuring the right things – the things that really influence the outcomes we want and reflected in our business transformation programme.'*

Tim Kidd, Operations Director, JANET (UK)

'The book is a great read but, more importantly, conducting *Value Management in practice within Logica has been a good business decision and certainly has improved our ability to justify investments and manage the returns.'*

Roel Wolfert, Global Head of Strategy & Marketing Financial Services, Logica

'What an amazingly clear way, Roger has, of bringing to together a wealth of tangentially related concepts into a consistent and focused "whole" that is easy to go out and implement. Read this book if you have a sense there must be a better way to improve the process you manage, but can't get the practical way to pull it together from reading all the standard management literature. I first met Roger Davies over thirty years ago when he was lapping up some really rather new ideas being offered by the consulting firm I represented. Even then he had a way of re-formulating what we were doing in a way that drove significant value from our ideas even before the paint was dry.'

Mark Elder, CEO SIMUL8 Corporation

'It is well understood that business success should not be left to chance. Most large organisations are bought into the ideas of Business Intelligence, in that they can analyse large quantities of data to build a picture of customer behaviour, however many are less au fait with understanding what drives that behaviour from a business dynamics perspective. In this book, Roger Davies not only clarifies the benefits of dynamic business modelling, he also explains in clear terms how to bring the two sets of techniques together, always with one eye on the financial drivers that underpin any organisation. This book is a must-read for any business strategist looking to achieve higher levels of value in their own organisation.'

Jon Collins, Founder, Inter Orbis

'This book provides new insights and practical application for Systems Theory and Dynamics Modelling in tackling some of the most important challenges in today's complex business environment.'

Joanne Egner, Managing Director, isee systems, inc.

'A very informative read covering a complex but critical subject with significant implications for the modern economy. Having applied this Value Management approach across the Financial Services Sector, I consider that a particularly powerful aspect is the ability to map and quantify revenue benefits. By focusing on business value, competitive advantage can be gleaned from risk management and even regulatory compliance, rather that treating them simply as inescapable cost burdens.'

Anita Bradshaw, Lead Consultant, Crowe Horwath Global Risk Consulting Ltd

'This book takes PMO best practices a step further by leveraging the proven V-model, used for critical process validation, and applying it to the financial planning and control functions of programme management. This is an essential read for anyone responsible for delivering benefit and value from change projects.'

Andy Jagger, Managing Director, Systems Ability Limited

'This book adds value to the field of performance management by including Dynamics Modelling and Business Intelligence in the context of value generation. It certainly makes a welcome change from some of the more academic offerings.'

Lee Jones Managing Director, Ventana Systems UK Limited

'The Value Management approach provides a clear and robust framework for assessing the business viability of the key investment decisions that organisations need to make to implement successful business change. I have used this approach successfully in a wide variety of key clients to help shape successful change programmes focused on delivery of business outcomes. Application of the techniques described in this book will elevate business case practice from administrative burden to a pragmatic and useful management toolset focused on genuine delivery of great outcomes.'

Martin Prior, Management Consultant, Logica

'The authors have managed to bring logic, insight and practical application together; it's very compelling and an asset for modern leaders of complex change, regardless of industry.'

Diahann Williams, Head of Human Resources,
Global Supply Chain Service Centre, BAT

Foreword by Tim Marshall

JANET (UK) manages and develops 'JANET', one of the world's leading research and education networks, providing services across the United Kingdom to the research, education and cultural communities. The network serves some 18 million users across the UK.

JANET (UK) has been recognised for innovation, operational efficiency and private–public integration. The company provides products and services to levels demanded by our academic and research customers, key players driving the UK's knowledge economy. To ensure continued quality JANET (UK) is undertaking a major programme to grow this innovative capability whilst also driving down the cost of delivery significantly. The company aims to combine the best of public and private sectors by partnering with private service providers, specifically to provide services not currently available from the commercial commodity market.

When I was appointed CEO in 2005, there were several major challenges facing JANET (UK), the response to which demanded a fundamental shift in the company's business model and ethos. A major factor which drove the need for change concerned future funding. The existing model provided top-sliced funds through the Joint Information Systems Committee (JISC), a body representing key customers. However, it was clear even before the turmoil in the financial sector that this centralised funding model was at risk due to changes to higher education funding. In future, JANET (UK) will need to maintain its differentiated service competitively in order to attract more of the institutional discretionary spending.

To accomplish this we identified five related work streams to incorporate into the JANET (UK) Transformation Programme:

1. Centralised service delivery: move from a regional to a centralised operation, providing improved service whilst also capturing economies of scale
2. Customer engagement: building on our greatest brand strength, trust, by proactively engaging with our customers to build the trusted relationships
3. Product portfolio: develop our product portfolio both to satisfy customer needs and provide demonstrable value for money
4. Commercial culture: develop increased customer focus in our people through greater commercial acuity
5. Management culture: deliver on promises through clear accountability

We also recognised the imperative to measure our performance in relation to meaningful objectives. We tried measuring various performance indicators, but were not convinced we had the key ones.

We were then presented with a different approach to performance management, from Logica and Impact Dynamics. This identified the cause and effect relationships that truly drove value for our stakeholders: these were then incorporated into a dynamics model which captured the uniqueness of our business. Key Performance Indicators (KPIs) were then defined and incorporated into a strategic Balanced Scorecard and subsequently cascaded into operational scorecards throughout the business. This gave us confidence that we were now measuring the factors that really influence the outcomes we want and which are clearly aligned to achieving our vision.

I am pleased to support the writing of this book, which offers the purpose, principles and advanced aspects behind the Value Management approach to performance management, together with practical application of the process through a case study outlining the development of our own business.

Tim Marshall
CEO JANET (UK)

Foreword by Lode Snykers

These continue to be demanding times for financial institutions. The dramatic market shocks of 2007–2008 have inevitably led to both governments and customers questioning what the financial institutions do for them. Regulators have moved to impose greater capital requirements, further reporting, and in some cases radical restructuring on banks, while customers' and the wider public's trust in banks has been dramatically undermined. So the new world demands more capital, more lending, and less risk while imposing major compliance and restructuring programmes. How can we help generate long term value for our clients against this backdrop?

Logica firmly believes that the route to sustainable profitability lies in innovation and partnership. This belief finds expression in our work with Roger Davies over many years, using his relentless focus on the measurable generation of value. Working with him has helped us work collaboratively with our clients to bring a clear understanding of how complex change programmes can establish and maintain focus on the end game. How will the business deliver value in the future from what we are doing and deciding today? His incessant demand is that we concentrate not only on complicated functional outputs, always a tendency for hard pressed programme managers, but also focus on the simple but elusive ultimate financial outcomes for the business. This is a discipline that can too often be overlooked in the heat of our day to day work, yet highlights the value that programmes deliver.

This book is not simply an academic study. We have gained clear advantage through the use of the tools and techniques Roger describes so lucidly in this book. The strength of ideas he describes here help us to build strong consensus with clients on how we will create value with them. We have then translated these ideas into clearly quantified, measurable and sustainable changes to business performance. That makes for a winning combination for our hard pressed finance sector clients.

Lode Snykers
Global Head of Financial Services, Logica

Preface

This book brings together a diverse set of subjects, concepts, techniques and tools and we owe it both to the reader and the many thinkers, on whose knowledge we have drawn, to explain how these are woven together into a coherent framework. The subject areas are shown as a mind map in Figure I.1 and are outlined in this section. The source references are listed in the Bibliography, which is subdivided to be consistent with Figure I.1. It is important to stress that the Value Management approach described in this book was not derived as an academic exercise but through evolutionary development spanning over 30 years of practical application.

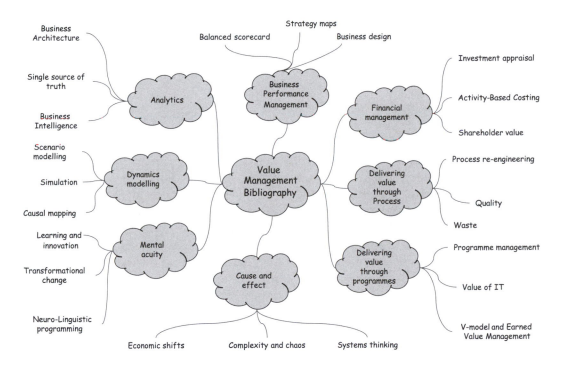

Figure I.1 Bibliography outline

Business Performance Management

Value Management is primarily concerned with delivering stakeholder outcomes, that is benefits, resulting from improvements in business performance through change programmes, which relate equally to major capital investments and *business as usual* operations. The leading business performance framework that has emerged over the last 20 years is the Balanced Scorecard, created by Robert Kaplan and David Norton of Harvard University (Kaplan and Norton 1996). The great advance instituted by the Balanced Scorecard was to broaden performance measures from a purely financial focus to other key stakeholder perspectives such as customers, staff and suppliers. From its inception, the creators stressed the need to build a scorecard around strategic objectives, together with alignment of, and causal linkage between, measures across perspectives in order to maximise value. These imperatives led to a profound innovation, the strategy map, comprising chains, called themes, of objectives linked causally to stakeholder outcomes. Although some distinctions between public organisations and private enterprises are necessary, the Balanced Scorecard is applicable across all sectors.

In order for a strategy to be effective, it is crucial to define the fundamental mechanism through which a business creates value – the business model. In its simplest form, a business model is defined by the value chain, the sequence of key activities which create and deliver value. Value Management draws on the work of Adrian Slywotzky and David Morrison (Slywotzky and Morrison 1997), who proposed reversing the traditional value chain from capability focus to customer-centric, and identified around 20 business designs which display distinct 'profit patterns'. Combined with other key thinking on business strategy, these archetypal business designs are a powerful aid in defining the objectives and strategic themes in a strategy map. Repeating patterns are used to shape, direct and implement action throughout Value Management.

Financial Management

Whilst recognising that not everything can be measured in monetary terms, Value Management operates on the strict premise that all outcomes can and must be related to the cost of achieving them. The relationship between outcomes and cost is *value*. For commercial enterprises operating in efficient markets, customers impose adherence to this relationship through competition, which is reflected in the profit and loss account. For the public sector we have to apply more tricky value for money measures, but in a world of finite resources the financial focus remains every bit as critical.

Financial business cases are central to Value Management and investment appraisal is a key skill in building them. There are three concepts related to achieving financial robustness in business cases: time value of money, causal assignment and cash is king. Discounted Cash Flow (DCF) techniques take into account the time value of money by computing the present value of cash inflows and outflows. Activity-Based Cost Management (ABC/M), with which we have been working since its inception, provides precise causal assignment of costs by quantifying true cost drivers and the means to influence them (Cokins 2001). Combined with advanced causal modelling, a similar approach can also be applied to revenue. DCF techniques strip out non-cash distortions to ensure that only real cash flows are included. This principle is also applied to advanced Shareholder Value Added (SVA) approaches in order to provide investors with more accurate projections of future business value.

Delivering Value through Process

In business, outcomes are enabled and costs consumed by processes. Value is created or destroyed through processes and the policies that govern them. Processes have acquired much greater recognition due to the dominance of Japanese methods, harnessing Total Quality Management principles taught by Deming, and later, the business process re-engineering (BPR) movement kick-started by Michael Hammer (1990). The key to delivering stakeholder outcomes is capacity, and Eli Goldratt provided us with a more precise means of managing capacity through the Theory of Constraints (TOC), which addresses the role of bottlenecks (Goldratt and Cox 1989). The quality technique Six Sigma, championed by Jack Walsh at General Electric, is now a major force for improving process value (Pande et al. 2000). Due to their importance, the Balanced Scorecard includes processes as a key part of the 'internal' perspective.

The value implications of processes go beyond efficient delivery of products and services to the very heart of removing poverty. Researching into the true drivers of economic growth, William Lewis challenged contemporary wisdom that poor countries only become rich through capital and education; arguing that productivity, driven through intense but fair competition and consumer rights, is far more significant (Lewis 2004). The key point is that capital and educational standards follow, rather than being prerequisites for, productivity, which is quicker and easier to achieve simply by implementing best in class processes, which are transferrable.

Processes also produce waste, which destroys value in two ways; it costs money to produce and it prevents us from delivering stakeholder outcomes by consuming capacity. However, the presence of waste also provides us with potentially the quickest and least expensive route to increasing value if we can remove it. Therefore, Value Management places great emphasis on the definition, source and elimination of waste. To do this we have to apply surgical precision to target the cancer without damaging the patient. This leads us to new ways of looking at causality, which we consider under cause and effect. The replication of excellence and removal of waste in processes are critical to recovery in our debt-ridden economies.

Delivering Value through Programmes

The record of value delivery from change initiatives is poor, particularly concerning Information Technology (IT), which underpins many programmes. Exhaustive research by Paul Strassmann (2001) exposed not only the absence of correlation between IT spend and Return on Investment (ROI), but in some cases an inverse relationship. Conclusions from this and other research converge on the need to *target, time* and *align* initiatives precisely to deliver strategic business outcomes, and not dissipate spend on wasteful, self-serving infrastructure and bureaucracy.

The most effective vehicle for delivering value through change is the programme. Programmes can comprise multiple projects or can be part of a larger portfolio, all of which have the same ultimate purpose: to deliver value to stakeholders. Best practice methods spanning projects, programmes and portfolios, together with related subjects, are provided through the UK Office of Government Commerce (OGC). The approach and tools described in this book are generic and compatible with the OGC's and other methodologies.

Two powerful practices are adapted from experience across defence and aerospace manufacturing, the V-model and Earned Value Management. The V Model framework, used widely in systems and software engineering, is extended to incorporate the two key stages in Value Management: building a baseline business case and subsequent value realisation. Earned Value Management provides tracking and management of cost and delivery for complex programmes.

Change only makes sense if the value it delivers is sustainable by becoming part of business as usual. Therefore, change programmes need to become integral to everyday operations and are inextricably linked to the Balanced Scorecard. As with the Balanced Scorecard, best practice programme management includes causal linkage to outcomes. In Value Management, we link benefits to specific programme phases dynamically in order to enable two things: optimising overall programme value and timely, corrective response to variances against the baseline.

Cause and Effect

Causality is central to Value Management; more specifically the explicit, quantified causal linkage between the programme and stakeholder benefits that the programme is intended to deliver. Traditionally, business cases divide benefits between 'hard benefits' such as a reduced headcount, which could be quantified in financial terms, and 'soft benefits', which could not. Soft benefits typically include staff motivation, customer satisfaction and innovation. As approval is normally based on financial criteria, often only hard benefits were included. This may have sufficed, just, when competition, pace of change and connectivity were limited and there was plenty of low-hanging fruit, but not now. However, this is still common practice, despite evidence that it is no longer viable. For example, shifting customer tastes, social networking and intense global competition mean that the degree to which staff are innovative and/or customers sticky, have profound effects on value, far outweighing simple cost cutting.

Given that they need to be considered, we either include these intangible factors on faith or we find a way to quantify them financially. Value Management chooses the latter. However, this commitment presents us with a fundamental dilemma: our conventional models for quantifying benefits do not equip us to deal with them. The solution lies in applying recent advances in systems thinking, which involves shifting our focus from linear, one-way causality to feedback loops which generate non-linear behaviours.

Fortunately, there is growing awareness of the need to apply these new systemic sciences thanks to some landmark books which have popularised the subject. Peter Senge initially raised mainstream awareness of systems thinking through *The Fifth Discipline* (1990). Senge and his team at MIT defined a small number of repeating causal patterns, called archetypes, such as 'eroding goals' and 'fixes that fail', which often provide a good starting point for diagnosing problems, and John Sterman's *Business Dynamics* (2000) provides a manual for applying systems thinking by making the transition to simulation, discussed further under dynamics modelling. Malcolm Gladwell, in *The Tipping Point* (2000), demonstrated how small, sometimes minute changes in everyday life can have massive effects. Gareth Morgan provided one of the clearest and most comprehensive descriptions of different causal perspectives in the context of business change in *Images of Organisation* (1997). Richard Koch added further practical application through *The Power Laws* (2000b). In *Deep Simplicity* (2005) John Gribbin summarised complexity theory as comprising just two things, starting conditions and feedback. These are just a taste of the wealth of literature in this emerging area.

It is crucial at this point to make a distinction between deterministic and non-deterministic sciences. Deterministic science relates to theory and application that enable us to achieve repeatable predicted results. Newtonian physics is a prime example, which has made our current technological world possible. Conversely, new sciences, most notably quantum physics and complexity theory, present us with a world in which we cannot predict outcomes, however sophisticated our models are. Yet the insights that they bring cannot be ignored and can be applied to business effectively, if done so with caution and wisdom. For example, whilst we cannot predict an exact weather pattern, we do know that climatic behaviour is highly dependent on starting conditions and feedback, which together produce the so called 'butterfly effect'. Businesses, markets and customers display similar complex behaviours. We can also apply the concepts to complex change programmes.

My mentors in systemic sciences, Dr Kim James and Dr Carole McKenzie, stressed the danger of making exact parallels between nature and business, whilst sharing some of the most powerful techniques that I have encountered for effective change, using metaphors derived from the systemic sciences. Systems thinking is a subset of complexity, some elements of which are deterministic and some which are not. In Value Management we use the deterministic elements, such as predictable causal patterns and feedback loops, to add precision and enable quantification where it would otherwise be meaningless. We use non-deterministic elements, such as emergence, to direct solutions to problems where exact outcomes cannot be predicted exactly, such as market and customer behaviour, but where quantitative insights are made possible through a combination of dynamics modelling and the predictive capability of advanced analytics.

The necessary sacrifice in making the shift to multidirectional, non-linear thinking is surrendering exact, absolute answers in exchange for patterns of greyness and embracing ambiguity. For example, we can put an exact revenue figure on a given percentage increase in sales, but we cannot make such a direct relationship to quantify *how* increased sales are enabled by better knowledge of our customers. However, this is the kind of challenge that we take on in Value Management. There are three tools with which we need to equip ourselves if we are to achieve this ability: mental acuity, dynamics modelling and analytics.

Mental Acuity

Thinking systemically does not come naturally to most of us. Before we can make use of systemic principles we need to shift the way problems are viewed. We perceive reality not as it is but through mental models which distort, generalise and delete information received through the senses. Understanding and changing mental models hold the key to developing the mental acuity and innovation needed for creating value. Neuro-Linguistic Programming (NLP) offers some of the most powerful tools available to enable the *value breakthroughs* needed in individuals and businesses. The originators of NLP, Richard

Bandler and John Grinder, modelled the best change practitioners and encapsulated their successful methods into learnable, repeatable processes (Bandler and Grinder 1982). There are very close links between NLP and systems thinking.

The key to applying systemic principles is to simplify problems using models, which capture critical aspects whilst ensuring causal precision. We refer to this approach as *precise simplicity*. We apply three NLP techniques in value breakthrough workshops to define the causal structure of problems: reframing, chunking and the Meta Model. Reframing ensures that we are tackling the right problem. Chunking directs us to the appropriate level. The Meta Model corrects distortions, generalisations and deletions in our mental models. This shift in approach demands a corresponding change in client engagement. The traditional management consultancy model, branded by the arrogance of packaged solutions, is replaced by the Action Learning principles of Reg Revens (1998), in which coach and client are comfortable in mutual exploration, each running the risk of being wrong. The key to this approach is *trust*.

Dynamics Modelling

The fundamental dilemma facing today's business leaders is managing the scope, pace and interdependent nature of change. The challenge is to find a way to model the future reliably. Traditional *historical* modelling approaches, even with large datasets and sophisticated forecasting, fail to provide adequate direction because the future no longer reflects the past. A powerful solution is to combine systems thinking with dynamics modelling. Systems thinking provides insights into causal patterns and dynamics modelling quantifies the predicted results which can be simulated under different scenarios. The Balanced Scorecard provides the ideal template for structuring both qualitative maps and quantitative models.

The importance of dynamics modelling lies in its capability to anticipate problems and/or see opportunities not visible by other means. Three dynamics modelling techniques are most important for Value Management: system dynamics, discrete event simulation and agent-based modelling. System dynamics closely mirrors systems thinking and is generally used to model strategic business behaviour. For this reason, we use it to apply causal dynamics to the Balanced Scorecard. Two of the leading system dynamics tools, iThink®, from isee systems and Vensim® from Ventana Systems, were used to produce maps and models featured in this book.

While designing computer-integrated manufacturing systems in the 1980s, we applied a new computer modelling tool called discrete event simulation (DES). Our coach, Mark Elder, later founded and became CEO of the SIMUL8 Corporation, which developed the leading DES tool, SIMUL8. DES proves very effective in modelling processes, particularly when there are complex interactions involved, such as supply chains.

Agent-based modelling (ABM) captures emergent behaviours where many objects interact with one another, such as markets, cultures and customer segments. ABM is becoming more important with the growth in social networking, which has transformed the way in which products and services either take off or fail.

Analytics

Managing data, and the transformation of data into information and knowledge for effective decision making, is arguably the most critical capability a business must develop to generate value. However, even with advanced IT it is impossible to track and respond effectively to all data. Therefore, competitive edge is not driven by how much data are analysed but knowing how much can be safely ignored. Only a small fraction of data is critical and these are usually time-dependent. The key is identifying, capturing and presenting the data that really counts, then acting upon it most effectively.

However, critical data must be derived from a full data set. The tool for managing corporate data is *Business Intelligence* (BI). Its importance is reflected by the rising spend in this technology over recent years. The most important purpose of BI is to provide a single source of truth from which critical information can be derived when needed and acted upon, and applications that perform this transition from data to knowledge. It is important that the technical architecture, supporting the data and information needs of the organisation, reflects the fundamental business design, discussed earlier.

The most pressing advance is what Gartner refers to as *next generation analytics*, which is defined as 'running simulations or models to predict the future outcome, rather than to simply provide backward looking data about past interactions, and to do these predictions in real-time to support each individual business action'. Gartner includes this development as one of the ten technologies and trends that they consider will be strategic for most organisations in 2011. In Value Management, we address this need by combining the predictive capability of dynamics modelling with the single source of truth and predictive analytics, provided by BI to deliver truly dynamic performance management.

Acknowledgements

In considering to whom I am indebted for the principles and techniques in this book, it soon became apparent that I had to go back a long time and include a great many mentors, coaches and sponsors who kept faith at critical times.

The journey began on a first degree course in engineering at the University of Bradford in the late 1970s. The school's visionary leadership included economic decision making as a core module which our lecturer, Roger de la Mare, introduced with the prophetic statement, 'If you want to make it in business, you will need to think like accountants.' He taught us to create and interpret company accounts until it became second nature; cost products from first principles and build complex investment appraisals using discounted cash flow techniques. It is a privilege now to sit on the Professional Advisory Board for the same university's School of Engineering.

Early into my postgraduate career, the UK economy entered the period of austerity of the early 1980s and I was given ample opportunities to apply this financial knowledge to product development and factory automation programmes, spanning high-volume batch manufacturing, petrochemicals and defence electronics. Plessey, a major defence company, invested heavily in research and I was included in pioneering work on Activity-Based Cost Management (ABC/M), IDED0 process modelling and computer simulation, all in the context of value delivery. I am particularly grateful to Steven La Pensee, who as general manager at Plessey Command and Control Systems, took a risk in appointing a young manager to Chief Mechanical Engineer and sponsored my proposal for a computer integrated manufacturing programme as part of an action learning MBA, awarded on delivery of benefits which were quantified and tracked using Value Management.

During my time in management consultancy from 1990, I am obliged to Elaine Fletcher, David Core, Martin Prior, Anita Bradshaw, Ruth Aaron, Nick Lawford, Malcolm Woodrow, Helen Gunn, Reis Braganza, Steve Lloyd, Nick Wensley, Andy Neal, Alan Munro, Andy Osborne, Ash Morris, Paul Montibelli, Steve Moss, Alan Pay, Tim Bharucha and the late Bill Reynolds, among others, who supported me in developing Value Management into a core value proposition, and some of whom provided collaborative assignments with Impact Dynamics Limited, since its foundation in 2002.

One of the most significant elements of the causal approach to Value Management is systems thinking, and I thank my mentors, Dr Kim James and Dr Carole Mckenzie, for teaching me both the theory and practical application in the management of change. I am also thankful to David Shephard, founder of The Performance Partnership, for his excellent courses in Neuro-Linguistic Programming; among the best training I have ever encountered.

A business book covering a complex subject like Value Management is of little use without case studies which demonstrate the principles in action. To this end, I am most grateful to Abby Cardall who supported the National Grid Metering example and Tim Marshall, CEO, and Tim Kidd, Operations Director at JANET (UK), who gave kind permission to use our work with them as the basis for a complete walk-through of the IMPACT framework. I also thank Symon Brown and Elaine Fletcher for supporting the use of these case studies, both of which were conducted with Logica clients and in partnership with Logica.

The Value Management Toolset™ is the result of over 20 years development and honing across numerous sectors and applications. The transformation into a commercial product required three key contributions which were greatly appreciated. First, Roel Wolfert, Global Head of Strategy and Marketing Financial Services at Logica, showed sufficient trust to fund licensing of the Toolset across Logica, which enabled further development. Secondly, the productisation was implemented by our development partner, David Richer, who consistently went the extra mile to perfect the software. Finally, our support partners, Systems Ability, not only provided essential infrastructure and technical expertise, but the founder Michael Dick and fellow Directors, Andy Jagger and Alistair Hamilton-Wilkes, also injected entrepreneurial direction.

Special thanks are extended to the two major contributors to this work, Elaine Fletcher and David Core, who provided depth and critical expertise, together with the review team Anita Bradshaw, Jon Collins, Joanne Egner, Mark Elder, Andy Jagger, Lee Jones, Dr Carole McKenzie, Andy Osborne, Mike Parker, Martin Prior, Patricia Thomson and Diahann Williams.

Dynamics modelling tools have transformed the capacity to find and exploit value-creating opportunities and form a core part of the approach covered in this book. The tool suppliers have been instrumental in incorporating the techniques within Value Management and we have used iThink® from isee systems, inc. and Vensim® from Ventana Systems, inc. for examples in this book. In particular, I wish to thank Joanne Egner, CEO at isee systems, inc., and Lee Jones at Ventana Systems UK Ltd, for their great support over many years, both of whom kindly reviewed the modelling chapters and provided invaluable feedback.

It is also important to acknowledge the many authors who have shared their knowledge, much of which has been incorporated in this work and referenced in the bibliography. In particular, I thank Gerald Bradley, author of *Benefits Realisation Management*, who kindly provided advice concerning, and permission to use, his style of glossary.

I would like to thank my son and co-author, Adam Davies, who in addition to producing material for the book, injecting the latest thinking drawn from his first degree in business, Masters in applied finance and extensive independent research, provided invaluable support in developing the Toolset. I am also grateful to my ever-patient partner, Jacqui McCulloch, for the seemingly endless proofreading and learning the art of indexing.

Finally, special thanks are extended to our publisher at Gower, Jonathan Norman, for his extraordinary level of support in reviewing material, market intelligence and clear direction throughout the production of the book.

Contributors

Two people in particular, with whom I have worked closely for over ten years, made significant contributions in both shaping and providing material for this book:

Elaine Fletcher is an established leader in benefits-driven Business Intelligence (BI), having pioneered the use of data mining and predictive modelling combined with Value Management across business scenarios in many industry sectors. Clean enterprise data and advanced analytics were significant omissions in the Value Management approach, whilst causal modelling was a key missing link for Elaine's approach to building enterprise BI solutions. Consequently, we have partnered with Elaine in her role as BI Practice Director at Logica, combining the strengths of dynamics modelling and BI to build the dynamic performance management solutions outlined in this book. Elaine is now a Partner within IBM's Business Analytics and Optimisation Group.

David Core is a seasoned consultant with particular expertise in the financial sector, business architecture and customer relationship management. David helped shape the more advanced causal techniques used in the IMPACT framework and incorporated within the Value Management Toolset™ and continues to work on its application to major infrastructural change in payments. He has worked in the finance sector for over 20 years, starting his career with the Inter Bank Research Organisation (IBRO), where he worked on the business case for electronic payments. Subsequently he developed card strategy and developed the use of analytical customer relationship management techniques for the TSB Group. More recently he has spent over ten years with Logica's financial services practice, working internationally on payments infrastructure refresh and bank transformations, always seeking to understand how target operating models will add value for stakeholders.

Review Team

It was deemed essential to subject the material to as wide a review as possible, and to that end the following review team represent expertise spanning all core subject areas of the book:

Anita Bradshaw is a management consultant with a long background in investment banking and specialist expertise in compliance, risk management and governance.

Jon Collins is a market research analyst specialising in analytics, author and social media expert.

Joanne Egner is managing director of isee systems, inc., a leader in system dynamics modelling.

Mark Elder is founder and CEO of the SIMUL8 Corporation, a leader in discrete event simulation and agent-based modelling.

Andy Jagger Andy is a director of Systems Ability, an infrastructure support enterprise, and has expertise in programme management and software development.

Lee Jones is co-founder and managing director of Ventana Systems UK Limited, a leader in system dynamics modelling.

Dr Carole McKenzie is an expert in cybernetics, artist and management coach and developed Aesthetic Intelligence with Dr Kim James.

Andy Osborne is a business consultant with a background in systems development and programme management.

Mike Parker is a management consultant with specialist knowledge in systems thinking and the financial sector.

Martin Prior is a management consultant and programme manager with specialist knowledge in Value Management.

Patricia Thomson is a management consultant with specialist knowledge in performance management and analytics.

Diahann Williams is a human resources director, specialising in change within large and complex commercial environments and a master practitioner in Neuro-Linguistic Programming.

Executive Questions

Executive question	Essence	Reference
What is the economic imperative addressed by this book?	**The need to create economic growth with fewer resources** The level of consumption used to generate economic growth in the past is now untenable and is undergoing a correction through austerity measures imposed by governments, markets and environmental limits. We must either learn to live with less wealth or create wealth with fewer resources. The latter will need to become the norm. If used and integrated more effectively, parallel advances in technology, processes and thinking offer an unprecedented opportunity to enable and sustain this essential shift.	Introduction Chapter 1 Critical Value
What must we do to grow wealth with limited resources and funding?	**Deliver greater value from change programmes** Programmes, which include all initiatives spanning operational improvements to major capital investments, are the vehicle by which change is implemented and value delivered to business stakeholders. Programmes are failing to deliver intended value and there is a poor correlation between spend and return on investment and value for money. A fundamental reason for this disconnect is poor causal linkage between programmes and the benefits which they are intended to deliver.	Chapter 1 Critical Value Chapter 4 Elusive Value
How does Value Management address the challenge of delivering greater value from change programmes?	**Value Management provides the means to deliver more benefit for less cost and risk** Value Management targets, times and aligns initiatives to maximise overall value. This is achieved by linking programmes explicitly to attributable benefits. This requires precise quantification of cause and effect relationships between programme deliverables, the drivers of business performance and consequential stakeholder benefits.	Chapter 7 Programming Value Chapter 8 Aligning Value
How do we link programme deliverables with performance drivers and benefits?	**Use strategy maps to develop a Balanced Scorecard** Benefits are reflected in business performance, the leading framework for which is the Balanced Scorecard. Strategy maps link objectives and measures through the perspectives of a Balanced Scorecard to reflect the business vision. Themes are specific cause and effect chains leading to financial outcomes. Strategy maps provide the foundation for modelling precise causal linkage between programme deliverables and the drivers and benefits which are tracked using the Balanced Scorecard.	Chapter 5 Intended Value Chapter 6 Modelling Value Chapter 7 Programming Value

Executive question	Essence	Reference
How do we define and quantify complex causal relationships between deliverables, drivers and benefits?	**Systems thinking and dynamics modelling** Conventional models using linear thinking are inadequate for dealing with the level of complexity associated with change in today's dynamic, global and competitive business environment. Deterministic elements of systems thinking are used to decode the complexity by defining feedback loops that drive non-linear behaviour, and dynamics modelling to provide quantitative precision.	Chapter 1 Critical Value Chapter 6 Modelling Value Appendix A Dynamics Modelling
How precise can we expect any casual business model to be?	**Approximately right rather than exactly wrong** All models are subsets of reality and therefore inherently wrong. The aim for models is to provide enough precision to design and implement programmes which deliver intended value. In order to achieve this, models should be simple yet causally precise, using systemic principles, with approximate but sufficiently correct data. This will not give us decimal point accuracy but patterns of cause and effect, providing an actionable margin of certainty. This approach to modelling is called precise simplicity.	Chapter 3 Precise Simplicity Chapter 6 Modelling Value Appendix A Dynamics Modelling
What is the value equation?	**Value = Benefits − Costs** The value equation provides the basis for quantification across all aspects of business. Value is the measure of degree to which benefits exceed the costs consumed in achieving them. Benefits are outcomes actually experienced by stakeholders and costs are what stakeholders must sacrifice in order to receive the benefits. Therefore, how value is interpreted depends on the stakeholder viewpoint and type of organisation.	Chapter 2 Defining Value
How is the value equation applied differently for private and public sector organisations?	**Profit for commercial businesses, value for money for public sector services** For commercial enterprises, value is ultimately reflected in the two sides of the profit and loss account, where both revenue and costbase are in financial units: *Profit = Revenue − Costbase* In the absence of revenue, public services can represent the equation as a quotient: *Value for money (VfM) = Benefits/Costs* VfM is a measure of stakeholder benefits for a given cost, and can also be expressed in terms of doing the right things, (effectiveness) and doing things right (efficiency): *VfM = Effectiveness × Efficiency*	Chapter 2 Defining Value

Executive question	Essence	Reference
How is the value equation applied for programmes?	**Discounted cash flow (DCF) analysis** DCF analyses calculate the net present value (NPV) of programmes, taking into account the time value of money. DCF analyses use only real cash flows to ensure that results are not distorted with non-cash items, such as depreciation. NPV is often more sensitive to both the magnitude and timing of programme benefits than programme costs. Therefore, the technique is more effective if programme phases are linked *dynamically* to the DCF analysis, which enables rapid assessment of, and response to, the impact of changes.	Chapter 2 Defining Value Chapter 7 Programming Value Chapter 8 Aligning Value
Why is alignment so important?	**Alignment focuses energy on intended value and minimises resistance to achieving it** Alignment is a state in which all business resources, programmes and cultural values are directed towards achieving the vision. It is also necessary to align value between stakeholders, to provide win–win situations, in order to ensure viability of the business in the long term. Value alignment is used to develop an implementation strategy, which optimises the structure and sequence of programme phases to deliver maximum overall value, expressed as NPV.	Chapter 8 Aligning Value
Why do targets fail to produce desired results?	**In order to meet targets people find the path of least resistance** Poor alignment of deliverables, drivers and benefits is a major reason behind the poor record of well intentioned, and seemingly logical, targets to deliver intended improvements in performance. This is a particularly challenging problem in the public sector, where targets are often used inappropriately as surrogates for commercial incentives. Rather than ensure that initiatives are universally beneficial, individual targets, often linked to rewards and penalties, are pursued at the expense of the overall business.	Chapter 6 Modelling Value
How do we align programme phases to maximise value?	**Optimise value dependence whilst respecting functional dependence** Functional dependence addresses the operational order in which certain tasks must be carried out. For example, you can not complete the roof of a house until you have built the walls. Value dependence determines the structure and sequence of phases that return the greatest value. For example, with care it may be possible to deliver early partial benefits or delay high front-end expenses, both of which can profoundly increase the programme value.	Chapter 7 Programming Value Chapter 8 Aligning Value

Executive question	Essence	Reference
How do mental models influence our ability to deliver value?	**By aligning our values, beliefs and behaviour to deliver value** Mental models are internal representations of how we perceive the world. They are a subset of reality filtered by distortions, generalisations and deletions, which limit our ability to respond most effectively to real-world events. Mental models can be changed in order to influence value most effectively by ensuring that we are tackling the right problem, at the appropriate level and with necessary precision.	Chapter 1 Critical Value Chapter 3 Precise Simplicity
How can we ensure that projected programme value will be delivered?	**Destruction test the business case** We subject the financial value model, underlying the business case, to extremes using sensitivity, risk, scenario and user analyses, in order to determine what it takes to destroy the financial NPV. Only after exhaustive destruction testing and problems that are exposed by the process are addressed is the business case submitted for approval. It then becomes the baseline against which the programme is managed from a value perspective.	Chapter 9 Valuing Certainty
How do we ensure that the approved baseline business case is delivered?	**Value realisation** Value realisation involves tracking deliverables, drivers and benefits and overall programme value. Deliverables tracking employs advanced Earned Value Management techniques. Tracking drivers and benefits is enabled by the Balanced Scorecard. Overall value tracking involves the dynamic linkage of the programme to a DCF analysis. The causal precision defined during the development of the baseline business case is used to correct negative variances and exploit unforeseen opportunities.	Chapter 10 Tracking Value
What is the best way to start a major programme?	**Use Proof of Concept (PoC) implementations** Big bang implementations, whereby complex, costly programmes are undertaken in a single chunk, rarely deliver intended value because of the inherent risk. We counter this problem by introducing PoC phases into the programme which deliver early benefits and reduce risk. PoC pilots exploit standard desktop applications and modelling tools, which provide inexpensive yet powerful solutions in their own right, and provide a proven specification and design templates for subsequent full implementation.	Chapter 1 Critical Value Appendix C Dynamic Performance Management
How can we rely on performance management information?	**Single source of truth** The single source of truth refers to information which is complete, correct and consistent across the entire business. It is achieved through Business Intelligence (BI), which can interrogate data to derive information and knowledge. Typically, BI solutions are limited to drilling *down* into more detailed data and rolling *up* operational data into summary reports for management. More advanced solutions drill *across* business functions and processes to reflect the true causal paths defined using dynamics modelling. This provides greater precision with which to pinpoint problems and direct effective action.	Appendix B Business Intelligence

Executive question	Essence	Reference
How do we respond sufficiently quickly and correctly in today's dynamic business environment?	**Dynamic performance management** Dynamic performance management is the capability to capture performance driver values and model the future impact of changes, together with potential responses, very quickly, even in real time. This is made possible by integrating the single source of truth and analytical power of BI with the predictive capability of dynamics modelling.	Appendix C Dynamic Performance Management

Introduction

The Shove Penny Story

When I was young, the family spent summer holidays in the old Victorian resort of Herne Bay on the north Kent coast. In the 1960s, the town boasted the second longest pier in Britain which was visited twice a day by the majestic paddle steamer Medway Queen. We had a beach hut, a boat and canoe and I enjoyed all the freedom I wanted. At only 11 years old I was allowed to row to the end of the pier in rough seas, clamber on the dangerous Hampton Rocks at low tide and undertake any number of dangerous activities. After all, I could swim so what could go wrong? To a small boy it seemed like heaven.

There was one place, however, that was out of bounds. About a mile away there were some amusement arcades. These unsavoury places, my parents said, encouraged all the wrong things, particularly gambling. But the pull for me was stronger than any tide, so I abused my freedom to visit these dens of iniquity. I loved the atmosphere; the ever-present smell of candy floss and the background drone of bingo calls overlaid with the pinging of the numerous pinball machines, which were the most popular amusement. Personally, I could not see the point of these 'flippers', a silver sixpence to make a lot of noise and with nothing to show for it but an occasional replay if you got enough points. No, my favourites involved making money to buy ice cream – sixpence bought a large Macari's 99 ice cream cone with a chocolate flake – and the best machine for this purpose, so I thought, was the shove penny.

The shove penny machines comprised several trays moving backwards and forwards with old pennies spread several layers deep. Crags of these large coins hung tantalisingly over the end just waiting for one more minute push to be tipped into the collection tray. It was all about skill and the keys were position and timing. You had to release your coin down the chute so that it fell flat on the tray, not on top of the other coins. Then as the tray moved back the new coin would be jammed against the backstop and push the other coins towards and over the precipice. I became expert and my good timing resulted in much *output*. Time and again a great clattering would be heard as the old coppers crashed down stainless steel slides.

But when I reached down to gather up the winnings there was nothing. Where did it go? What was hidden from the player, unless you looked carefully, was that on each side of the tray coins were being pushed into a very different chute, which led into the machine for collection by the arcade owner. Each side of the tray was longer than the front which meant that it was much easier for coins to be pushed off the sides.

> In truth, I never won sufficient money to buy even a single scoop cornet, let alone a 99, using the shove pennies. I was more successful on the roulette wheel, a game of pure chance. However, a strange fascination lingered; I could get my coins in the right place at the right time: if only the sides of the tray had guides directing all the coins towards the front, I would be a millionaire, I thought.
>
> When we defined Value Management as targeting, timing and aligning investment and operations to maximise stakeholder value, I remembered these old shove penny machines.

A dominant theme in the UK over the last decade has been the abysmal correlation between spending on public services and the improvements actually experienced by the recipients of each service. Just like the shove penny machines, the vast proportion of resource and effort was wasted. Vast sums of money were poured in. Some was dissipated in self-serving bureaucracy before reaching any programmes. Some paid for direct waste, such as nugatory work, duplication and fixing avoidable problems. Some was directed to *outputs* that had very little or no effect on the intended *outcomes*. The poor linkage between spend and outcomes has been particularly common and severe across all sectors where Information Technology (IT) is concerned; research by Sessions[1] puts the annual cost to the UK economy being around US$200 billion. Imagine the difference if we could redirect this waste.

The Challenge

Our current economic landscape presents us with five seemingly irreconcilable challenges:

- Increased competition from major developing economies, such as China and India, in our traditionally competitive strongholds, including our remaining manufacturing industries and high technology sectors such as IT
- Growing numbers of young people on welfare, combined with ageing populations demanding pensions and health care means increased demand for public services from a declining productive workforce
- Unsustainable public debt to bail out banks and weather the recession, demanding cuts or shifts in funding of essential services
- Dwindling natural resources forcing up prices to levels that render existing business models untenable
- Limits on ecological capacity to support growth even if the resources were there to fuel it

Manipulating the arithmetic or spinning statistics will not change the facts. For Western economies, this all boils down to one essential truth:

We either learn to live with less wealth or find ways to create wealth with fewer resources.

---

1   Sessions, R. 2009. *Cost of IT Failure: What does IT failure cost us annually? A lot.* Available at http://simplearchitectures. blogspot.com/2009/09/cost-of-it-failure.html, accessed 20 December 2010.

The overall message in this book is positive and is founded on three fundamental premises:

1. Economic growth with reduced consumption is quite possible, and will have to become the norm
2. The shift needed will demand much more value from change programmes
3. We can deliver far greater value from change programmes, right now

To achieve this, we must undergo a transformation in the way we define and manage programmes intended to deliver value. Parallel advances in technical architectures, open standards and programme management techniques have led to more reliable delivery of improved business *functionality*. However, these advances have not been reflected in delivery of either intended outcomes or financial returns.

Poor implementation is more common than technical limitations. The most cited reasons for programmes failing to deliver value include lack of executive support and/or buy-in from key users, loose requirements definition, weak programme management and plain wishful thinking. In this book we argue that, whilst correcting these problems is a perquisite for success, they are also symptoms of more fundamental repeating patterns causing failure time and again. We will define these failure patterns and build the solutions into a repeatable framework. We will also demonstrate how these shifts in thinking and process can be applied to exploit IT to provide dynamic performance management; in which the latest correct, complete and consistent data give accurate historic performance, whilst dynamic models, capturing changes over time based on true cause and effect, provide reliable future predictions.

Why we have Written this Book

This book was written to stress the need, define the theoretical basis, outline the process and explore the full potential for delivering far greater economic value from change programmes, spanning operational improvement to strategic business transformation. It is intended to provide a concise manual which will enable immediate application and early results.

Who we have Written the Book For

The book is aimed at executives *directing*, programme managers *driving* and people tasked with *delivering* intended value at any level in the organisation.

Objectives of the Book

As a direct result of reading this book you will be able to apply the two key stages of Value Management:

1. Baseline business case: target, time and align change programmes to deliver maximum intended value to stakeholders with speed and certainty.

2. Benefits realisation: track and respond to changes during and beyond implementation to ensure that the programme remains on purpose and on value.

Structure of the Book

This book is designed to be an easy read of a highly complex and contentious subject. To this end, the book is structured using the 4MAT System pioneered by Bernice McCarthy, designed to span all preferred learning styles.[2] The system targets Jung's four personality archetypes, used by the Myers–Briggs Type Indicator (MBTI) and many other profiling methods. When learning, each type adopts a dominant questioning style as follows:

*   Introvert: *why* are we doing this and why is it important?
*   Extrovert: *what* is it and what does it do?
*   Feeler: *how* does it work and how can I apply it immediately?
*   Thinker: *what if* I did this, what would and wouldn't happen?
*   The book is divided into four parts, each of which focuses on one of these questions:

Part I Problem (Why?)

Part I spells out the need for a new urgency to drive value from change, provides a clear definition of value, presents the causal thinking necessary for unlocking value and concludes by exploring precisely how programmes fail.

Chapter 1 states the critical significance of value in the new economic reality, defines common myths relating to change programmes and outlines key advances spanning technology and process, together with thinking which when combined and applied effectively can significantly improve value outcomes.

Chapter 2 defines value in simple and precise terms, providing a quantitative foundation for increasing stakeholder value from change programmes; which translates into Return on Investment (ROI) for commercial enterprises and Value for Money (VfM) for public sector and not-for-profit organisations.

Chapter 3 presents shifts in thinking required for Value Management, introduces the concept of precise simplicity as the practical means of structuring causal thinking and outlines key techniques which support the approach.

Chapter 4 defines precise causes of, and outlines corresponding archetypal solutions for, six repeating failure patterns of programmes to deliver against value expectations.

Part II Principles (What?)

Part II describes solutions to the six repeating failure patterns defined in Part I as the core principles of Value Management and structures these concepts into a practical framework.

---

2   McCarthy, B., McCarthy, D. 2006. *Teaching Around the 4MAT® Cycle: Designing Instruction for Diverse Learners with Diverse Learning Styles*. Thousand Oaks, USA: Corwin Press.

Chapter 5 stresses the need for outcome focus through precise linking of programme deliverables to benefits, together with unambiguous ownership.

Chapter 6 harnesses the power of recent advances in systemic thinking to build causal models which define the most critical drivers of performance and value.

Chapter 7 consolidates the most successful approaches to programme management and links benefits to specific programme phases dynamically.

Chapter 8 covers value alignment and developing an implementation strategy that optimises both the magnitude and timing of value delivery.

Chapter 9 shows how to provide certainty that the programme delivers intended value by defining clear criteria for success and conducting exhaustive risk analysis.

Chapter 10 concerns tracking deliverables, drivers and benefits to ensure that the programme remains on purpose and on value.

Chapter 11 structures the six Value Management principles into a repeatable framework, IMPACT.

Part III Process (How?)

Part III shows how the IMPACT Value Management framework has been implemented in practice.

Chapter 12 walks through each phase in the IMPACT framework using a real case study.

Appendices: Precision (What if?)

The appendices demonstrate how the latest advances in dynamics modelling and Business Intelligence can be combined to provide truly dynamic performance management.

Appendix A describes how dynamics modelling tools and techniques are used to provide precision in quantifying cause and effect relationships and determine the most important measures in the business.

Appendix B describes how BI is applied to provide correct, complete and consistent underlying data and business rules, together with predictive analytics using vast datasets.

Appendix C demonstrates how dynamics modelling and BI are combined to enable business agility through dynamic performance management.

The book is purpose-driven. At the start of each chapter we define the intended outcomes for the reader and conclude with the essence of what the chapter covers. Examples and real case studies are included to provide clarity and add credibility to the approach, which is the result of over 30 years research, development and, most of all, practical application.

▌ *Problem*

In Part I we first state the crucial role that value plays in the fundamental economic and business challenge; creating, distributing and sustaining wealth with diminishing resources. We assert the critical role of change programmes in achieving this imperative. Three common myths relating to delivering value from programmes are exposed. We describe parallel advances in technology, process and thinking that when used effectively together take away all excuses for failing to deliver value. We then define the Value Equation to provide a foundation for quantifying value and consider how it can be applied across several key perspectives. We discuss new ways of thinking in creating value and key skills and, finally, apply these thinking skills to define repeating patterns of failure which direct us to repeatable solutions.

1 *Critical Value*

Objectives

After reading this chapter you will be able to:

- Recognise and avoid three myths related to creating value through change programmes
- Identify opportunities for applying advances in technology, processes and thinking to create value

The Economic Wake up

The Nightmare Story

You wake up in a cold sweat. That has to be the worst nightmare you have ever had. It is still clear in your mind. The Earth has warmed up so much that coastal defences around the world have been overwhelmed by the sea. The Thames barrier has been breached like a child's sandcastle. Your new London apartment, which your insurance company refused to cover against flooding because it was built on a floodplain, is under water and you are loaded with debt from the heady days of cheap credit. Still dazed, your radio alarm bursts into life with the 06:00 news.

The top story covers latest research proving beyond doubt that the environmental cynics were right all the time, the calculations were wrong, global warming is a con trick; carbon emissions have no effect on global warming. In fact, it turns out that CO_2 is good for the planet.

It also transpires that massive debt is the miracle to end recession and drives new, unfettered growth after all. The credit crunch was just a one-off aberration that will never happen again. Borrowing is back and it's good for us. The Dickensian idea that what you spend must be in relation to the value that you create is dead. House prices are rising rapidly again. The Prime Minister announces that we are back to uninterrupted economic growth.

A great calm warms your entire body. You relax and plan the loan for that new 4 × 4 you promised yourself.

As I write this book, there is great speculation over the validity of dire global warming predictions. Leading academics have allegedly been manipulating data which has left a large credibility gap. Although for most scientists it seems highly unlikely that global warming is a myth, let's just suppose that the Nightmare Story was true. Where would that actually leave the human race in respect of our economic and biological survival? The uncomfortable answer is, 'largely the same'. Even if environmental issues disappeared, and ignoring human and ethical arguments, the resources needed for fuelling the growth to support exponentially rising populations and expectations of the new super economies are rapidly running out. Consequently, in purely economic terms, scarcity will result in reduced availability or cost increases to levels which render many existing business models unviable. The natural Law of 'limits to growth', defined by Donella Meadows[1] dictates that propelling prosperity though unfettered consumption, with or without cheap credit, is unsustainable.

We cannot sustain increased prosperity using the current
proportional level of resource consumption.

Developed countries are holding on to the hope that promised levels of income and pensions can be sustained with debt and a return to growth, whilst becoming increasingly uncompetitive against the major developing countries, notably China and India. If we add back the environmental truths and the economic risks of high levels of debt, we are faced with a new reality: either we learn to live with less wealth or we find ways to create wealth with fewer resources.

The first alternative is not practical, at least not without a fundamental shift in human nature. The history of the human race is one of endeavour to drive economic growth. Developing nations are determined to experience the benefits of growth and are now driving the pace. Creating more from less is the only option in the long term and for Western economies it is critical. If *economics* is the study of wants and needs, then the relationship between acquisition and the consumption of resources required to attain them is *value*. Ultimately, wealth is generated from value creation. Therefore if we are to continue to improve our standard of living, through economic growth with less resource, we need to create and manage value more skilfully.

Value is the measure of more for less.

The primary message of this book is a positive one: that it is perfectly possible to achieve growth with sustainable consumption of resources through precise targeting, timing and alignment of investment in people, process and technology. Programmes have a core role in this transition because they are the vehicle by which change, and more importantly intended outcomes from change, are realised. However, it is no longer enough to throw money at problems when most of the effort is dissipated in waste. This was never the solution but the futility was hidden by readily available money, energy and raw materials.

Another essential shift is for change programmes to be incorporated within 'business as usual' operations, which is now in itself the management of change, rather than the protector of stability. This means that changes to the business drivers and outcomes are

---

1   Meadows, D.H, Meadows, D.L., Randers, J., Behrens, W. 1974. *Limits to Growth: A Report for the Club of Rome's Project on the Predicament of Mankind*. London: Pan Books.

no longer wishful figures in an archived business case, but daily tracked measures within a dynamic performance framework.

Value Management is the transition from wishful thinking to causal certainty.

Record of Failures

It is not hard to find instances of programme failure. In Britain alone, there are the jaw-dropping headline cases, such as the £12.7 billion IT overhaul of the NHS[2] that has been riddled with technical issues and the London Olympics which has seen its original 2007 budget triple from £2.4 billion to £7.2 billion. It is feared that neither of these major programmes is likely to deliver anything like the benefits claimed. The more general picture is also one of programmes failing to realise the value upon which their approval was gained.

A large proportion of change programmes still fail to deliver expected benefits.

Although the failure to deliver value relates to all types of programme, because IT forms a major catalyst for change much research into the problem has centred on IT. There is a difference in opinion regarding the real extent of IT failure: some estimates suggest roughly a third of technology-related projects are unsuccessful,[3] while a recent Standish Group Chaos report implies that only a third (32 per cent) of IT projects are successful.[4] More specifically the Standish Group's report for the 2009 period found that in addition to 44 per cent of projects being challenged in some fundamental way, 24 per cent were cancelled before they were completed, or never used. Less optimistic findings can also be found suggesting failure rates as high as 68 per cent.[5] With regard to the impact on shareholders, research from Tata Consulting finds that 41 per cent of organisations failed to realise the expected ROI from their IT projects.[6] The higher rates of failure bear out our own experience. The overall picture is one of unacceptable levels of failure.

Recognising that IT is critical to business and the economy as a whole, this failure prevents us from growing and sustaining wealth individually and globally. To put this cost into financial perspective, calculations by Roger Sessions of ObectWatch estimate

2   Rose, D. 2009. Computer glitches in NHS IT system force patients to wait six months. Available at http://www.timesonline.co.uk/tol/life_and _style/health/article6856103.ece, accessed 23 October 2009.

3   Saucer, C., Gemino, A., Reich, B. 2007. The Impact of size and volatility on IT project performance. *Communications of the ACM*, 50(11): 79–84.

4   Standish Group. 2009. *CHAOS summary*. Available at http://www.standishgroup.com/newsroom/chaos_2009.php, accessed 20 December 2010.

5   Ellis, K., IAG Consulting. 2009. *Business analysis benchmark: The impact of business requirements on the success of technology projects*. Available at http://www.iag.biz/images/resources/iag%20business%20analysis%20benchmark%20-%20full%20report.pdf, accessed 20 December 2010.

6   Tata Consulting Services. 2007. *Research survey*. Available at http://www.tcs.com/AboutUs/Research_Survey.html, accessed 2009.

that the annual world wide cost of IT failure is as high as US\$6.2 trillion.[7] This level of waste is just not sustainable, but also offers a massive opportunity.

Common Programme Value Myths

The Welfare Benefits Story

During the late 1990s the UK government was enthusiastic in exploiting opportunities for electronic government as a way of reducing burgeoning public sector costs. An area singled out for exploiting the new technologies was administration of the UK welfare benefits system. Benefits comprised some 70 types of welfare streams, called chimneys. Chimneys were managed using hugely expensive and inefficient manual processes. They were also run independently, despite the fact that one stream triggered one or more others. These links were manual and allowed for colossal error and fraud. For example, people on Income Support would be automatically eligible for Housing Benefit but when Income Support ceased so should the associated Housing Benefit, in principle. However, claimants would frequently continue to receive the benefit payments to which they were no longer entitled simply by failing to notify the appropriate authority. When the process eventually caught up, there was little or no way of retrieving the money, the responsibility being deemed to reside with the government. The Department of Health and Social Security (DHSS) quaintly referred to this loss as 'leakage'.

The DHSS launched a Business Process Re-engineering (BPR) programme, the largest and most ambitious in Europe at the time, to transform the administration of the UK benefits system. The focus was directed on cost savings in running the system. Benchmark indicators of savings claimed in other major programmes were the principal justification. Consequently, elegant process maps and scenarios detailing every life event of all conceivable claimants were devised using the most sophisticated tools available. The programme was run diligently, in this case under PRINCE2™. However, no one questioned the validity of a narrow cost saving focus.

As the business case, using Value Management, was developed it became clear that the few millions potentially saved in process efficiencies were eclipsed by the billions lost in fraud and errors, which the new processes were not tackling. The final value model demonstrated that the financial case was not viable on operational cost savings alone and the programme was shelved, with the result that further futile spend was avoided but the opportunity to correct these flaws was lost.

---

7   Sessions, R. 2009. *Cost of IT Failure: What does IT failure cost us annually? A lot.* Available at http://simplearchitectures. blogspot.com/2009/09/cost-of-it-failure.html, accessed 20 December 2010.

There are three common myths related to creating value through change programmes which we will illustrate through the Welfare Benefits Story case study:

- Myth 1: value correlates with spend
- Myth 2: wishful thinking will do
- Myth 3: big bang implementation is best

Myth 1: Value Correlates with Spend

The first myth is that big changes demand big investments and, more dangerously, that big spend correlates directly to value. Whilst the first assumption can be true, the second most certainly is not. This is the stuff of spin where politicians boast about protecting spending on public services, such as health, education and policing. However, it is the *outcomes* from spend that need to be protected, and these cannot be guaranteed by the size of the spend itself. This message is, of course, highly contentious and we do not say this lightly. Paul Strassmann, a leading authority on the value of IT, has devoted much research to the correlation of spend in IT and ROI. Not only did this research expose a poor correlation between financial results and IT spend, but also in some cases increased spending on IT corresponded to reduced ROI.[8] We will demonstrate that precise targeting, timing and alignment of investment is far more critical than the size of spend.

Myth 2: Wishful Thinking Will Do

This myth comes in various guises, such as 'everyone else is doing this so we should too', 'the claimed savings of this fad are £x million so we can expect £y million in our case' and 'the benefits will follow automatically'. The Welfare Benefits Story above illustrates several manifestations of wishful thinking. The first concerns poor targeting and lack of precision in defining what value the change was intended to deliver, and to whom. For example, in this case the entire programme was initiated on the unsubstantiated premise that process *efficiency* was the most significant issue. This blinded the team from pursuing much greater potential outcomes from improved process *effectiveness* of integrating the chimneys. This common situation arises because effectiveness benefits, such as improved service and revenue generation, are generally more difficult to define and quantify than cost savings, typically involving simple headcount reduction. However, of the numerous strategic programmes to which we have applied Value Management, the achieved effectiveness benefits far outweighed cost savings in most cases.

The first problem concerns imprecise starting conditions.

The second problem relates to poor or misdirected assessment of the value status of the programme during and after implementation. In this example, the value opportunity for shifting emphasis from reducing headcount to addressing the integration between

---

8   Strassmann, P. 2001. Technology and the bottom line – making the connection. Butler Group conference and exhibition, Marriott Hotel, Heathrow, 20–21 June 2001, conference paper.

welfare chimneys was exposed quite early in the programme. However, the programme board continued to focus on cost savings because this was their measure of success. This pattern also occurs when the programme cost or margin becomes the dominant measure, rather than overall value. For example, in major defence contracts programme managers are assessed by their ability to maintain a defined margin. Such is the pressure for and pain of failure in not delivering these margins that monthly reports become smokescreens behind which problems are hidden until much later when a myriad of other circumstances can be blamed.

The second problem concerns failure to collect and act upon accurate feedback.

Myth 3: Big Bang Implementation is Best

Some lessons you never forget. My father encouraged me to use woodworking tools before I started school and to learn by making mistakes. I did, and still have the scars to prove it. Quietly watching me throwing 'a hissy', together with the saws, hammers and chisels in frustration at my repeated failures, he would just calmly repeat, 'measure twice cut once' and I wrote this on Adam's first toolbox. This brings us to the next myth, the delusion of a big bang approach. Caught up in the euphoria and revolutionary appeal of business process re-engineering, the welfare benefits programme was initiated to develop a single solution using an 'all or nothing' model. This was despite the immense complexity of the challenge and cost of failure.

Here we need a shift in approach with some corroboration from science. The discovery of modern quantum theory in the 1920s brought us the greatest leap in our understanding of, and approach to, causality in the physical world since Isaac Newton. Two key principles of quantum physics are wave-particle duality and uncertainty. The first humbles us to realise that there is no single way of measuring a situation or developing a solution. The second teaches us to expect the unexpected. The key message from quantum theory for business transformation is not to reject Newtonian laws – they are more relevant than ever – but to recognise the need to develop and test multiple options. In Value Management we apply these principles by building proof of concept models which enable us to develop multiple solutions and inject pragmatic levels of certainty by testing them to destruction before committing to a full solution. We measure twice and cut once.

Advanced modelling techniques and computer tools enable us to develop and test options cost effectively with speed and certainty.

Advances Applied in Value Management

HISTORICAL CONTEXT

The approach to Value Management described in this book was founded while working on computer-integrated manufacturing programmes during the late 1970s. A key observation looking over the subsequent 30 years is that fundamental challenges and underlying principles have not changed. For example, investment appraisals demanded discounted cash flow analyses in order to be credible with financial directors, from whom approval was being sought. We were grappling with the inadequacy of absorption-based standard costing systems to provide true attribution of benefits to proposed programmes. Managing capacity to meet uncertain and fluctuating demand was just as critical as it is today, together with cooperation between hierarchical functions to deliver value through cross-functional processes. Managing performance consumed far more time reconciling inconsistent data sources than using information to create value; a pattern we still see in most of our clients' businesses, even with IT we could only have dreamed of then. However, the greatest challenge was, and is still, how to model and quantify the complex cause and effect relationships linking portfolios of programmes to measurable financial outcomes, and then maintaining the motivation, commitment and governance through people at all levels within the business to deliver intended benefits.

The next observation concerns the consistency of issues across very different sectors, industries and applications, most of which are manifested as repeating patterns. Importantly, this consistency holds true between private and public sectors. For example, all the above issues are just as relevant and critical for public services as they are for commercial enterprises in the private sector. Just as the issues can be modelled as archetypal patterns, so can the solutions; a characteristic that we exploit in Value Management.

What have changed dramatically are the technologies, tools, techniques and methods available to diagnose the problems, design and implement solutions and incorporate them into business as usual operations. It is now appropriate to outline key advances across a spectrum of disciplines and how they are applied in Value Management. We approach this in two parts:

1. advances in technology and process
2. advances in thinking

Advances in Technology and Process

During the previous three decades, key advances in IT and business processes have emerged which are of direct and massive significance to creating value. In Table 1.1 we summarise these advances and their application to Value Management.

Table 1.1　Advances in technology and process

Area	Advance	Value Management application
IT	Advances in hardware and software engineering standards, architectures and programme management, when applied effectively, have resulted in more reliable delivery of technical functionality.	We apply key IT development disciplines, such as verification and validation, in the framework (see Chapter 11). We trace benefits to the technical functionally and associated business capability, which enable the benefits, through precise cause and effect linkage (see Chapter 7).
Business Intelligence	From a Value Management perspective, the most important advance in IT is Business Intelligence (BI). BI can interrogate and makes sense of large, complex data sets and provide timely and accurate information as an easily accessible single source of truth for business managers to track current performance, and compare this against historical performance.	We use BI to provide current and historic actual data for value realisation (see Appendix B). BI is combined with advanced predictive modelling to provide dynamic performance management (see Appendix C) so that on-target improvements in value from incremental change programmes become a business as usual fact.
Business process focus	There is now universal recognition of the critical role of processes in delivering value. By targeting process we are focusing on the activities that actually generate the value and incur costs. The core process by which a business delivers value to its customers is called the *value chain*.	We define the value chain as the starting point for the causal approach (see Chapter 5). Process elimination and simplification are primary means for deriving reduced cost and increased revenue benefits (see Chapter 6).
Activity-Based Costing (ABC) and Activity-Based Management (ABM) Combined these are referred to as Activity-Based Cost Management (ABC/M)	ABC assigns cost drivers to activities in order to provide a precise causal relationship between what, to whom and how processes deliver, that is products, customers and channels, and how much resource is consumed in each combination. ABM examines how cost drivers can be influenced to deliver more stakeholder value for less cost.	We apply ABC and ABM principles to relate key drivers to activities at the 'point of power', where greatest value can be created both to reduce costs and increase revenue (see Chapter 6). Cost driver behaviour is quantified causally using dynamics modelling (see Appendix A).
Modelling value	Although dynamic simulation tools have been available for some time, in the past they were expensive, difficult to use and suffered from poor user interfaces. This situation has changed dramatically. Many relatively inexpensive (typically £1000 to £5000) dynamics modelling tools are now available with the result that complexity can be harnessed to generate extraordinary value.	We combine dynamics modelling and financial analysis to build more precise and robust business cases (see Appendix A). We combine dynamics modelling with BI to provide dynamic performance management (see Appendix C).

Area	Advance	Value Management application
Programme management	Over the last 20 years there has been an increasing emphasis on applying structured project, programme and portfolio management. Principal among these for the UK are PRINCE2™, Managing Successful Programmes (MPS), Portfolio, Programme and Project Offices (P3O) and Management of Value (MoV) from the Office of Government Commerce (OGC).	We ensure compatibility with these methods by providing a generic framework which emphasises explicit links between the programme deliverables and intended business benefits. To this end we use the best material available from all disciplines, incorporating a precise linkage to benefits (see Chapter 7).
Performance management	Since the early 1990s, businesses have undergone a transition from using historical financial accounts to future focused metrics within a performance management framework. The most widely used approach and the one we adopt for Value Management is the Balanced Scorecard (BSC). Other similar approaches are the European Federation of Quality Model (EFQM) and Baldrige Model.	We use strategy mapping within a performance management structure as the foundation for dynamic business models to link programme deliverables explicitly to business benefits. BSC is most widely used but the causal approach is generic to any performance management framework (see Chapter 5).
Governance	In addition to effective processes, we also need clear organisational structures and governance to make them work. Business governance is essentially about ownership, and the appropriate allocation of accountability. Governance recognises the need for clear leadership and management of processes.	We define unambiguous ownerships and 'failure is not an option' relationships between owners of benefits, drivers and programme deliverables (see Chapter 5). We apply strong process governance through the IMPACT – intention, model, programme, alignment, certainty, track – framework which is generic and compatible with any methodology (see Chapter 11).

Advances in Thinking

Technology and process advances provide the potential for significant improvements in value delivery from change programmes. However, although many of these are being applied the expected level of improvement has not materialised – why is this? The answer lies in our flawed mental models which dictate the assumptions and beliefs that prevent us from the necessary shifts in thinking. Conversely, if we change the way we perceive problems to reflect reality more precisely, we will be able to exploit these advances much more effectively. This applies to both individuals and groups.

The easier value opportunities for reducing cost and/or increasing revenue, so called 'low-hanging fruit' such as simple headcount reductions and automation are usually exhausted. The remaining value opportunities often go undetected or are considered too woolly to quantify. This is largely because conventional approaches focus on surface level events and fail to identify opportunities requiring exposure of relationships deeper within the chains of cause and effect that drive value.

Consequently, in order to release significant additional value we need a means of enquiry into these underlying causal relationships. This requires two things: a repeatable process for effective thinking and tools to deal with the complexity. There are two closely related advances which provide both process and tools:

1. Neuro-Linguistic Programming
2. systems thinking

Neuro-Linguistic Programming

Neuro-Linguistic Programming (NLP) was developed in the 1970s by Richard Bandler and John Grindler, who modelled the best change experts in their field, to determine the distinctions that accounted for their consistent success in achieving profound positive outcomes for their clients. They translated their discoveries into a number of processes that can be learnt and techniques that deliver repeatable permanent results.

NLP comprises a set of processes and techniques for achieving excellence.

NLP is now widely used across many areas in business, notably interpersonal communications, sales, coaching and training. However, the ability most relevant to Value Management is to produce radical shifts in performance by re-programming limiting perceptions and transform them into mental models which enable clients to release latent potential through change. This process is called a value breakthrough.

Systems Thinking

Systems are things that maintain their existence and function as a whole through the interaction of their parts. The human body, environment, societies and families are all systems. So are markets, businesses and transformation programmes. Recent advances in systemic sciences provide powerful insights and applications for Value Management, which we will be exploring in Part II. Some aspects of systems thinking are deterministic and enable us to achieve repeatable predicted results, which is important in quantifying causal relationships between programmes and intended benefits.

Other elements, relating to complexity, are non-deterministic and cannot be used to predict exact results. However, despite being immersed in Nobel Prize-winning mathematics, some fundamental principles can be applied in business, as metaphors. For example, complex systems, such as weather, are sensitive to starting conditions and feedback. These principles translate into two complementary concepts upon which the Value Management approach is structured: *right first time* and *tracking and correction*.

Right first time refers to an achievable, best condition, or state, from which value can be created most effectively. These starting conditions are defined with the development and approval of a baseline business case, which forms the value datum from which to implement the programme, and includes prerequisites and resources required to achieve success.

Tracking and correction refers to the process of measuring progress, assessing the value status against the baseline, and implementing the most effective action in order to ensure that the programme remains on purpose and on value against that purpose. The *baseline business case* becomes a vital programme management tool. Paradoxically, the most critical role of the business case is not to be proved right, but exposing variances that most affect value so that corrections can be put into place immediately, *when* they are most effective. In Value Management, we refer to the tracking and correction process as *value realisation*.

Value Breakthroughs

Value breakthroughs provide a repeatable process and tools for essential changes in thinking and are founded on six key principles, which mirror the solutions needed to address repeating failure patterns that we discuss in Chapter 4:

1. Commitment
2. Cause and effect
3. Timeline
4. Congruence
5. Specificity
6. Feedback

Commitment

Commitment is arguably the most critical characteristic in Value Management but is a word that we often use with casual abandon. We delude ourselves that because we say that we are committed we mean it and because of the human tendency to believe what we want to believe, we also take the word of others when they say that they are committed to something. Ask why we continually buy the spin dished out by politicians, even after they perpetually fail to deliver on promises. Outcomes are purpose driven, meaning that their achievement is in alignment with purpose. Dan Pink[9] identifies purpose, along with autonomy and mastery, as key to motivation for cognitive tasks. True commitment comprises two components:

1. Dedication to achievement of a purpose driven outcome;
2. Total ownership of the achievement of the outcome.

Value Management is a demanding discipline which means not hiding behind tick boxes, mistakes by other people, the economy, due diligence or any other protection mechanism or excuse.

---

9   Pink, D. 2010. *Drive: The strange truth about what motivates us.* Available at http://www.goodreads.com/videos/list_author/96150.Daniel_H_Pink, accessed 9 December 2010.

To cause intended outcomes we must have full and aligned commitment to purpose.

Commitment to outcomes is also a collaborative undertaking. In change programmes there will be at least two roles. First, responsibility for delivering new business capabilities, *deliverables*, typically lies with the programme manager. Secondly, for the realisation of *benefits*, enabled by the deliverables, will usually be the responsibility of an appropriate senior business manager. This relationship is often unclear: for example, who is ultimately accountable for the benefits, the programme manager or the business managers in whose function the benefits are intended to be manifested?

In Value Management the answer is *both*. This recognises the critical dependence between deliverables and benefits. If there is, as is often the case, even subtle resistance from key people in the programme, the intended benefits will not be achieved. Although disagreements, doubts and even some confusion concerning *how* outcomes will be achieved can be useful because they encourage the right questions, once decisions are made total commitment is essential, despite any lingering doubts. The important prerequisites are faith in the purpose and willingness to suspend doubt in achieving the outcome. Commitment is driven through clear ownership and a willingness to 'stick with it' until the end; sadly often the winner is not the one who is right, but always the one who is left! Commitment is covered in Chapter 5.

Everything but total commitment is sabotage.
David Shephard, Performance Partnership

Cause and Effect

Life is not fair, it is causal. In Value Management, cause and effect is the basis upon which we build the entire framework. NLP is also founded on the Law of Cause and Effect, expressed in terms of results and reasons as shown in Figure 1.1.

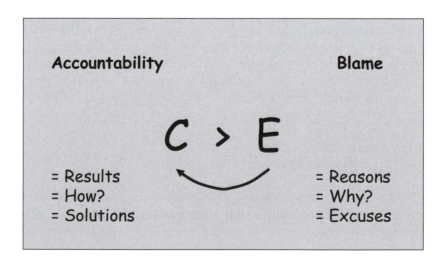

Figure 1.1   The cause and effect equation

Figure 1.1 highlights the distinction between blame and accountability:

- Blame is the apportionment of failure;
- Accountability is the ownership of solution.

The key to this NLP presupposition is that we need to remain *in cause* at all times. We ask not *why* something failed but *how* we are causing failure and *how* we fix it, right now. When we ask a *why?* question we are subconsciously searching for reasons and places to offload blame with a mindset in the past. Conversely, by asking *how* we are failing we are taking ownership of results with a future perspective.

In Value Management blame is of no practical use because it does not promote solutions. This does not mean that we excuse failure, far from it; it means that we assign accountability for success. In order for accountability to work, we must remove all excuses. Therefore, in Value Management we approach challenges by dovetailing two *extreme* questions:

1. What must be done to achieve intended outcomes, assuming that all necessary resources were available but no excuses are acceptable?
2. What resources would have to be available to provide certainty that the intended outcomes will be achieved?

In Value Management, ownership is placed squarely at *points of power* where effective resources can be *authorised* and *deployed*. We cover cause and effect and ownership in Chapters 5 and 6 when considering deliverable, benefit and driver owners.

Timeline

We cause the outcomes that we direct most attention on. This is called the law of attraction and it works at a subconscious level. Therefore, it is important to feed the subconscious mind with what we desire, rather than what we don't want – this law is impassive and we could get either result. For example, most diets fail because we are focused on wanting to lose weight, so we only attract 'wanting to lose weight' in a never-ending cycle. Instead, to harness the law of attraction we must focus on how we will look and feel when we have attained our target weight; then the target weight is what we attract. The law is used most effectively when intended outcomes are defined in time. Time itself has value. In value breakthroughs timelines are crucial and the most effective way to use a timeline is to *learn* from the past and *align* the future.

We cause outcomes by attracting them through focus.

In Value Management, the timeline is derived by linking benefits explicitly to milestones in the programme plan which then provide the focus for achieving the benefits. Time value of money is accounted for in discounted cash flow techniques for investment appraisal. Programme linkage is covered in Chapter 7.

Congruence

In NLP, congruence refers to consistency between beliefs, values and actions. This means that we 'walk our talk'. Change is the process of energy exchange and congruence is the means by which most energy is generated and directed effectively to achieve defined outcomes. The most effective way to achieve congruent energy of change is by *aligning* values. Values are those things that are most important to us and therefore what we find easiest to devote both time and effort to. For business it is crucial to promote shared values because this provides a double whammy; strong group energy can be generated and the minimum of this energy is dissipated through conflicts.

Energy and commitment are driven by the degree to which our values are aligned.

In Value Management, congruence is achieved through exhaustive reviewing of value models across the business and by aligning the benefits in the programme plan through an implementation strategy. Value alignment is covered in Chapter 8.

Specificity

It is generally known that the subconscious mind can achieve seemingly impossible results through its ability to deal with immense complexity, far in excess of the level manageable by the conscious mind. However, what is less well appreciated is that in order to cope with complexity, the subconscious must have simple instructions. In this respect, the subconscious mind is like a child's. It is one of the great paradoxes of the human mind that explains the power of one-liners, spin and why a single memorable message is far more effective than a 'death by PowerPoint presentation'. In *The Tipping Point*, Malcolm Gladwell refers to this phenomenon as the 'stickiness factor'.[10] Additionally, the more specific the instructions, the greater certainty there is that intended outcomes will be achieved.

The subconscious mind acts on simple, specific and repeated instructions.

Therefore, the key to creating value lies not in detail or sophistication but *specificity*. The subconscious mind does not recognise negatives; for example, try not to think of a blue tree. Consequently, as the law of attraction dictates, it is important to ensure that instructions are positive. We must define precise measures and defined levels of achievement for performance management because we get what we measure. For this reason there is a critical distinction between targets and standards:

- Targets are aspirations the achievement of which is desirable;
- Standards are levels of achievement below which is unacceptable.

---

10   Gladwell, M. 2000. *The Tipping Point: How Little Things can Make a Big Difference*. London: Abacus.

In Value Management we adopt the principle of *precise simplicity*, covered in Chapter 3, and apply it by defining criteria by which achievement is defined and ensure certainty by destruction testing, explored in Chapter 9.

Feedback

An attribute of successful entrepreneurs is persistence in focusing on a clearly defined vision and ability to respond effectively to changing circumstances in order to achieve the vision. A key presupposition of NLP is that there is no such thing as failure, only feedback, which is used for learning and correction. An important purpose of planning is to provide the means by which feedback and correction can be coordinated effectively.

Success and failure are simply feedback.

In Value Management, feedback is reflected in *tracking* changes in drivers and the consequential benefits and implementing corrective action in order to remain on purpose and on value. Tracking is covered in Chapter 10.

Essence

The principal learning from this chapter is summarised below:

- Value Management represents a shift from wishful thinking to causal certainty
- Redressing the current failure level of programmes to deliver value provides a massive opportunity
- Many programme failures can be traced to three myths: value correlates with spend, wishful thinking will do and big bang implementation is best
- Value Management applies and combines advances in technology and process, together with advances in thinking
- Advances in technology and process span: IT architecture and standards, BI, process focus and Activity-Based Management, programme management, governance and dynamics modelling
- Advances in thinking include NLP and systems thinking which are combined in value breakthroughs

2 *Defining Value*

Objectives

After reading this chapter you will be able to:

- Define value as a simple universal equation
- Define the concept of value from several different, complementary perspectives
- Apply the value equation consistently across perspectives

A Universal Definition for Value

In our value breakthrough workshops, delegates are asked to define business value. We generate some interesting responses which typically include: quality, importance, worth, utility, market price and the favourite, what customers are willing to pay. Although technically correct, these and similar definitions leave us with three fundamental problems. First, they are inconsistent. For example, how do we reconcile quality, utility and market price and consolidate them into a common usable measure? Secondly, they do not support precise quantification; how do we quantify utility or quality? Thirdly, there is no reference to the cost of achieving these results. For example, how can we assess value if we do not know the cost of providing the intended utility or achieving the desired market price? Before we define value for practical application within Value Management, we need to define some key distinctions.

Inputs, Outputs and Outcomes

The first distinction concerns inputs, outputs and outcomes. The failure to recognise and act upon the implications of differences between these components is a major reason why initiatives fail to deliver intended value, because focus is misdirected and misaligned:

- Inputs are things that consume resources and generate cost in the production of outputs;
- Outputs are things that are produced through the consumption of resources;
- Outcomes are the benefits to stakeholders, which include shareholders, customers, staff and suppliers, delivered through the outputs.

The Late Train Story

Imagine, if it is not already the case, that you are one of life's hardiest warriors, the rail commuter. It is 07:30 on a Monday morning in January. You intend to catch your usual; 07:40 into the city, which takes 45 minutes on a good day. It is raining. After queuing for ten minutes to buy a ticket, you find that there is another inflation-busting fare increase. People are bunched up under the station canopy, built in 1900 and leaking, in an attempt to stay dry. You know that if you remain with everyone else, the probability of getting a seat reduces from low to virtually zero. So at 07:35 you venture into the rain and make your way to the far end of the platform where it is marginally less crowded and the last carriage sometimes has seats. At 07:36 a muffled voice comes over the tannoy to announce that the 07:40 has been cancelled due to driver illness. There is hardly a murmur, it's Monday and we are British.

You stay where you are, wet and angry. People catching the next train, due in at 07:55, now fill the platform even more. At 07:53 the loudspeaker bleats another unwelcome message; the next train comprises eight coaches instead of the usual ten, but they apologise for any inconvenience to your journey, as if there is a possibility that you will not notice the difference. You move down the platform but have lost your strategic position near the doors. The train arrives and the crush to board commences. People are already standing in the aisles. As you reach the doors you say, 'after you' to the person nearest to you as you enter. What you are thinking is, 'If you get the last seat I'm afraid you are going to die', but they are quite safe. You resign yourself to nearly an hour of utter purgatory, standing. The guard announces that he will be checking tickets ('let him try' you huff audibly) and that if he can do anything to assist in your journey he is located in the centre of the train (seated).

You unravel your newspaper as far as you dare, and there, on the front page, is the lead article; 'Record investment in railways'. The article explains how the government is committed to public transport, and because safety is at the top of their agenda, they are funding upgraded signals and 600 miles of replacement track, somewhere, this year. Suddenly, mention of signals alerts you the location, Clapham, where another Monday some years ago, weekend signalling work was left unfinished and resulted in many deaths. When, after many jerky stops and starts, you arrive a further ten minutes late, you catch the gist of a further apology as you walk along the platform.

Another great start to the week.

Now let's unpick these components from the Late Train Story. Inputs are resources used or engaged in running the railway, which include staff, trains, rails, stations, signals and power and so on, all of which consume money. The important point is that inputs do not necessarily deliver what stakeholders want by just being there. For example, more staff at the station does not necessarily translate into less queuing for tickets. In the Shove Penny machine, which we introduced at the beginning of this book, inputs are the coins that are fed onto the sliding trays; some land on other coins, some miss the tray altogether and some make it onto the tray and push other coins, but because these are not connected to the overhanging coins, the desired effect is still not achieved.

Outputs are the means by which stakeholder outcomes are delivered, and for railways outputs are 'journeys' (equivalent to flights in aviation or voyages in seafaring). Again, the delivery of outputs does not guarantee that stakeholder wants and needs are actually met. For example, is there a train when you need it and get you to that critical meeting on time? Outputs can also be negative, for example, carbon emissions from diesel locomotives and jet engines. Outputs are the coins that are pushed into chutes; some go to the winning tray but most end up in the side chutes.

Outcomes are what stakeholders actually experience. Intended outcomes will normally relate to the highest purpose of the business; in the case of train operators delivering passengers or freight to desired destinations undamaged, comfortably and when needed. Outcomes are the coins that are finally corralled into the winning trays. There are several stakeholders but for now let's consider you, the customer, and your priorities, which include:

- Availability of a train when you need it in order to achieve your intended outcome, for example getting to work on time, catching your holiday flight and so on
- Reliability, that is, faith that the train you want will actual turn up and you do not have to catch an earlier train just to be on the safe side
- Convenience in booking or buying a ticket, parking at the station and so on
- The train turns up on time and arrives at your destination on time
- Getting a comfortable seat
- Smooth journey, without violent swaying and sharp braking
- Confidence that you will arrive safely and actually do arrive safely
- Affordable cost proportionate to the outcome

Rather lower in your priority list are:

- Polite apologies at the start of the journey for not delivering your outcomes
- Guards offering assistance which has no bearing on meeting your outcomes
- More polite apologies at the end of your journey for not delivering your outcomes

When standing up on the wrong, overcrowded train for which you have paid a premium because you are obliged to travel during peak times, you might be forgiven for being underwhelmed at the news concerning extra investment for railways. More succinctly, you don't give a damn how many signals are erected or rails replaced this year, the fact is that not one of your desired outcomes has been met. Yet where in the article did it mention how specifically these replaced rails and upgraded signals would contribute to your desired outcomes, precisely by how much and specifically when? The answer is nowhere. The presupposition is that by spending some money and outputting something, desired outcomes will somehow result. In this book we refer to this *input* focus as 'marks for trying'.

Conflict between inputs, outputs and outcomes tend to get worse where ill-conceived targets are involved. For example, some train operating companies have adopted the common practice of missing out scheduled intermediate stations when trains are running late because they are measured on achieving the final destination on time. The train operator achieves the target, but passengers arrive at their destination even later because they must take next train *back* to the station they have just zoomed through; the output is met but not the outcome. We discuss the implications of inappropriate targets in Chapter 6.

Some argue that it is impossible to commit to outcomes when the linkage is so long and intangible. The same argument was made concerning the value of quality in manufacturing, an error which cost the UK very dearly. However, most programmes have poor or no definition of how promised outcomes will be achieved and consequently fail to deliver them. How much better would it be if investments could be defined in terms of linkage between programme deliverables and intended outcomes? This does not require multiple decimal point accuracy, but clear causal precision which can be measured, tracked and managed.

Differentiating between inputs, outputs and outcomes is critical to Value Management and it is worth practising this skill across as many situations as possible until it becomes second nature. Some further simple examples are given in Table 2.1, noting that we have not included how these relate to value at this point:

Table 2.1   Distinction between inputs, outputs and outcomes

Organisation	Input	Output	Outcome
Enterprise	Costbase	Product/service	Revenue/margin
Health	Operating theatres	Operations	Patient health
Police	Officers	Arrests	Crime level/fear of crime
Education	Teachers	Qualified students	Sustainable employment

There are several key issues in Table 2.1. First, the examples demonstrate that it is relatively more difficult to define, let alone deliver, outcomes than inputs or outputs. For example, in the case of the police, deployment of officers, an input, is done through resource management and costs are controlled through budgets. Keeping track of arrests, an output, involves detailed compliance with legal procedures. Although these tasks require heavy administration, they are clearly defined. Conversely, it is extraordinarily problematic to define and analyse crime levels. The same difficulty is encountered in health care, teaching and generally across all sectors.

Secondly, the table illustrates the fundamental difference between private and public sectors. For commercial enterprises operating in efficient markets, the degree to which desired stakeholder benefits are met is reflected in revenue, and associated margin in relation to the cost of sales, from customers who exercise real choice. Businesses have to be concerned with delivering intended outcomes to customers because ultimately, they have to attract sufficient custom to survive. Although this relationship is affected by distortions in the market, such as monopolies and/or cartels and so on, the essential outcome measure, revenue, remains clear and operates as a surrogate for successful customer outcomes. Conversely, public organisations do not have a revenue component driven by free choice and face a dilemma of how to measure and declare their outcome performance. Governments use various devices to encourage market efficiencies, such as funding caps, pseudo competition, league tables and targets. The problem is that all these can be mutually opposing. For example, the pursuit of targets without adequate funding, and/or appropriate context, often leads to game playing and manipulative behaviour which counters delivery of stakeholder outcomes.

This leads us to the next issue, the problem of focusing on particular measures to the exclusion of others. If we focus purely on minimising inputs through budgeting, we risk the effects of under-capacity and corner cutting. For example, overzealous cost containment in the privatised UK railway infrastructure contributed to several horrific, but completely avoidable, fatal accidents involving substandard track. If we focus on delivering outputs, we risk delivering the easy ones to make up the figures. For example, if hospitals are measured by the number of operations, and are penalised for underperformance against this measure, there will be a tendency to favour easier, quicker procedures. Surely, the answer is simply to shift our focus from inputs and outputs to outcome measures. Unfortunately, this will not cut it either. It results in achieving one outcome at the expense of others, and/or manipulation of the statistics. For example, after much self-congratulation about reducing violent assaults, a previous British government was forced to apologise for over-favourable knife crime statistics.

The key conclusion from these observations is that not only do we need to take into account measures relating to all three components – inputs, outputs and outcomes – but also *align* the measures causally in such away that they work together to deliver value to stakeholders. This is difficult enough in the private sector, where the challenge is to convert products and services, which are outputs, into the intended outcome of greater sales at higher margins. The process demands knowledge of what customers want and need, even if they don't know it themselves yet. This explains the increase in Customer Relationship Management (CRM) systems which aim to capture customer knowledge, and enable businesses to offer value propositions which target specific, profitable market niches and customer segments.

Quantifying the linkage between inputs, outputs and outcomes in the public sector is even more difficult. For example, how should police resources be deployed in order to make arrests and secure subsequent prosecutions that result in reduced crime and fear of crime? This fundamental question raises issues which are constantly in the news and very politically charged. Do we need more police officers on the beat or detectives following leads, more legwork or more technology and so on? What types of crime should resources be focused on and how are arrests being reflected in a reduction in this type of offence? It soon becomes apparent that imposing broad targets will not provide the level of precision needed. Whilst Value Management does not pretend to offer packaged solutions to these complex challenges, it certainly can help to *direct*, *drive* and *deliver* solutions which result in the greatest value to stakeholders.

> *Input, output and outcome measures must be aligned through the cause and effect relationships between them.*

Effectiveness and Efficiency

The second distinction concerns the fundamental difference between *effectiveness* and *efficiency*. These two terms are often used synonymously but are very different, and this misuse is the source of more confusion than just about anything else in both business and human endeavour. Peter Drucker[1] provided arguably the most succinct and useful definitions:

- Effectiveness is doing the right things
- Efficiency is doing things right

Effectiveness is the degree to which intended stakeholder outcomes are delivered. Because outcomes are delivered through outputs, it follows that effectiveness is a measure of the extent to which outputs achieve desired outcomes. An effectiveness mindset is needed to deliver good customer service. Conversely, efficiency is the relationship between inputs and the outputs that they produce; it is a measure of outputs produced for a given level of inputs. An efficiency mindset is needed for good productivity and cost control.

For example, if we were to apply this distinction to the Late Train Story, imagine that in an effort to improve services the train operating company upgrades its signalling system, an input, enabling more train journeys per hour, an output, for the same operating cost. The company has therefore improved its efficiency. If by virtue of these extra train journeys more passengers are able to arrive at their destination on time, then the signalling upgrade will have also increased effectiveness. It is important to recognise that an increase in efficiency does not necessarily mean an increase in effectiveness and visa versa. It may be the case that the extra trains are at inconvenient times or consist of fewer carriages and thus the additional train journeys fail to translate into desired customer outcomes.

It is crucial to define effectiveness, that is what outcomes are needed, before planning for efficiency, otherwise we risk doing the wrong things well. For example, we have witnessed the spectacle of robotic production lines manufacturing products that nobody wants and storing them in just in time (JIT) warehouses; the same warehouses that the JIT system was intended to eliminate. Unfortunately, this kind of situation is all too common.

The Value Equation

For practical purposes, we use money to provide a universal measure of worth; a common unit. It must be stressed that not everything can, or should, be measured in money; for example, what financial figure do we assign to human life? In practice however, almost everything will have an economic footprint of some sort. Therefore, we need a single measure that defines this footprint precisely in the context of benefits relative to the costs of achieving them. This measure is *value*. We condense the key distinctions into the value equation as emblazoned in Figure 2.1.

Value is the degree to which benefits exceed the cost of realising them.

---

1   Drucker, P. 1993. *The Effective Executive: The Definitive Guide to Getting the Right Things Done.* New York: HarperBusiness.

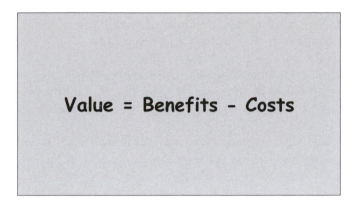

Figure 2.1   Value equation

This equation tells us that from whichever stakeholder viewpoint we are looking, value is the difference between benefits and costs incurred to achieve them. Benefits are what the stakeholder ultimately wants, or dis-benefits that they do not want. Benefits are stakeholder outcomes. Costs are what stakeholders must sacrifice personally, and/or the programme must spend on behalf of stakeholders, in the expectation of achieving the benefits. Costs relate directly to inputs. Therefore, because benefits or outcomes and costs or inputs can be used interchangeably for practical purposes, the value equation can also be written:

Value = Outcomes – Inputs

This definition of value not only holds true for all of the above and, incidentally, every interaction of the universe, but also provides us with an equation from which we can anchor all our subsequent thinking. Because value is stakeholder-specific, we need to define value as the difference between outcomes and inputs, measured in the context of a given stakeholder perspective for a defined situation and timescale. Also, in order for the value equation to be valid, both benefits and costs must be expressed in the same units, ideally financial terms. This presents a problem for the public sector and not-for-profit organisations, when the satisfaction of outcomes does not readily translate into monetary measures, such as revenue.

Value for Money

Value for money is a very commonly used term and the subject of considerable confusion. A useful definition of value for money from the Improvement and Development Agency (IDeA) which in its procurement guidance defines best value for money as the 'optimum combination of whole-life costs and benefits to meet the customer's requirement'.

More specifically, value for money is widely used to describe the optimal balance between outputs and inputs. Good value for money gives *efficiency* (the ratio of an activity to the resources input), *economy* (the purchase of goods or services at lowest cost) and *effectiveness* (the extent to which objectives are achieved).[2]

The value equation can be expressed as a quotient to reflect value for money in a simplified form which relates benefits, that is, outcomes, directly to costs, that is, inputs (costs and inputs are taken to be the same thing for practical purposes and objectives are synonymous with outcomes):

$$Value\ for\ money = Benefits/Costs$$

or

$$Value\ for\ money = Outcomes/Inputs$$

Now let us decompose this relationship into two further components relating to effectiveness and efficiency. Effectiveness concerns the extent to which stakeholder outcomes are delivered by the outputs:

$$Effectiveness = Outcomes/Outputs$$

Efficiency is the relationship between what the business outputs and the input resources consumed in the transformation:

$$Efficiency = Outputs/Inputs$$

When we combine these relationships we get:

$$Value\ for\ Money = (Outcomes/Outputs) \times (Outputs/Inputs)$$

$$Value\ for\ Money = Effectiveness \times Efficiency$$

This insultingly simple relationship provides massive power in our quest to deliver value from change programmes. First, it tells us that in order to realise value, we must take into account both effectiveness and efficiency. Secondly, we now have a quantitative route to linking inputs that we consume, not only with the outputs produced, but also with the outcomes that those outputs deliver to stakeholders.

Returning once again to the Late Train Story, we could express value for money as:

$$Value\ for\ money = (Seated\ timely\ journeys)/Journeys) \times (Journeys/Cost)$$

$$Value\ for\ money = Seated\ timely\ journeys/Cost$$

---

2   North West Network. 2011. *Glossary: value for money.* Available at: http://www.nwnetwork.org.uk/glossary/term/118, accessed 7 January 2011.

Whilst, as with any other indicator, it would be dangerous to use this measure in isolation, it does provide the foundation for a high-level outcome focus towards which other performance drivers can be linked. In Part II we develop this linkage and in Appendix A we use it to build dynamics models.

Stakeholder Perspectives

Stakeholders are people who have some relationship with the business and stand to gain or lose depending on how it behaves and performs. From a business perspective, we use the term stakeholder to describe all those different people who interact with the business and are the recipients of value from the business. There are three key categories of stakeholder. First, there are people who have an ownership or direct interest in the fortunes of the business, such as shareholders in a commercial enterprise or government, on behalf of taxpayers in the public sector. Secondly, there are people who buy, use or are affected by the outputs from the business. These include customers who want the outputs because they lead to achievement of their desired outcomes, and people who have to live with pollution, who do not want the output because it results in unwanted outcomes. Finally, there are people who provide input to or are *engaged* in the transition of inputs into outputs, such as staff and suppliers. Stakeholders are of primary importance in Value Management because they are the recipients and owners of benefits, and they will figure strongly throughout this book.

Value is only relevant in the context of a stakeholder. It is clear from the definitions volunteered at our workshops that value is in the eye of the beholder. For example, what value do motorists associate with their car? Cars are designed to perform the same function. However, for one person, travelling in comfort is the most important attribute. For another, it is the status that they perceive people attach to the vehicle. The components in the value equation also depend on the stakeholder perspective. For example, considering the Late Train Story, if the stakeholder is the customer, cost relates to the price that must be paid to purchase their intended outcome. Conversely, for the train operating company, cost relates to the resources needed to deliver the same customer outcome. Business stakeholders can be categorised into four different types, as shown in Figure 2.2 (separating staff and suppliers).

Stakeholders are recipients of value from the business.

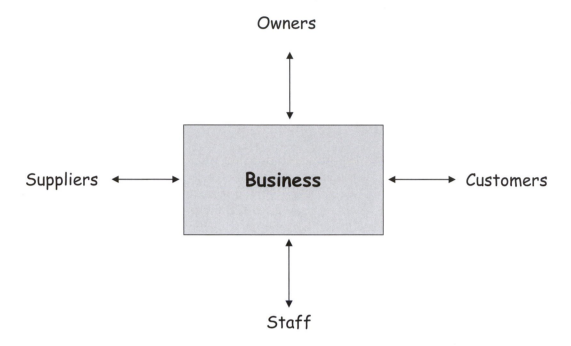

Figure 2.2   Stakeholder perspectives

Market, social and environmental forces also impact stakeholder interactions with the business. For example, competition and cultural attitudes influence customer behaviour and the cost of labour, and physical limitations on natural resources affect the price availability of raw materials. It is important to make a distinction between the stakeholder role and the actual entity assuming the role. An entity can have multiple stakeholder perspectives. For example, an employee will have a *staff* perspective but may also own shares in the employing company and assume an *owner* role too; the government can be an owner, on behalf of taxpayers, a customer or supplier.

> *The purpose of a business is to deliver value to its stakeholders.*

How value is experienced and measured will vary significantly for each stakeholder. For example, shareholders may be primarily concerned with ROI, customers with satisfaction in relation to the price paid, and staff in remuneration and career prospects in relation to their sacrifice in time, effort and family life. These are very much generalisations and it is important not to stereotype or pigeonhole stakeholders or their perception of value. Nevertheless, the point is that all these are manifestations of the value equation from the specific stakeholder perspective.

> *Each stakeholder is consciously or unconsciously building the*
> *value equation from their own viewpoint.*

If a business is to remain sustainable, the systems and processes that it adopts must be aligned; in other words, work together towards common economic goals. However, this economic alignment is not enough to ensure long-term successes. For a business to sustain value creation, the value itself must be balanced across the stakeholders, not necessarily equally but certainly equitably. The reason for this equitable distribution of value has nothing to do with ethics or political ideology. It is strictly business, or to be more precise, sustainable business.

Value must be balanced equitably across stakeholders in
order for the business to remain sustainable.

Once again, this principle is supported and explained by systems theory. Systems, of which businesses, markets and economies are complex examples, live or die through the interaction of their parts. In the case of businesses, a critically important part is its stakeholders. For example, if employees do not perceive that they are treated fairly, their dissatisfaction will be reflected in poor customer service, resulting in reduced revenue and increased cost through churn, sickness and absenteeism. The negative effect on profit reduces shareholder return and with it the ability to make the investment needed to sustain the business. It follows that benefits must be defined more precisely as the outcomes that are most important to stakeholders.

Value as a Process

The means by which value is continually delivered to stakeholders is through processes. Value is created or destroyed as a result of business processes. Thus the quality of the processes and our ability to follow them consistently will define the value we can create repeatedly for our stakeholders.

Processes provide the means by which we can repeat success.

The Further Education Story

A new term has emerged over recent years to describe an expanding group within the UK working age population – NEETS (Not in Employment, Education or Training).

Many of these predominately young people have left school with no or minimal qualifications, often grown up in households where there is no working adult and tend to have little self-esteem, motivation or ambition. NEETS represent a tragic waste and pose a particularly difficult challenge for government because they are neither readily employable nor suited to traditional education, which tends to impose rigid age windows and all or nothing qualifications. A more flexible approach is needed to break this vicious circle.

In response, government education bodies and further education colleges are structuring courses to provide a much more modular approach, whereby qualifications can be built up in stages and added over time. For example, a student can apply for a state-funded starter course in computer skills and on successful completion, is awarded credits which are of immediate value for gaining a job and provide the prerequisites for the next level.

There is currently a high drop-out rate on these courses and much debate about how effective they are in the real job market and contribution to the economy.

Consequently, the challenge of the further education *process* is to deliver fulfilled, competent and motivated people who contribute to the economic needs of the nation.

A process can be defined as comprising one or more activities which transform inputs into outputs, enabled by resources under the influence of controls. This definition of a process is represented simply and elegantly by IDEF0 as shown in Figure 2.3.

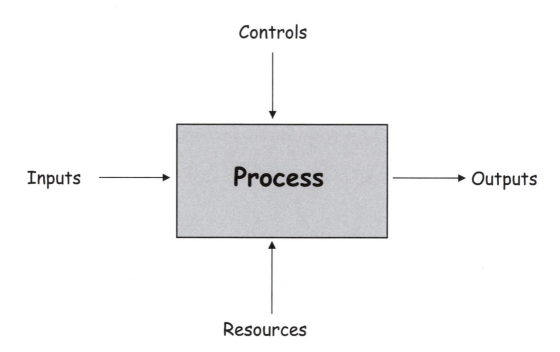

Figure 2.3   Process as defined by IDEF0

IDEF0, Integration Definition for Function Modelling, originated in the US aerospace industry and remains one of the most powerful and widely used process modelling tools. IDEF0 is a process mapping technique specified in Draft Federal Information Processing Standards Publication 183 (FIPS 183). It has a precise syntax. Using a top-down approach, activities, together with material and information flows, are disseminated from a high-level context diagram to increasingly detailed lower levels.

Inputs to a process are the objects which will undergo the transformation into outputs, such as raw materials, bought in goods and services and people. Process is the transformation. Outputs are the result of the transformation. Resources are the means by which the transformation takes place. Controls are the formal and/or informal rules under which the transformation takes place. An example of process for the Further Education Story is shown in Figure 2.4.

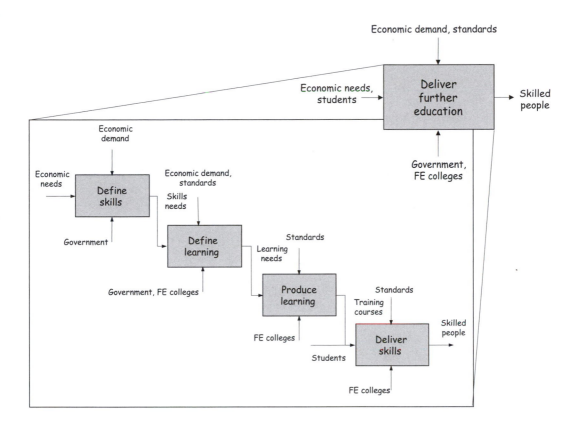

Figure 2.4   Further education process

In this example, the elements that make up the further education process are defined as follows:

- Inputs: for example students with prerequisite qualifications, credits, acceptance letters to a specific course and financial grants.
- Process: for example course of learning modules and examinations intended to result in the award of credits for successful students.
- Outputs: for example successful students, deemed to be skilled people evidenced through award of credits, or unsuccessful students who fail to acquire credits.
- Resources: for example government bodies, lecturers, FE college, faculty, laboratories, course notes, computer systems, and so on
- Controls: rules by which the transformation is necessitated and governed, for example, market demand for particular trades, the syllabus and academic, trade or regulatory standard.

A process transforms inputs into outputs using resources under the influence of controls.

The Missing Element

This definition focuses on the outputs from a process but does not address the value created from these outputs. This is problematic from a value perspective. The Shopping Story illustrates why.

The Shopping Story

Shopping in the supermarket on a Saturday morning in the 1980s we would see all the checkouts manned and busy, trolleys laden with life's essentials topped off with the recently arrived premium ice cream tubs. But when it came to paying, the experience was anything but smooth. The protracted process of fumbling for the cheque book and guarantee card, or proffering a credit card that then had to be carefully inserted into the 'zip-zap' machine, all took precious time.

This process was clearly ripe for innovation and so Electronic Funds Transfer at the Point of Sale (EFTPOS), was born. But rather than the banks and credit card operators, developments were led by smaller players who saw the opportunity and could move quickly to exploit it. In response, the banks set up a new company, EftPos UK. Its task was to create a single national business model and infrastructure that would allow us all a few seconds more leisure on Saturdays, whilst reducing the costs of payment processing for banks and retailers.

EftPos UK successfully resolved many complex business and technical issues, and created a whole new infrastructure that could process card payments in a fast, secure and highly reliable way. Collectively, over £100 million was spent by the banks on the programme, and much more by the individual banks in parallel internal developments to connect to this new infrastructure.

Sadly, only 5,000 such transactions took place using the EftPos UK solution and then the whole thing was switched off, never to be used again. It had been overtaken by wider market developments.

EftPos UK was a well-run programme and applied the best practices of the day to ensure clear definition of what was to be built. There were demonstrable benefits from what could be achieved with the new infrastructure. There was no shortage of resources, whether money or talented and committed individuals working on the programme. What was promised was actually delivered. So what went wrong? Let's answer that question from a value perspective. The following are simplified definitions for EFTPOS as a process:

- Inputs: shoppers at the checkout waiting to pay
- Process: card payment initiated at the point of sale (EFTPOS)
- Outputs: shoppers with completed payments
- Resources: EFTPOS systems, checkout clerks, payment clerks, funds and so on
- Controls: regulatory standards, bank policies, fraud check criteria and so on

Despite there being clearly defined inputs and outputs, adequate resources and best practice controls, the industry spent a great deal of money on something it never used. Intended value was not delivered. If the elements within this definition of process were right and it was implemented correctly, it follows that that there must be something missing from our definition of process. This missing element is outcomes. Outcomes refer to the degree to which stakeholders benefit in terms of what is most important from their specific viewpoint.

Outcomes are benefits to stakeholders.

The problem for EftPos UK was that none of the expected benefits – faster, cheaper and lower risk payments in retailers – that had been identified were actually achieved. A number of the key stakeholders decided that there were better ways to achieve the desired outcomes and pursed those alternatives. Because the programme was committed to outputs rather than outcomes, the programme was not corrected to reflect these external changes and continued in the futile pursuit of outputs that nobody wanted.

The EftPos UK story illustrates that defining an output is insufficient to ensure that value is created. We have to define not just the outputs, but the outcomes that a process will deliver to the business stakeholders. This leads us to a value-focused definition of process within a business context as shown in Figure 2.5.

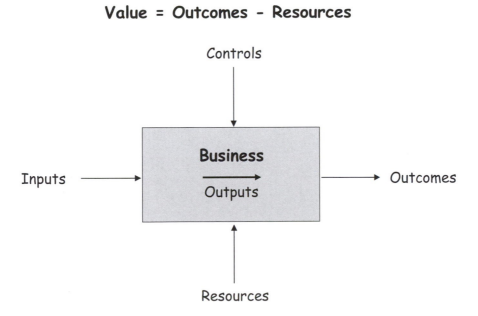

Figure 2.5   Value definition of process

*The value of a process is the degree to which stakeholder
outcomes exceed the cost of inputs and resources.*

In order to be consistent with the value equation and ensure that all costs are accounted for, the input component in the equation includes any costs associated with inputs undergoing transformation, which may be zero, in addition to the resources needed to *complete* the transformation. For example, in the case of the Shopping Story, no cost is attributed to shoppers, the cost of customer acquisition and retention being covered by other processes. All costs are incurred as a result of resources engaged in the transaction. However, for the Further Education Story, grants represent a cost associated with students before courses start, whereas the cost of lecturers is incurred during the course itself. This subtlety is more obvious for manufactured goods, in which case raw materials are inputs that undergo a transformation and must be purchased before the transformation takes place, whereas a machine tool is a resource which consumes cost during the transformation. In practice, this complication does not cause a problem when applying the value equation; the important thing is to make sure that all costs are included.

Value as a Business

This leads us to extend process to an entire business. A business delivers value to its stakeholders through the operation and interaction of one or more processes. The core process within a business is called the value chain, which defines the essential activities needed to create value to customers, the stakeholder, to which products and services are aimed, as shown in Figure 2.6.

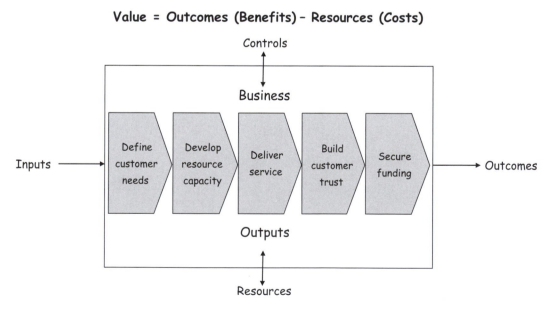

Figure 2.6   Value as a business

The purpose of a business is to deliver value to its stakeholders.

Other stakeholders, such as staff and shareholders, are also potential recipients of value in accordance with the value equation. However, the sustainability of value to these stakeholders is dependent on continued satisfaction of customers. Despite being a simplification which will be manipulated in the real business environment, for example through cartels, monopolies and political intervention, this structure provides a firm basis for outcome focus.

Value as a Balanced Scorecard

The combination of process and stakeholder perspectives of a business is encapsulated in the Balanced Scorecard, which is the leading performance management framework. A typical Balanced Scorecard comprises four perspectives, often called quadrants, as shown in Figure 2.7.

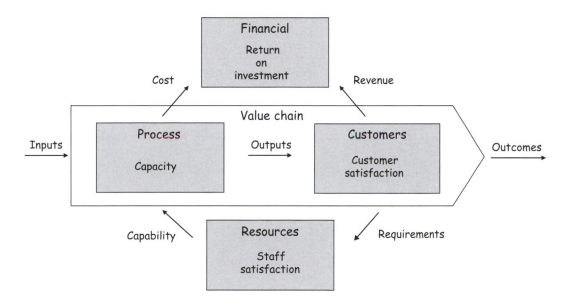

Figure 2.7   Value as a Balanced Scorecard

There is a clear mapping between the process elements and Balanced Scorecard perspectives as outlined below (titles in brackets denote the original naming convention and arrows in the figure show the causal flow in creating value most frequently used):

*   Financial: the financial view is centred on the profit and loss account for private enterprises and accountability for expenditure in relation to service delivered in the public sector, that is, value for money. Shareholders, private equity companies

and government (on behalf of taxpayers) are all instances of owners, and effectively impose controls on the business through profit targets and/or budgets

- Customers: focusing on the perceived value delivered from the customer viewpoint. Customers are also the intended recipients of outcomes derived from the business outputs, that is products and services
- Resources: (learning and growth): focusing on the degree to which people engaged in the business are appropriately skilled and motivated, and have appropriate systems with which to deliver value now and drive innovation necessary to sustain future value. Staff are usually the principal resource enabling value creation
- Process (internal): the value chain and supporting activities that deliver value to customers for a cost that enables sufficient returns to sustain investment from shareholders, taxpayers and so on

The Balanced Scorecard combines process and stakeholder perspectives of a business.

The Balanced Scorecard is used as a foundation for the performance management element of Value Management.

Value as a Programme

There is much debate concerning the distinction between projects, programmes and portfolios. These distinctions are important when considering implementation and will be revisited later. However, from a Value Management perspective, they all relate to one single aim; delivering value to stakeholders through change. Consequently, we will cover them all under the single heading *programme*.

A programme is the means by which value is delivered through change.

The Shopping Story illustrates the vital need for a clear understanding of how value will be created through change programmes. To clarify the difference between simply achieving a change and creating value, let us define the process elements in relation to a programme. It is useful to consider a programme as a process through which inputs and resources create some form of output, whilst controls ensure the success of the programme. We can translate these into programme components as follows, noting that the list does not yet include outcomes:

- Inputs to a programme are typically a statement of requirements defining a new system, product or service for the business which define some new capability.
- Resources are the people, facilities, IT platforms and products and other services that may be used to deliver the programme.
- Controls are the governance and funding structures used to manage the programme and can account for resource consumption, activities, decisions and progress against schedules.
- Outputs are the high-level programme products which enable new, or release latent, capabilities for use by the business in compliance with requirements, referred to as *deliverables*.

In recent years, there has been significant investment in documenting best practice in running programmes. For example, the UK Office of Government Commerce (OGC) promotes PRINCE2™, Managing Successful Programmes (MSP™) and Portfolio, Programme and Project Offices (P3O®) Increasingly later versions of these methodologies place more focus on the importance of benefits management and most recently, the OGC has included Management of Value (MoV™). As the EftPos UK story illustrates, defining an outputs is insufficient to ensure that value is created. We have to define not just the *outputs* but the *outcomes* that a programme will deliver.

A programme is a process for delivering value to stakeholders by implementing change.

A programme *outcome* is a measureable business benefit created by exploiting new capabilities enabled by programme outputs. So, in the case of EftPos UK it was not the responsibility of the programme or even the infrastructure operating company to sign up retailers, issue cards and promote their use as a substitute for cheques. All of those activities were part of the everyday business of the banks, and they had already found an easier way of achieving those business outputs. If we extend the process analogy to the purpose of the wider business, we see that a programme deliverable is not an end in itself but a new resource that can be used by the business to fulfil customer needs. This is shown in Figure 2.8.

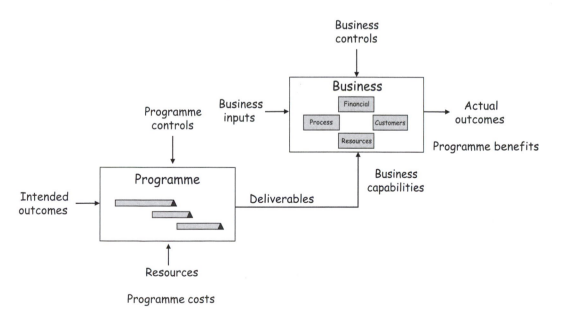

Figure 2.8 Value as a programme

There are two key implications from this definition of a programme.

1. There must be a direct link between programme management and wider business performance management, if value from a programme is to be quantified and controlled effectively.
2. An appropriate performance measurement framework is needed as an integral part of the programme design in order to measure outcomes and manage the programme to deliver them.

We shall see later how the link between programme management and wider business management is reflected in the Balanced Scorecard, ownership and governance.

Programme and business are linked through value delivery.

Investment Appraisal

The financial value of a programme is determined using investment appraisal techniques, the most powerful being Discounted Cash Flow (DCF) analysis. DCF analysis provides a particularly precise quantification of value for two reasons. First, it deals with real cash and ignores non-cash accounting manipulations, notably depreciation, which distort the purity of the appraisal.

Secondly, DCF analysis takes into account the time value of money. This is important because, as we will demonstrate later, timing is often the most critical factor in programme value. The time value of money recognises that £1 today is worth more than £1 in a year's time for one of two reasons, because either £1 *owned* today can be invested at an interest rate, or £1 *borrowed* today will incur interest. In order to take the time value of money into account, cash flows are discounted on a compound basis over the life of the programme to compute the present value using the equation:

$$Present\ Value = Cash\ Flow \times Discount\ Rate$$

$$Discount\ Rate = 1/(1 + r/100)^n$$

- r is the interest rate at which the £1 could be invested or cost of capital for borrowing it expressed as a percentage
- n is the year number in the programme for the cash flow.

Other factors, such as inflation and currency fluctuations, can also have a major influence on the value of money over time. Conventionally, inflation is excluded from DCF analyses on the grounds that it affects everything equally and therefore its effect is neutral. However, sometimes this is not the case. For example, the price of some commodities, such as oil, can inflate disproportionately. Accountants use sophisticated techniques, which are beyond the scope of this book, to arrive at the discount rate. The important point is that we need to apply DCF techniques to quantify the financial viability of a change programme, in order to apply sufficient financial rigour. There are two complementary DCF analysis techniques:

1. net present value
2. internal rate of return.

NET PRESENT VALUE

Net Present Value (NPV) is the *present* value of all future cash flows related to the programme. More specifically, it is the present value of all cash *inflows* minus the all cash *outflows*, that is the net cash flows. NPV addresses the question, 'What is today's monetary value of this programme?' A NPV analysis of a simple programme implemented in the first three years of a six-year life is shown in Figure 2.9. Annual cost savings which are directly attributable to the programme start in year 2 and build up to a maximum value of £800,000/annum. The cost of capital, or interest rate, upon which the discount factor is calculated is 10 per cent. The NPV row is shown as the *cumulative present value* of the net cash flows, and the NPV for a programme life of six years is £885,000. By convention, DCF analyses often include a conceptual Year 0 with a discount factor of 1, to represent initial investments. This is not included in this example because there are no initial costs. The NPV analysis also quantifies the payback (more correctly discounted payback) expressed in time, for example number of years. The NPV is often called a J-curve (as presented in Figure 2.9) which also shows the payback as about four years.

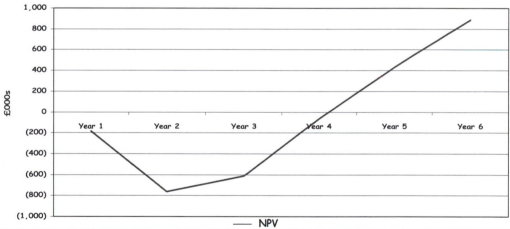

Description	Year 1 (£000)	Year 2 (£000)	Year 3 (£000)	Year 4 (£000)	Year 5 (£000)	Year 6 (£000)
Programme cost	(200)	(800)	(200)			
Annual s aving		100	400	800	800	800
Net cash flow	(200)	(700)	200	800	800	800
Cost of capital	10.0%					
Discount factor	0.91	0.83	0.75	0.68	0.62	0.56
Present value (PV)	(182)	(579)	150	546	497	452
Net present value (NPV)	(182)	(760)	(610)	(64)	433	885

Figure 2.9   Net present value J-curve

INTERNAL RATE OF RETURN

Internal Rate of Return (IRR), also referred to as the *yield*, is the discount rate at which the present value of future cash inflows equals that of cash outflows. IRR addresses the question, 'At what interest rate would this programme have zero NPV? Calculations for the simple example programme are tabulated in Figure 2.10 which shows an interest rate of 43.5 per cent, the IRR for a six-year programme life.

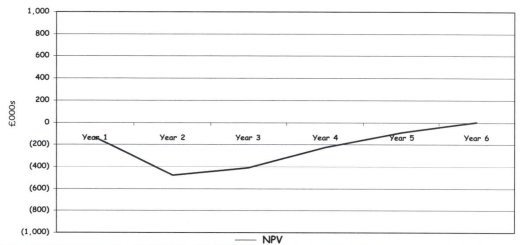

Description	Year 1 (£000)	Year 2 (£000)	Year 3 (£000)	Year 4 (£000)	Year 5 (£000)	Year 6 (£000)
Programme cost	(200)	(800)	(200)			
Annual saving		100	400	800	800	800
Net cash flow	(200)	(700)	200	800	800	800
IRR	43.5%					
Discount factor	0.70	0.49	0.34	0.24	0.16	0.11
Present value (PV)	(139)	(340)	68	189	131	92
Net present value (NPV)	(139)	(479)	(412)	(223)	(91)	0

Figure 2.10 Internal rate of return

There are advantages associated with both DCF measures and management accountants tend to have strong views on which to use. In essence, NPV returns an absolute value of programme value over time, whereas IRR provides a metric related to the ROI. NPV and IRR can return conflicting results. For example, one programme may have a greater NPV and the other a higher yield. This is mainly due to the timing and magnitude of cash flows. Generally, IRR favours programmes with smaller initial investments and more front-ended positive cash inflows, which tend to be lower risk, and for this reason IRR is often preferred. Conversely, programmes with large but late benefits could be eliminated using IRR whilst the NPV is favourable. In Value Management, we use both NPV and IRR.

Despite each measure's caveats, DCF valuation is central in the context of change programmes because it quantifies the criticality of timing on resultant value.

Accounting for Changes in Value for Money

Earlier in this chapter we defined value for money as:

$$Value\ for\ money = Benefits/Costs$$

As well as being useful for any business, this measure is critical for quantifying value in non-commercial organisations which do not have a revenue component and benefits are not defined in financial units. However, DCF analyses use only pure cash flows. This means that financial investment appraisals for public sector and not-for-profit programmes often include only costbase savings. This does not present a problem of units if the programme is concerned with improved *efficiency*, where the intention is to deliver the same or greater *output* for the less *cost*. For example if an IT solution enables more efficient use of resources, the investment cost of the technology is assessed against the reduced costbase resulting from a smaller headcount. Of course, there will normally be major management and political challenges relating to how this can be achieved with the implication of job losses and so on, but this is a separate issue.

However, units *are* a problem if the focus includes *effectiveness* improvements, where the intention is to deliver greater non-financial *outcomes*, such as improved service, the achievement of which requires investment, and/or increased operational costs. In this case, the DCF may well be negative, and therefore apparently unattractive from a financial perspective. There are essentially three ways in which we address this problem.

First, we can include *efficiency* benefits that outweigh the investment and increased operational costs and pay for the improved *effectiveness*. Very often, this is quite possible through the use of advanced systemic techniques which we discuss in Chapter 6. For example, some years ago, we built a value model covering a command and control system for one of the UK's largest police forces. Working with senior detectives, we developed an overwhelming financial case, largely based on the prevention and/or early detection of crime through advanced crime pattern analysis capability provided by the new technology. Treating prevention, detection and prosecution as a *process*, the work demonstrated how major improvements in inputs, outputs and outcomes were possible through more precise targeting of resources, enabled through intelligence. The NPV was not only positive but transparently very favourable and was duly approved in its entirety by the governing police authority.

Secondly, we can increase the scope to include benefits that can be quantified in financial terms. For example, in the same assignment, we considered including the reduced cost of crime to society, or specific stakeholders within society. In practice, this option can, and did in this case, prove difficult to translate into measurable cash flows. For example, reduced burglaries might eventually be manifested in reduced insurance premiums to householders, but this would be after a long period and be difficult to incorporate within an investment appraisal for a police command and control system. However, systemic approaches often reveal benefits that would otherwise remain unseen. For instance, in a health care assignment we modelled future care policies for dealing with an increasing elderly population for a county council. The systemic model quantified cost savings due to reductions in repeat hospital admissions, by revising the existing policy of discharging patients early to free up beds. This finding, outside the original scope of work, was an example of efficiency benefits driven by improvements in effectiveness; getting things right first time.

In the first two options, the focus is in achieving a positive NPV as the primary measure for programme value. The third option is to accept that a negative NPV is the necessary price for improving stakeholder outcomes. In this case, we consider the least costly alternative which delivers the greatest value for money and it is useful to combine the NPV J-curve with value for money, as shown in Figure 2.11 (the value for money units are indicative only).

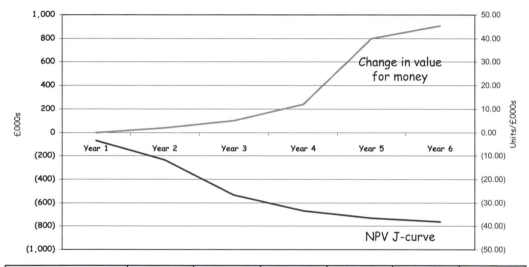

	Year 1	Year 2	Year 3	Year 4	Year 5	Year 6
Net present value (NPV)	(68)	(233)	(534)	(671)	(733)	(761)
Change in value for money	0.00	2.00	5.00	12.00	40.00	45.45

Figure 2.11 NPV versus change in value for money

The important point concerning Figure 2.11 is not to distort the NPV calculation with any factors, weightings or other manipulations that detract from pure cash. The value is managed in the same way as if the NPV were positive. The difference is that we are linking the NPV with value for money. In practice, we would provide precise cause and effect traceability showing how the investment is being translated in improved value for money. We would also provide the capability to map other related performance measures against the NPV.

Programme Value Linkage

Value Management places great emphasis on precise causal linkage between programme deliverables and benefits that are attributable to the deliverables. Consequently, in Part II we build this linkage dynamically to the programme plan, enabling us to see how NPV and IRR can fluctuate dramatically in response to the timing of milestones. This programme linkage is shown in Figure 2.12.

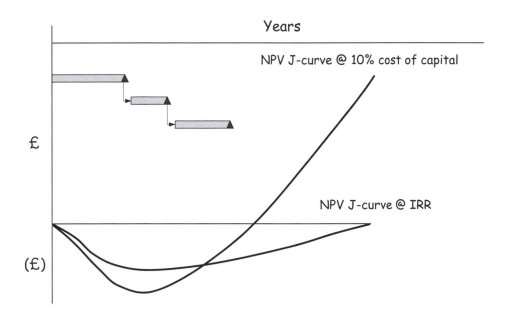

Figure 2.12 Programme value linkage

It follows that for this linkage to be valid, we must have precise assignment of benefits, for example reductions in business costbase and/or increase in revenue, to the programme phases, outputting deliverables that enable the benefits. Activity-Based Cost Management (ABC/M) provides a powerful means of cost assignment using cost drivers. A similar approach can also be applied for revenue, using revenue drivers. Programme linkage is covered in Chapter 7.

Essence

The principal learning from this chapter is summarised below:

- The value equation is: Value = Benefits – Costs
- Expressed as a quotient in terms of inputs, outputs and outcomes, the value equation becomes:

$$\textit{Value for money} = \textit{Effectiveness} \times \textit{Efficiency}$$

- Effectiveness is doing the right things, efficiency is doing things right
- Value depends on the perspective of specific stakeholders, such as shareholders, customers and staff
- Business value is delivered through processes; the primary process for a business is the value chain
- The Balanced Scorecard provides a performance management framework which links process with stakeholder perspectives
- A programme is the vehicle by which additional business value is delivered through change
- To be effective, programmes must incorporate change into business as usual; therefore the Balanced Scorecard becomes a critical component in realising value
- Programme value is quantified using discounted cash flow techniques which take into account the time value of money

3 *Precise Simplicity*

Objectives

After reading this chapter you will be able to:

- Recognise how mental models influence our own behaviour and the behaviour of others
- Use advanced techniques to replace limiting patterns with mental models that enable us to see and exploit value-creating opportunities

The Meaning of Precise Simplicity

Creating business value involves both *mindset* and *process*. Successful business start-ups often create great value through entrepreneurial spirit and a 'do whatever is necessary' mindset with very little process. The challenge for these fast-growing businesses is recognising when process becomes necessary to sustain growth. Conversely, many large, established companies owe their continued success to clear *processes* which deliver value efficiently. Here the challenge is not to lose creativity and initiative in 'tick box' bureaucracy; process should release capacity for innovation, not constrain it.

Value Management is the integration of mindset and process.

There are copious process methodologies concerning change, programme and benefits management and we will cover some of the most important in this book. However, even the best methodologies will, and do, fail to deliver intended value without the mental commitment, belief and clarity of thinking necessary to enable change. Therefore, this chapter is devoted to the shifts in mindset essential to deliver value from change, together with the tools to achieve them.

Mindset is needed to generate essential vision and energy;
process to direct that energy to achieve the vision.

Over the last three decades, we have made quantum leaps in our understanding of how the human mind works. Significantly, this recent knowledge converges with some of the greatest spiritual and philosophical wisdom gathered over the centuries. One of the most profound revelations is the link between consciousness and reality. We perceive a fixed physical reality that our conscious minds can relate to and enable us to interact with. However, recent advances in psychology, complexity theory and quantum physics support the opposite view, postulated by Siddhãrtha Gautama, the Buddha, 2,500 years ago; that there is no fixed reality. Rather, the reality that we experience is influenced by our *mental models*, which can be a vastly filtered subset of the real world.

> *We co-create our reality with natural laws through mental models.*

A corollary of this shift in thinking is that we can have significant influence on outcomes as long as we work with true *causality*. Our ability to influence outcomes is also influenced by the quality of our mental models and the degree to which they align with causal laws. The important implication from a Value Management perspective is that whereas a sound process can be of great value, it is much less effective if it is incongruent with the mental models of people engaged in the change process. This is one of several reasons for the failure of government-driven targets to deliver intended step improvements in public services, such as health care, policing, social welfare and education.

Because models have such a profound effect on our ability to cause outcomes, Value Management is constructed around the ability to build and act upon models that most effectively represent real cause and effect, and consequently enable us to deliver intended results by aligning with universal causal laws. As we shall illustrate, change works primarily at a subconscious level. The subconscious mind follows simple, precise, specific instructions and mental models are most effective if they are also simple, precise and specific.

Value Management is founded on the principle of precise simplicity. In considering the significance of this concept, it is important to make two key distinctions. The first concerns the difference between simple and easy:

- Simple is the degree to which *selecting* a choice is clear;
- Easy is the degree to which *achieving* a selected choice is effortless.

It is simple to choose peace as wiser than war but not easy to achieve. Similarly, simple models are not necessarily easier to produce and the simple insights that they bring are often the most difficult to address, concerning issues that have been intentionally or unintentionally avoided and become embedded within culture.

> *It is easy to make something simple complicated; the real challenge is making something inherently complex simple.*

The second distinction is precision versus detail:

- Precision is the degree to which a model reflects reality;
- Detail is the level of data used to model reality.

Intuitively, we associate precision with problems broken down into smaller and smaller parts and increasing decimal points. Sometimes fine detail and many decimal points of accuracy are essential to define a subject or problem adequately. For example, consider a situation where a manufacturer is experiencing a high level of customer complaints. Management information indicates that complaints are related to a particular product or range of products. The management information system is sufficiently detailed that the fault is traced to a particular component, sub assembly, production plant and then finally machine, which it turns out was not correctly calibrated. In this instance, this increasing level of detail, called vertical drilling, led directly to the cause of the problem.

Conversely, the root cause could be a poor procurement specification generated by a department well outside the scope of the vertical drill, and which no end of detail would diagnose. So, detail adds complexity which can not only obscure the key underlying situation but also delude us into believing that we are in control when we are not. We see this pattern regularly in performance management scorecards and dashboards, where measures are defined in great detail and weighted to several decimal places, yet fail to reflect the true dynamics of the business in a way that enables value creation. We revisit the difference between detail and precision in the context of Business Intelligence (BI) in Appendix B.

Precise simplicity is the mindset and process of using the simplest models possible with sufficient precision to enable us to cause intended outcomes.

Mental Models

The human mind can only process seven, plus or minus two, bits of information at any one time. We deal with this limitation by using filters to simplify our view of the world. By applying these filters it means that we experience the world not as it actually is, but through our own personal internal representation of it. Also, because we all filter information differently, we see and experience the world differently from each other. This difference can be used to create value, through the 'energy of difference' as seen in high innovation businesses, or wasted in conflict, bureaucracy or over-regulation. Because of the need to work together, we develop similar worldviews made up of similar filters. This convergence is reflected in cultures, which hold the key to real change.

It is crucial that we are aware of the filters that we use ourselves and recognise those that are being used by other people, whether conscious of them or not. We also need to know how the filters affect behaviour. The NLP communications model, shown in Figure 3.1, provides a useful tool for explaining how filters work.

Data relating to external events are received through one or more of the five senses: sight, hearing, touch, smell and taste. The data is then filtered in three key ways: scope, level and precision. Scope concerns the overall context with which we process the data. Using a map analogy, have we got the right map? For example, in the film *Meet the Fokkers*, the hapless Gaylords are trying to follow a shortcut in Florida to head off a sulking Jack Byrne, using a map of Detroit. Level relates to the detail at which the data is received and is equivalent to the scale of the map. A large-scale road map of Scotland will get us to the right part of the planet, but is of limited value if we are trekking across the Trossachs. Precision is the degree to which data received represents reality. For example, to get off a mountain safely in mist we need a map that shows us where the footpaths are, and a compass with which to orientate the map correctly to find them. This filtering injects *distortions, generalisations* and *deletions* (explained later).

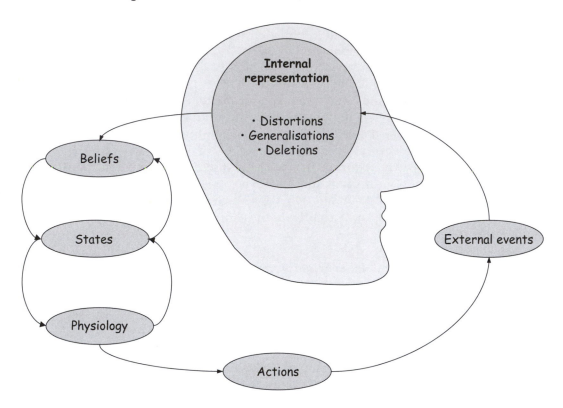

Figure 3.1   The NLP communications model

Information derived from the filtered data is then held as an internal representation, which inherits the limitations injected by the filters. Internal representations determine *beliefs*, which drive mental *state* and dictate our *physiology*; all of which operate in both directions. Physiology then influences our external actions which cause subsequent events, forming a complete feedback loop. (We will be exploring feedback loops in detail in Chapter 6.)

For example, suppose as a child we were bitten by a dog. We believe that all dogs bite, so when we see a dog we feel fear and our body stiffens. We shoo the dog away, the dog reacts by showing its teeth and your expectations are confirmed ready for the next dog encounter. This sort of reinforcing pattern is happening all day every day in one form or another in normal life. This both protects and limits us.

Mental models are formed through two key mechanisms:

1. *Inherited*, for example from parents during childhood or 'experts'
2. Programmed by repeated experience or exposure, by ourselves or witnessed in others, to similar *references*

Consequently, mental models can easily become self-reinforcing; driving the same beliefs, states and behaviours, producing the same results to similar problems which confirm the mental model, however flawed. Therefore, it follows that if we want to change outcomes we first need to change the mental models that drive limiting behaviours;

we have to break the vicious circle which perpetuates sub-optimum results. There are three strongly related skills employed in Value Management to shift limiting mental models relating to how we filter information:

1. Reframing: helps us define the right *scope*
2. Chunking: helps us operate at the right *level*
3. Meta Model: helps us get the right degree of *precision*

Reframing

One of the most critical skills needed for creating value is reframing. Reframing is the process of changing the meaning with which we represent a situation, so that we change our behaviour in addressing the problem and thus the outcome. Used inappropriately it is called spin. The best place to practice skills in recognising spin is by listening to politicians. (When I was young my mum called it *lies* but what did she know about the complexities of modern politics!) Unchallenged acceptance of this kind of manipulation can be very dangerous, even fatal. Inconveniently, God has not updated the universal laws of cause and effect to accommodate advances in spin. When engineers make a mistake, rails still crack, exhibition roofs still collapse and people still die. As we are interested in real value derived from true causality, it is important to define a distinction between spin and reframing as we apply it in Value Management:

*   Spin is manipulation of the truth with an intention of installing a desired mental model.
*   Reframing is challenging our installed mental model with an intention of getting closer to the truth.

There are two types of reframing which we apply depending on how the presenting problem is expressed:

1. context reframing
2. meaning reframing

CONTEXT REFRAMING

A problem is frequently presented in the form, 'It's too big, small, slow and so on' This structure is called a comparative deletion because the context in which the problem is expressed is missing. For example, a client says, 'We are losing business because we are *too* slow to respond to our customers.' In this case, we challenge the context by asking questions such as, 'Too slow for whom?' We have shifted the context by forcing causal enquiries which replace the deletion, in this case the customer. This can lead to significant revelations. For example, in this case, we may want to challenge which specific customers are causing us to provide such a rapid response and then question if they are of high enough value to warrant the cost of providing that level of service. Activity-Based Costing (ABC) is an immensely powerful tool for exposing this kind of pattern.

In context reframing, the circumstance within which the problem is presented is
shifted and the original meaning challenged in relation to this new perspective.

MEANING REFRAMING

A problem is also often presented in the form, 'When *this* happens, it *means* that.' This structure is called a complex equivalence because the underlying premise is that one thing automatically infers another, which may not be true. For example, a client says, 'When our suppliers fail to deliver it *means* we are not important to them.' In this case, we challenge the underlying assumptions and explore different meanings within the same context by asking questions such as, 'How does failure to deliver on time translate into indifference towards us?' This question forces causal challenges such as: 'Could it be that on these occasions the supplier is dealing with our poor specification at their own cost, because we are such an important customer to them?'

In a meaning reframe, the meaning of the presenting problem
is challenged in relation to the same context.

Reframing is very important for strategic positioning. For example we need to ask the questions, 'What business are we in?,' a context reframe, and 'What do we mean to our customers?' – a meaning reframe.

Chunking

Chunking refers to the level at which a problem, challenge or situation is being viewed. In business, chunking is important to determine at what level the issue resides or decisions are required. We cannot resolve problems with high-level causes by examining and tweaking fine operational details. Conversely, broad, high-level changes are not necessarily going to succeed if the cause is embedded at a lower level of the operation. In fact, it can be very wasteful and potentially disastrous to address a change in policy which completely misses a problem in an operational process. It could also be that the problem resides at the same level but in a different department. Therefore, chunking is conducted in three directions:

1. Chunking up to investigate increasingly higher level purpose or cause;
2. Chunking down to home in on specific lower level options or causes;
3. Chunking across to find alternative options or causes.

The easiest way to demonstrate the principle of chunking is decision making. For example, suppose that we are considering buying a car:

CHUNKING UP

To chunk up we ask the questions, 'For what purpose?' and 'What will this do for you?' A chunking up question will reveal the next level of requirement, such as a means of transport. If we keep asking the same question we eventually get to the highest value driving the decision, for example freedom, status, economy and so on.

CHUNKING DOWN

To chunk down we ask the questions, 'What is an example of?' and 'What specific type of car do you need?' Having established the purpose, we ask the chunk down question to find the options. For example, we may consider saloons, smart cars and 4 × 4s. If our highest value is freedom, it might point to buying a 4 × 4, or if it is economy, we would pitch for a smart car.

CHUNKING ACROSS

To chunk across we ask the question, 'What is another example of?' 4 × 4s are great but they are expensive and the government is making noises about road tax, so you want to consider other options. The chunking across question reveals alternatives that still meet your value. For example, some 4 × 4s may have lower CO_2 emissions than others, and therefore incur less tax and environmental damage.

Chunking is very powerful for reaching agreement. If there is disagreement it is usually in the detail. Consequently, we chunk up to the level at which all parties can agree and chunk down one level at a time to gain agreement.

If the devil is in the detail then God is in the vision.

Meta Model

Problems are usually presented to us as a surface structure which is highly filtered. One of the most powerful solutions for addressing this challenge is a form of structured questioning, called the Meta Model, which drills under the surface of the presenting problem to the deep underlying structure, where the cause is likely to reside. From this deeper understanding of underlying causal dynamics, more effective decisions can be made. This same process works at an individual, group or business level; the Meta Model was actually developed by modelling the structure of questions behind the success of Virginia Satir[1] in family therapy. We apply the Meta Model throughout Value Management. The Meta Model reinstates information relating to three filters which undermine precision:

1. distortions
2. generalisations
3. deletions

---

1   Bandler, R., Grinder, J. 1975. *The Structure of Magic*. Palo Alto, USA: Science and Behavior Books.

DISTORTIONS

Distortions are perceptions in which our internal representations of the world differ significantly from reality, and can result in inappropriate responses. For example, suppose that we are walking along a narrow mountain pass and see what we believe to be a snake; we leap sideways and slip into the ravine below, all for the sake of a piece of string. Distortions often manifest themselves as misinterpreting intentions or more generally, attributing the wrong meaning to what we are seeing around us. In a commercial context, this may result in deriving the wrong conclusions from customer or staff behaviour. Distortions can obscure problems and opportunities alike. For example, customer complaints are often interpreted as costly problems when in fact they provide opportunities for service improvement and additional sales.

A distortion is often presented as a form of cause and effect or equivalence. An example of cause and effect is, 'We are experiencing high error rates *because* of poor staff motivation.' This could have been stated as 'High error rates *means* we have poor staff motivation.' Cause and effect implies a time delay between the reason and the result, whereas with equivalence the link is instantaneous.

Distortions are corrected by challenging the causal relationship. For example, 'How specifically are high error rates being caused by poor motivation?' The three key words in this response are *how, specifically* and *caused*. The reason that *how* is used rather than *why* is because *how* returns more reliable and precise results. Suppose we asked '*Why* is poor staff motivation making high error rates?' The answer tends to focus around blame and excuses, such as 'Because people are demoralised by the low pay award and do not feel valued.' This may be true but it is not causally useful in this form.

Conversely, by structuring the question around *how*, adding specificity and stressing causality, we are more likely to get the operational explanation 'Since the new pay award, key staff responsible for incoming quality have been absent, sampling has been cut and more faults have slipped through to the shop floor.' We are now in a much stronger position to find out if the problem is motivation, weak management, domestic problems or the winter flu epidemic.

GENERALISATIONS

In a generalisation, one phenomenon is taken to represent everything else in a similar category. Verbally, generalisations take the form of statements such as: every time x happens we get y, all x are y, x is always y. Unchecked generalisations can be extremely dangerous because they can cloud objectivity and stop us from looking for distinctions and qualifications. In business, an example of a generalisation would be, 'every time we invest in R & D it turns out to be a complete waste of money.'

Generalisations are corrected by challenging the universal presupposition and probing for specific instances that break it, together with causal distinctions. For example, we could simply reply, 'Every?' We could then explore more deeply such as, 'Have there been any occasions when R & D has paid off? What did we do differently then which made these cases successful?'

DELETIONS

Deletions filter out key information. This leaves the mind to retain a small manageable amount of selective information. Although essential to cope with real-life complexity, deletions can lead to important items not being observed, for example threats or opportunities being missed in one area of a business due to some management fixation in another area. Very often deletions are presented in the form of missing sources and general vagueness. For example, '*They* say it is unacceptable?'

Deletions are corrected by reinstating the missing information and injecting specificity. For example, we would respond, 'Who specifically is saying that it is unacceptable? What specifically are they saying is unacceptable? What specifically is it that they find unacceptable?'

Aching Curiosity, Truth and Ownership

In this chapter we have discussed the need for precise simplicity, and the role of mental models as well as the mental techniques used to counter some of the disadvantages of how our brains are wired. However, if we are going to apply these things then often there is going to have to be a substantial shift in thinking, culture and business practices. As we get deeper into the Value Management process, we will be encouraging people to reveal contentious, and potentially dangerous, information concerning what is actually going on. Three driving forces are needed to provide people with the energy and motivation to go through the necessary discipline:

1. Aching curiosity: is a child-like, uncompromising determination to get to get to the bottom of the real cause.
2. Dedication to truth: is commitment that the answer obtained actually represents reality unfiltered by spin or manipulating of the facts, however painful.
3. Ownership: is acceptance of absolute responsibility for cause and total commitment to the solution.

> *Lies that life is black and white spoke from my skull ... Ah, but I*
> *was so much older then, I'm younger than that now.'*
> 'My Back Pages' by Bob Dylan

Essence

The principal learning from this chapter is summarised below:

*   Precise simplicity is the mindset and process of defining and working with the simplest mental and physical models possible which contain sufficient precision to enable us to cause intended outcomes
*   We perceive and respond to the world through mental models
*   Mental models filter real-world information through distortions, generalisations and deletions

- Problems are normally presented as surface events after being filtered
- Problem causes and value-creating opportunities generally reside at the deep structure level
- In order for us to derive effective solutions we need ways of reinstating the deep structure
- Three key tools for achieving this result are the reframing, chunking and the Meta Models
- Reframing ensures that we are addressing the right problem, chunking the right level and Meta Model the appropriate causal precision by correcting distortions, generalisations and deletions
- The necessary mental shifts require curiosity to get to the cause, dedication to the truth, whatever the findings, and ownership of solutions

4 *Elusive Value*

Objectives

After reading this chapter you will be able to:

- Define repeating patterns which account for much of the failure to deliver intended value from programmes
- Recognise underlying causes of the failure patterns
- Apply archetypal solutions to each pattern

Record of Failure

There is abundant research documenting failure of programmes to deliver value, together with views concerning the reasons. Research commissioned by Computer Associates[1] concludes that the main cause of budget overspend is poor forecasting. The report also suggests that scope creep, together with problems relating to interdependencies and conflicts between multiple projects, are also significant factors.

These problems also reflect a lack of visibility and effective control by executives over programmes. According to the same research, 40 per cent of IT directors lack adequate visibility regarding the projects that they are implementing. This is blamed on the failure to utilise appropriate tools to manage and measure initiatives. Compounded by the complexity of today's programme portfolios, poor measurement undermines attempts to identify strategic projects. The report found that for 60 per cent of the firms surveyed, less than 50 per cent of their programmes were considered to be strategic.

A significant finding was that only a quarter of companies surveyed appeared to carry out a ROI-based calculation in order to link projects to the business value they expected to deliver. This observation was also echoed by recent research by IAG Consulting,[2] who concluded that firms with poor business analysis capability have three times more project failures than successes.

> *A major factor in programme failure is inability to link programmes to business value and then manage them effectively to deliver the value.*

---

1   Research from Computer Associates conducted by Loudhouse. 2007. Press release. Available at http://www.ca.com/gb/press/release.aspx?cid=155480#, accessed 23 October 2009.

2   Ellis, K. and IAG Consulting. 2009. *Business Analysis Benchmark: The Impact of Business Requirements on the Success of Technology Projects*. Available at http://www.iag.biz/images/resources/iag%20business%20analysis%20benchmark%20-%20full%20report.pdf, accessed 20 December 2010.

When we combine research and best practice with our own experience, spanning hundreds of programmes and applications across both the private and public sectors, two disciplines stand out as both the source of, and solution to, the failure of programmes to deliver intended value:

- Baseline business case: prior to implementation, gaining approval based on precise causal linkage between new business functionality delivered by the programme and value outcomes to stakeholders
- Value realisation: managing the realisation of actual value delivered during and post implementation against the baseline

Repeating Failure Patterns and Solutions

A central message of this book is that *we cause* programmes to fail in delivering intended value though inadequate application of these two key disciplines. However, in order to find effective solutions we need to apply principles covered in previous chapters to define precisely and specifically *how* we cause this failure. To this end, we have identified six repeating failure patterns. The first five relate to baseline business case and last concerns value realisation:

- Failure pattern 1: inadequate specification of stakeholder outcomes
- Failure pattern 2: unrealistic quantification of benefits
- Failure pattern 3: poor causal linkage between programme phases and benefits
- Failure pattern 4: poor value alignment
- Failure pattern 5: imprecise criteria for success and inadequate provision for risk
- Failure pattern 6: inadequate tracking of benefits and overall programme value

Failure Pattern 1: Inadequate Specification of Stakeholder Outcomes

Despite advances in processes and tools, programme management is still often narrowly focused on programme *outputs* rather than the stakeholder *outcomes* that the outputs are intended to deliver. Emphasis remains on delivering against functional requirements, on time and within budget. Two vital elements are omitted; delivery of benefits, in the form of stakeholder outcomes, and the overall value of the programme. Both these elements should be reflected in a robust business case, reflecting the financial case of undertaking the programme.

There are two parts to this repeating failure pattern. First, requirements capture is poor and technically, rather than business driven. Although business users are consulted, their involvement is often insufficient, typically due to other commitments or lack of ownership, and the process is not performed effectively. This leads to a set of requirements that have not been fully reviewed by key users, that is, beneficiaries, who are subsequently expected to realise the benefits. As a result, programmes are progressed against requirements that are poorly defined, loosely owned or just plain wrong.

Requirements of functional outputs from the programme are often not adequately defined.

Secondly, even if the requirements are clearly defined, with full involvement and ownership from the business community, and subsequently delivered, this still may not lead to intended stakeholder outcomes. This is because the functional requirements result in outputs that do not deliver the required outcomes. To illustrate, consider a programme which increases the number of surgical operations conducted in a health authority responding to government efficiency targets. The focus on number of operations leads to a boost in productivity, by performing more simple procedures whilst pushing the more demanding operations to the back of the queue. Despite meeting the target by increasing the number of operations it is able to perform, that is its outputs, the programme does not necessarily achieve the desired outcomes of the neediest stakeholders, such as people waiting for complex and expensive operations.

Functional outputs, even when adequately defined and achieved,
often fail to deliver stakeholder outcomes.

The inability to specify stakeholder outcomes, and the business capabilities needed to cause them, is a failure of both process and mindset. When a new programme is set up there is usually a scoping study to determine the feasibility of the change programme. If approved, the next phase is often detailed requirements capture comprising workshops and interviews. This generates a user requirements document from which the functional specification and system design can be derived. Despite increasing use of methodologies for defining programmes and benefits, it is still rare for requirements to be challenged rigorously against their ability to deliver stakeholder *outcomes*. This mindset failure is manifest in a premise that if the requirements are correctly specified, benefits will follow automatically. Often, they do not.

Precision Question

What are intended stakeholder outcomes, what new business capabilities are required to deliver them and who is accountable for success?

SOLUTION

The solution to this recurring problem is to define precise intended stakeholder outcomes, that is benefits, specify the new business capabilities, that is programme deliverables, needed to cause the benefits and assign clear ownership to both deliverables and benefits. Outcomes are expressed as objectives within the Balanced Scorecard and cause and effect chains which link the objectives, called *themes*, define the strategy for achieving the vision. The shift in thinking from a functional focus to outcome-centred awareness and the definition of strategic themes is expanded in Chapter 5.

Failure Pattern 2: Unrealistic Quantification of Benefits

Another reason that benefits are not realised in practice is because we have not determined precisely the drivers of value which must change in order to *cause* the intended outcomes. These drivers translate into business performance measures in the Balanced Scorecard, the poor definition of which results in unrealistic quantification of benefits.

As discussed in Chapter 2, DCF techniques measure programme value in the context of achieving acceptable NPV, yield, and payback. However, often in an attempt to meet predefined criteria, projected benefits are manipulated, even fabricated, because they are difficult to define and/or quantify. As DCF analyses demand benefits to be quantified financially, business cases tend to include only hard benefits, such as reduced headcount, and omit benefits perceived to be intangible. Consequently, only a proportion of the total benefits related to any programme are accounted for. For example, consider a business case for an automated loan system within a bank. It is likely that reduced manual labour is central to the financial case. Less likely to be included is the extra revenue generated from customers by virtue of significantly reduced response times, or the effect it would have on staff who, no longer engaged in manual processes, can redirect effort into value added activities.

Typically, only a proportion of total programme benefits are accounted for in business cases.

The problem is that often tangible benefits alone are insufficient to make the business case viable. There may be awareness of potential intangible benefits but it is assumed that they cannot be meaningfully quantified. Consequently, there is a tendency to inflate the estimated tangible benefits, and leave the intangibles unquantified. This leads to a double whammy; inflated tangible benefits are not delivered and potential intangible benefits squandered because they are not measured and tracked. 'What is not measured cannot be managed.'

Poor quantification of benefits leads to manipulation and
failure to capture full potential programme value.

Precision Question

What business performance drivers must change in order to cause intended stakeholder outcomes?

SOLUTION

The solution is to ensure that strategic themes in the Balanced Scorecard are defined explicitly through the linkage between drivers and benefits using cause and effect mapping and subsequent dynamics modelling of the business. Causal mapping will be explained, and dynamics modelling introduced, in Chapter 6.

Failure Pattern 3: Poor Causal Linkage Between Programme Phases and Benefits

This problem is encapsulated in the most feared question from a CEO, 'OK, so precisely how much money will I get and when will I get it?' Suppose that stakeholder outcomes are defined, together with the causal linkage to key business drivers. There is another level of linkage that is frequently neglected, the explicit causal connection between specific programme phases and the business drivers that result in benefits. The term *phase* is used to include any programme breakdown, such as projects, work packages, stages and so on, which output partial or complete deliverables. Although phase costs may be monitored closely, the business benefits attributable to each phase are not generally measured and managed with anything like the same rigour, if at all.

Benefits are not generally linked to programme phases.

This raises two issues. The first relates to the *magnitude* of benefits attributable to each phase. Some phases deliver more benefits than others and without quantifying the contribution of each phase, it is not possible to optimise the programme structure around value. The second problem concerns benefits *timing*. Later, we will demonstrate that even modest slips in a programme schedule can have greater impact on value than significant cost escalation. What might appear as a relatively immaterial slip in a milestone may have critical consequences for the programme value as a whole, due to dependencies between phases. This is especially true of large, high-risk programmes with substantial front-end investment and slow build up of benefits; the CFO's nightmare.

Precision Question

What level of benefits and costs are attributable to each specific programme phase and when will the value be delivered?

SOLUTION

The solution to this problem has two parts. We first link deliverables to drivers and benefits through quantified causal threads. Then we attribute benefits across programme phases in a process called benefits attribution. At all times, we ensure that the causal linkage is traced to the strategic themes in the Balanced Scorecard. These techniques are covered in Chapter 7.

Failure Pattern 4: Poor Value Alignment

Alignment refers to an optimum condition whereby all business resources are directed to achieving the vision, of which there are two aspects: business alignment and programme value alignment. *Business alignment* refers to convergence of objectives and measures at all levels within the organisation, providing a clear line of sight on the vision from any viewpoint. *Programme value alignment* is concerned with directing this business convergence to programmes, which are optimised for realising greatest benefits most quickly at least cost and minimum acceptable risk.

Poor business alignment results in the different parts of the business pursuing local objectives and targets which oppose each other and counter the vision. This is often caused by conflicting criteria for success. For example, a procurement department may have measures focusing on minimising price, which drive demanding contracts with suppliers. In response, suppliers cut corners on quality in order to maintain their own margins, and this conflicts with quality measures within operations.

Poor programme value alignment is manifested as sub-optimal programme design from a value perspective. This is often as a result of a technical rather than a value focus. For example, suppose a retail bank is implementing new products across its branch network. From a technical perspective, the entire communications infrastructure would be completed before training staff and launching the products for sale. However, there may well be opportunities to implement key branches first or launch products using partially manual processes, which bring forward significant cash inflows.

Precision Question

What is the optimum business and programme alignment that delivers greatest value, most quickly at acceptable risk?

SOLUTION

The solution for business alignment is to cascade the Balanced Scorecard to management, operations and even individuals, across the business and extend strategic themes through all these levels. The solution for programme value alignment is modelling to ensure that programme deliverables *cause* positive changes in key drivers and benefits through themes. Changes in drivers and benefits are then attributed to phases so that we can determine the optimum structure and sequence of phases for value. The key output from the programme value alignment process is an implementation strategy. We explore value alignment in Chapter 8.

Failure Pattern 5: Imprecise Criteria for Success and Inadequate Provision for Risk

The next two patterns are very closely related. Failure pattern 5 concerns the definition of precise criteria for success, together with assessment of risk, and the final pattern tracking the degree to which value is delivered against these criteria. To put them into the appropriate context, it is useful to compare best practice for managing programme *outputs* with a typical approach to ensuring that *benefits* are delivered.

For functional outputs, well-managed programmes follow a structured method built around two disciplines, ensuring that defined requirements are fully incorporated and that they are implemented correctly. The first discipline is *verification*, the second is *validation*. Requirements are defined and translated into a design, which is built and tested against the defined requirements. Any changes are, or should be, properly assessed and documented as part of a formal change control process. As individual modules are built they are tested against test scripts which can be traced back to approved requirements. Once complete, the system is tested as a whole for both technical compliance and user acceptance. Test scripts contain precise *criteria* by which compliance with requirements is measured.

Now consider how programme *benefits* are typically managed. The scrutiny applied to technical requirements is rarely extended to benefits and business cases do not contain the level of precision afforded to functional requirements. Also, it is even rarer for benefits to be assigned measures against which the business case can be tested.

There are rarely precise criteria for measuring delivery of benefits.

A similar comparison can be made in relation to risk. Where technical functionality is concerned, models and/or prototypes are often built in order to test compliance and reduce inherent risk. For example, in aerospace this is taken to extremes; simulation and prototyping is used to test new aircraft to destruction. Not only is performance validated under normal operation, but more importantly, destruction testing determines how to deal with extraordinary conditions and what it takes to break all the fail safes. This same rigour is generally not applied for benefits and value in change programmes, but why not, when value is business-critical and the tools are there?

The level of risk assessment for functional outputs is not applied for programme value.

Precision Question

What are the precise criteria through that we can be certain of delivering intended value and what would it take to destroy the financial viability of the programme?

SOLUTION

The solution to this failure pattern is to define very specific measures by which to assess actual and forecast benefits and overall value at all stages in the programme development and implementation. These measures take three forms; measures that tell us whether programme deliverables are on track, measures that we use to track drivers and benefits and measures that track overall programme value. We use models with dynamic causality to destruction test the financial case and build a Balanced Scorecard comprising the most critical measures. The 'test script' for benefits is the Balanced Scorecard.

Failure Pattern 6: Inadequate Tracking of Benefits and Overall Programme Value

Closely linked to the previous failure pattern is inadequate monitoring and assurance of success, which relates to the inability to *track* value delivered during and post implementation. Oakland and Tanner[3] explain, 'The research indicated that this is an area where there is scope for improvement within many organisations. In particular, the area of setting clear measurable objectives for the change and evaluating their achievement may be singled out for attention.' In the previous pattern we stated that appropriate measures for programme success were often lacking. However, even if measures are in place, they are only of use if supported by a rigorous value realisation process which monitors actual and forecast status against the baseline business case. This is rarely done.

More commonly, after approval of the business case, the emphasis shifts to delivery of compliant technical outputs on time and within budget. The implicit assumption is that projected benefits will happen automatically. However, as we stated earlier, delivery against requirements is no guarantee that intended benefits and overall value will be realised. The business case is seldom, if ever revisited. Sometimes a Post Implementation Review (PIR) is conducted to determine whether benefits were actually achieved, but by this time the horse has bolted. What is absent is the perpetual tracking of programme benefits and overall value, together with corrective action needed to remain on purpose and on value.

Benefits and overall programme value are rarely tracked, assessed and corrected.

Precision Question

During and post implementation, how do we define the status of the programme value, correct negative variances and exploit positive changes?

SOLUTION

Tracking for value is incorporated as an integral part of the entire programme management process, which involves the monitoring and correction of three aspects of the programme – deliverables, drivers and benefits and overall programme value. Deliverables are tracked using advanced earned value techniques to complement best practice project management. Drivers and benefits are tracked using the Balanced Scorecard. Programme value is tracked using DCF analysis. Deliverables, drivers, benefits and programme value are all linked dynamically using causal models, which are vital in assessing the impact of changes and directing effective action.

Essence

The principal learning from this chapter is summarised below:

* Research, best practice and direct experience converge on the need for excellence in two disciplines and to redress the failure of programmes to deliver intended value: building baseline business cases and value realisation

---

3   Oakland, J.S., Tanner, S. 2007. Successful change programs. *Total Quality Management*, 18(1–2): 1–19.

- There are six repeating patterns relating to these disciplines which account for much of the failure of programmes to deliver intended value:
  1. Inadequate specification of stakeholder outcomes
  2. Unrealistic quantification of benefits
  3. Poor causal linkage between programme phases and benefits
  4. Poor value alignment
  5. Imprecise criteria for success and inadequate provision for risk
  6. Inadequate tracking of benefit and overall programme value
- Through analysis of these causal patterns we can define archetypal solutions which are now explored in greater depth in Part II

▌▌ *Principles*

We concluded Part I by defining six repeating failure patterns, all of which have their root in poor cognition and definition of causal linkage between programmes and the benefits that programmes are intended to deliver. For each failure pattern we outlined corresponding archetypal solutions. In Part II we take each pattern and discuss the principles behind the solution, providing both theoretical foundation and practical application. We then structure the principles into a Value Management framework, IMPACT, which provides a practical approach for delivering value from change programmes.

Value Management is a non-linear process and rather than treat it as a set of strictly sequential steps, it is more appropriate to adopt those parts of the framework which offer most value, in the context of any methods being employed.

Part II builds the ability to link new business capabilities output by the programme, which we refer to as *deliverables*, to outcomes actually experienced by stakeholders, *benefits,* by quantifying key measureable factors, *drivers*, and the cause and effect relationships between deliverables, drivers and benefits. It is crucial to define terms precisely. Consequently, those terms that are most critical in this process, which are also included in the Glossary at the end of this book, are described in greater depth below. Other terms will be expanded where appropriate in each chapter:

Benefits (Outcomes)

Benefits are stakeholder outcomes. In a commercial enterprise, the key benefits are increased revenue and/or reduced costbase, the two sides of the profit and loss account. Other stakeholder outcomes, such as good customer experience and motivated staff, are also essential in the context of sustaining adequate ROI, without which nothing else is possible. For public sector and not-for-profit organisations, the focus is on value for money, rather than profit, although sustainability is still ultimately dependent on financial performance and affordability. This is even more pertinent when governments are forced to reign in public spending. Benefits are lag indicators, that is, they are the result of a change in one or more drivers. In Value Management, we use the terms benefits, outcomes, stakeholder outcomes, outcome measures and lag indicators or measures synonymously.

Stakeholders

Stakeholders are people who interact with the business and/or are the recipients of outcomes from the business. Outcomes can be negative, for example, people living near to a factory belching poisonous fumes are stakeholders, as are the shareholders who stand to gain a return on their investment. To be effective, a stakeholder must both own the outcome and have the power to influence it. This presents us with a problem, for example, customers do not generally have any direct control over the business. Therefore, for practical purposes, stakeholders are named individuals within the business who represent the external stakeholders. For example, in a commercial enterprise, where there is real competition, a customer stakeholder may be the budget owner of the account that serves them. In the public sector, the equivalent role may be the most senior person interfacing with the appropriate regulator. In Value Management, we use the terms stakeholders and benefit owners synonymously.

Deliverables

Deliverables are high-level programme products which enable new business capabilities, or release latent existing resources, needed to deliver stakeholder outcomes, that is, benefits. For example, for banking, straight through processing (STP) would be a deliverable which enables the bank to achieve the outcome of selling more business with a lower costbase. Deliverables will be major milestones in programmes. In Value Management, we use the terms deliverables, business capabilities and programme products synonymously.

Drivers (Performance Drivers)

Drivers are measurable factors which are influenced by deliverables. Generally, drivers fall into the resource, process or customer perspectives of the Balanced Scorecard, discussed in Chapter 2. For example, call centre staff churn rate (resources), time to offer new quote (process) and number of new customers (customers). Drivers are generally lead indicators because they must change before benefits, that is lag indicators, are realised. In Value Management, we use the terms drivers, performance drivers and lead indicators or measures synonymously.

Beneficiaries

Beneficiaries are people who will have a new capability they can exploit as a result of a programme deliverable. Beneficiaries are at the *point of power* where the change in driver actually takes place and their business will be changed in some way once the programme deliverable is operational. Beneficiaries own changes in drivers. In Value Management we use the terms beneficiaries and driver owners synonymously.

Phase

Phase is a generic term used to define a chunk of work which outputs one or more whole or partial deliverables within a project, programme or portfolio. Precisely what a phase refers to depends on the level at which we are working. For example, for a work package within a project, phases might be the high-level tasks, whereas at project level, phases would be work packages. For a programme, phases could refer to complete projects and for a portfolio, a phase could be an entire programme. The crucial point is that a phase outputs a defined deliverable, which is linked causally to changes in drivers, which in turn result in benefits, either in its own right or by enabling other deliverables.

Strategy Map

A strategy map is the causal framework for developing a Balanced Scorecard within the context of a business strategy. Strategy maps are critical to Value Management because they form the basis for causal mapping and subsequent dynamics modelling. Strategy maps are described in more detail in Chapter 5. However, it is useful at this point to define the key components that we use to build strategy maps as shown in Figure II.1:

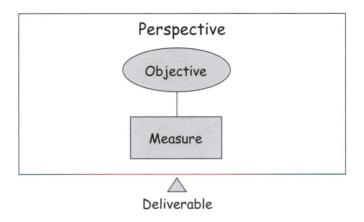

Figure II.1   Strategy map key

Perspective

Perspective, also called quadrant, is a stakeholder viewpoint within which performance criteria are categorised for the Balanced Scorecard. Typically, there are four perspectives, referred to in this book as financial, customers, resources and process. Where scores are used, perspective scores are rolled up into an overall Balanced Scorecard score.

Objectives

Objectives are strategic intentions, ideally expressed in an action context, such as, 'know our customers', 'deliver excellence' and so on, although we sometimes deviate from this ideal in diagrams for the sake of brevity. In a strategy map, objectives are linked within and across perspectives in chains of cause and effect called themes. Objective scores are rolled up into perspective scores.

Measures

Measure is the general term used to describe precise criteria through which we quantify performance. There are two types of measure, lead and lag indicators. Lead indicators, also called performance drivers or drivers as defined above, must happen first in order to cause lag indicators, which are measures of outcome, that is, benefits. Measure scores are rolled up into objective scores. Measures are changed causally by deliverables, as defined above. Two other commonly used terms, which are the source of much confusion, are Key Performance Indicator (KPI) and Performance Indicator (PI). KPI is often used to denote measures included within a strategic level Balanced Scorecard, whereas PI refers to measures in tactical and operational level Balanced Scorecards. Both KPIs and PIs can comprise lead and lag indicators.

Causal Relationships

Causal relationships are cause and effect links between deliverables, drivers and benefits. The relationships can, and generally are, many-to-many, that is a deliverable can influence several drivers and/or any one driver can be changed by the effect of several deliverables. The key to Value Management is defining and quantifying these relationships specifically and precisely.

Causal Storylines

The most effective way to identify, define and quantify causal relationships is using real stories from real people. To this end, causal stories are complete chains of causal relationships, expressed as a story and corroborated with a calculation which quantifies the storyline. In their abbreviated form, storylines read as IF–THEN statements between deliverables, drivers and benefits. For example, IF straight through processing (deliverable) automates the payment process THEN there will be fewer errors (driver); IF fewer errors THEN there will be reduced correction costs (benefit).

Themes

Themes are complete chains of cause and effect relationships between objectives and measures within a Balanced Scorecard. At the highest level, themes define business strategy. Themes can also define causal links between Balanced Scorecards that are cascaded at various levels within the business, to provide a clear line of sight through aligned objectives and measures.

5 *Intended Value*

Objectives

After reading this chapter you will be able to:

- Define key outcome objectives
- Build strategy maps that link objectives within a Balanced Scorecard performance management framework
- Define chains of cause and effect, themes, that provide specific focus linking to financial objectives
- Identify business capabilities that will be enabled by programme deliverables which are essential to cause benefits
- Define the partnership between benefit and deliverable owners
- Map deliverables precisely to objectives

Precision Question

What are intended stakeholder outcomes, what new business capabilities are required to deliver them and who is accountable for success?

Outcome Focus

Most programmes still focus on inputs and outputs. *Input* focus concentrates on delivering the programme on budget; *output* focus on delivery of timely functionality compliant against specification. Conversely, outcome focus is most concerned with delivering intended benefits in relation to the resources consumed.

In other words, outcome focus is about delivering the overall programme value. For a programme, benefits result from *deliverables*, which are new business capabilities.

> *Outcome focus represents a shift from accounting for what is spent to accountability for value that the spend delivers to stakeholders.*

Outcome focus is both the mindset and process of clearly defining intended benefits, together with the causal means by which the benefits are achieved, then retaining that clarity throughout the life of the programme. Therefore, outcome focus comprises two essential components as shown in Figure 5.1:

- Intention: this is the precise definition of outcomes together with what is needed in order to enable the benefits. Intention is about doing the right things.
- Attention: this is the perpetual measurement, feedback and correction to ensure that outcomes are realised. Attention is about doing things right.

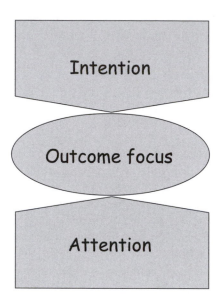

Figure 5.1   Outcome focus

Intention is a strong word. It does not mean wish, aim, target or marks for trying. Intention means commitment to a standard of achievement and that anything below that standard is deemed to be unacceptable. Standards require unambiguous measures against which to assess achievement, together with a 'failure is not an option' commitment. This combination of precise definition and total commitment is evident in safety-critical industries, such as airlines and nuclear power, where standards cannot be compromised legally, morally or commercially. In Value Management, we apply this level of commitment to value delivery from programmes; financial health is business-critical.

Attention also has strong meaning. We get what we direct our focus to, whether this is what we most want or most fear. In business, this translates into, 'we can only manage what we measure'. Therefore, combined with clear intention, we need to be specific about what that intention will look, sound and feel like, defined as precise *criteria* for success.

Outcome Focus in Private and Public Sectors

Traditionally, the commercial private sector has been most concerned with making profit in order to deliver acceptable returns to shareholders, whilst the public sector focused on accountability for spending taxpayers' money. If only it were that simple. In today's complex world, with integration of, and interdependence between, public and private sectors, these distinctions are not only less significant, they can be outright dangerous.

For example, several fatal crashes involving poorly maintained infrastructure in the privatised UK railway industry were partly blamed on the pursuit of profit at the expense of safety. Conversely, there is still massive waste in the public sector that would have been driven out in commercial enterprises through the profit motive.

The challenge is to balance the best of private and public sectors to optimise value.

We stated earlier that for a business, whether private or public, to remain sustainable there must be equitable, although not necessarily equal, value across stakeholders. In other words, there must be sufficient win–win so that stakeholder behaviour is mutually supportive. Outcome focus provides this by considering how the interests of all stakeholders are met. In Part III we demonstrate through a case study the integration of private and public sectors to generate the greatest overall, sustainable value to all stakeholders.

Channel Tunnel Story

After the Channel Tunnel opened, the shiny new Eurostar train fleet was soon packed with passengers enjoying smooth, high-speed journeys from London to the heart of Paris and back. Business travellers enjoyed the speed and sophistication of the trains, with mobile phone coverage all the way, whilst the leisure market boomed as a long weekend in Paris or Brussels became more practical and affordable.

Soon, Eurostar became a victim of its own success. The volume of sales enquiries in its burgeoning Ashford call centre grew rapidly, and lost call rates rose. A greater capacity was needed urgently, and the solution seemed obvious; get a bigger call switch (a simple technology issue). However, the visionary call centre manager was not convinced that the challenge was that simple and instigated the development of a business case.

He was right. The value-based study of the call centre operation and Eurostar's wider business strategy revealed a more complex picture. Although there was a problem with call volumes, other issues became apparent. Call durations were rising, driven by more complex customer requirements and in turn, queues were growing leading to lost calls. These problems drove declining customer satisfaction and lost business.

However, Eurostar had ambitious goals to build repeat business, driven by crossover trade from business to leisure, and to increase cross sales and up sales. This was reflected in the business strategy which projected new revenue streams, developed by offering customers a range of ancillary services such as hotel booking and tickets for local attractions. The increasing importance of the Internet in travel and leisure markets was expected to drive a new distribution mix, changing both the predicted volumes for the centre, the type of calls to be handled, and consequently, the skills mix required for the agents. In outcome focus language, Eurostar's objective was to 'own the destination' in the eyes of its customers, that is, to provide for all their needs whilst in Paris, ensuring that they had a memorable visit all thanks to Eurostar.

Standing back from the *surface* operational problem had made it possible to see a richer picture against which both short- and long-term solutions could be directed. Applying skills-based routing techniques and a new team structure relieved the immediate pressure, and allowed time to develop a robust, long-term technology platform that supported the wider Eurostar business strategy.

Front line managers, such as the Eurostar's call centre manager, are beset by today's operational issues, in this case, average wait times, call durations, absence rates, team rosters and many more. It is natural and right that they develop an operational mindset to get work done as efficiently as possible. This is classic input and output thinking to ensure that capacity meets demand and therefore it must be an integral part of the programme design to ensure that requisite operational functionality is delivered.

However, by shifting to an outcome focus, not only were these operational imperatives met, but the value model directed solutions that delivered far greater value across the business stakeholders. Customers got better deals, staff greater satisfaction and the company was able to make more money through the direct sales channels. This was achieved through a combination of reframing the problem from just the need for a bigger call centre switch, chunking up to a more strategic, customer-centric perspective, and using Meta Model questions to match solutions against the key value propositions.

Mission, Vision and Objectives

MISSION

Business is purpose driven and the highest purpose of a business is its mission, which is usually articulated in a mission statement that answers the essential question, 'Why is the business in existence?' This is simple but not easy. Some years ago we built a Balanced Scorecard for an international military client whose main operations involved the planning and running of inter-service exercises, with the aim of maintaining battle readiness. We began the workshops, attended by senior officers from several countries and spanning all the armed services, by establishing the mission. We learned that it was defined in a thick document which described in detail what they did, *inputs*, and what the *outputs* were, such as completed exercises and reports. After several workshops, the *outcome* mission was condensed to one line; to maintain peace in their geographic theatre. For Eurostar, the mission was to transform the journey into part of a great customer experience of visiting cities served by the company.

A mission defines the primary purpose of the business.

VISION

The vision defines *where* a business will be within a defined time frame. This is often expressed as profit, size of organisation, market share, the number 1, 2, 3 and so on, in the market or 'to be the supplier of choice' for a product or service. The vision then provides a foundation upon which value propositions are formulated. Value propositions generally fall under the three categories defined by Treacy and Wiersema:[1] product leadership, operational excellence or customer intimacy. For Eurostar, the vision was 'to own Paris'. This emotive phrase expressed the intention for Eurostar to provide a portal through which customers purchased all travel and entertainment services, in support of delivering their overall experience.

The vision describes where the company will be when success is achieved.

OBJECTIVES

Objectives are those things that must be achieved in order to realise the business vision. For the Eurostar direct sales business, the objectives centred on capacity to meet call volumes and efficient utilisation of agents. These were extended to include more effective targeting of propositions, greater sales conversion rates, customer retention, particularly the high-value business customers, and greater overall customer value.

Objectives define what specific achievements are needed to achieve the vision.

Essential Value Dynamics

The core tenet in Value Management is explicit causal linkage between programme *deliverables* and *benefits* experienced by stakeholders. It follows that we need to define the essential causal process by which this value is created by the business. In *The Profit Zone*, Slywotzky and Morrison[2] identify 22 named profit models which define the highest level mechanisms by which enterprises make money. For example:

- General Electric (GE) is a customer solutions profit model which involves investment in understanding customer needs against which to target high-value propositions
- Pharmaceuticals have a blockbuster profit model, demanding large up-front risk with extraordinary returns, but only if they are first in the market
- Microsoft has a de facto standard profit model, with a locked in customer base (although that is now being challenged by players offering new operating systems, such as Google)

---

1   Treacy, M., Wiersema, F. 1995. *The Discipline of Market Leaders*. London: HarperCollins.

2   Slywotzky, A., Morrison, D. 1997. *The Profit Zone: How Strategic Business Design will Lead You to Tomorrow's Profits*. Chichester: Wiley.

The value chain describes the core process through which value is generated. Slywotzky and Morrison propose that the traditional value chain, starting with assets and core competencies, is reversed to become customer-centric. A customer-focused value chain for Eurostar is shown in Figure 5.2.

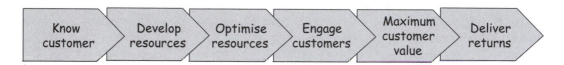

Figure 5.2   Customer-focused value chain

If we combine a customer-focused value chain with a Balanced Scorecard, we define the essential value dynamics of the organisation as shown for Eurostar in Figure 5.3. We also refer to this as a value chain strategy map.

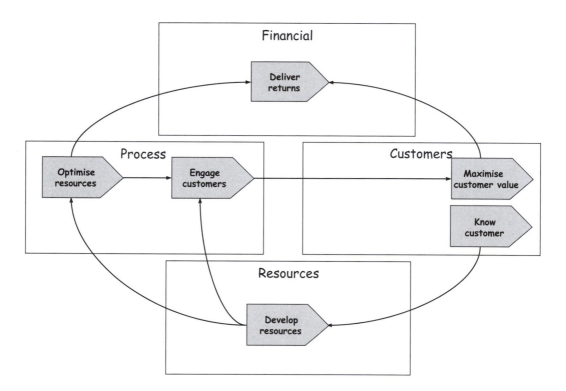

Figure 5.3   Essential value dynamics (value chain strategy map)

Strategy Maps

Kaplan and Norton[3] define a strategy as a set of hypotheses about cause and effect. A strategy map links key objectives causally through the perspectives of a Balanced Scorecard. A high-level strategy map for Eurostar is shown in Figure 5.4.

Strategy defines how success will be achieved.

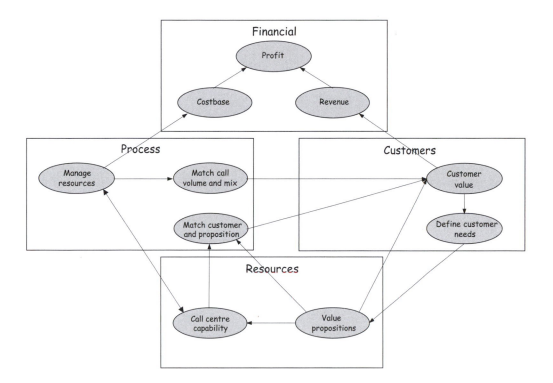

Figure 5.4   Strategy map for Eurostar

In Value Management we present strategy maps differently from the most common approach in which objectives are linked in a vertical thread through the perspectives in the order resources, process, customers and financial. The structure as shown in Figure 5.4 is used to facilitate conversion of the strategy map into a cause and effect map and dynamics model in which causation operates in feedback loops.

Themes

The power of strategy mapping lies in themes, which are focused chains of cause and effect linking objectives, and associated measures, through the Balanced Scorecard perspectives

---

3   Kaplan, R., Norton, D. 1996. *The Balanced Scorecard: Translating Strategy into Action*. Boston, USA: HBS Press.

to financial outcomes. Themes read as stories. For Eurostar, there were two key themes reflecting the cost and revenue components of the profit and loss account:

1. customer value theme
2. operational efficiency theme

CUSTOMER VALUE THEME

Knowledge about the market and customers enabled precisely targeted value propositions, with higher sales value. In addition, close matching of propositions to customers resulted in more repeat sales with higher sales value sustained over longer periods due to better customer retention.

OPERATIONAL EFFICIENCY THEME

By defining precise value propositions targeted to customer segments, each agent could be trained to be more productive, handling more and a greater range of calls, thereby requiring fewer resources to provide the capacity needed to cover call volumes and mix. Precise propositions also enabled agents to be more effective, so increasing the conversion rates for customers and sales which, in turn resulted more precise knowledge concerning customer needs. The operational efficiency theme for Eurostar is shown in Figure 5.5.

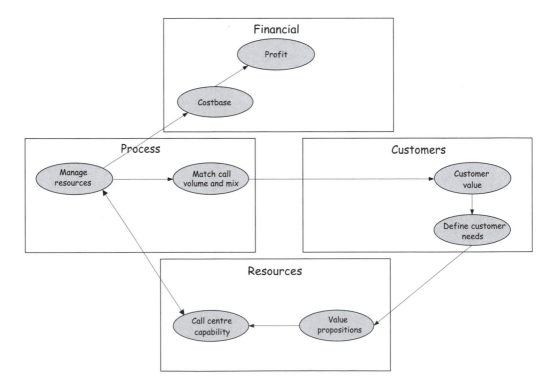

Figure 5.5   Operational efficiency theme for Eurostar

It is important to recognise the mutual interdependence between the themes; targeted value propositions, enabled by precise market and customer intelligence, increased revenue for a reduced costbase; that is, both effectiveness and efficiency.

Deliverables

Deliverables enable new business capabilities that are needed to achieve the objectives. These may include resources which are not currently being used effectively, in which case a deliverable may be staff qualified with new skills, or completely new business capabilities requiring IT solutions. Deliverables become programme outputs. Usually, programme outputs are defined as functional capability. For example, typical deliverables for Business Intelligence (BI) programmes may include reports. However, what is important is the *value* that can be created as a result of the deliverables, in this case, reports. Here we need to be specific. For example, as a direct result of applying the information contained in a marketing report we can offer the best value propositions to customers, thereby increasing sales and profit.

Deliverables enable business capability that causes benefits.

However, it is inherently difficult, and usually unhelpful, to assign specific benefits to a single low-level item, such as a report. There are two reasons for this. First, we end up with a set of complex piecemeal benefits which are impractical to manage. Secondly, value creation is dependent on a combination of capabilities working together. For example, in order for report information to be translated into value, we must also be able to configure products and services, both to meet customer needs and be profitable, and then promote them effectively. The report is only one component in the total capability needed to deliver benefits to stakeholders.

In Value Management, we overcome this dilemma by *chunking* deliverables up to a level at which they can be most readily translated into business capabilities that cause benefits. So we combine the lower-level outputs into a single deliverable, such as targeted customer propositions.

Deliverables are derived by asking, 'How will we cause objectives to be achieved?' For Eurostar, the key deliverables were defined as follows:

- switch capacity
- management information
- customer and destination information

Switch capacity referred to the ability to handle the increasing call volumes without losing calls. Management information included resource management which enabled the call centre manager to optimise deployment of agents in order to maximise utilisation and contain costs. Customer and destination information, which included a data warehouse, enabled Eurostar to match value propositions to customers.

Deliverable Independence

It is also important at this early stage to define deliverables to be as independent as possible from a value perspective. There are several reasons for this that will become more apparent in subsequent chapters. First, it is much easier and more effective to attribute benefits to deliverables: we cover this in Chapter 7. Secondly, deliverable independence enables value alignment, examined in Chapter 8, and reduces risk, which we discuss in Chapter 9. Finally, it is much easier to track and correct negative variances, the subject of Chapter 10, if deliverables have a degree of autonomy.

Deliverable independence is also achieved through the chunking up process, by combining functionality to a level at which benefits can be attributed to specific deliverables. The aim is not to eliminate dependencies between deliverables, which are both inevitable and essential, but to identify benefits attributable to each specific deliverable operating independently or in conjunction with dependent deliverables operating in alignment.

Value Ownership

A consequence of the switch to an outcome focus is that the level of engagement of key stakeholders in programmes has to change. Tension between the typical operational and programme management mindsets, focused on outputs, can be a problem. Many large organisations find running programmes tricky, not because they do not have robust programme management methodologies and processes, but because of a failure to work in partnership with stakeholders effectively. The key is to set up a governance structure which can stand the various strains that the programme will create. Outcome focus is achieved through a total commitment between those accountable for delivering business capability, deliverables owners and recipients of the outcomes, the business stakeholders, as shown in Figure 5.6. In practice, deliverables owners will be programme managers and benefits owners key people within the business representing both internal and external stakeholders.

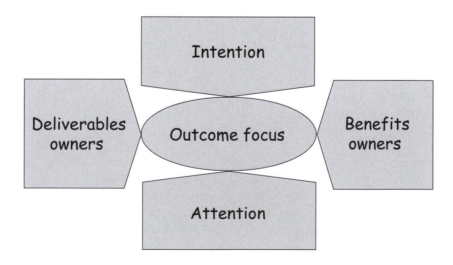

Figure 5.6   Value ownership

Building Certainty

The core tenet in Value Management is delivering intended stakeholder outcomes from change programmes with *certainty*, through precise causal linkage of deliverables to benefits. The partnering commitment between deliverable and benefit owners is maintained throughout the life of the programme, by ensuring at each step that deliverables will result in the intended benefits. Financial benefits will be achieved through the interaction of changes defined in themes. Therefore, certainty is injected by mapping deliverables against each theme. At this stage, deliverables are mapped against objectives in each theme. Deliverables–objectives mapping in the operational efficiency theme for Eurostar is shown in Figure 5.7:

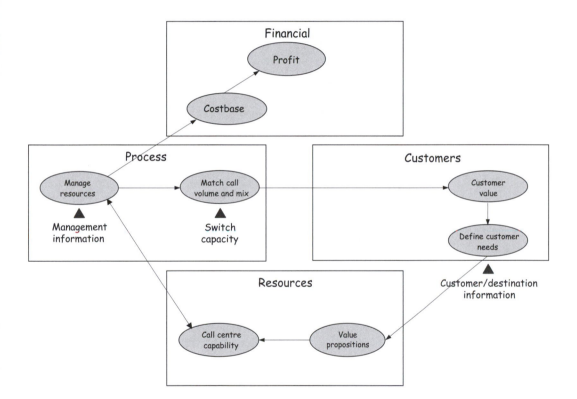

Figure 5.7   Deliverables–objectives mapping

This mapping process builds certainty by exerting the discipline of ensuring explicit links between deliverables and the outcomes. We add precision to this initial map as we work through the Value Management framework, leading to full alignment and exhaustive risk analysis.

Essence

The principal learning from this chapter is summarised below:

- The first significant reason for the failure of programmes to deliver intended value is lack of clarity, precision and management of stakeholder outcomes
- The solution is a shift in mindset and process from an emphasis on managing only inputs and outputs to an outcome focus
- Outcome focus demands two components: intention, which provides clarity of purpose, and attention to ensure precise measurement, feedback and correction
- The mission, vision and objectives define the purpose, destination and prerequisites for achieving the vision
- The essential value dynamics of a business is the highest level definition of how value is created and is founded on a customer-centric value chain
- A strategy map is a hypothesis of how the objectives and associated measures are linked causally to deliver the vision
- Themes are causal chains through the strategy map that provide explicit linkages to financial outcomes
- Deliverables enable business capabilities needed to deliver intended stakeholder outcomes
- Accountability for value delivery is governed through a total commitment partnership between deliverable and benefits owners

6 *Modelling Value*

Objectives

After reading this chapter you will be able to:

- Develop qualitative causal maps that define key drivers and which can subsequently be developed into precise quantitative simulation models
- Define key feedback loops which direct us to the points of highest leverage for change, enabling greatest return at least cost and risk most quickly
- Add precision to themes by converting loops into causal trees
- Inject further certainty by mapping deliverables to specific driver measures

Precision Question

What business performance drivers must change in order to cause intended stakeholder outcomes?

Significance of Modelling

Our ability to influence outcomes is determined by our mastery of cause and effect. All human achievement is the result of our endeavour to understand and apply the universal laws of cause and effect. To be of practical value, we need the ability to reproduce desired effects by creating the causes that produce them. For example, Newtonian physics provides a reliable means of repeating similar results in the physical world. Recent advances in systems theory now enable us to define, quantify and employ causal relationships within a business to create value, eliminate waste and repeat success. These relationships often take the form of repeating archetypal patterns which have corresponding archetypal solutions.

Models provide the means by which we apply cause and effect to create value.

These recent advances in understanding complexity confirm what spiritual leaders have surmised for millennia; that ultimately, everything is connected causally. However, because we are unable to process all these relationships simultaneously, we simplify the world using models. Therefore, the aim of modelling is to represent reality with sufficient precision to enable us to achieve intended stakeholder outcomes. Specifically, in Value Management there are four reasons for modelling:

1. Exposing problems and opportunities
2. Directing value-creating solutions
3. Defining criteria for success
4. Measure twice cut once

EXPOSING PROBLEMS AND OPPORTUNITIES

Modelling enables us both to see problems and, just as importantly, to define their underlying causes. In Value Management, problems and opportunities are simply two sides of the same coin. For example, if you have a problem that is haemorrhaging money then you also have the opportunity to rectify the problem and prevent losing value. Alternatively, if you have an opportunity to increase revenue then the problem can be expressed as 'How we are not exploiting this opportunity to create more value, right now?'

DIRECTING VALUE-CREATING SOLUTIONS

Once we have exposed opportunities or problems, modelling can direct us to effective and efficient solutions. By defining the causal structures, we can target solutions to those areas where we can achieve quickest and greatest positive effect for least cost and risk. This is called *leverage* and it is one of the most important principles in Value Management.

DEFINE CRITERIA FOR SUCCESS

Modelling also enables us to define specific measures against which the degree of success is assessed, negative variances are corrected and positive changes exploited. These measures are used in performance management frameworks, such as the Balanced Scorecard.

MEASURE TWICE CUT ONCE

Whenever we take action to invoke change, we are subject to risk. In today's complex, interconnected environment, implementing major change on a trial and error basis exposes businesses to unacceptable levels of risk and consequential cost. Another key reason for employing modelling is that it allows us to make mistakes and test outcomes within an inexpensive environment. We refer to this process as 'what-if?' modelling or 'sandboxing'. It also provides us with the certainty that solutions will deliver the intended value.

Expectations and Limitations of Modelling

Before exploring modelling further, it is crucial to set expectations and define boundaries within which models are valid. If we expect complex business models, combining process, culture, legislation, customer behaviour, and so on, to give us the exact absolute results achievable in engineering, we will be sorely disappointed. The focus in Value Management is not trying to build models that are exactly right but that tell us more precisely how we are wrong, causally. This shift in emphasis ensures that we concentrate on corrective solutions and is most effectively achieved by modelling *patterns* of cause and effect, rather than absolute results. It is important to recognise that all models come with a health warning because they limit our ability to interpret causality, by presenting only a subset of reality. Therefore, we discuss modelling in the context of how to minimise and counter these limitations.

We also need to reiterate the distinction between deterministic and non-deterministic approaches. Deterministic techniques apply sciences, such as Newtonian physics, which enable us to achieve predictable results repeatedly. Non-deterministic approaches apply new sciences, such as complexity theory, from which we can derive valuable insights and direction, but not absolute results. Value Management makes great use of systems thinking, which is a subset of complexity theory, and contains both deterministic and non-deterministic elements.

The deterministic components include causal patterns, involving feedback loops, which can be simulated using dynamics modelling to provide greater precision in quantifying links between programmes and benefits. Whilst the results will not be exact, they provide boundaries within which we can operate with a degree of certainty. Non-deterministic elements include emergent behaviours derived from many interactions between 'agents' in complex adaptive systems, such as markets and customer segments. These systems can display widely different results due to minute changes in starting conditions and/or chance interactions. Despite this unpredictability, by understanding key drivers we can hone our solutions and avoid pitfalls. In Value Management, we take great care in applying these different models appropriately and use the different approaches to complement each other, corroborating and challenging results.

Types of Models

Models come in two basic forms:

1. Mental models: internal representations of cause and effect through which we filter all input that we receive through our five senses, which was discussed in Chapter 3.
2. Modelling tools: devices which enable us to process more information than we are capable of handling in our brains and are based on our mental models.

MENTAL MODELS

In Part I we discussed mental models and the limitations that they create through scope, level and precision filters. By applying these filters we experience the world not as it actually is, but through our own personal internal representation of it. Also, because we all filter information differently, we see and experience the world uniquely. This diversity can be used to create value, through the 'energy of difference', or wasted in conflict or over-regulation.

Because of the need to work together, we develop similar worldviews made up of similar filters. This convergence is reflected in cultures which hold the key to real change. Cultures are habits of beliefs, values and behaviours adopted by groups, including businesses. Often it is necessary to break out of these cultural habits in order to adapt to new challenges, and this can prove far more difficult than implementing technological solutions. We also discussed powerful structured techniques, reframing, chunking and the Meta Model, which are used to 'shake' established mental models and break through negative cultural barriers to creating value.

MODELLING TOOLS

Modelling tools refer to the physical models that we use to simulate reality, either statically, as explored in this chapter, or dynamically, covered in the Appedices. In Value Management, modelling tools include spreadsheets, accounting packages and specialised business modelling applications. Spreadsheets are ideal for processing *detail* complexity, involving large volumes of data with simple relationships. Over the last two decades, dramatic advances have led to relatively inexpensive modelling solutions capable of simulating *relational* complexity, involving smaller amounts of data but with intricate relationships. At the same time, enormous amounts of information can be stored, retrieved and applied to these business models through Business Intelligence (BI). In addition to developing even more robust modelling tools, the challenge now is learning how to utilise more of the vast potential already available through existing tools.

Modelling Approaches

In addition to types of models, we need to consider different approaches associated with modelling. Essentially, there are two approaches to modelling from a Value Management perspective in the context of quantifying cause and effect:

1. linear thinking
2. systems thinking

LINEAR THINKING

Linear thinking models the world by presupposing that cause and effect are proportionate and operate in one direction. A percentage change in a driver measure results in a proportionate, linear change in the outcome measure, as shown in Figure 6.1. The great benefit of linear thinking is that it is intuitive and simple. In many situations useful models can be developed quickly, cheaply and are easily understood. When there is limited information with which to ascertain deeper cause and effect relationships, linear relationships often provide the most practical starting point.

The tool which champions linear thinking is the spreadsheet. Although capable of non-linear computation, most applications within business are still linear in nature; in particular virtually all accounting applications. The spreadsheet has enabled us to build models with large volumes of data to several decimal places and *detail* complexity which can easily delude us into believing that this is the same as precision. Linear thinking derives cause and effect by focusing on simple relationships between surface-level events using large volumes of data. There are two fundamental limitations associated with most linear modelling tools which we need to be aware of from a Value Management viewpoint:

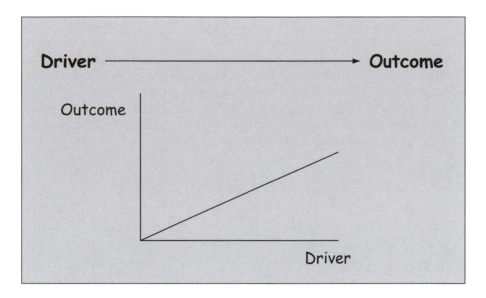

Figure 6.1   Linear thinking

1. proportional (linear) relationships
2. one-way logic

Proportional relationships form the foundation of linear thinking and work on the premise that if a certain quantity of driver is resulting in an *outcome*, then if we double the driver quantity we will also double the outcome. Linear thinking presupposes that large improvements in performance can *only* be effected by large, expensive changes in the organisation. As humans, we are naturally wired to assume that big problems have built up over a long period and require big solutions over a similar time frame.

Closely associated with linear relationships is the concept of one-way logic, whereby everything is assumed to work in one direction as shown in Figure 6.1, where the driver influences the outcome without an effect in the opposite direction. For example, in order to reduce overall production costs (outcome), a company might decide to squeeze suppliers on price (driver); resulting in a quick saving and bonus for the procurement manager. One-way logic would not take into account that in order to maintain their own margins suppliers cut corners on quality, resulting in rework and greater overall production cost, thereby putting more pressure on reducing the suppliers price.

Linear relationships and one-way logic are often acceptable assumptions for practical purposes. However, they can combine to give dangerously erroneous results. Like mental models, linear thinking tools can blind us with the same filters as mental models. Worse still, we create measurement systems that actually support the erroneous thinking. In effect, the tools become an extension of our mental models that remain unchallenged, even when there is evidence that they are wrong. The challenge is to know when to use the simplicity of linear thinking, duly recognising its limitations, and when to use more precise models.

Laundry List Management

In performance management, linear, one-way thinking leads to what Barry Richmond[1] called the laundry list. All factors deemed to have an influence on a desired outcome are linked individually to the objective. This simple approach is often used for building Balanced Scorecards; the factors are given weightings to account for their different levels of influence. Factors may be several layers deep and weightings to several decimal points. A laundry list for the Eurostar story is shown in Figure 6.2.

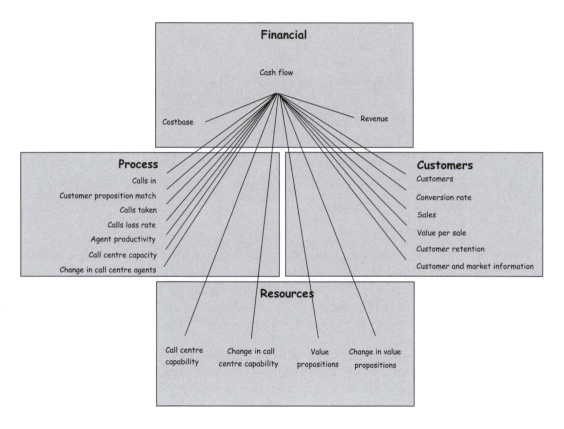

Figure 6.2   Laundry list management

The laundry list provides a useful starting point by considering factors that need to be examined from different perspectives. However, the fundamental limitation with this approach is that it does not define the interconnectedness *between* the different factors. Consequently, it does not pass what we call the 'So what?' test; how specifically does a given change in one factor change one or more other factors in a causal chain linked to financial outcomes? The ability to answer this question is important for three reasons. First, we need to know which factors provide most leverage and so where to target our deliverables. Secondly, we need to know that a positive change in one factor is not at the

---

1   Richmond, B. 2004. *An Introduction to Systems Thinking with iThink*. Lebanon, USA: isee systems, inc.

expense of adverse effects in the others, but is in alignment with them. Finally, we need to translate all change into financial terms. This leads us to the systems paradigm.

SYSTEMS THINKING

The solution to these limitations is systems thinking – the term can mean different things so it is important to define what we mean here. In Value Management systems thinking is the study of things that comprise a number of parts which work together as a whole, called 'systems'. Examples include the human mind and body, economies, societies and businesses. Systems thinking is diametrically opposite to linear thinking in two key ways. First, cause and effect is modelled as a series of feedback loops rather than one-way flows. These loop structures can give rise to disproportionately large effects from small causes over equally disparate time frames. Secondly, linear tools tend to infer causal relationships by using large detailed data sets to determine *correlations* between events. Conversely, systems thinking focuses on true causal relationships between relatively few variables and is more concerned with underlying causal *patterns*. Peter Senge,[2] who brought systems thinking to the mainstream attention of business, observed that some of these patterns are so common that they are archetypal in nature.

Systems thinking models below surface level events to underlying patterns of cause and effect.

Feedback Loops

There are two types of feedback loop:

1. reinforcing
2. balancing

REINFORCING LOOP

Reinforcing loops are either vicious or virtuous circles. For example, in Figure 6.3 unpaid debt incurs greater interest payments, which in turn increases the debt, creating a vicious circle. The plus sign implies that all factors are moving in the same direction, all up or all down. A typical graphical plot for a reinforcing loop is exponential growth. If we substitute debt for savings we would get a virtuous circle with exactly the same structure, although generally with a much shallower curve. There are also cases where reinforcing loops cancel each other out. For example, initiatives that create positive growth in one department may cause exponential decline in another resulting in overall zero gain to the business.

2   Senge, P. 1990. *The Fifth Discipline: The Art and Practice of The Learning Organisation*. London: Century.

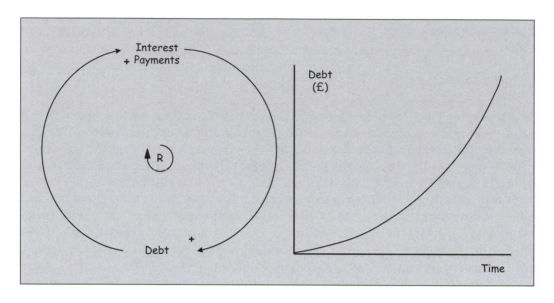

Figure 6.3   Reinforcing loop

BALANCING LOOP

In the absence of any counter effect, reinforcing loops will run out of control. Balancing loops provide this control function, without which the world would not exist. In balancing loops, either one or an odd number of factors work in the opposite direction to the others, denoted by a minus sign. Balancing loops are goal-seeking, meaning that they operate towards either an explicit or implied aim. The degree of control is driven by essentially two things: first, the action in relation to the gap between the current system status and goal, and secondly, the delay between the need for action and change in the system.

For example, referring to Figure 6.4, imagine you have just woken up in a strange hotel and overslept because you couldn't figure out the automated alarm call. You are rushing to prepare for a 09:00 client meeting and stagger into the shower, turning it on hoping that the mixer is set to the right temperature. It isn't! The water is scalding. You say '*@#$ – oh bother!', lunge for the mixer control and turn it wildly towards cold. But nothing seems to happen so you turn it some more. Suddenly, the water changes to freezing. So you turn the mixer the other way and continue this caper until the water matches your body temperature.

If there is not much temperature differential or you can stand extremes, small mixer changes result in the smooth plots in Figure 6.4. If not, the plot is more like wild fluctuations. Unfortunately, economies, housing markets and many examples in business, such as supply chains, behave more like the latter than the former. In fact, in many cases, apparently logical attempts to control the balancing loop end up amplifying the error.

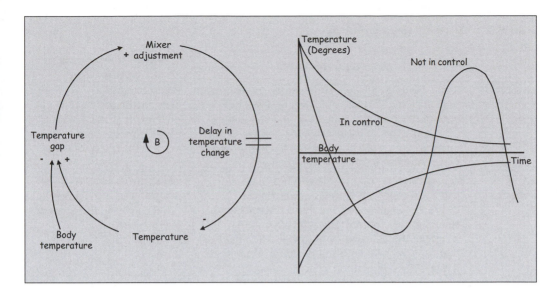

Figure 6.4   Balancing loop

Systems Laws

As we stated earlier, systems thinking is a subset of complexity theory, which covers a vast subject area and extends beyond the scope of this book. However, it is useful to summarise some essential laws derived from this new knowledge which are most relevant to Value Management. Some are not strictly laws but are in themselves subsets of much more complex principles. The statements are valid within the context in which they are described here and can be treated as laws for the purpose of practical application.

Table 6.1   Systems laws

Law	Description	Value Management application
Law of separation	Cause and effect can be separated in space. For example, seemingly sensible actions in one part of the business can result in negative outcomes in one or more other parts	We apply this law to interrogate, find and address true causes, rather than just the symptoms, that is effects
Law of delays	There is often a delay between a change in one part of the system and the consequential effect in another. For example, the effect of an inappropriate action to solve a problem may not become apparent for some time, during which period the problem is made worse by continuing the same incorrect response	We apply this law to minimise the time it takes to address problems, realise benefits and respond to risk

Table 6.1   Systems laws *concluded*

Law	Description	Value Management application
Law of leverage	Small changes can have large effects, for example, seemingly small variances in accuracy of stock can have disproportionate effects on manufacturing productivity. In an extreme when a system becomes unstable, very small changes can flip the system one way or another into a completely new form	We apply this law to target action to those parts of the business that have greatest positive influence on value
Law of connectivity	A single change in one part of the system can affect many other parts of the system disproportionately and the more relationships in the system the greater this effect becomes. For example, the complexity of globalisation means that financial problems in one country can effect the entire world economy	We apply this law to align programme deliverables in order to create the greatest overall value
Law of flexibility	A system must be sufficiently flexible to interact effectively with its environment. A corollary of this law is that the part of the system with the greatest ability to change has greatest influence over the overall system. For example, the most successful businesses possess the agility to respond quickly to market demands for new *outcomes*, such as improved customer service or product functionality	We apply this law to build agility into solutions which enable the business to respond to changing stakeholder needs and wants
Law of redundancy	Flexibility comes with the price of additional capacity needed to deliver a given level of outcome. For example, in order to provide a defined level of customer service, spare capacity is needed in order to respond to variations in demand without deterioration. The laws of flexibility and redundancy tend to operate together	We apply this law to remove real waste whilst providing sufficient capacity to realise stakeholder outcomes
Law of energy exchange	Open systems, such as businesses, exchange energy with their environments in order to sustain them. For example, successful businesses treat customers as partners with whom needs, wants and ideas are exchanged	We apply this law to ensure that proposed changes are consistent with external drivers and for developing win–win solutions between stakeholders
Law of self-organisation	Complex systems, called Complex Adaptive Systems (CAS), find their own order. For example, much behaviour within a business *emerges* by informal rules which reflect the culture. An important point about CASs is that meddling with them by imposing controls without understanding the causal patterns that drive them often creates more problems than it solves	We apply this law to design policies and processes that encourage collaboration and understand group behaviour such as teams and market segmentation
Law of organisational closure	Complex systems close in on themselves in relation to their environments. For example, many organisations tend to 'protect' themselves against external changes such as shifts in technology, markets or public opinion, rather than responding positively to the new needs	We apply this law to ensure that vision and objectives are fitting and sustainable with an appropriately wide context

Why Targets Fail

The systems approach goes a long way to explaining why well-intentioned targets so frequently fail. Few things have invoked contention in the UK like government targets. The concept seems simple enough; define measures that drive the behaviour you want, throw loads of taxpayers' money at the problem then reward compliance and punish failure. However, an understanding of systems thinking and the systems laws outlined above explains how the target culture has failed to achieve desired improvements in public services. There are two interacting reasons from a causal perspective:

1. system manipulation
2. misalignment between drivers and outcomes

SYSTEM MANIPULATION

The corollary of the adage that 'we cannot manage what we cannot measure' is that we get what we measure and, like electricity, we find the easiest way to achieve targets. So, if we measure police performance by the number of arrests or hospital performance by the number of operations undertaken, both output measures, we should not be surprised when these targets are met by increasing convictions in minor offences and simple medical procedures, at the expense of addressing more complex cases. This situation is exacerbated by linking these kinds of measures to budgets and/or pay, bonuses and so on. We are human, we respond to pain and pleasure.

MISALIGNMENT BETWEEN DRIVERS AND OUTCOMES

Systems thinking tells us that drivers and outcomes are separated in both time and space. The time dimension is reflected in two types of measure which we defined in Chapter 2, to recap:

1. Outcomes are lag indicators that reflect the degree to which we *have* achieved intended objectives. Examples include increased revenue and/or reduced costbase.
2. Drivers are lead indicators that signify whether we *will* achieve intended outcomes. Examples include sales pipeline and conversion rate for revenue and error rate for costbase.

Another reason for failure of targets to deliver expected results is misalignment between lead and lag measures. Focusing on either one type or the other creates system manipulation and/or data which may result in short-term local gains but at the cost of overall sustainable value within the entire system.

Unintended Consequences

In practice, system manipulation and causal misalignment tend to work together. For example, in an attempt to improve how quickly patients could be seen by general practitioners (GPs), the UK government introduced a target which rewarded primary care surgeries for making appointments within 48 hours. So what do they do? They *only* allowed for appointments within 48 hours: people who needed to plan ahead, such as those in full-time work, could not book in advance. This came as a complete surprise to the government and is an example of unintended consequences resulting from a flawed system design, in this case created through an ill thought-out policy.

In Value Management, we resolve these problems through the definition and management of precise cause and effect links between measures in the context of the entire business. Success relies on another important phenomenon which we observe in our clients; people who do the actual work generally show great commitment and common sense to do the right thing. Often they succeed *despite*, not as a result of, bureaucratic meddling. This is largely because they can see both causes and effects more clearly; a characteristic of critical importance in this approach to performance management. It was to their great credit that many surgeries continued to cater for longer-term bookings, despite the risk of being penalised for it. Our local GP's surgery is one of the best run organisations I have encountered, and I have never been refused a long-term booking. Excellence is certainly not confined to the private sector.

The Role of Capacity

Closely related to the problem of failed targets is the issue of capacity. Capacity refers to the resources available to create value, and meet targets in the process. Resources include not only people and things needed to do work but also items necessary to translate that work into value, for example, customers. It is no good supplying a gap in the market unless there is a market for the gap. Consequently, demand can refer both to wants from customers and the call on customers' capacity to buy, that is, the size of the market.

If there is insufficient capacity to meet demand, no end of manipulation, spin or plain denial will change the fact that there will be competition for scarce resources. The greatest challenge facing mankind has always been, and remains, the management of limited resources. Take school places. During the 1980s as a centrepiece of their policy the UK government introduced legislation that gave parents the right to choose which particular school to send their children. Just try it! The reality is that this law gives parents no more than the right to *compete* with other parents for limited school places.

When popular schools are over-subscribed, which is now the norm in the UK, some form of selection is used. The most common is the catchment area, which arguably favours the wealthy middle classes who migrate to price-inflated properties within catchment areas for the best schools. To counter this, some authorities have used lotteries, which level the playing field for poorer children. Or does it? One result of this policy when it was piloted was to increase the demand for private school places; an unintended consequence working completely against the government's intention to increase social mobility through education. It is also significant that where grammar schools still exist, that is selection designated by ability, demand is even greater despite government efforts to eradicate them.

The key point is that the fundamental issue behind failure to meet intended stakeholder outcomes is providing and managing capacity. In Appendix A we explore this challenge in greater depth through the context of dynamics modelling.

Stories

The most effective method for capturing complex cause and effect relationships and feedback loops is by using stories. In Value Management workshops, participants are asked to walk through their key issues as stories. There are three reasons why stories are so effective. First, they are personal and create energy whilst providing a vehicle for taking an objective view to emotive problems. This is done by asking the storyteller to relate the story as if they were outside the situation, looking in. In NLP we call this being *dissociated* which means there is less negative emotional energy relating to the current problem and that, in turn, releases the energy to *associate* with the future solution. Secondly, people find it much easier to articulate and relate to problems and opportunities if they are expressed as stories, so it is possible to gain a good insight very quickly. Thirdly, stories are causal by nature. In a gripping novel, we are captivated by the prospect of finding out how the story unfolds and ends. This is natural causal thinking.

Stories are also best told when there is a plot. In Value Management workshops, the plot is directed through a set of precise questions.

- What are the key issues preventing success?
- How are these issues caused?
- If you had total authority, all necessary resources but no excuses for failure, what would you do to prevent or improve the situation and what would you need to be certain of success?
- What measures would you need in order to be certain that you will achieve and have achieved success?

The Meta Model is then applied to the stories in order to add precision by addressing any distortions, generalisations and deletions. (We provide a real example of how these questions are used to build a dynamics model in Appendix A.)

Cause and Effect Mapping

The stories are then woven into a cause and effect map which comprises the factors and relationships that make up the complete causal story for the scope of the programme. This will include causal loops, which normally account for non-linear behaviours and other items feeding into and resulting from the loops. The factors in the map include measures relating to benefits, key drivers that result in benefits and other items that are needed to complete the map. The cause and effect map for Eurostar is shown in Figure 6.5, which links all the measures that we included earlier in the laundry list, Figure 6.2, into a set of causal relationships.

It is very useful to identify the key reinforcing and balancing loops and reference them explicitly. Precision built into cause and effect mapping at this stage pays dividends later when we translate the qualitative maps into quantitative simulation models, which we cover under dynamics modelling in Appendix A. The reinforcing loops drive growth and are likely to contain the highest leverage points for revenue. For Eurostar there were five principal reinforcing loops:

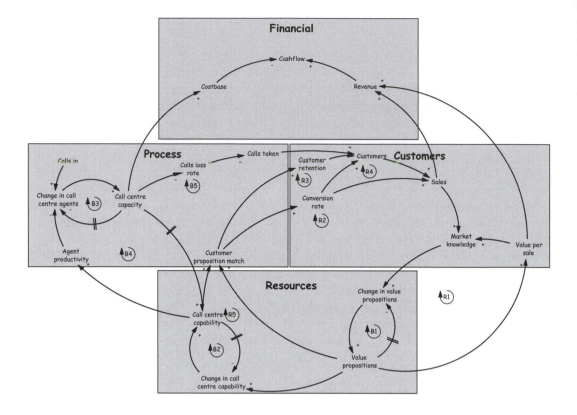

Figure 6.5   Cause and effect map for Eurostar's call centre

1. R1: building value propositions
2. R2: converting sales
3. R3: retaining customers
4. R4: customers and sales
5. R5: effective agents

Reinforcing loops frequently have a compounding effect, as is the case in the Eurostar example. Good value propositions result in a close match with customer needs which drives the acquisition of customers, ability to retain customers, sales conversion and value per sale. The map also directs us to the leverage point in these loops, that is, customer and market information.

Balancing loops tend to be explicit management controls or constraints in the system. For example, balancing loops B1, B2 and B3 are local management of value propositions, call centre staff capability and call centre capacity, respectively. B4 links B2 and B3; staff capability increases productivity per agent which reduces the number of agents needed to meet capacity requirements. Conversely, the greater the capacity the more opportunity there is to train staff to become more capable. B5 is a system constraint; as sales increase through the reinforcing loops, there is increased likelihood of lost calls for a given call centre capacity which in turn reduces sales. This is what is called a 'limits to growth' archetype and is one of the most common causal patterns.

It is useful to build the cause and effect map using the Balanced Scorecard framework for three reasons. First, the approach defines stakeholders. Secondly, it assigns the location and ownership of drivers and benefits. Thirdly, it provides the relationships supporting the strategy maps developed in the previous chapter from which Balanced Scorecard weightings can be derived. Defining the structure and weightings takes the Balanced Scorecard beyond being a measurement tool to a fully causal control panel, in which strategies and specific actions can be traced explicitly to changes in drivers and benefits. It is this quantitative linkage that leads to value realisation and dynamic performance management, described in Appendix C.

Causal Loop Diagrams

It is often difficult to identify specific feedback loops from a complex cause and effect map. Causal loop diagrams are explicit definitions of feedback loops and provide greater clarity by isolating only those factors in the loop. It is often valuable to combine related loops in the same diagram so that interactions between the loops can be seen explicitly. The reinforcing loops for Eurostar are shown in Figure 6.6.

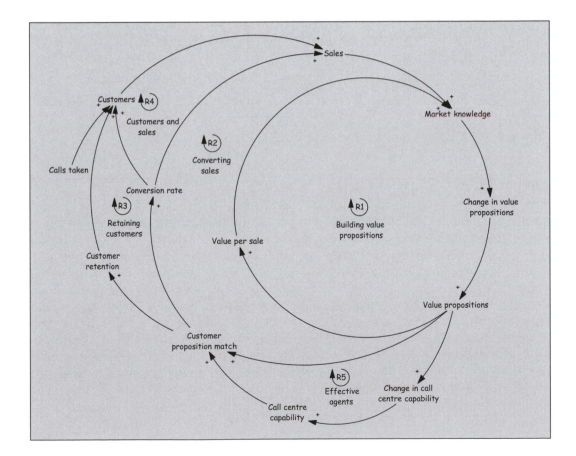

Figure 6.6   Causal loop diagram for Eurostar's call centre

Causal Trees

Loops are very powerful but it often proves easier to communicate cause and effect in a left to right format. Causal trees convert causal loop diagrams into a more easily digested horizontal tree representation. This is achieved by pivoting a single item and opening the loops around it. Things to the left of the item are component causes and things to the right effects, or uses. This process can be performed in two directions; working backwards results in a causes tree, working forward a uses tree. Causal trees are invaluable for tracing the paths of *themes* in the Balanced Scorecard. A causal tree for Eurostar, focusing on market knowledge, is shown in Figure 6.7, observing that items in brackets denote a complete loop, as in the case of R1 shown in the figure.

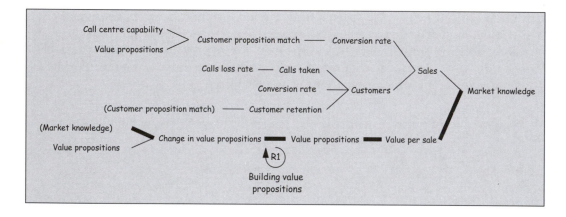

Figure 6.7   A causal tree for Eurostar's call centre

Driver Ownership

Earlier, we defined a stakeholder as an owner of benefits, that is the objective outcomes or lag measures. We now need to define ownership of the drivers, or lead measures. In Value Management, we often refer to driver owners as beneficiaries. A beneficiary is someone who will have a new capability to exploit as a result of a programme deliverable. Their business will be changed in some way once the programme deliverable has been completed. The important characteristic of a beneficiary is that they are at the *point of power* where the actual change will take place. This is like saying a General is accountable for the overall victory, that is the benefit, whilst officers in the field own delivery of each tactical success, i.e. the drivers. These battles must be part of the overall strategy. In the Eurostar example, the marketing director was identified as the programme sponsor, that is the benefit owner, and the call centre manager, the driver owner.

Building Certainty

In Chapter 5 we mapped deliverables against objectives in themes. We can now overlay the deliverables against specific underlying drivers, defined in the cause and effect map, which influence the objectives. This discipline of mapping injects certainty, by ensuring that there is a clear causal linkage between deliverables and specific performance drivers that must be changed in order to achieve objectives. The deliverable–driver mapping for the Eurostar operational efficiency theme is shown in Figure 6.8.

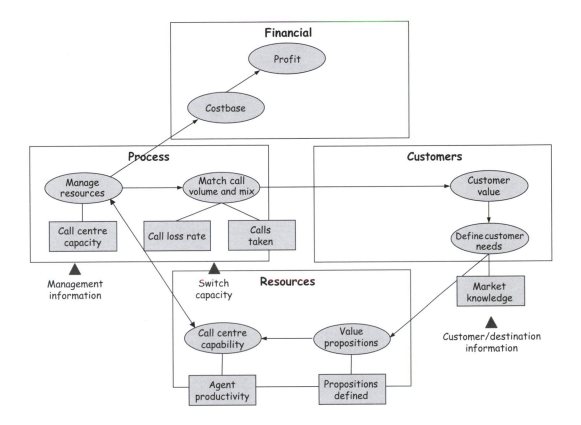

Figure 6.8   Deliverables–measures mapping

Essence

The principal learning from this chapter is summarised below:

- Models are the means by which we simplify reality to make sense of cause and effect in order to create value
- In Value Management, we use models to expose problems and direct appropriate solutions from the confines of a simulated environment, in which we can afford to make mistakes

- Models come in two basic forms, mental models and modelling tools
- In Value Management, there are two fundamental approaches to modelling: linear thinking and systems thinking
- The fundamental limitations associated with most linear modelling tools concern linear relationships and one-way logic
- The solution to these limitations is systems thinking which models cause and effect as a series of feedback loops
- Primary reasons for failure of targets to deliver expected results include manipulation of the system and poor alignment of lead and lag performance measures
- Complex feedback loops can be converted into casual trees to represent the cause and effect dynamics more clearly
- Certainty is injected by mapping deliverables to specific drivers, which are in turn linked to objectives

7 *Programming Value*

Objectives

After reading this chapter you will be able to:

- Quantify benefits attributable to deliverables and specific programme phases
- Quantify development and support costs attributable to programme phases
- Quantify overall programme value
- Profile value over the life of the programme

Precision Question

What level of benefits and costs are attributable to each specific programme phase and when will the value be delivered?

Portfolio, Programme and Project

In this chapter, we describe how to design the organisational structure for implementing change that creates intended value. The best practice for delivering change has converged in recent years to include three key terms: portfolios, programmes and projects, defined by the Office of Government Commerce (OGC)[1] below:

- Portfolio: is the totality of an organisation's investment (or segment thereof) in the changes required to achieve its strategic objectives.
- Programme: is a temporary, flexible organisation created to coordinate, direct and oversee the implementation of a set of related projects and activities, in order to deliver outcomes and benefits related to the organisation's strategic objectives.
- Project: is also a temporary organisation, usually existing for a much shorter duration, which will deliver one or more outputs in accordance with a specific business case.

PROJECT

Projects focus on the cost, timing and compliance of project outputs. In other words, the purpose of projects within a programme is to deliver new or latent business *capabilities* that enable intended stakeholder *outcomes* within defined timescales and cost. A project

---

1   OGC. 2008. *Portfolio, Programme and Project Offices P3O®*. Norwich: The Stationery Office.

can also deliver benefits in its own right. PRINCE2™[2] has become a widely adopted best practice, especially within the public sector. PRINCE2™ provides a structured framework and process for defining, planning and managing projects. A particular strength of PRINCE2™ is product-based planning, which means that plans are structured around delivery of *outputs*, rather than *input* tasks. In Value Management, programme outputs are referred to as deliverables. As the OGC definition implies, a project can and should be supported by a business case in its own right. However, the more common situation for strategic change is several projects running in parallel, in which the deliverables have critical dependencies between them. Therefore, in order to ensure overall value the projects need to be managed as a whole.

PROGRAMME

The vehicle for managing related projects is a *programme*, which encompasses the projects that output deliverables and a framework for measuring the changes in business benefits. An established best practice for programme management is Managing Successful Programmes MSP™ from the OGC.[3] A programme is equally concerned with the cost, timing and compliance of deliverables from its component projects. However, as MSP™ stresses, this is in the context of the higher purpose of a programme; to deliver benefits within an overall business vision. MSP™ introduces two key concepts beyond project management. The first is a *blueprint*: this is what the business will look like when the strategic vision is realised and provides the basis for defining what new capabilities the programme must deliver. The second is *tranche*, which is a major chunk of tasks within the programme that delivers part of the blueprint and associated benefits. In Value Management, we use the term *Target Operating Model* (TOM), adapted from transformation programmes in the financial sector, to be synonymous with blueprint, and programme *phase* as a generic term meaning the same as tranche.

PORTFOLIO

In recent years there has been increasing interest in managing all investments and initiatives within an organisation as a coherent whole. This brings us to portfolio management. Again, the OGC offers a best practice, Portfolio, Programme and Project Offices P3O®, which introduces two major insights which are of particular relevance to Value Management. First, change must include *business as usual* (BAU), meaning that benefits are only realised when change becomes part of BAU; in Value Management, we refer to this as the *point of power*. Secondly, projects, programmes and BAU are inextricably linked and it is essential that all initiatives are integrated in order to optimise value. This means managing dependencies between projects and their outputs. So, portfolio implies a higher-level organisation in which programmes, their component projects and BAU are integrated to deliver the strategic business vision. Portfolio management places emphasis on coordinating dependencies across programmes, projects and BAU, a critical aspect of Value Management encapsulated in an implementation strategy which we introduce in Chapter 8.

---

2   OGC. 2009. *Managing Successful Projects with PRINCE2™ Manual*. 2009 Edition. Norwich: The Stationery Office.

3   OGC. 2007. *Managing Successful Programmes MSP™*. Norwich: The Stationery Office.

In practice, these distinctions can get blurred in both naming and nature. For example, we have managed equally strategic initiatives which are called projects in some client organisations and programmes or portfolios in others. We have seen strategic programmes consume vast resources and deliver no benefit whatever. Conversely, minor projects, fixing some seemingly low-level operational problem, can cause massive returns because of compound reinforcing effects through the organisation, that is, leverage. In Value Management, we are less concerned with what we call an initiative or how strategic it is, than with the extent to which it returns value to stakeholders. In this context, programmes and portfolios are chunked up levels of project with the same purpose, to deliver stakeholder benefits and overall value. Consequently, we apply the same causal attribution process to projects, programmes and portfolios and we use the term *programme* to cover any level. The framework is completely generic and works equally at project, programme or portfolio levels, individually or across all three.

The common thread through projects, programmes and portfolios is value.

The Business Banking Story

As a key part of their five year strategic vision, a major UK bank was undergoing a transition to a TOM where business functions required by business banking were the same as, or very similar to, those provided by the systems, applications and processes used in the retail bank. It was particularly focused on the radical overhaul of existing business systems, which comprised a combination of expensive and loosely integrated retail, wholesale and home-grown systems, applications and processes.

The overall aim was to remove the high degree of duplication and complexity which was contributing to an unsustainable cost/income ratio of around 70 per cent, compared to 60 per cent or lower in competitor organisations. It supported a medium-term objective to reduce its cost/income ratio towards 50 per cent over the following three years. The programme initiative demanded close collaboration between the business banking study team and Group IT team, who between them defined the high-level requirements.

The programme contained considerable risk and the financial business case, which needed main board approval, was proving difficult due to the level of complexity and challenge of quantifying benefits. Value Management was applied to support the business case with a cause and effect analysis, enabling precise linkage between the TOM deliverables, value drivers and business benefits, validated by the business.

The TOM clearly demonstrated how business banking could eliminate many of its own specific processes by reusing and sharing Group processes, mainly with retail banking. This could be achieved by migrating onto the same IT platform and effectively having all (streamlined) back office processes serviced by Group operations. This provided the basis for setting technology requirements.

The Transformation Programme Plan was created through a 'sequencing strategy' workshop which developed the ordering and timing of pilots, technology and process transitions and migration (of accounts) to the new platform. This was used as a basis to develop a comprehensive plan with some 25 stakeholders, and on to a finalised programme. The executive approved the programme which became one of the most successful in the bank.

Designing For Outcomes: Target Operating Model

In Chapters 5 and 6, we mapped deliverables against the outcomes and causal drivers respectively. We now define programme deliverables more precisely and incorporate them into a value-focused programme design and high-level plan. We have seen that to ensure programmes deliver stakeholder *outcomes* rather than simply functional *outputs*, we must not only manage the programme cost, time and compliance, but ensure that the programme deliverables result in the intended benefits.

A critical tool in this process is the TOM. The TOM describes how business will be conducted in the future once our programme has delivered new capabilities to the organisation. As such, it represents a new operational state, or blueprint, that will be different from today. The TOM is divided into three layers, as shown in Figure 7.1:

1. business model
2. operational model
3. technology model

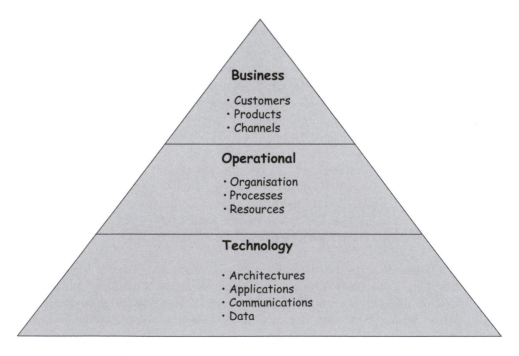

Figure 7.1   Target operating model

BUSINESS MODEL

The business model is the fundamental mechanism by which a business creates value, as discussed in Chapter 5. It describes which customer segments will be targeted with which specific products, services and channels.

OPERATIONAL MODEL

The operational model describes the organisational structure and resources used to support the business model, the processes that will be used to deliver the products and services and the facilities required to house and support these operations.

TECHNOLOGY MODEL

The technology model describes the applications, communications, infrastructure and data required to maintain the operational model, together with the logical and physical architecture on which they are built.

Defining Programme Deliverables

The TOM provides the basis for defining programme deliverables in the context of *all* levels within the business. Whilst many programmes create some part of the TOM during the design process, it is critical that all three layers are considered to ensure alignment. Developing the TOM ensures that a proper understanding is developed not just of what the programme needs to achieve, but how BAU will be different in the future. In turn, this gives us a measurement framework for value that the programme will generate in the future.

The target operating model is a value focused business design.

Key deliverables for the bank were derived from the TOM as follows:

- D1 Straight through processing (STP): enabling the bank to process a transaction automatically from cradle to grave, which reduced cost, through decreased manual handling and injection of errors, whilst improving responsiveness to customers
- D2 Simplified processes: re-engineered processes by reducing the number and resource consumption of activities, thereby decreasing the associated effort, particularly manual input, whilst releasing resources for value added work
- D3 Securities process: identification and rejection of high-risk transactions using automated techniques that reduced the cost of manual intervention, whilst increasing the capacity to filter out otherwise undetected risk
- D4 Online real time: enabled customers to conduct their own transactions with minimal or no manual support from the bank, which reduced the cost of transactions to the bank whilst improving perception of service to customers

- D5 Eliminated processes: processes that were completely removed, together with the cost of resources consumed in supporting them, thereby reducing cost whilst releasing resources for value added activities
- D6 Eliminated IT: IT systems that were completely removed, together with the maintenance and support costs associated with them
- D7 CRM: acquisition of data relating to customer circumstances and behaviour, which enabled the bank to generate greater value through more precise targeting and promotion of value propositions to customers
- D8 Common products: products configured so that they could be offered to both retail and business banking customers, thereby reducing the cost of supporting multiple product variants and gaining economies of scale

It is important to note that deliverables can span all three levels of the TOM. For example, CRM will include channels in the business level, processes in the operational layer and IT in the technology layer.

Programme Value Attribution

A fundamental requirement for projects, programmes and portfolios alike is to quantify intended benefits, together with costs associated with achieving them; the difference being value. Consequently, we need to quantify benefits and costs attributable to the work packages, projects and initiatives and so on, which will produce the deliverables. As we stated in the definition at the beginning of Part II, the term *phase* refers to a high-level chunk of plan that outputs one or more complete or partial deliverables. Phases can include entire programmes within portfolios, projects within programmes or work packages within projects, depending on what level we are working at.

In Value Management, we attribute costs and benefits explicitly to programme phases.

Programme Value Dimensions

In Chapter 2 we quantified the financial worth of a programme using DCF analysis, of which there are essentially two variants, NPV and IRR or yield. Programme value, as quantified by DCF, is determined by the interaction of two dimensions relating to cash flows:

1. magnitude
2. timing

Magnitude refers to the *size* of either programme costs or benefits within a defined accounting period to which the discount factor is applied, for example months, quarters or years. Timing relates to *when* the cash flow is applicable. A core tenet of DCF analysis is the time value of money, manifested through the use of a discount rate which devalues later cash flows exponentially due to the effects of compounding. This means that programme value can be extremely sensitive to the timing of cash flows. We examine the implications of timing more comprehensively in the next chapter. For now, we simply need to recognise the importance of timing as well as magnitude.

If we want to determine precise programme *value*, that is programme benefits minus programme costs, we need to quantify how costs and benefits are distributed across programme phases. There are two complications. First, we are interested in *benefits*, yet phases tend to be designed around functional *outputs*. Secondly, there are usually strong dependencies between phases, which affect both how costs are incurred and the realisation of benefits.

Functional and Value Dependence

In Value Management, we resolve this dilemma by recognising and respecting two types of logical dependence:

1. functional dependence
2. value dependence

Functional dependence is the recognition that there is a logical *operational* order and sequence in which tasks must be conducted. For example, we cannot construct a roof on a house until we have erected the walls. Functional dependence is the bread and butter of sound project management and is achieved through network diagrams and PERT – programme evaluation and review technique – charts. Functional dependence is derived from the question, 'What must be in place before a subsequent phase can be done?'

Value dependence is the degree to which *value* attributable to one or more deliverables is released by a phase and the extent to which this release is dependent on deliverables output by other phases. This recognises that value is not necessarily realised in the same proportion that functionality is implemented. For example, some houses on a development may be cheaper to build yet command a disproportionately high price. Value dependence is derived from the question, 'What structure and sequence of phases delivers maximum programme value?'

As stated earlier, value is driven by both the *magnitude* and *timing* of programme costs and benefits. Sometimes, functional dependence does not allow any flexibility in either magnitude or timing. For example we cannot erect the walls until we have dug the foundations. However, suppose we are implementing a new international payments product within a bank. Functionally, we need to implement the payments infrastructure before we can generate revenue from the value added service offered to customers. However, not all customers have the same value and the cost of implementation may vary greatly across geographies. In this case, there is scope for optimising both the magnitude and timing of value without violating functional dependencies, by appropriate roll out. In the next chapter we use the distinction between functional and value dependence to define deliverables and design the programme to maximise value, in an *implementation strategy*.

Programme Benefits Attribution

Ultimately, we need to answer the question from the CEO and/or CFO, 'What benefits will I get and when will I get them?' Benefits are driven by programme deliverables which are output by programme phases. Therefore, in order to answer this question we need to know what benefits are attributable to each specific programme phase. This requires two steps:

1. attributing benefits to deliverables
2. attributing deliverables to phases

Attributing Benefits to Deliverables

This step involves tracing the causal chains that link programme deliverables to benefits. Most methods for deriving value from change address the fundamental need to assign benefits to programme outputs. Before describing the approach used in Value Management, it is appropriate to cover two of the most powerful and widely used techniques:

1. benefits dependency map
2. benefits dependency network

BENEFITS DEPENDENCY MAP

Benefits dependency mapping is a technique proposed by Gerald Bradley for benefits realisation management.[4] A benefits map chains enablers, business changes, intermediate benefits and end benefits to strategic objectives. The approach is used by MSP™ and provides strong linkage to other aspects of this OGC best practice. Scorings and weightings are used to prioritise the changes.

BENEFITS DEPENDENCY NETWORK

This is a similar framework targeted at IT programmes proposed by John Ward and Elizabeth Daniel of Cranfield University.[5] A benefits dependency network links IS/IT enablers, enabling changes, business changes and benefits to objectives. The approach recognises different levels of difficulty in providing precise measurement, particularly financial measures, and provides several means of evidential change, such as simulation, benchmarking and pilot implementations.

Cause and Effect Linkage

Value Management adopts an approach called *cause and effect linkage*. The approach is founded on the sometimes contentious premise that all change can and should ultimately

---

4   Bradley, G. 2010. *Benefit Realisation Management: A Practical Guide to Achieving Benefits Through Change*. Second Edition. Farnham: Gower.

5   Ward, J., Daniel, E. 2006. *Benefits Management: Delivering Value from IS & IT Investments*. Chichester: Wiley.

be translated into financial measures. This presupposes that areas which are notoriously difficult to quantify financially, for example staff motivation, customer satisfaction or mandatory compliance, can be traced explicitly to financial outcomes. There are three reasons for adopting this uncompromising stance. First, for virtually all our clients across both private and public sectors, only financial measures will do; soft factors may be recognised but are trumped by hard financial figures, even when 'intangibles' are potentially more significant. Secondly, increasingly it is the soft and intangible factors which have the most leverage. For example, in times of austerity and radical budget, rebalancing the elimination of waste becomes more critical than ever; but waste can be subtle and obscured behind 'soft' factors such as lack of trust, internal conflicts and game playing. Thirdly, and paradoxically, the need to quantify all factors financially drives the discipline of precision for 'soft' measures. The challenge is how to translate all changes into financial outcomes? The answer is through the integration of systems thinking and dynamics modelling.

The cause and effect linkage approach aims to combine simplicity with precision. Simplicity is achieved by condensing causal chains to just three terms, as defined in detail at the beginning of Part II and summarised below:

1. Deliverables: programme outputs, which enable new, or release existing latent, capabilities.
2. Drivers: all non-financial factors that must change in order to result in benefits.
3. Benefits: financial outcomes, in commercial enterprises reflected in the two sides of the profit and loss account and in public organisations the cost of delivering stakeholder outcomes; value for money.

Precision is injected by linking the components with reference to cause and effect maps, developed in Chapter 6, using systems theory and practice. The resulting structure for the bank is shown in Figure 7.2.

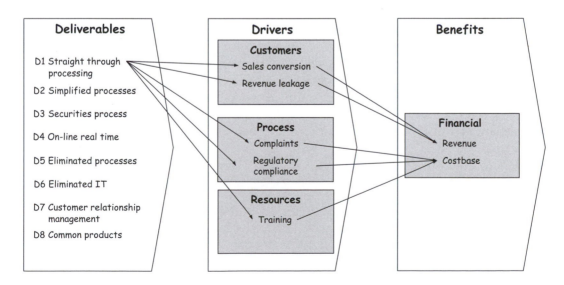

Figure 7.2   Cause and effect linkage

Drivers are lead measures derived from the customer, process and resources perspectives of the Balanced Scorecard. Benefits are lag measures within the financial perspective. This selection process is a simplification, because a Balanced Scorecard normally contains a mixture of lead and lag measures in each perspective, and integrity is maintained through reference to the causal mapping covered in Chapter 6. Each causal thread reads as a *storyline*. The storylines are then combined and interlinked into complete chapters which make up the financial business case. The storylines are articulated in tabular form as shown in Table 7.1.

Table 7.1   Cause and effect linkage storylines

Deliverable	Causation	Driver	Calculation	Benefit
Straight-through processing	Faster service increases cross-sales by 5%	Cross-sales conversion	2K leads per year × 5% conversion × £10K value per sale	£1m/year revenue
	Less errors avoid current arrangement fees loss of 4%	Revenue leakage	£5m arrangement fees per year × 4% loss	£200K/year revenue
	Less errors reduces customer support by 20%	Customer complaints	90 customer support FTEs × £60K per year salary × 20% reduction	1.08m/year costbase
	Less compliance problems reduces audit staff cost by 5%	Compliance issues	£2m per year audit staff cost × 5% reduction	£100K/year costbase
	Less manual processes require 2% less training	Manual process training days	£14m per year staff cost × 5% training × 2% saving	£14K/year costbase

There are several key points to note referring to this case study example:

- Measures and storylines are derived using themes from the cause and effect map, which is developed through workshops and/or interviews;
- Each storyline thread has a calculation, or reference to a calculation, in order to provide a full quantitative audit trail;
- A change to the driver is important for subsequent performance tracking and benefits realisation;
- Benefit values are additive and care is needed to avoid double counting.

Whilst following a strict discipline of quantification, Value Management recognises that many, if not most, of the amounts are subject to estimation and, in the extreme, plain guesswork based on experience. This renders the process vulnerable to a challenge that values are simply fantasy and therefore of no practical use. This is not our experience. The key is to have the appropriate people committed to the process. In fact, the process of constructive challenge is a great way of building commitment to the values agreed upon. It is the old adage that it is better to have an estimate than to simply throw one's hands up and say we can't estimate because it's too hard! We are not aiming for decimal point accuracy but patterns of cause and effect which provide a rich picture. Considerably greater precision is provided when the cause and effect map is translated into a dynamics model, which we explore in Appendix A.

The key to developing a valid cause and effect linkage is being
approximately right rather than exactly wrong.

A common concern from clients is the apparent level of work involved in the technique, particularly given the degree of quantification demanded. Our consistent experience is that this material is completed very quickly. This is usually achieved through workshops; but not always. In the case of the bank example, a seasoned business manager was assigned to help us build the cause and effect linkage table. He turned up at 10:00 on a Friday morning and we had prepared for a very long day. However, after half an hour of the technique, his very first exposure to it, Andy said, 'OK I get it, now buy me a cappuccino then p*** off and let me get on with it,' By 16:00 that afternoon, he had documented 250 storylines, complete with calculations, which did not change much despite being subjected to subsequent rigorous 'destruction testing' by the many stakeholders. My kind of client!

Benefit Profiles

The cause and effect linkage is developed into a database from which a number of benefit profiles can be derived providing graphical 'bangs per buck' views of the sources and causes of benefits. A benefit profile for the bank, in this case, plotting revenue and costbase benefits versus deliverables, is shown in Figure 7.3.

Figure 7.3 illustrates a very typical situation; namely a Pareto, that is 80–20 rule, effect whereby the contribution to benefits is dominated by a few deliverables, in this case straight through processing and securities process. Similar profiles can be generated to determine the distribution of benefits by stakeholder, beneficiary, driver, phase and so on. These analyses are crucial for value alignment because they enable us to distribute deliverables across phases, in order to build a value-optimised implementation strategy. We cover this process in the next chapter.

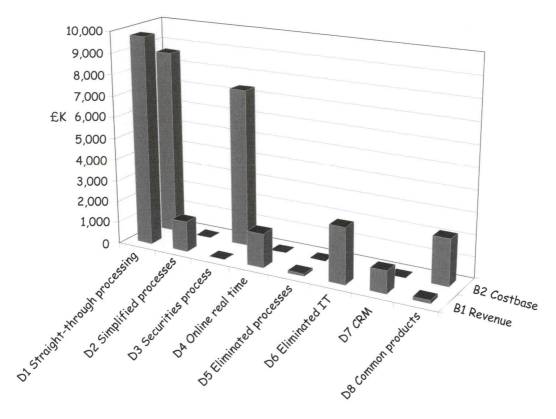

Figure 7.3   Benefits profile

Traceability to User Requirements and Functional Specification

It is crucial that the traceability between the programme deliverables and lower-level requirements is also explicit and auditable. This is achieved by mapping deliverables against user requirements and/or functional specification documentation, as the solutions are developed and implemented. This is often in the form of a compliance matrix, which is used to *verify* that all prerequisite requirements are included and that they are *validated*. This is shown diagrammatically in Figure 7.4.

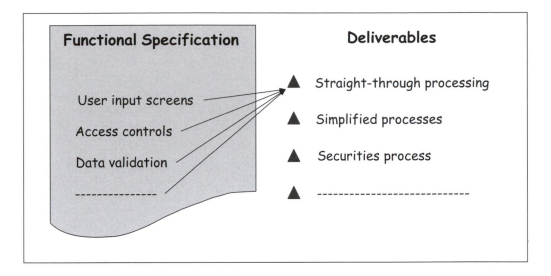

Figure 7.4   Mapping deliverables to control documentation

ATTRIBUTING BENEFITS TO PHASES

Once quantified against deliverables, we need to assign benefits to specific programme phases by addressing the very precise question, 'What proportion of benefits attributable to each deliverable or partial deliverable output from a phase will be realised as a result of that phase?' This process applies the principle of value dependence, defined earlier in this chapter and will be expanded in Chapter 8 in the context of programme value alignment.

Programme Cost Attribution

So far, we have considered the benefits side of the value equation for programmes. We now turn our attention to programme cost. Phases consume resources and incur cost in order to produce deliverables. Then, after being completed, most deliverables must be supported on an ongoing basis. Consequently, there are two types of programme costs which we attribute to each phase:

1. development costs
2. support costs

DEVELOPMENT COST

Development costs are incurred in order to produce the deliverables. They are regarded as non-recurring cost because they cease at the end of development and include initial outlay for physical assets, such as plant and machinery, staff engaged in the programme, installation costs and initial user training. The cumulative cost of a phase within a programme, for example a project, typically displays an S-curve profile over the life of the project, as shown in Figure 7.5, although this can be influenced by large one-off costs. It is important to note that this only covers the output of the project deliverable(s) which is not the entire project life from a value perspective.

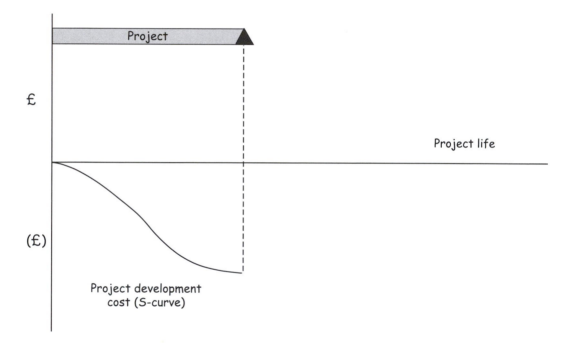

Figure 7.5   Cumulative cost S-curve

SUPPORT COST

Support costs relate to programme-specific items required to ensure that the deliverables continue to provide the capability needed to enable intended benefits. Typical support costs include operational running costs, maintenance and any ongoing training. They also include any additional staff needed to provide the new capabilities made possible by the programme. The typical profile for cumulative support cost is a continuous increase from the output of the deliverable(s) to the end of the defined project life, as shown in Figure 7.6, although this smooth curve can be influenced by warranty periods, fluctuating maintenance expenditure and so on.

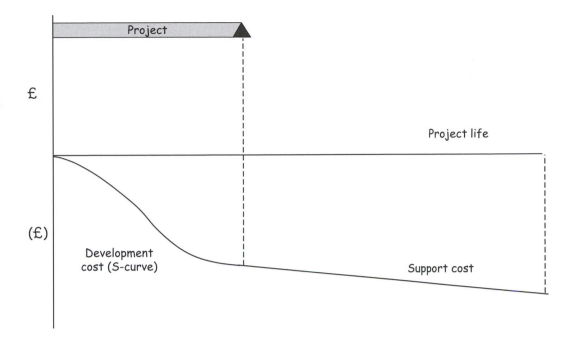

Figure 7.6   Cumulative support cost

Initial Programme Design

In Value Management, programmes are designed around value, which is derived from changes in performance drivers caused by deliverables. Therefore, the most effective first step is to build the programme around the deliverables. This is consistent with PRINCE2™ which advocates an output-based planning approach, whereby work packages are defined around key products. Therefore, the programme structure comprises a phase for each deliverable. The programme structure is then reflected in the high-level plan, in which each group of work needed to output a deliverable is chunked up to a single level. This is shown for the first three deliverables for the bank case study in Figure 7.7.

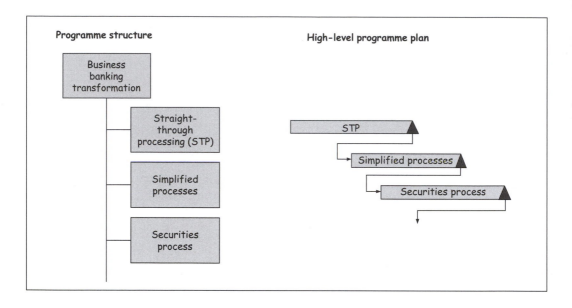

Figure 7.7 Programme structure and high-level plan

Building Certainty

Finally, we need to provide certainty that the programme is financially viable. In Chapter 5 we injected certainty of value by ensuring that deliverables targeted objectives, with reference to the strategy map. Then, in Chapter 6 we instilled further precision by mapping the deliverables against specific driver measures underlying the objectives. So far in this chapter we have quantified financial benefits and costs which are attributable to each deliverable, then assigned benefits to the high-level programme phases that output each deliverable. We now bring the costs and benefits together in order to determine the overall programme value, using DCF analysis. A DCF analysis for the bank is shown in Figure 7.8 (for simplicity only the first three phases are shown).

There are several key observations illustrated in Figure 7.8 (the build up of costs and benefits are shown as linear in order to make the picture easier to follow).

- Programme costs accumulate immediately, are often front-loaded and are committed whether subsequent benefits are realised or not
- Deliverables can enable benefits in a number of ways:
  - Cause benefits completely independently of other deliverables
  - Cause no benefits in their own right but enable one or more other deliverables to cause benefits
  - Cause some benefits independently and enable one or more other deliverables to cause benefits
  - Cause no benefits until one or more other deliverables are completed
  - Cause some benefits independently and increased benefits as other deliverables are completed

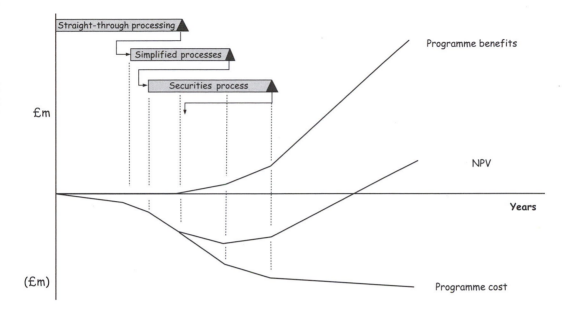

Figure 7.8 Programme discounted cash flow analysis

- No benefits are realised until at least the first deliverable is output, and then only if, as in this case, some benefits are attributable to the deliverable independently, that is they are not dependent on other deliverables
- Benefits tend to build up slowly even after the entire compliant deliverable is output, due to the need for learning time, data accumulation and so on, for example, CRM will only be translated into benefits when sufficient customer data are collected and the skills are available to exploit the information
- The net cash flow for each period, that is the difference between benefits and costs for each month, quarter, year and so on, is adjusted for its time value by a discount factor in order to produce a cumulative Net Present Value (NPV) plot, often referred to as a *J-curve*
- In order to model the complex interaction of both magnitude and timing effects on value, it is necessary to link programme phases *dynamically* to the J-curve

Essence

The principal learning from this chapter is summarised below:

- A programme is currently the most effective vehicle we have for implementing change to deliver business value
- In Value Management, we recognise two types of dependence: functional and value
- Functional dependence focuses on the operational order in which things must be done, value dependence on the order that returns the greatest value

- In Value Management, we combine functional and value dependence in order to deliver maximum programme value, which is reflected in the DCF J-curve
- Programme phases are linked dynamically to the J-curve

8 *Aligning Value*

Objectives

After reading this chapter you will be able to:

- Define business alignment and programme value alignment
- Align objectives and measures throughout the business by cascading the Balanced Scorecard and extending themes through these levels
- Define which combination of programme deliverables offers the greatest value using value magnitude alignment
- Structure and sequence programme phases in order to deliver this value most quickly with least risk using value timing alignment
- Combine magnitude and timing components of alignment into an implementation strategy which optimises overall programme value

Precision Question

What is the optimum business and programme alignment that delivers greatest value, most quickly at acceptable risk?

What is Value Alignment?

Value alignment refers to the state in which all levels of the business, together with programmes, are focused on and working directly towards a common vision. Value alignment is required to operate in the two dimensions that we introduced in the last chapter, magnitude and timing, to ensure that the maximum overall value is realised. There are two aspects to value alignment:

1. business alignment
2. programme value alignment

Business alignment refers to convergence of objectives and measures at all levels within the organisation, providing a clear line of sight on the vision from any viewpoint. Programme value alignment is concerned with directing this business convergence to programmes, which are optimised for realising the greatest benefits most quickly at least cost and acceptable risk. The two aspects of value alignment work in unison. Business alignment provides the essential business environment within which stakeholder value can be most readily created, the key output from which is a cascaded and aligned Balanced Scorecard. Programme value alignment ensures that programmes deliver the full potential value in the shortest time and with least risk, through an implementation strategy.

BUSINESS ALIGNMENT

Thus far we have considered the Balanced Scorecard in the context of the highest level in the business. This is important because the Balanced Scorecard is developed around the strategy for delivering the vision, defined as themes, which connect objectives and measures in the strategy map. This level was also used to develop the corresponding cause and effect map and dynamics model.

However, to be truly effective it is necessary to propagate the Balanced Scorecard throughout the business, ensuring that performance measures align with themes in the strategy map. Niven[1] concludes that, if implemented effectively, cascading may pay the biggest dividends of all. A Balanced Scorecard, or any performance management framework, should be holographic in nature, whereby from any point in the business there are clear objectives, precise measures and causal threads which lead to the vision. Consequently, the strategy map should be represented at all levels within the business, providing an unambiguous line of sight, through the objectives and measures to the vision. This leads us to the challenge of cascading the Balanced Scorecard through the various levels in the business. There are essentially two ways in which this can be done, and these are combined in Value Management to provide the broadest possible picture of the business:

1. hierarchical cascade
2. causal cascade

Hierarchical Cascade

Typically, in a hierarchically cascaded Balanced Scorecard, measures at the highest level are designated KPIs, to denote their strategic significance. The KPIs are then broken down into one or more lower levels of Performance Indicators (PIs), which often reflect the organisational structure of the organisation. For example, the Balanced Scorecard used to manage IT outsourcing within a UK motoring organisation followed a cascade which reflected the different services. So, the customer perspective had an objective, maintain high availability, with two underlying KPI measures, system availability and application availability. The KPIs were then decomposed into PIs covering the availability of the specific applications. The significance of each application was reflected in the weightings leading to the KPI scores. A hierarchical cascade is shown in Figure 8.1.

1   Niven, P. 2002. *Balanced Scorecard Step-by-step: Maximizing Performance and Maintaining Results*. New York, USA: Wiley.

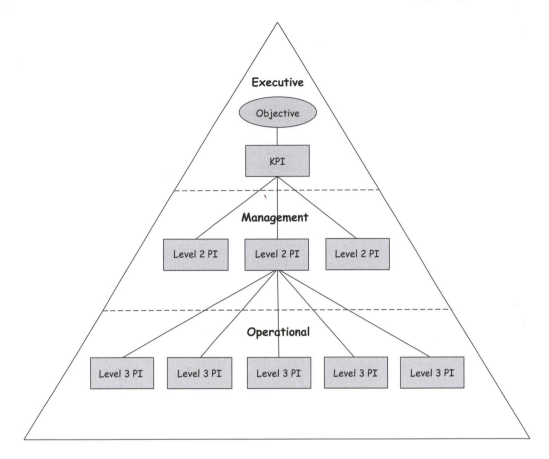

Figure 8.1 Hierarchical Balanced Scorecard cascade

This approach is generally the most intuitive to implement because the cascade mirrors the organisation. It is also important for management purposes. For example, a department manager needs to know how *all* the areas within their responsibility are performing, how these compare and link their performance to personal Balanced Scorecards for individuals. Ultimately, individual performance is reflected in the staff appraisal regime.

However, this structure has two limitations. First, it promotes the presupposition that measures are also hierarchical in status, that is, KPIs are more important than PIs, and the lower the level, the less important a measure is. In Value Management, higher-level measures are simply nearer to the intended outcome, but not necessarily more important. As the law of leverage dictates, lower-level measures can not only have effects which are completely disproportionate to their apparent status, but are generally at the point of power where actual changes are initiated.

Secondly, the structure imposes the same constraint that we discuss when we consider Business Intelligence (BI) solutions in Appendix B; the vertical drill and roll up does not necessarily reflect true cross-functional causality. The best way to explain this is through the 'So what?' test, stated as, 'So what effect will there be in one or more strategic outcomes as a direct result of a given change in a departmental or individual measure?'

It is usually difficult to give a precise answer to this question because the hierarchical and causal links are not the same.

Causal Cascade

In a causal cascade structure, Balanced Scorecards are developed for different levels and follow the themes, so that every objective and measure has a direct cause and effect connection to strategic outcomes. In effect, the strategy map is extended throughout the business. Themes are mapped through all levels, providing a clear line of sight from each measure to the vision, as shown in Figure 8.2.

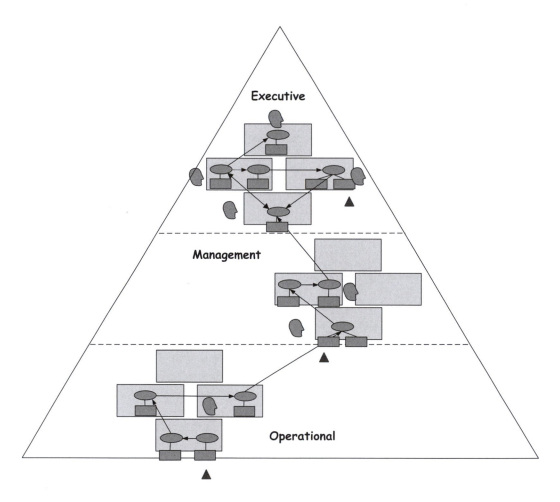

Figure 8.2   Causal Balanced Scorecard cascade

There are four key observations from Figure 8.2. First, the themes do not necessarily follow the same perspectives and/or objectives. In this example, an objective in the customer perspective at the operational level feeds into a different objective in the resources perspective at the management level. Secondly, the theme contains only those specific measures for each objective in the chain that actually contribute to the theme's strategic outcomes. For example, an objective may have five measures but only two of these contribute to the specific theme. Thirdly, programme deliverables (denoted by the triangles) are mapped against measures, to provide a complete picture of how the theme's strategic outcomes will be achieved. Finally, driver and benefit owners (denoted by the heads) are also defined for the theme, remembering that the owner of a driver at a point of power at the operational level can have the greatest overall influence on the outcomes.

The degree of specificity in the linkage between measures is derived from the cause and effect map and dynamics model, and it is important that these are synchronised with the Balanced Scorecard. More specifically, by ensuring consistency between the Balanced Scorecard and dynamics model, we can use the former to assess past and present performance and apply the latter to make future predictions, incorporating necessary corrective action. This is covered in Appendix C. Figure 8.3 shows the causal connections between specific measures in the theme, as they would appear in the cause and effect map, and quantified in the dynamics model.

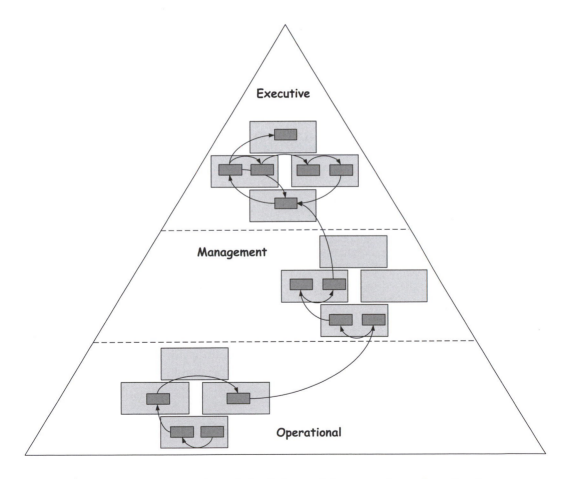

Figure 8.3   Causal map and model – Balanced Scorecard synchronisation

Programme Value Alignment

The vision is caused through business capabilities enabled by programme *deliverables*; remembering that deliverables are provided by business as usual as well as by major change initiatives. Therefore, the focus in Value Management is to drive the vision and maximise overall value by aligning programme deliverables in both magnitude and time. In the last chapter we introduced the distinction between functional and value dependence in relation to programme design and implementation. Functional dependence refers to *operational* relationships between deliverables. For example, a brick wall cannot be built until the foundations are completed. Value dependence involves a strategy by which phases are structured and sequenced to deliver the greatest *value*. For example, we build the houses that represent the greatest realisable value first. In Value Management, we maximise the overall value of the programme by optimising value dependence whist respecting essential functional dependence. This process is called programme value alignment and the key output is an implementation strategy.

Programme Value Alignment Road map

It is appropriate to review how we have reached the point where we can achieve programme value alignment. In Chapter 5 we defined the vision and mapped deliverables against specific *objectives* needed to achieve the vision. In Chapter 6 we identified the highest leverage through which change can be effected and mapped the deliverables to specific *drivers*. In Chapter 7 we attributed financial benefits to deliverables and assigned benefits, together with development and support costs, to major programme *phases*. This enabled us to quantify cash flows and gave us an initial DCF analysis.

Now, we consider how to structure and sequence the programme phases that output deliverables in order to maximise benefits and overall value. We achieve this by reordering, decomposing, and/or redefining phases to output whole or partial deliverables, and *aligning* them into an implementation strategy which maximises programme value, taking into account risk, always within the context of the vision.

Programme value is expressed as a DCF J-curve, which quantifies the difference between programme benefits and costs adjusted for the time value of money. The J-curve is driven by both the *magnitude* and *timing* of programme costs and benefits. Value magnitude is concerned with the size of programme benefits and costs, whilst timing relates to how they are phased within the programme. Therefore, an implementation strategy maximises overall value by optimising the magnitude and timing of value attributable to programme phases. A road map for developing an implementation strategy is shown in Figure 8.4 and demonstrated in the next case study.

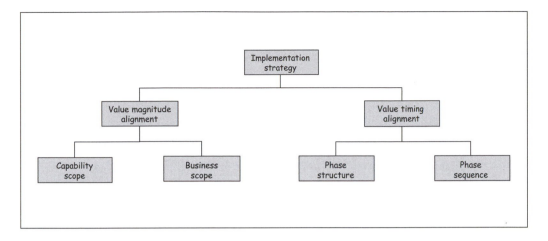

Figure 8.4   Programme value alignment road map

The New Banking Product Story

A major UK bank owned one of the largest high street networks and market share for retail business. However, it had a comparatively smaller share of the business banking market and was undertaking an urgent strategy to raise its profile to be within the top five in the UK. In addition to introducing new business banking products, the bank wanted to exploit its branch network to cross-sell existing products, currently sold centrally. The most important of these was Invoice Discounting (ID), which involved the bank managing payment of supplier invoices on behalf of clients, mainly small and medium-sized enterprises (SME).

A programme team was assigned with a brief to introduce ID into the branch network as a matter of urgency. The team identified three key deliverables within the programme:

- Branch electronic network: installing a dedicated electronic network across the branches to enable automation of the service
- Process changes: essential process changes within branch operations to facilitate the new product
- Product sales skills: capability of branch staff to cross-sell ID to both new and existing customers

The initial business case was based on a programme plan comprising three projects, mirroring the deliverables, sequenced in typical functional dependence as shown in a simplified version in Figure 8.5.

Although the NPV was positive, after analysing the results the programme team made several observations relating to delivered value. First, there was minimal concurrent working between phases, rendering the programme inherently long. Secondly, no benefits were realised until the entire programme was completed, concluding with the product sales training. Thirdly, because the most expensive phase, branch electronic network, was implemented first, the programme incurred high early negative cash flows.

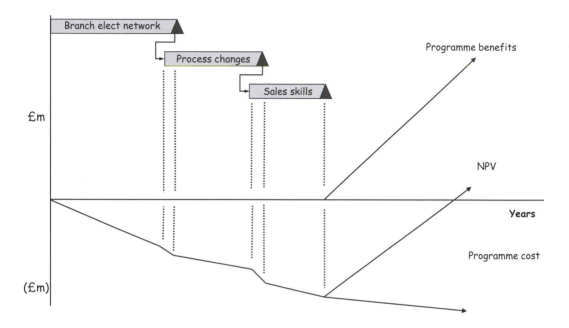

Figure 8.5   Functional dependence

We refer to this dependence as *functional* because the links are driven purely by the intuitive *operational* order in which the outputs are implemented. In this case, process changes would naturally be implemented after the technology is available and training would only be done when everything else is completed, so that new practices are started whilst they are fresh in peoples' minds. The team then considered how the programme design could be changed in order deliver optimum value, using value alignment.

Value Magnitude Alignment

Value magnitude alignment targets the greatest potential *size* of programme benefits, in relation to programme costs, and is achieved in two ways, referring to Figure 8.4:

1. capability scope
2. business scope

CAPABILITY SCOPE

Capability scope is the degree to which capabilities, enabled by each deliverable, are implemented in terms of value. In the new product case study, it was possible to introduce a semi-automated version of ID with limited capabilities. This was an example of capability scope. It is important to quantify phase costs and benefits separately, in order to compute the *value* of each option, as illustrated in the following examples:

- Phase costs: measured as the proportion of development and support costs that would be incurred for full implementation. For example, development of the semi-automated ID was approximately 40 per cent of the cost of a fully functional version.
- Phase benefits: measured as the proportion of maximum periodic, for example annual, benefits attributable to the deliverable. For example, the semi-automated ID represented approximately 60 per cent of the annual benefits attributable to ID implemented with full capabilities.

> *Capability scope refers to the proportion of full capability enabled by deliverables that is implemented within a given part of the business, in terms of value.*

BUSINESS SCOPE

Business scope refers to the degree to which capabilities are implemented within the business and customer base, in terms of value. In the new product case study, it also made sense to limit implementation of the semi-automated version of ID within carefully selected branches. This was an example of business scope. Business scope is measured in the same way as for capability scope. For example, operating within selected branches represented 30 per cent of the cost of rollout across the entire branch network, whilst representing 50 per cent of potential business customer value.

> *Business scope is the degree to which capability is implemented within the business, in terms of value.*

Business scope operates in two dimensions, as shown in Figure 8.6:

1. business level scope
2. business lateral scope

Business level scope is concerned with the hierarchical position within the business at which the capability is implemented. When considering level in Value Management, we make a distinction between *status* and *causal* influence. Status relates to the level of authority and *organisation*, for example, whether capabilities are deployed at operational, tactical or strategic levels in the business. Causal influence is less obvious; it refers to the degree of *leverage* that a capability has on value outcomes, completely irrespective of the formal hierarchical or process location. Sometimes status and causal influence are the same. For example, a strategic BI solution can only be used effectively at the point where there is sufficient authority to act on the insights that it exposes.

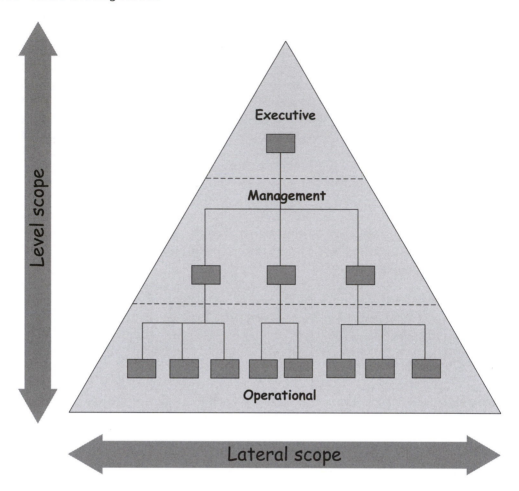

Figure 8.6   Business scope

However, this is not always the case. For example, in defence electronics manufacturing, components are sourced, stored and scheduled using Enterprise Resource Planning (ERP) and directed into kits comprising all the parts needed to complete a particular sub-assembly at the appropriate build stage. However, when parts are missing, automation is overridden by progress chasers, called expeditors in the US, who rob full but lower-priority kits to replace missing components on higher-priority work. Because ERP systems are very sensitive to the accuracy of inventory, this practice soon undermines the integrity of the entire manufacturing process. In this case, seemingly innocuous actions at the operational level can have profound effects on the entire business. Lateral scope is concerned with the degree to which change is implemented *across* the business at the appropriate levels.

Watzlawick et al.[2] articulated the need to determine the appropriate level for dealing with a problem, as to whether we need *revolution* or *evolution*. In systemic terms, revolution involves changing the *structure* of a problem, for example, major shifts in polices, organisation or processes, whereas evolution adjusts the elements working within the overall structure. The penalty of getting this wrong can be severe. For example, repeatedly changing managers of underperforming departments without resolving a fundamental flaw in the business will not only fail to solve the issue, but impose the cost of change and resentment. Conversely, poor productivity within an otherwise efficient and fair process does not call for a new company-wide policy on diversity, which might be effective in the former case, but just some strong local management. Reframing, chunking and the Meta Model, discussed in Chapter 3, provide powerful tools for tackling this challenge.

Capability and business scope can be combined in terms of both programme costs and benefits, to deliver maximum value. For example, the benefits for introducing semi-automatic ID in the selected branches was 60% × 50% = 30% of the fully functional product operating in all branches. The cost was 40% × 30% = 12%. In other words, by focusing on 12 per cent of the final programme costs it was possible to return 30 per cent of the benefits. As in this case, even modest early returns can have a significant effect on the NPV due to the time value of money. What we looking for in value magnitude alignment are 'sweet spots' where the meeting of deliverables and business drivers present the most leverage to create value. This is shown in Figure 8.7.

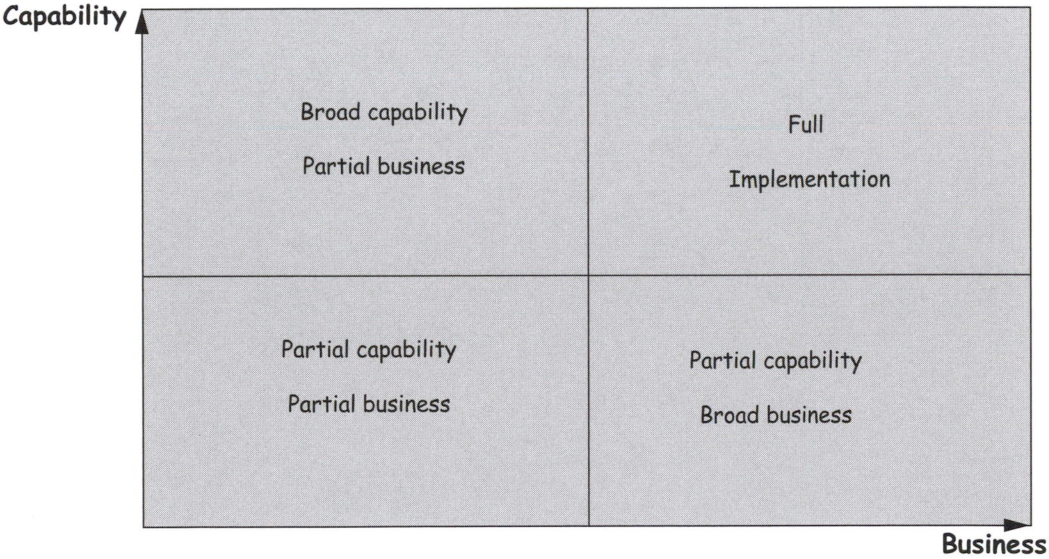

Figure 8.7   Value magnitude alignment

2   Watzlawick, P., Weakland, C. E., Fisch, R. 1974. *Change: Principles of Problem Formulation and Problem Resolution*. New York, USA: Norton.

Value Timing Alignment

Whilst magnitude alignment maximises the potential *size* of programme value, timing alignment is concerned with *realising* this value most quickly with least risk. Value timing alignment is achieved in two ways, referring to Figure 8.4:

1. phase structure
2. phase sequence

PHASE STRUCTURE

Phase structure relates to how value attributable to deliverables is distributed across phases. There are several ways in which this can be done. First, we can structure phases to output more than one whole or partial deliverable, as shown in Figure 8.8.

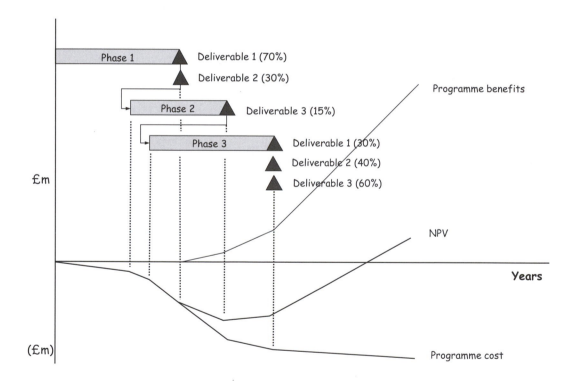

Figure 8.8   Phase structure – multiple deliverables per phase

In this case, rather than each phase outputting a single deliverable, as in the initial structure, phases are designed to result in benefits attributable to more than one partial deliverable. The specific part of each deliverable to be output would be selected as a result of value magnitude alignment and reference to benefits profiles covered in the previous chapter.

Sometimes, we need to be even more precise in determining when benefits attributable to each partial deliverable will be realised. To achieve this level of definition, we can decompose larger phases into to a greater number of smaller phases for each deliverable, as shown in Figure 8.9.

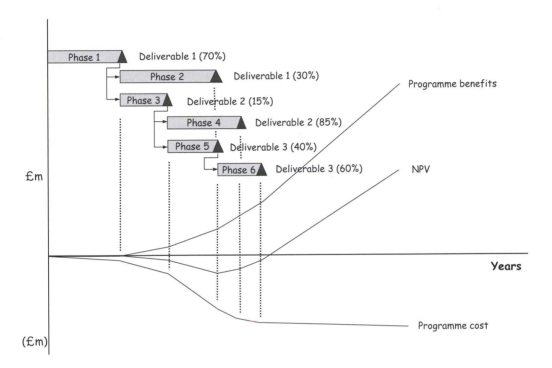

Figure 8.9 Phase structure – multiple phases per deliverable

The difference between these examples is that by using multiple, more precisely defined phases we have realised some benefits earlier, resulting in a significantly more favourable NPV J-curve. We can combine the approaches to produce an increasingly more defined delivery profile. It is important to stress that in all cases, the proportions shown against each phase represents the benefits attributable to each phase, which may be different from either the proportion of cost or operational implementation.

PHASE SEQUENCE

Phase sequence refers to how programme phases are ordered to deliver value most quickly. This aspect covers both the *order* in which phases are arranged, taking into account functional dependencies, and *concurrence*, that is the level of parallel working between phases. For example, in the new product case study, the team initially restructured the programme in three key ways. First, the programme was shortened by introducing greater concurrence between the three projects. Secondly, the minimum essential process changes were implemented as soon as functionally possible, enabling branches to sell ID sooner, albeit with some manual intervention, in a number of carefully selected branches.

Although the semi-automated version was less attractive and more costly to operate, early benefits provided a 'quick win'. Thirdly, the most expensive phase, branch electronic network, was sequenced later in the programme, taking pressure off early negative cash flows, as well as reducing the overall operational risk. The resulting NPV, shown in Figure 8.10, was greatly increased from the initial structure in Figure 8.5.

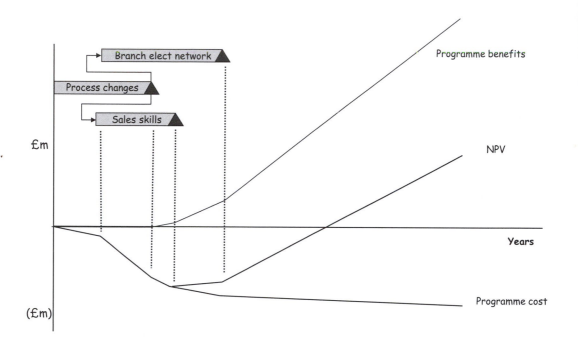

Figure 8.10 Phase sequence

The early negative cash flows increased because the work was front loaded. However, this was more than compensated by benefits which accrued much earlier through the introduction of a manual version of the product, rather than waiting until completion of the electronic network enabled full automation.

Programme Value Dynamics

As we have shown in Chapter 7 and the above examples, programme costs and benefits behave in very different ways. We now need to consider how these differences are critical to programme design from value and risk perspectives. The first essential difference is that for each phase, development costs are incurred before any deliverables are output and support costs subsequently expended. Conversely, for benefits to be realised, deliverables must not only be output but also operationally effective. Secondly, whereas costs are generally incurred in full as resources are consumed, irrespective of whether any benefits are achieved, benefits tend to build up to a maximum over time. For example, CRM requires significant up-front investment, but will not generate additional revenue streams until the customer knowledge has accumulated to the point where it can be used effectively to match value propositions with customers.

A key implication of the dynamics of programme costs and benefits is that the odds are stacked against delivering intended value. More frequently, costs escalate and benefits are reduced through the manifestation of risk: the J-curve takes a hike to the right and falls over. However, this common pattern can be greatly mitigated through value alignment and careful programme design reflected in an implementation strategy.

Integrating Quick Returns with Sustainability

This brings us to the need to integrate early returns with long-term sustainability. One of the most effective ways to increase the programme NPV is to bring forward whole or partial deliverables that result in significant early benefits. Applied wisely, this approach can also reduce risk in three ways. First, realising benefits early not only improves the NPV, due to the time value of money, but also means that whatever happens later these benefits are not lost, as would be the case if all benefits were dependent on a big bang delivery later in the programme life. Secondly, early benefits can fund subsequent development. Thirdly, early implementation can be used to eliminate functional and organisational risks by ironing out problems, proving success and reducing resistance to change. The practical means by which this integration is achieved is by implementing Proof of Concept (PoC) solutions, which deliver early returns and reduce risk, prior to full implementation. We discuss the use of PoC in Appendix C.

The key to maximising value whilst minimising risk is to integrate quick returns with long term sustainability, made possible through value alignment.

Implementation Strategy

Value magnitude and timing alignment are combined to produce an implementation strategy which optimises value by outputting precisely *targeted*, *timed* and *aligned* deliverables. An implementation strategy aligns both the magnitude and timing of benefits to maximise the overall value of the programme, taking into account risk. A simplified version of the final implementation strategy for the new banking product case study is shown in Figure 8.11.

An implementation strategy maximises programme value by targeting, timing and aligning deliverables.

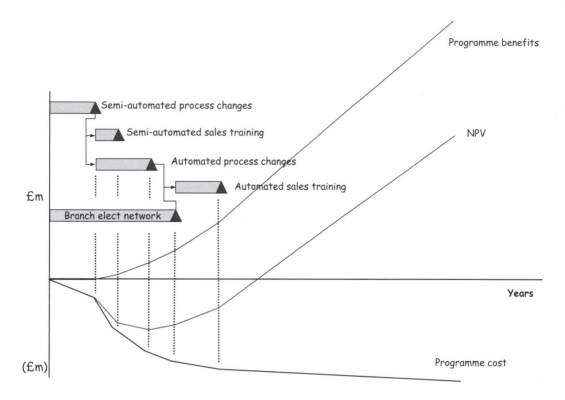

Figure 8.11 Implementation strategy

The new product implementation strategy applied both magnitude and timing alignment. The semi-automated ID product was rolled out to selected branches; examples of capability and business scope respectively. The process and training elements were duly decomposed into smaller, more precisely defined phases, an example of phase structure using multiple phases. Finally, phase sequencing was used by ordering the phases to deliver early positive cash flows from the semi-automated ID, prior to full implementation after completion of the branch electronic network.

The implementation strategy forms the basis for a baseline business case and value realisation plan, the two key tools for approving and tracking the programme. However, before we produce these documents we need to be certain that intended value will be delivered. This is the subject of the next chapter.

Essence

The principal learning from this chapter is summarised below:

* Value alignment refers to the state in which all levels of the *business*, together with *programmes*, are focused on and working directly towards a common vision
* Business alignment refers to convergence of objectives and measures at all levels within the organisation, providing a clear line of sight on the vision from any viewpoint

- Programme value alignment is concerned with directing this business convergence to programmes, which are optimised for realising greatest benefits most quickly at least cost and acceptable risk
- Programme value alignment is expressed in terms of the *magnitude* and *timing* of value which is delivered through programme design
- Value magnitude alignment is concerned with quantifying elements of capability and parts of the business which represent greatest value for implementation
- Value timing alignment determines how phases are structured and sequenced in order to deliver greatest value, most quickly with least risk
- Magnitude and timing value alignment are combined into an implementation strategy which optimises the programme by value delivery

9 *Valuing Certainty*

Objectives

After reading this chapter you will be able to:

- Ensure that intended value is delivered by combining the disciplines of certainty management and risk management
- Improve the certainty of business cases using complementary testing techniques and modelling extremes
- Quantify and manage the effect of key risks on programme value by developing a causal risk register
- Produce a baseline business case which takes into account the effects of risk and provides complete transparency for tracking

Precision Question

What are the precise criteria through which we can be certain of delivering intended value and what would it take to destroy the financial viability of the programme?

Value Assurance

Much is made in programme management of the need for technical and quality assurance, the means by which fitness for purpose in solution design and adherence to standards is ensured. In addition to these critical disciplines, which relate to deliverables, Value Management places equal emphasis on ensuring that intended *value* is delivered or exceeded, that is, *value assurance*.

Value is *created* through the output and deployment of deliverables to change performance drivers and cause benefits. Value is *destroyed* by the manifestation of risk. Therefore, value assurance requires two complementary disciplines:

1. Risk management: preventing, mitigating against and dealing with the manifestation of risks that undermine value delivery;
2. Certainty management: focusing on delivering intended value.

RISK MANAGEMENT

Risk relates to *uncertainty* and risk management the means of dealing with that uncertainty, defined more precisely below:

- Risk is the combination of the probability and impact of effects from potential negative circumstances on intended outcomes which increase costs, decrease benefits and/or extend timescales.
- Risk management is the mindset of due diligence and process of anticipating potential problems, taking steps to prevent the problems happening in the first place and mitigating against the effects if the problems do materialise.

In recent years, there has been increasing emphasis on the need to manage risk as a key part of programme management. This is mirrored by advances in supporting frameworks, such as Management of Risk M_o_R® from OGC,[1] and tools, such as @RISK from Palisade[2] for Monte Carlo analysis, which quantifies boundaries of probable outcomes by calculating permutations of uncertainty across selected variables. A key tool for containing risk in programme management is the *risk register* which defines and tracks the exposure of those risks deemed to be most significant.

When considering risk management, we need to make a distinction between essential redundancy and waste. We must make sure that we allow sufficient contingency or spare capacity, that is redundancy, to allow for unavoidable but measured uncertainty. Conversely, we must not allow ourselves to fall into the trap of 'padding' to support, even promote, the lack of provision for avoidable risks, that is waste. We have seen many instances where risk management is used as an excuse for inaction rather than as a tool for ensuring stakeholder outcomes.

CERTAINTY MANAGEMENT

Although it is essential, there are several potential problems with relying solely on risk management as the means to ensure value delivery. First, there is a tendency for the process to become an *end* rather than a *means*, whereby risk management becomes the main focus, over the outcomes. This leads to the second pitfall, in which risk becomes a self-fulfilling prophesy blaming outside circumstances. This justifies excuses and leads to a 'we told you that risk x might happen and it did so we were right' mentality. Finally, because risk is a scalar, that is it only has quantity, it covers any number of potential problems and it can prove difficult to see the wood for the trees.

All these tendencies can blur focus and/or lead to poorly targeted measures which stifle the ability to deliver outcomes. For example, we have seen major programmes where risk management was undertaken as a science yet not one single outcome was achieved. Nevertheless, because the risk management process was conducted so 'thoroughly', with ten out of ten audits, the programme was deemed to be a success. This is 'marks for trying' at its worst.

---

1   OGC. *Management of Risk M_o_R®: Guidance for Practitioners Book*. Third Edition. Norwich: The Stationery Office.

2   Winston, W. 1995. *Simulation Modelling Using @RISK*. New York, USA: Duxbury Press.

Value Management counters these issues by combining risk management with a focus on *certainty* and *certainty management* which are defined below:

- Certainty is the probability that intended outcomes, manifested as value, will be delivered when promised.
- Certainty management is the process of directing resources on the delivery of intended outcomes, correcting *causally* for potential and manifested *risks*, combined with a 'failure is not an option' mindset which never loses focus on the outcomes.

Certainty is not a simple reciprocal of risk. This is easily tested: if we took all defined risks out of the equation, would we be certain of delivering intended value? We would not, because of all the other factors contributing to uncertainty, many of which we would not include as risks. Certainty, therefore, is the degree to which we can be sure of delivering intended value under the totality of anticipated and unanticipated circumstances. Certainty management combines the risk management process, whereby the entire programme team are alert to anything that threatens intended outcomes, with a mindset to act effectively as soon as possible.

The reason that certainty management is so important is that it is *outcome*-focused. Certainty is a vector, it has direction as well as quantity, the specific outcome being measured as benefits. Consequently, it is focused on moving *toward* something positive, that is the outcomes, rather than only moving *away* from any number of negative risks. The other primary attribute of certainty management is that it is *causal* in nature. For example, earlier we quantified explicit cause and effect linkages between deliverables and the programme phases. Finally, in certainty management there are no excuses; owners must take full responsibility for managing risks from whatever source. The key tool in certainty management is the *value realisation plan*, which we cover in the next chapter.

Risk management is the means by which we inject certainty.

We now examine risk management in more detail from three perspectives:

1. programme risk dynamics
2. value testing
3. causal risk register

Programme Risk Dynamics

Programme risk dynamics refers to the effect of risk on value over time. In practical terms, we measure the effects of risk as changes in NPV and IRR. As with alignment, the effects of risk operate in the two dimensions, *magnitude* and *timing*. When we analyse risk as the interaction of timing, as well as magnitude, effects on DCF we can get some counter-intuitive findings which we demonstrate using a simple, single deliverable and phase programme, as shown in Figure 9.1.

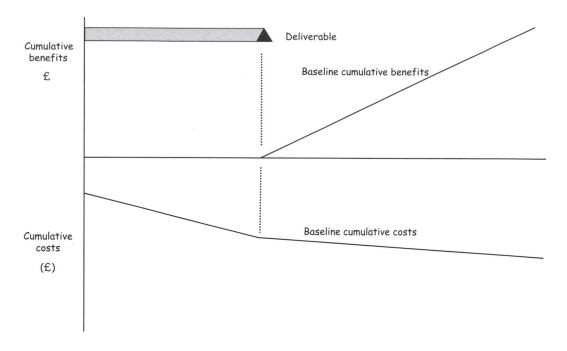

Figure 9.1   Risk dynamics – programme baseline

Figure 9.1 represents a baseline business case in which we have separated the NPV J-curve into its two key components, programme costs and programme benefits, so that we can study the effects of risk on each component separately. There are also some simplifying assumptions as defined below to make the effects easier to follow:

* Benefits are assumed to accrue as soon as the deliverable is output at the phase end, resulting in a linear cumulative plot; in reality they would take time to build up to a maximum annual value.
* Development costs are assumed to be equally distributed along the full duration of the phase, resulting in a linear cumulative plot rather than the more realistic S-curve.
* Annual support costs are assumed to accrue equally from the output of the deliverable, also resulting in a linear cumulative plot, whereas contractual and warranty effects would normally delay the onset of some support costs which may also change over time.
* In all cases the effect of discounting, which would also alter the plots, is omitted.

However, the important risk dynamics are equally applicable even with these simplifying assumptions and are likely to be even more severe in reality.

Magnitude Risk

Magnitude risk relates to both programme benefits and programme costs. Benefit magnitude risks are manifested through failure of deliverables to cause intended outcomes, in essentially one, or a combination of, two ways:

1. Deliverables fail to be compliant with the specification which remains valid;
2. The environment within which the deliverables will operate has changed, rendering the specification invalid and reducing effectiveness of the deliverables.

The effect in both cases is to depress the benefit component of the J-curve vertically downward. Cost magnitude risks usually manifest as increases in programme development and/or support costs. Increased development cost depresses the part of the plot relating to the phase, whilst increases in support cost depress the part of the plot after the phase end. The effects on both benefits and costs are shown in Figure 9.2.

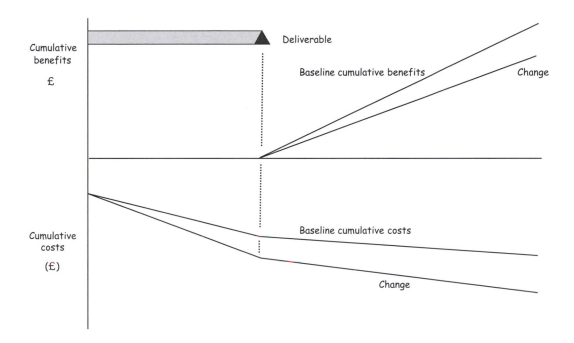

Figure 9.2   Magnitude risk effects

Timing Risk

Timing risk also relates to programme benefits and costs, and in both cases is normally the result of slip in one or more programme phases. The effect of slip on programme benefits is to shift the plot to the right. The programme cost effects can be more complicated. Development costs continue to grow at the same rate due to the 'marching army' effect, whereby the development team is retained until the phase is completed and consumes the same level of costs. The exception is where the phase is fixed price, or there are one-off expenditures (not shown), in which case the same overall cost is spread over a longer period or delayed into later periods. Support costs shift to the right in the same manner as benefits. These effects are shown in Figure 9.3.

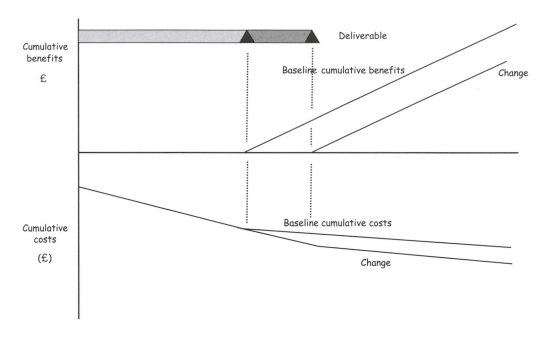

Figure 9.3   Timing risk effects

Combining Magnitude and Timing Risks

The more general situation is that magnitude and timing risks combine to give a result, as shown in Figure 9.4.

Benefits are not only depressed vertically but shifted to the right. Development costs continue for longer at a faster rate due to increased magnitude, combined with the marching army effect of slip. Support costs also increase at a faster rate due to an increase in magnitude. However, because they are incurred later as a result of slip, this can sometimes have a positive influence on the DCF. Overall, these combined effects can, and often do, have a devastating effect on both NPV and IRR. Risk has a double whammy, shearing effect on programme value by forcing benefits down whilst increasing cost. It is useful to overlay the risk on the NPV J-curve so that the full effects can be seen, as in Figure 9.5 in which the risk component is depicted as the dark grey.

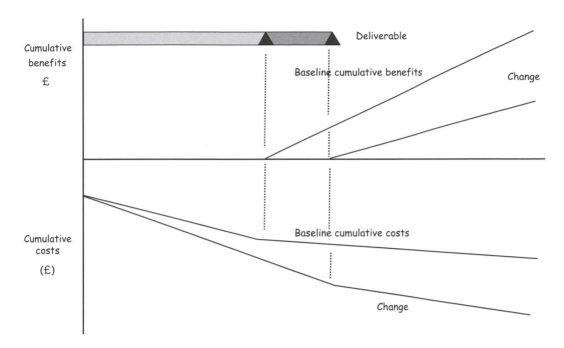

Figure 9.4   Combined magnitude and timing risk effect

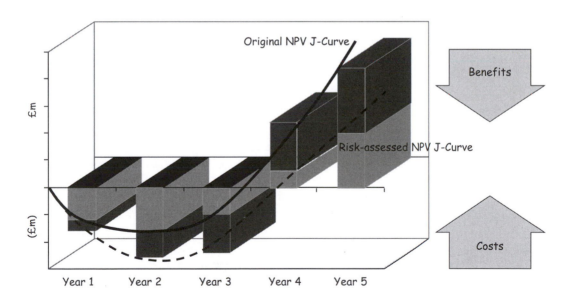

Figure 9.5   Risk overlaid onto the NPV J-curve

Value Testing

The aim of value testing is to provide certainty that intended value is delivered and determine the level of risk that is acceptable in achieving this end. In safety-critical engineering, such as aircraft design, where catastrophic failure is not an option, products are tested to destruction in order to determine acceptable operating limits. As a nervous flyer I was greatly reassured when, in the days when it was possible to visit the cockpit, a chatty pilot calmly reassured me that a 747's wings can flex 11 feet. In Value Management, we apply the principle of destruction testing by exercising the financial model to extremes, within which intended value is delivered by asking the question, 'What would have to happen to break the business case?' There are essentially four techniques that we use for testing value, as shown in Table 9.1.

Table 9.1   Value testing techniques

Analysis	Question	Purpose
Sensitivity analysis	How is programme value affected by changes in one or more factors?	Criticality/leverage
Monte Carlo analysis	What are the bounds of value when key variables are exercised between extremes across many permutations?	Robustness
Scenario analysis	How is programme value affected by possible future circumstances?	Future proofing
Supplier and user reviews	Are all deliverables, drivers and benefits aligned and do they have unambiguous ownership?	Commitment/governance

Sensitivity analysis quantifies the effect on value of changes in one or more variables, either individually or in combination. With the appropriate tools, such as the Value Management Toolset™ outlined later in the book, the technique is fast, easy and particularly powerful for exposing high leverage points and counter-intuitive behaviours. For example, sensitivity analysis often demonstrates that programme value is far more sensitive to apparently small slips in timescale than significant increases in programme cost; a counter-intuitive pattern which takes some courage to deliver, when the counsel is to increase cost in order to get back on schedule. (Reporting slip generally involves less pain to programme managers than cost increases.)

In Monte Carlo analysis, selected variables are attributed ranges of values, typically minimum, expected and maximum. The value model is then exercised over the full range of values for each of these variables using many permutations. The output is *bounds* of programme value reflecting the extremes of the variables operating interactively, with different values, as shown in Figure 9.6. The technique is more involved than sensitivity analysis and generally requires specialist software, such as @RISK from Palisade.

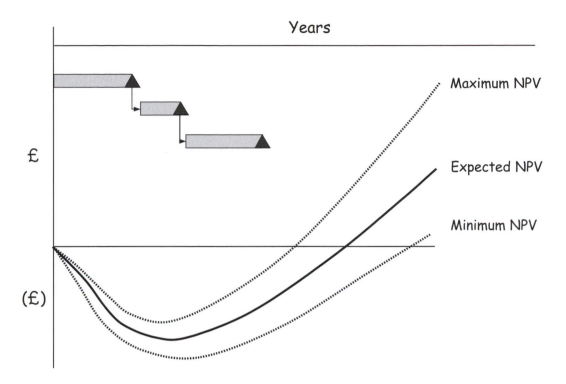

Figure 9.6   Monte Carlo risk analysis

Scenario analysis considers the value implications of potential future situations, such as a significant market shift or introduction of new regulation. For example, how would more stringent privacy laws impact the value of a CRM programme, the success of which is dependent on acquiring intimate customer information? The key to scenario analysis is to think the unthinkable and model it.

Supplier and user reviews stress test the commitment and partnership between owners of deliverables, drivers and benefits. This is usually achieved through structured workshops, in which all causal assumptions and calculations are walked through and challenged in an environment of total openness and transparency. It is important to encourage views that challenge obvious or majority views. To this end, we request inclusion of known sceptics and even cynics. Converting destructive conflict into creative 'energy of difference' often produces the most committed converts. Despondency is almost always the result of lack of genuine involvement or over-exposure to hackneyed management hype, colloquially known as 'bullshit', both of which this process reverses.

Causal Risk Register

One of the most important tools in programme management is the risk register, which defines and tracks the most significant threats, together with action to prevent, mitigate against and deal with them should they manifest themselves. The most common approach to quantifying the level of exposure is as a weighted score comprising two components:

1. Probability: probability of a defined risk occurring;
2. Impact: impact of the risk in the event that it does occur.

Probability is expressed as a score or percentage. Impact is usually also represented using a subjective score based on perceived level of severity, for example a scale of 1 to 10 where 1 is defined as a minor delay with minimal cost implications and 10 is a major budget overrun and/or late delivery causing political embarrassment or damage to the brand. The *exposure* for each risk is then derived by multiplying probability and impact to produce a weighted score. This approach is effective in three ways. First, it imposes the discipline of anticipating risks and defining them precisely. Secondly, it provides quantification of relative exposure, enabling risks to be prioritised. Thirdly, the inclusion of impact introduces some consideration of causality.

In Value Management, the cause and effect linkage approach, described in Chapter 7, is used to quantify the effects of risk explicitly. This is done by treating each risk as an *unintended* deliverable which is then linked to performance drivers to cause negative benefits. This approach works because a deliverable is business capability, so in the case of risk the deliverable is effectively an imposed negative capability, expressed in both magnitude and timing. Again, precision is the key. For example, rather than define a risk as 'a minor slip', it is defined more precisely as: slip in phase 3 of 1 month. We then use the value model to quantify the impact on value of this risk.

The causal risk register is initiated from the start so that risks may be defined during programme development and finalised as part of value testing. As with other deliverables a named owner is assigned to each risk, commissioned to prevent it, mitigate its effect and deal with the consequences if it is manifested.

The Mission Critical Outsourcing Story

The Federal Commonwealth Law Enforcement Board (CLEB) is responsible for countering fraud, such as money laundering, in Australia. CLEB was reaching a final decision concerning options for the future management of their operational IT services. A major driver behind the decision to change was cost and CLEB commissioned the development of a business case with which to compare the financial alternatives. The essential choice boiled down to continuing to manage IT in-house or outsource the services to a third party.

The mission-critical nature of the services meant that it was particularly important to factor risks into the investment appraisal. Consequently, the value model incorporated a causal risk register which quantified the financial effects of key risks on both IT suppliers and users assuming that the current service level was maintained. The specific effect of risk was quantified in terms of cost, incorporated into the DCF analysis and displayed as an overlay on the NPV plot as shown in Figure 9.7.

The initial DCF analysis of costs, which excluded the effects of risk, appeared to render the decision to outsource easy, as shown by the light grey plot in Figure 9.7. However, once risks had been quantified and overlaid onto the DCF, the dark grey component in Figure 9.7, a very different picture emerged. Examples of risk that accounted for such a marked difference included: configuration management, business continuity, security, capacity management, specialist expertise and disaster recovery.

The facility stayed in-house.

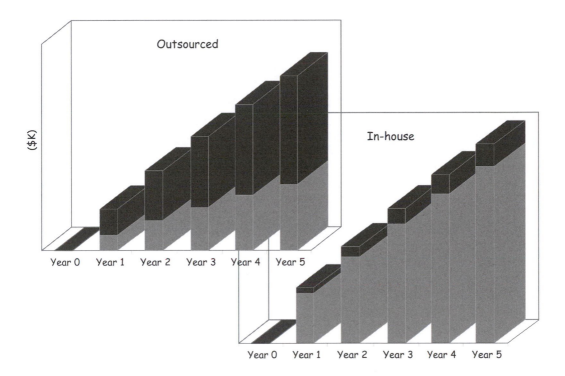

Figure 9.7   Comparison of value effects of risk

Baseline Business Case

The key output from the value assurance process is a baseline business case. This is derived from the implementation strategy, developed during value alignment, and incorporates the effects of risk as quantified through the process described in this chapter. A critical discipline that we apply in Value Management before baselining is to subject the business case to the full rigours of financial professionals in the organisation. This typically involves submitting the value model, including all the assumptions and calculations for scrutiny by the Chief Financial Officer (CFO). We use the term 'CFO-proof' to describe the standard of completeness, correctness and consistency to which the material must adhere. Ideally, a representative from finance is involved throughout the programme development process, together with subsequent tracking of value realisation which is the subject of the next chapter.

Essence

The principal learning from this chapter is summarised below:

- Value assurance is concerned with ensuring that intended value is delivered and combines the complementary disciplines of risk management and certainty management
- Certainty management maintains focus on intended outcomes whilst risk management provides the means to anticipate and deal with threats to value delivery
- Risk dynamics is the quantification of the effects on value of changes in magnitude and timing of programme costs and benefits
- Value testing is concerned with the application of risk dynamics, by exercising the business case to extreme changes in key variables, determining the limits within which delivery of intended value is assured
- Value testing comprises sensitivity analysis, Monte Carlo analysis, scenario analysis and supplier and user reviews
- The results of value testing are incorporated into a causal risk register which provides precise quantification of risk exposure
- The baseline business case takes into account the effects of risk exposure and provides complete transparency to enable exhaustive scrutiny for approval and subsequent through-life audit

10 *Tracking Value*

Objectives

After reading this chapter you will be able to:

- Recognise common, often subtle patterns that prevent effective tracking and how to avoid them through strong governance
- Develop a value realisation plan incorporating the process for tracking deliverables, benefits and overall programme value
- Track deliverables using Earned Value Management
- Track benefits and causal drivers using the Balanced Scorecard
- Track overall value by linking the programme phases dynamically to a DCF analysis

Precision Question

During and post implementation, how do we define the status of the programme value, correct negative variances and exploit positive changes?

Context: Feedback and Correction

In Part I we introduced two complementary concepts derived from complexity theory, upon which Value Management is founded:

1. Right first time: starting conditions most suited for delivering intended value;
2. Feedback and correction: responsiveness to changes in order to ensure delivery of intended value.

Right first time refers to an ideal condition, or state, from which value can be created most effectively, with the minimum of essential redundancy and no waste. Essential redundancy is spare capacity needed to ensure a defined level of outcome. Waste is unneeded consumption, that is nugatory work, rework and duplication. The principles covered so far in Part II are all concerned with right first time, and concluded with the development and approval of a baseline business case, which forms the value datum from which to implement the programme.

Feedback and correction refers to the process of measuring progress, assessing the value status and implementing the most effective action, in order to ensure that the programme remains on purpose and on value. Tracking value focuses on perpetual feedback and correction. The baseline business case becomes a vital programme management tool, the most critical role of which is not to be proved right but to expose variances that most affect value so that corrections can be put into place quickly, when they are most value effective.

> *The baseline business case becomes a live document through which value variances of the programme are exposed and corrective action directed effectively.*

The Value Tracking Challenge

Best practice approaches and support tools have greatly improved the tracking of cost, time and compliance for projects. However, despite greater interest in benefits management, the precise tracking of drivers, benefits and overall value is still the least practiced area of programme management. There are three main reasons for this situation.

First, it is the most difficult. To be effective, precise performance measurement is essential to quantify changes. Often the necessary measures are not currently used by the business and are therefore not readily available. Even if they do exist, neither the infrastructure needed for capturing measure values on a sufficiently frequent basis nor skilled resources capable of using the results to direct effective action, are likely to be in place. In both cases considerable initial investment and ongoing expenditure is required. Value Management addresses this problem in two ways; through cause and effect modelling which reduces the number of measures to a manageable level, and by incorporating BI solutions, covered in Appendix B, that can provide timely, clean data with which to populate measure values. Skilled resources are also grown in parallel with the development of these solutions.

Secondly, even if change is measured the next challenge kicks in; how we know whether the change is the result of the programme and would not have happened anyway. This argument is a favourite excuse for not undertaking tracking at all and completely misses the point that it is the feedback and correction process, and not whether the programme was the complete cause, that is important. Value Management addresses this challenge through cause and effect linkage, by assigning specific changes in drivers and benefits quantitatively to programme deliverables. This does not eliminate the inevitability that change happens independently of the programme but it does filter out much of the noise, rendering causal relationships between deliverables and outcomes more traceable.

Thirdly and most significantly, measuring change exposes under-performance which introduces perceived threat. It is generally much safer and comfortable to provide an audit trail of due diligence afforded by a complex, detailed business case and reports than draw attention to adverse variances. Often this pattern is subtly supported by senior management for the same reasons. In Value Management, we refer to this as 'marks for trying'. Whereas the first two challenges can be dealt with through process, this third issue requires both process and a shift in mindset from fear of reporting variances to an emphasis on it. This means that the board and entire team focus perpetually on two key questions:

1. Are the intended benefits still on *purpose*?
2. Are the programme deliverables still on *value*?

The first question challenges whether any fundamental internal or external changes dictate a shift in programme purpose and intended outcomes. Internal changes include variations in strategic direction. External changes include shifts in the market or the introduction of new legislation. The second question challenges whether programme deliverables are on time, cost and compliance such that intended benefits and overall programme value will be realised.

The entire team become business people encouraged to be cognitive of anything that challenges either the outcomes or the capacity of the programme to cause these *outcomes*. This is counter-intuitive. Conventional wisdom has wired us to focus on delivering the *outputs* of each specific work package and not be distracted by challenging the experts. Value Management is not conventional wisdom.

The Reporting Myth

The Defence Programme Reporting Story

A major UK defence company (Defence) supplies advanced military technology to the British Ministry of Defence and friendly governments around the world. Defence was, and remains, one of the most successful companies, attracting the best people and delivering world-beating products. The programme values ran into hundreds of millions of pounds. The avionics technology that set the products aside was cutting edge, highly complex and carried significant risk. Consequently, the reporting structure reflected the need to manage this complexity and risk.

Absolutely critical for Defence and similar programme-based enterprises is strong programme management and tight reporting. This was reflected in the monthly reports which comprised over 20 pages. These reports, far more complex than those typically used for PRINCE2™, covered all aspects of the programme and sections were linked in order to account for the complex interdependence.

There was one page, however, that dominated focus for the monthly programme board meetings. This page covered the financials. Each programme was structured around delivery of a target margin to the company and because programmes were fixed price any escalation in cost eroded the margin. Programme costs were managed using Earned Value Management (covered later in this chapter). In order to cover the risk, several layers of contingency were used – technical, programme and management – requiring increasingly higher levels of authority to use.

Despite the sophistication of the reporting process, careers, reputation, bonuses and survival ultimately depended on delivering the margin and considerable pain was associated with reporting negative variances in this key measure. Consequently, the monthly reporting cycle became a process for 'protecting' the margin.

It was generally recognised that it was no more painful to report reduced margin later in the programme than immediately after it was known. In fact, the later in the programme bad news was declared, the greater the opportunity for excuses, such as someone else had caused the problems. This situation created a pattern of problems being obscured in the reporting process for as long as possible, with the result that when they were exposed it was much more difficult to correct them and regain lost margin, if at all.

The Defence case study is an extreme example of a very common pattern; one or more targets become so dominant that behaviour and reporting is manipulated to show success in achieving the targets, even if this is at the expense of the truth. Instead of addressing adverse variances in the leading drivers that would result in success, effort is focused on spinning reports. We witness this behaviour in one form or another in virtually every performance management and/or programme management regime we see, across every sector. In many cases reporting becomes a bureaucratic exercise in which boards are presented with thick reports containing mostly superfluous information which is used to detract subtly from the really important issues. This pattern is a reinforcing causal loop as shown for Defence in Figure 10.1.

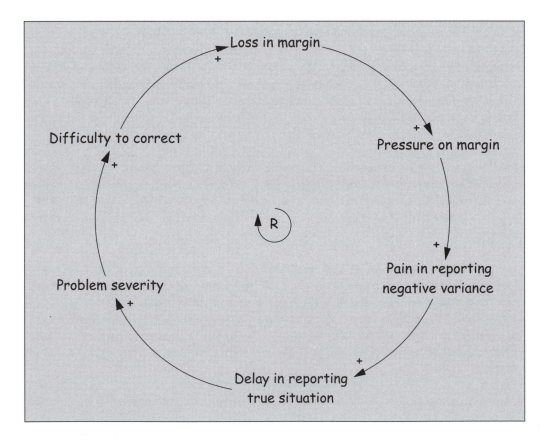

Figure 10.1 Delaying the reporting of bad news

One of the major challenges facing complex programme-based companies, like Defence, is managing the interdependence between the different functions and associated technologies. Defence programmes required six key functions: systems, software, electrical hardware, mechanical hardware, manufacturing and integrated logistics support. If an error was generated in one function, this could be proliferated and exacerbated across one or more other functions. For example, advanced avionics involves real-time computation resulting in high processor utilisation. This generates heat which reduces electrical hardware life unless kept within operational limits. Temperature is controlled using fans (simple mechanical technology). However, if fans are under-specified in error the high-technology avionics overheats and will not meet specification. The usual solution, bigger fans, may not be possible due to tight physical constraints, especially if space provision was not designed in from the start. Typically, over 80 per cent of the cost is committed during early stages of design and is not easily changed subsequently.

A dynamics model was developed, which simulated the generation and proliferation of errors within and across functions through the programme life cycle. The model quantified the effect on costs attributable to errors over time and demonstrated that cost due to errors, that is nugatory work, rework and duplication, could be reduced exponentially through early detection. In fact, the model demonstrated a counter-intuitive insight that in some cases it was more cost-effective to allow errors and detect them early, than consume the extra time and resources needed to get a perfect design first time. This is a case in which feedback is more effective in achieving the intended outcome than trying to achieve ideal starting conditions.

The important point from the Defence story is the critical need for changes in both mindset and process concerning the way in which problems are perceived, reported and dealt with. The required shift is to do what is cost-effective to prevent avoidable errors in the first place, that is right first time, make provision for correcting the level of unavoidable errors and engender a culture in which perpetual problem reporting and correction becomes culturally embedded. This is an example of applying the principle of feedback and correction. What is interesting about the Defence case study is that not only were people willing to declare and quantify these patterns, but also when these radical findings and solutions were presented to the Operations Director, they were completely consistent with his own intuition, based on extensive experience.

Value Governance

Before we discuss specific techniques for tracking, it must be stressed that success in value realisation demands exceptionally strong governance, the most important element of which is accountability. In Chapter 5 we stated the critical need for clear, committed ownership manifested in the partnership between deliverable and benefit owners. PRINCE2™ and MSP™ provide powerful frameworks for project and programme management respectively, which emphasise strong ownership, and include templates for reporting. The techniques described in the remainder of this chapter are completely generic and complementary to these or any other programme management approaches.

Value Realisation Plan

The key tool for tracking, correcting and delivering programme value is the *value realisation plan* (VRP). The purpose of the VRP is to ensure that both programme costs and benefits are actively managed so that the intended programme value is delivered. This document is often referred to as a *benefits realisation plan*. However, the term 'value' is used to recognise the importance of overall programme value, comprising both programme *benefits* and *costs*. The VRP comprises three parts which reflect the components of the value equation for programmes:

Programme Value = Programme Benefits − Programme Costs

1. deliverables tracking
2. benefits tracking
3. value tracking

Deliverables Tracking

This part of the VRP is concerned with tracking the programme deliverables through the phases which output the deliverables. This includes development and support costs, timing of whole and/or partial deliverables, compliance of whole and/or partial deliverables with specification and capacity to generate intended benefits, taking into account any changes. Deliverables tracking focuses on ensuring that business *capabilities* are delivered on time and budget, demanding project management skills, such as incorporated within PRINCE2™, and similar approaches.

EARNED VALUE MANAGEMENT

One of the most effective techniques for managing programme costs is Earned Value Management (EVM). EVM is used extensively within the aerospace and defence sectors because it is particularly well suited to complex, high-risk programmes. It has also been used within Value Management successfully across both private and public sectors. The technique can be used in combination with, and complements, PRINCE2™. EVM provides a means of measuring cost, timing and compliance quantitatively using the cumulative cost curve, as shown in Figure 10.2.

Key EVM components are described below with reference to Figure 10.2 (full terms[1] are also defined where appropriate):

- A cumulative cost curve, usually an S-curve plotted over time, is first derived for the programme and baselined as the baseline costs, full-term Budgeted Cost of Work Scheduled (BCWS), and the total designated Baseline at Completion (BAC) which corresponds in time to the end of the programme.
- For each reporting period the expenditure up to that point, time now, is plotted as actual costs, full term Actual Cost of Work Performed (ACWP).

---

1   Webb, A. 2003. *Using Earned Value: A Project Manager's Guide*. Farnham: Gower.

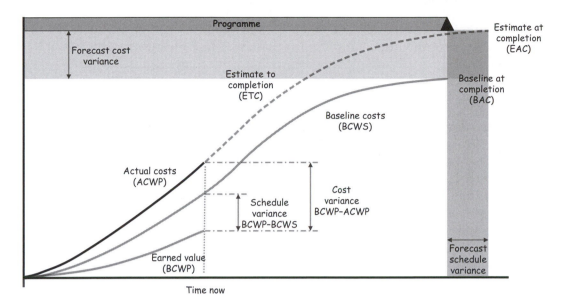

Figure 10.2 Earned Value Management

- The entire remainder of the programme is re-planned to determine the Estimate to Completion (ETC) costs, and the actual plus forecast total designated Estimate at Completion (EAC).
- For each reporting period the earned value, full term Budgeted Cost of Work Performed (BCWP) is calculated to reflect the real proportion of valuable work completed at time now.
- The difference between actual costs and earned value is called cost variance, and provides an acid test of the degree to which the programme is on budget.
- The difference between baseline costs and earned value is called schedule variance and represents the degree to which the programme is on time, in terms of cost.
- The difference between BAC and EAC is the forecast cost variance of the programme.
- The relative positions on the time axis gives the forecast schedule variance.

There are numerous ways to determine the earned value, a common example being estimates by the team of value added work completed to date. The problem with this, and similar assessments of work done, is that it tends to encourage wishful thinking. In Value Management, we favour computing earned value as a relationship between EAC and BAC as follows:

$$\textit{Earned Value} = \textit{Actual Costs} \times \textit{BAC/EAC}$$

This simple calculation derives earned value by factoring the actual spend by the degree to which the latest expectation of cost to complete varies in relation to the original baseline. The key to achieving an accurate earned value is realistic and truthful estimates of the outstanding work, which must take into account changes, error corrections and so on, to be meaningful. It is important not to fall into the trap of simply re-baselining the programme to obscure negative variances. It is far more effective to expose the full extent of variances and deal with them accordingly, even if this means terminating the programme.

The Government Accounts Story

A large UK Government department was the second to introduce commercial financial information and accounting systems, duly adapted for public sector cash accounting. This was a £10 million programme. The first such system, recently implemented in a similarly large department, failed spectacularly attracting much negative media publicity. An audit deemed the principal reason for failure to be poor programme management.

Consequently, there was considerable pressure on the programme board, chaired by the Head of Finance, to ensure accountability to the Treasury for both the multi-billion pound budget and delivery of benefits of the new system as projected in the business case, developed in accordance with the *Treasury Green Book*.[2]

Late delivery was not an option because of the annual financial accounting cycle. So it was essential that the board was provided with an accurate and precise assessment of status, forecast and risk during the monthly PRINCE2™ board meetings. In addition, the chairman needed to be alerted immediately to adverse developments between the monthly reviews in order to prepare his briefings to the Under Secretary.

The programme comprised a large in-house team covering some 13 strongly interdependent work streams, spanning a diverse set of disciplines distributed over many locations across the UK.

Value Management was used to track the business case on a monthly basis. The programme cost and schedule were tracked using EVM as a means to coordinate the complexity. The overall programme EVM report was disseminated to EVM reports for each individual work stream. This provided a precise assessment of the contribution of, and also diagnosed problems with, specific individual work streams. This case study illustrates the generic and powerful nature of EVM which can be applied within any sector as part of the value realisation process.

Benefits Tracking

Benefits tracking is concerned with monitoring the delivery of actual stakeholder outcomes. For commercial enterprises, where customers have a real choice, this is ultimately reflected in increases in revenue and/or reductions in costbase; in other words

---

2   TSO. 2010. *The Green Book: Appraisal and Evaluation in Central Government.* Available at http://www.hm-treasury.gov. uk/d/green_book_complete.pdf, accessed: 31 December 2010.

the two sides of the profit and loss account. For public organisations, the equivalent measure of success is value for money, the level of benefits delivered for a given level of costs. The most effective means of tracking benefits is to plot measures relating to lead and lag measures in themes that were defined earlier in Part II. This is shown for the Eurostar operational efficiency theme, which we covered in Chapter 6, in Figure 10.3.

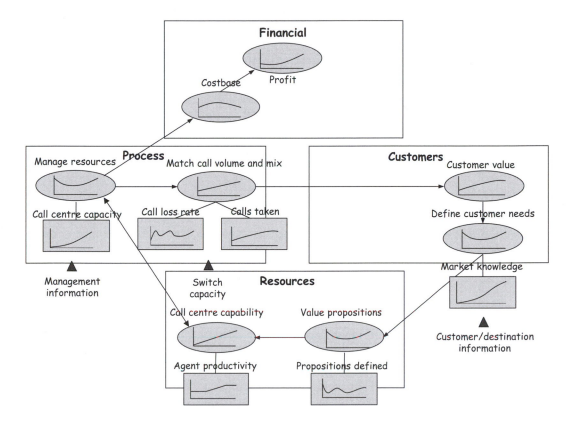

Figure 10.3 Benefits tracking – strategy map

Figure 10.3 shows a helicopter view of theme-specific Balanced Scorecard scores for measures and objectives plotted over time. The key point is that the causal path linking the measures is shown explicitly. This means that the point(s) in the chain which account for variances can be identified quickly and corrective action targeted most effectively. The thumbnail graphs shown represent planned profiles which are derived from the cause and effect linkage covered in Chapter 7, implementation strategy developed in Chapter 8 and taking into account risks addressed in Chapter 9. In Appendix A we inject even greater precision into the profiles using dynamics modelling.

Measure values are converted to scores for the Balanced Scorecard and can be presented in a number of ways. Two of the most important presentations for Value Management are:

1. individual measures
2. linked measures

INDIVIDUAL MEASURES

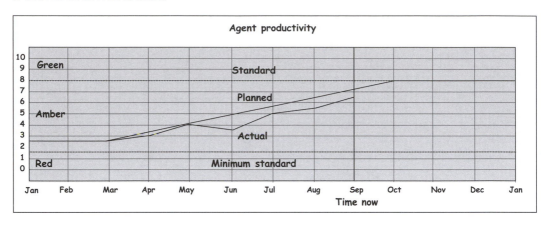

Figure 10.4 Benefits tracking – individual measure

This presentation provides the status for an individual measure in relation to the standard required and the planned route for achieving the standard. The term standard is used, rather than target, to emphasise intention; targets are negotiable, standards are not. Figure 10.4 shows the plot for an individual measure, in this case a lead indicator, agent productivity. There are four plots:

1. Standard: the level of performance deemed necessary to *sustain* the vision; scores on or above which are shown as green in the commonly used Red–Amber–Green (RAG) view.
2. Planned: refers to the intended scores deemed necessary to *achieve* the vision, which typically build from a current level to the standard, as shown in this example.
3. Minimum standard: the level below which performance is *unacceptable* and anything on or below this score would show as red in the RAG view in a Balanced Scorecard.
4. Actual: relates to *realised* scores up to time now.

The difference between standard and minimum standard is the operational tolerance. This does not imply that this amber range is acceptable, but rather that it is operationally viable in the short term.

LINKED MEASURES

This is a parent–child presentation which provides the status in relation to causal connectivity between measures in the strategy map. This is usually most effective if plotted within the context of a specific theme. Figure 10.5 shows scores for the two measures, Call loss rate and Calls taken, that contribute to the objective match call volume and mix for the Eurostar operational efficiency theme shown in Figure 10.3. This display communicates two essential pieces of information. First, the degree to which measure scores correlate with the score for the related objective. These relationships are influenced by the respective weighting allocated to each measure. Secondly, it pinpoints

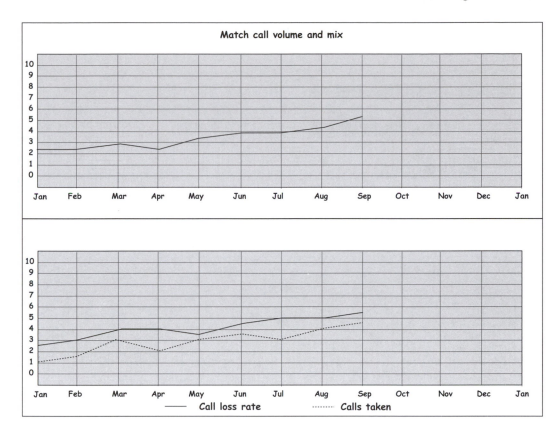

Figure 10.5 Benefits tracking – linked measures

which specific measure is responsible for under- or over performance, so that action can be targeted precisely to correct negative variances or exploit positive changes.

Value Tracking

Deliverable and benefits tracking concern the monitoring and correction of variances in programme costs and benefits, respectively. Value tracking combines these two techniques to track overall programme value in accordance with the value equation for programmes. Programme value is measured as a DCF analysis which, as discussed in Chapters 8 and 9, is driven by the magnitude and timing of costs, benefits and risks. Therefore, value tracking is concerned with the status of the causal linkage between programme phases and the benefits, attributable to deliverables output by the phases, together with costs of developing and supporting the deliverables. Programme value is expressed as a NPV J-curve. This is shown in Figure 10.6. Only three phases are shown for simplicity:

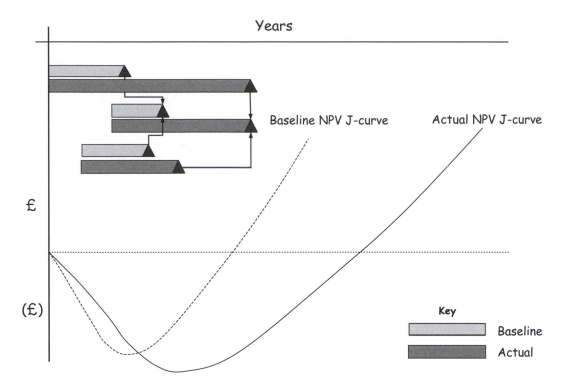

Figure 10.6 Value tracking

Figure 10.6 comprises two parts. The top part shows the actual status of the programme plan (dark grey phases) against the approved baseline (light grey phases). The lower part presents how the plan status is reflected in the NPV J-curve. The causal connection between phases and benefits was initially derived in Chapter 7. These links were maintained during alignment covered in Chapter 8, and risk analysis discussed in Chapter 9, the final result being a baseline business case, incorporating the risk-assessed implementation strategy. The links are also maintained throughout the programme life so that we can track the value dynamically.

Essence

The principal learning from this chapter is summarised below:

- Value Management draws on complexity theory which boils down to two essential elements, starting conditions and feedback, which reflect the two stages of the framework
- Starting conditions refer to the state from which value can be created most effectively; in Value Management, this involves the development of a *baseline business case* through processes covered in the first five chapters of Part II
- Feedback concerns tracking value status and implementing the most effective actions in response to change ensuring *value realisation*, which is the subject of this chapter

- Value realisation integrates deliverables, benefits and value tracking, which are incorporated into a *value realisation plan*
- Deliverables tracking is concerned with the cost, compliance and timing of new business capabilities needed to cause intended stakeholder benefits
- A powerful tool for deliverables tracking is Earned Value Management (EVM) which provides precise measures of progress for complex programmes
- Benefits tracking relates to monitoring and correcting variances in planned changes to causal drivers which lead to benefits
- Benefits tracking is conducted using the Balanced Scorecard and is most effective when measures are tracked as causal chains defined by themes in the strategy map
- Value realisation is founded on explicit causal relationships between deliverables, drivers and benefits
- Value tracking provides dynamic causal linkage between programme phases and the discounted cash flow (DCF) analysis

11 *IMPACT*

Objectives

After reading this chapter you will be able to:

- Manage programmes to deliver intended stakeholder outcomes and overall programme value
- Repeat success by applying the Value Management principles within a structured Value Management framework, IMPACT – intention, model, programme, alignment, certainty, track

---

The First Maths Lesson Story

The new intake of 11-year-olds shuffled into the playground on that first dank September morning, failing to obscure their nerves with loud behaviour and exaggerated laughter. Suddenly, the tallest man they had ever seen barked instructions for silence, 'You are at secondary school now, behave like it and follow me.' They filed into the old hall and were allocated to their forms.

The next day, they had their first maths lesson. Most hated the subject and were horrified to see that their teacher was the same imposing figure that had corralled them so brutally the day before. The classroom was in the old building and still had bench desks from the 1920s. It felt like something out of a Dickens novel. They sat down, shaking with trepidation. Then something magical happened. 'Forget what you were taught in primary school', he began, 'mathematics is about just three things.' Then he pointed to three cardboard posters above the blackboard on which he had written in large green letters: STATEMENT–METHOD–RESULT.

He then proceeded to explain in clear language, as if he were talking to grown-ups, that the way to approach a problem was by first stating your purpose, then working through the method and finally comparing the result against the purpose to make sure that it made sense. He made them use this approach for every sum until it became habit. It did. For the first time ever they got sums right, every time.

It would be many years before I grasped the full significance of what Mr Cleaver had taught us during that first term, when I recognised this problem solving structure as the V-model

---

used for systems and software engineering. Variants are also known as the Test Operate Test Exit (TOTE) Model, the Deming cycle and double-loop control or learning. It is one of the most powerful frameworks for achievement and is the foundation for Value Management.

What we owe people who touch our lives with knowledge is immeasurable.

In this chapter we consolidate the principles covered so far in Part II to build a generic, repeatable framework which combines two complementary concepts: double-loop control and the V-model. The resulting framework, IMPACT, encompasses the two fundamental stages of Value Management; baseline business case and value realisation.

Double-loop Control

Previously, we asserted that despite significant advances developing best practices, programme management still often focuses mainly on delivering technology outputs. However, it is stakeholder outcomes that are the primary *purpose* of a programme whilst outputs are the *means* by which the outcomes are realised. In the value equation as applied to programmes, *purpose* translates into benefits and *means* the new business capabilities enabled by deliverables. Therefore, it is important to measure success in achieving both stakeholder outcomes (benefits), which is about 'doing the right things', and enabling outputs (deliverables) on time, cost and quality, which concerns 'doing things right'. The process of managing both outcomes and outputs is called double-loop control and is shown in Figure 11.1.

Double-loop control manages both components in the value equation.

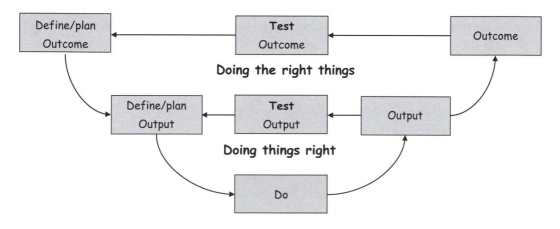

Figure 11.1 Double-loop control

Both loops are defined by the Deming quality cycle of continuous improvement: Plan–Do–Test-Act.[1] Plan includes definition of requirements, Do is ideally a small scale change which is then tested and adjustments made before the cycle is repeated. Test, also referred to as Check or Study, involves comparing actual results with those expected. Act concerns making the necessary adjustments to close the gap identified in Test. The lower loop involves classic project management disciplines of ensuring compliance against requirements (quality), expenditure against budget (cost) and adherence to delivery targets (timescales). The outer loop challenges whether the programme is still delivering adequate value to stakeholders, that is the right benefits in relation to purpose. Notice that changes to *outcomes* are achieved through changes to *outputs*. A particularly powerful aspect of double-loop control is the ability to manage value in the context of both internal and external changes. Internal changes include failure to produce compliant outputs on time or punitive budget overruns. External changes include major market shifts or new regulation.

Double-loop control manages both internal and external changes.

The V-Model

A powerful framework for the practical application of double-loop control is the V-model, which is widely used for major systems and software development. The most proficient systems engineer that I have worked with used the framework for orchestrating all aspects of programme structure, ownership, documentation and planning. The V-model provides double-loop control by assuring two aspects of the development process, *verification* and *validation*. Verification ensures that we build the product as intended – doing things right. Validation ensures that we build the right product to satisfy stakeholder's needs – doing the right thing. The overall testing process is often referred to as V & V – verification and validation. The horizontal arrows are shown as two-way. This is because outputs and outcomes are tested against criteria defined in test scripts (left to right flow) and changes incorporated within the definitions and plans ready for the next iteration of the cycle (right to left flow), as shown in Figure 11.2.

Verification ensures that the output is built as intended; validation
ensures that the output performs as intended.

1   Lepore, D., Cohen, O. 1999. *Deming and Goldratt: The Theory of Constraints and the System of Profound Knowledge.* Great Barrington, USA: North River Press.

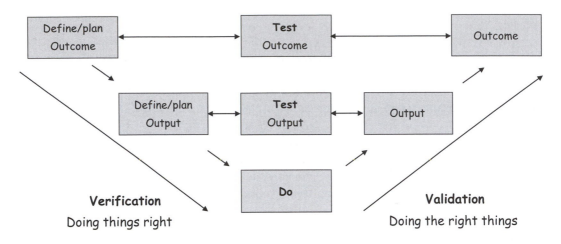

Figure 11.2 The V-model

In Value Management, we use the V-model for managing both the programme deliverables and benefits. Therefore, it is useful to consider how verification and validation is applied to each of these elements in turn and then how they are combined to provide a complete framework which incorporates the six principles covered in Part II.

The V-Model for Programme Deliverables

For programme deliverables, verification involves testing that *all* user requirements are incorporated into system design and build. In a real development programme additional phases are normally included, such as functional specification, module design and unit design, but the essential flow remains the same. Validation involves testing that outputs from the build phase actually perform as required. A key principle of the V-model is that verification and validation are defined in the form of test scripts at each phase, before build. This imposes the discipline of defining the criteria for success during each step of the process, thereby reducing risk, speeding development and reducing cost. Testing covers verification, by ensuring that all requirements are incorporated within the test scripts and validation, by proving that test results are as intended.

The V-model ensures that deliverables meet user requirements.

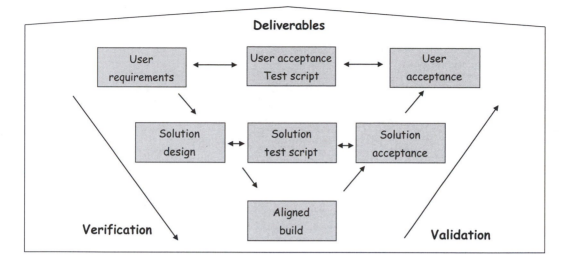

Figure 11.3 The V-model for deliverables

Limitations of the V-Model for Deliverables

From a value perspective, the V-model as used for software development has a fundamental limitation: it focuses on programme *outputs* rather than stakeholder *outcomes*. Therefore, it only addresses the output components in value equation. The implication of this constraint is that even if the deliverables from a programme incorporate the defined requirements (verification) and operate entirely as intended (validation), there is no certainty that intended stakeholder benefits will be realised; there is no closed loop with which to ensure this. In effect, the V-model for programme deliverables is the inner loop of Figure 11.1. To put it even more strongly, we need to kill the illusion that a software/system project will inevitably deliver benefits. This leads us to the V-model for benefits.

The V-model as applied to system development omits stakeholder outcomes.

The V-Model for Programme Benefits

The V-model can also be applied very effectively for programme benefits. In this case, verification involves defining and aligning *all* benefits, drivers and actions precisely to ensure that the intended benefits are delivered. In the case of the V-model for deliverables, predictability that user requirements are met is provided by the precision of design relationships between modules, units and components. When the V-model is applied to benefits, the equivalent relationships are causal threads between drivers and benefits. Therefore, validation involves testing that changes in drivers are as expected and that these changes result in intended benefits.

The V-model aligns actions with drivers and benefits.

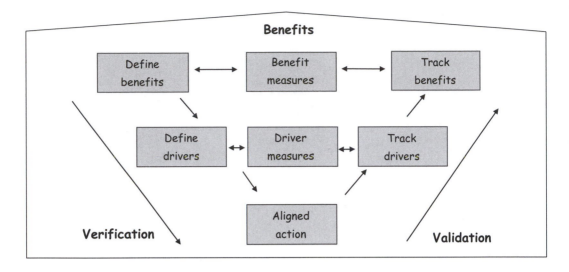

Figure 11.4 The V-model for benefits

Limitations of the V-Model for Benefits

The V-model as used for benefits has the opposite limitation to that for deliverables; it focuses on outcomes and excludes the means and cost for achieving them through programme deliverables. The V-model for benefits is the outer loop in Figure 11.1. However, as dictated by the value equation, we need to ensure that benefits are balanced against associated costs and that the functional requirements have been met through the deliverables.

The V-model as applied to benefits omits deliverables.

The IMPACT Framework

In Value Management, we overcome the limitations described above by combining the V-models as applied to programme deliverables and benefits into a single integrated structure. The resulting framework, IMPACT, provides double-loop control between deliverables and benefits. The IMPACT phases mirror the Value Management principles covered in Part II; intention, model, programme, alignment, certainty and track as shown in Figure 11.5.

IMPACT injects certainty in delivering programme value.

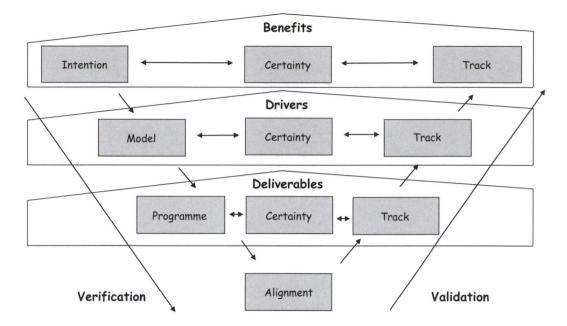

Figure 11.5 IMPACT Value Management framework

Programme Whole Life Value

IMPACT supports both the business case baseline and value realisation stages of Value Management. The verification process builds a robust financial business case which, after approval, becomes the baseline. The validation process tracks all three components which we connected in the cause and effect linkage, that is deliverables, drivers and benefits, using the value realisation plan as described in the previous chapter. The IMPACT framework is iterative, supporting perpetual feedback and timely corrective action to ensure that the programme remains on value and on purpose.

IMPACT injects certainty of delivering value throughout the programme life.

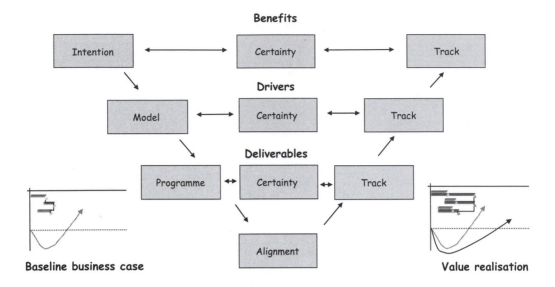

Figure 11.6 Value Management life cycle

Compatibility with Related Methodologies

IMPACT is designed to be completely generic. Consequently, it is complementary to any best practice methods and tools, including the OGC best practice series: PRINCE2™, Managing Successful Programmes (MSP)™, Portfolio, Programme and Project Offices P3O®, Management of Risk M_o_R® and Managing of Value MoV™.

Essence

The principal learning from this chapter is summarised below:

- The core element that underpins Value Management is precise, explicit quantification of the causal links between programme deliverables and stakeholder benefits
- The Value Management framework supports this cause and effect linkage by applying two key concepts, double-loop control and the V-model
- Double-loop control provides the means to manage both benefits and the deliverables through which intended benefits are realised
- The V-model is one of the most powerful frameworks for designing and managing programmes and applies double-loop control through verification and validation
- The V-model as applied for system development is enhanced to incorporate drivers and benefits to from the Value Management framework, IMPACT
- IMPACT covers the whole programme life by supporting the key Value Management stages, baseline business case and value realisation
- Baseline business case delivers a robust, risk assessed and approved financial business case

- Value realisation ensures delivery of benefits to stakeholders and overall programme value
- The IMPACT framework is completely generic and can be used with any methodology

The Story so Far

It is appropriate to take stock of what we have covered so far in the book and how it has led us to the point at which we can develop dynamic performance management.

In Part I, we reasoned that in order to remain competitive in the post-credit crunch world, businesses must generate more from less with greater certainty from change programmes, which to date have a dismal record of delivering intended outcomes. Ideally, programmes should be self-funding. This can be achieved by combining advanced theory, tools and thinking in a causal approach called performance breakthroughs. The first prerequisite is to define *how* we are failing to deliver intended value from programmes, right now. To this end, we defined six recurring failure patterns, together with their causal diagnoses and corresponding solutions.

In Part II, we transformed these failure patterns into phased solutions within a Value Management framework, IMPACT, which is founded on the V-model. In turn, this provides a structure for developing a baseline business case and subsequent value realisation. The six phases of IMPACT are:

1. *Intention*: define stakeholder outcomes, that is benefits, the new business capabilities, that is deliverables, that enable benefits, and assign committed benefit and deliverable owners who form a 'failure is not an option' partnership
2. *Model*: define key drivers, together with the cause and effect relationships which link them, through which necessary change can be achieved and consequential value delivered
3. *Programme*: link benefits explicitly and precisely to programme phases using causal connections derived in the model phase
4. *Alignment*: align measures using causal chains throughout the business and optimise the structure and order of programme phases to maximise value delivery
5. *Certainty*: define precise criteria by which success will be measured, then test the business case to destruction, in order to determine extremes within which success is certain
6. *Track*: monitor the value status of the programme, and use causal linkages to correct negative variances and exploit positive opportunities

In Part III we undertake a journey through the entire IMPACT framework using a case study.

PART III *Process*

We introduced this book by stating a conviction that the economic growth needed to meet our expectations of wealth is no longer sustainable using current levels of resource consumption. This new reality is the result of five fundamental and related drivers: debt, cost, demographics, competition and environmental survival. We argued that greater prosperity can, and must be achieved from more *effective* and *efficient* use of fewer resources. We postulated that as economics is the *study* of how wealth is created and distributed, value is the *measure* of wealth creation which is reflected in the value equation, defined in Chapter 2, which boils down to two key relationships:

$$Value = Benefits - Costs$$

$$Value\ for\ Money = Effectiveness \times Efficiency$$

For Western economies the imperative to create more from less represents a major challenge because traditional responses to redress economic imbalances, such as reducing cost by shedding labour and automation and/or maintaining markets through technological advantage, no longer provide the same corrective effect in today's climate. The emerging super economies will always beat us on labour costs. Unemployment is not only politically prohibitive but imposes a double whammy; it wastes potential value creating resources and depletes real wealth through welfare payments. Both product and process advantages are quickly copied, even overtaken; technical superiority is no longer the sole prerogative of the West.

Clearly, we need to do something differently, but what? Three key themes emerge from both the research and cross-sector experience behind this book. The first is innovation. This includes products and services offering differential value, commanding premium prices needed to fund and sustain future innovation, together with the business models and processes that deliver this value most productively. More subtly, innovation also includes policies and business rules which enable the innovation process, whilst protecting consumers and other stakeholders from market distortions and abuses. Innovation requires customer knowledge, a creative workforce to translate the market intelligence into value propositions and delivery processes which meet or exceed expectations. In the UK, with one of the most diverse, tolerant and eccentric workforces in the world, we have few excuses concerning innovation.

The second theme is a far greater commitment to elimination of waste. Waste does not only relate the obvious, headline-grabbing examples, such as late, over-budget public investments, banking collapses and long-term unemployment, all of which must be fixed. It also includes four categories of less visible non-value adding activities, nugatory work, rework, duplication and managing the waste that these represent. Our direct experience confirms that, taken as a whole, this effort can account for up to 80 per cent of resources engaged in work. Therefore, waste represents a significant opportunity if this proportion could be reversed. With skill and commitment, much of this misdirected effort can be eliminated to deliver a double benefit, reduced cost and resources released to generate more wealth. However, it will take great commitment, together with a new way of looking at, and measuring, what we do and how we do it.

The third theme concerns the integration of private and public sectors. The important point here is that both innovation and waste relate to both sectors, albeit in different ways. For example, purely from a value perspective, profit motivation drives growth through innovation, but the market cannot be relied upon to distribute value generated equitably across stakeholders, and ultimately, imbalances lead to waste. Conversely, whilst the public sector can intervene where markets do not operate optimally, the inherent lack of market accountability subjects this sector to the risk of delivering poor value for money. It is generally recognised that some things are more effectively delivered under commercial market drivers, and others need the support of public funding. The challenge is to combine the advantages of both mechanisms to mutually support each other, the economy and society. The common thread in achieving this integration is commitment to aligned performance standards reflected in value delivery. Having applied Value Management across private and public sectors in equal measure, we can assert that this is a completely realistic goal.

> *The three key prerequisites for our future wealth are mastery of innovation,*
> *elimination of waste and value integration across private and public sectors.*

The vehicle for achieving this essential transition where it counts, at a business level, is the change programme. Programmes span improvements in business as usual operations to strategic business transformations, and to be effective, must be managed as an aligned portfolio, whereby all initiatives are linked causally to a vision. As we have demonstrated using advanced systemic techniques, contribution to value creation is more important than the status within an organisation.

This brings us to the subject of the IMPACT case study, JANET (UK), which already excels in innovation, operational efficiency and private–public integration. The company provides unique products at exceptional service levels demanded by their academic and research customers, who are driving the knowledge economy. JANET (UK) is undertaking a major programme to grow this innovative capability, whilst further significantly reducing the cost of delivery. They also combine the best of public and private sectors, by partnering with private service providers where commercially optimal, whilst employing public funding where superior service is not commercially viable, but essential to power the knowledge sector upon which our future prosperity depends. Put simply, take JANET (UK) out of the picture and we have a major problem, maybe not now, but in the future when we pass the critical point beyond which we can no longer compete with our key economic rivals. JANET (UK) combines clear purpose with customer-focused service, innovation and entrepreneurial drive. We now step through the IMPACT Value Management framework for the business transformation programme, designed to equip JANET (UK) for the future economic landscape.

After reading this part of the book you will be able to implement key phases of the IMPACT Value Management framework.

12 *JANET (UK) Transformation Programme Case Study*

The JANET (UK) Story

JANET (UK) provides one of the world's leading research and education networks serving 18 million users. Operating as JANET (UK) the company is constituted as the JNT Association, a company limited by guarantee and owned by the four categories of members: the UK higher and further education funding bodies, the higher education institutions and research councils, the further education colleges and individual members. Accountability is derived through an annually reviewed Service Level Agreement with the Joint Information Systems Committee (JISC).

There were several reasons why JANET (UK) needed to change. Most critical was the growing pressure to reduce the cost of service provision from both the government, committed to stringent cuts across public funding, and user institution customers who, in a challenging financial environment, become increasingly discerning in what they require. In response to these shifting market dynamics, JANET (UK)'s CEO, Tim Marshall, was driving the transition from a largely centrally funded model to one where there was more choice for customers who would pay for specific value-added services. It followed that such a model would attract a variety of variable revenue streams.

Tim and his team were clear what was needed to achieve this change: understanding and acting upon customer needs through high trust relationships, driving the market through innovation, value-driven partnerships with customers, suppliers and staff and delivery on promises. The board was equally clear on the essential programmes needed to effect the change, which spanned customer intimacy, product development, delivery processes and culture.

A primary component in achieving the shift to a commercial model was the development of a Balanced Scorecard to reflect the new value dynamics, with which to track and correct performance across the company. It was decided to build a dynamics model with which to define and quantify the most critical performance measures. The model evolved through a number of workshops with senior JANET (UK) staff.

Intention

Key outputs from this phase were a strategy map which connected key objectives and deliverables, defined as new business capabilities needed to achieve the objectives. The context within IMPACT is shown in Figure 12.1.

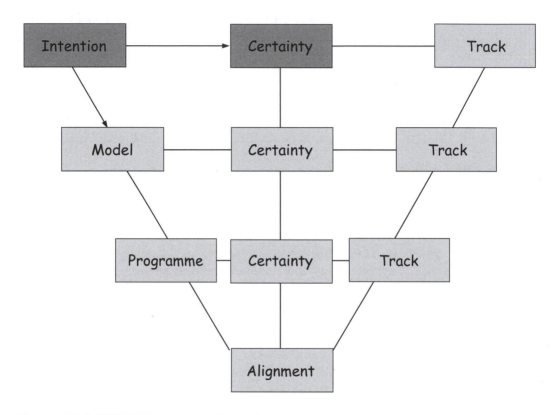

Figure 12.1 IMPACT context – intention

Mission, Vision and Objectives

JANET (UK) has a very clearly defined purpose, direction and values. The mission, vision and strategic objectives, as stated in JANET (UK)'s corporate plan 2010–2012, are defined below:

MISSION

To provide outstanding and distinctive information and communication services to the UK's research, education, training and cultural communities.

VISION

Through JANET (UK)'s activities, everyone working and studying in the UK's research, education, training and cultural communities will have services that enable collaborative working and the acquisition and exchange of information, ideas and knowledge.

STRATEGIC OBJECTIVES

The vision will be achieved through four strategic objectives, summarised below and defined at a more precise level in the corporate plan:

- To sustain and develop a world-leading research and education network and essential services
- To deliver valued services to our users effectively and efficiently
- To develop our people to deliver excellent services
- To influence and support policy development

Values

JANET (UK) also has very clear and practised values which are defined in the corporate plan and summarised below:

- Trusted advisors: providing trusted advice, respecting partners and ethical commitment to promises
- Professional partners: creating value to stakeholders through grounded solutions and ensuring the skilled capacity to deliver shared innovation and success
- Effective communicators: listen to understand stakeholder needs, acted upon using precise communication with genuine two-way feedback
- Responsible innovators: collaborative innovation through wide consultation and commitment to the highest standards for relevant, sustainable solutions

Stakeholders

Stakeholders are recipients and owners of benefits. JANET (UK)'s key stakeholders, reflected in the Balanced Scorecard, are:

- Government: providing central funding, referred to as top slice funding through the JISC
- Customers: education, research, local council and cultural bodies using JANET (UK)'s services
- Staff: all employees within JANET (UK)
- Suppliers: providing capacity in partnership with JANET (UK)

Value Chain

The customer-centric value chain for JANET (UK) comprises five core activities shown in Figure 12.2.

Figure 12.2 JANET (UK) value chain

Strategy Map

A strategy map defines key causal relationships through the Balanced Scorecard. The strategy map for JANET (UK) was built at two levels. The first level represented the essential value dynamics reflecting core value chain activities, as shown in Figure 12.3.

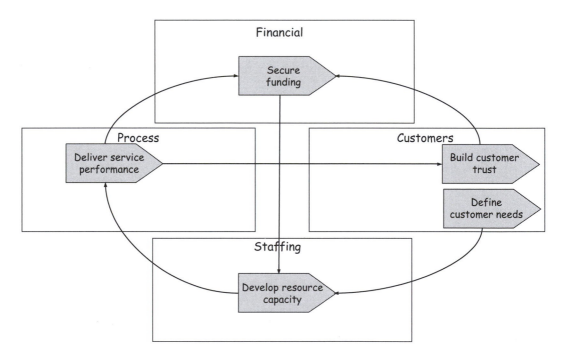

Figure 12.3 JANET (UK) value chain strategy map

The second level strategy map comprised specific objectives for achieving the JANET (UK) vision as shown in Figure 12.4 (the Resources perspective was called Staffing in this case study).

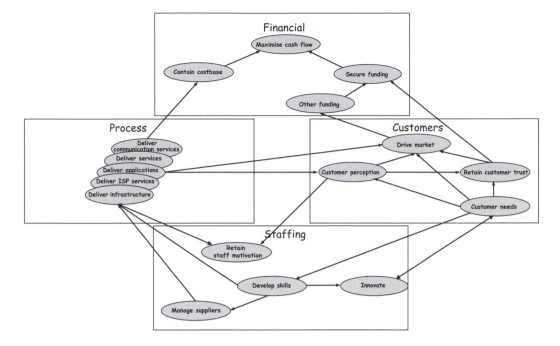

Figure 12.4 JANET (UK) objectives strategy map

Deliverables

Deliverables are programme outputs expressed in terms of new business capabilities that *cause* changes in *drivers* and result in *benefits*. JANET (UK) developed a high-level programme definition, reflecting changes needed to achieve the vision. The essential deliverables from the programme were defined during the early workshops as follows:

- Central service delivery: efficient and effective delivery of customer value
- Customer engagement: trust-based responsiveness to customer and market needs
- Product portfolio management: serving customer needs through innovation and pragmatism
- Commercial culture: creating passion and capability to promote JANET (UK) and JANET (UK)'s products
- Management culture: building the capability to deliver on promises

Strategic Themes: Objectives

Strategic themes are the key cause and effect chains through the Balanced Scorecard routed to the financial perspective. Themes provide the focus for ensuring that the strategic objectives are achieved and manifested in financial outcomes. For the intention phase, themes link objectives within the Balanced Scorecard, and for JANET (UK), five themes were defined:

1. Customer perception: the market is driven from customer needs and customer perception of delivery against those needs (shown in Figure 12.5)
2. Innovation: innovation is driven from and drives customer needs
3. Customer trust: customer trust secures overall funding and releases the knowledge needed to develop new sources of revenue
4. Staff motivation: staff motivation is driven from skills development and the ability to deliver excellence
5. Supplier management: supplier management drives delivery of quality and cost

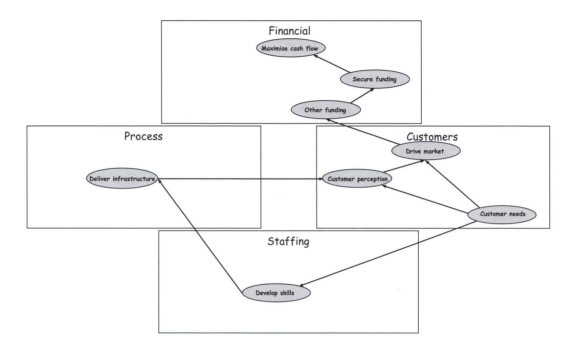

Figure 12.5 JANET (UK) customer perception strategic theme

Customer Perception Theme

The customer perception theme, which for clarity focuses on JANET (UK)'s main product infrastructure, reads as a story, referring to Figure 12.5:

* Customer needs: defining precise customer needs determines both opportunities for selling more of the current services and potential future direction
* Develop skills: provides the capabilities needed to deliver customer needs
* Deliver infrastructure: translates capability into capacity to deliver the demanded quantity and expected quality of service to the customer
* Customer perception: reflects the degree to which actual service delivery is perceived by JANET (UK)'s customers
* Drive market: manifestation of meeting the customer's needs in terms of the value of JANET (UK)'s services demanded

- Other funding: a key outcome includes new revenue streams
- Secure funding: new revenue streams contribute to overall security of funding
- Maximise cash flow: measures the financial value of the strategy

Building Certainty: Deliverables–Objectives Mapping

This final step injects certainty that the deliverables target objectives precisely. The deliverables–objectives mapping for the customer perception theme is shown in Figure 12.6.

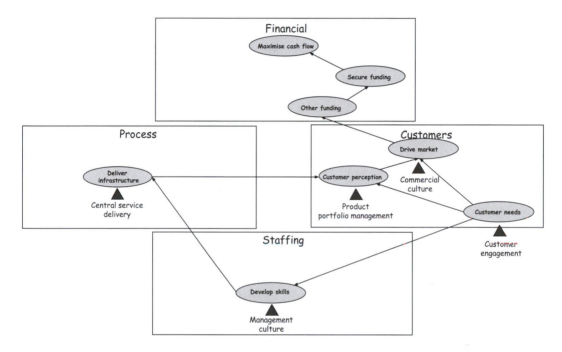

Figure 12.6 JANET (UK) deliverables–objectives mapping

Model

In addition to a *qualitative* cause and effect map, key outputs from this phase included a dynamics model, which defined feedback loops and *quantified* precise measures, together with the relationships between them. The context within IMPACT is shown in Figure 12.7.

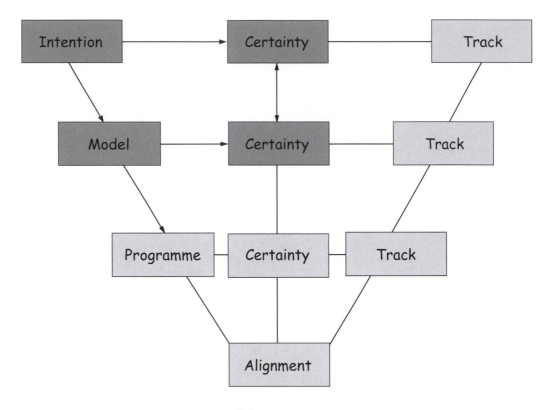

Figure 12.7 IMPACT context – model

Cause and Effect Map

The strategy map was translated first into a *qualitative* cause and effect map, then a *quantitative* dynamics model. The cause and effect map defines relationships in the strategy map more precisely as a set of interconnected feedback loops, which account for the most significant dynamic behaviour. The cause and effect map for JANET (UK) is shown in Figure 12.8.

The cause and effect map contained a number of key causal feedback loops which were specifically referenced for traceability:

- R1 Innovation
- R2 Performance staff motivation
- R3 Customer staff motivation
- B1 Customer perception
- B2 Resource capacity management
- B3 Service capacity management
- B4 Customer responsiveness
- B5 Staff motivation sensitivity

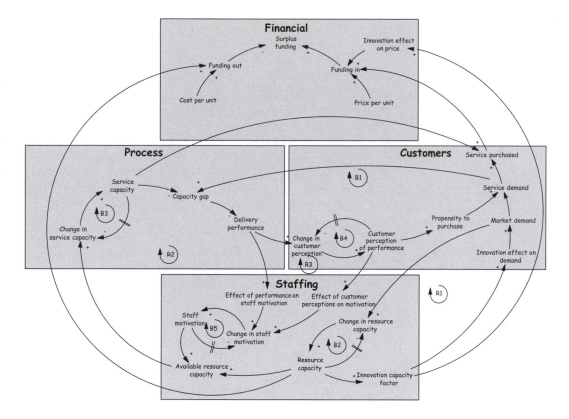

Figure 12.8 JANET (UK) cause and effect map

Dynamics Model

A dynamics model *quantifies* the causal relationships by translating the cause and effect map into a state transition representation, in this case a system dynamics model. The model comprised two levels, an overview which reflected the essential flow in the strategy map, and a lower level containing more detailed underlying structure. The high-level dynamics model for JANET (UK), with the four most complex feedback loops indicated, is shown in Figure 12.9.

This high-level model defined the essential dynamics for JANET (UK)'s value chain and provided insights into specific characteristics of the business. For example, future funding, particularly new commercial revenue streams, is extremely sensitive to responsiveness to customer needs.

The high-level model was broken down into further detail (not shown) to provide sufficient precision to define measures which quantify objectives. The detail comprised two forms. First, the structure was expanded to cover underlying causal dynamics. For example, resource capacity was decomposed into three specific items: contract management, skills development and innovation. Secondly, dimensions were added to account for important distinctions within the causal structure. Three dimensions were used: customer base, performance and service.

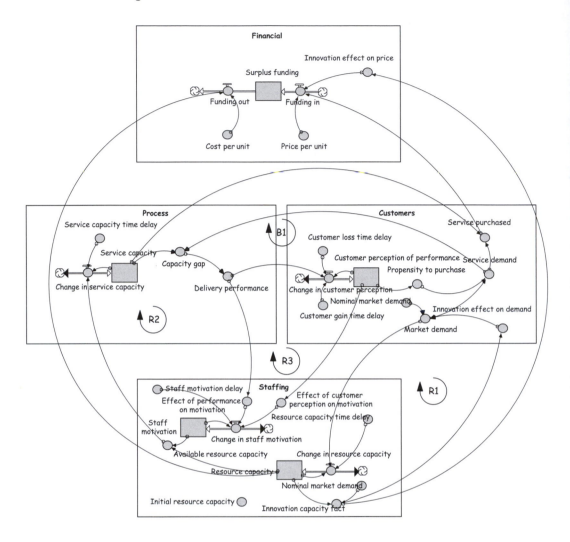

Figure 12.9 JANET (UK) high-level dynamics model

Causal Loop Diagrams

With a complex map and/or model it can be difficult to follow the feedback loops, and it is often helpful to use causal loop diagrams. Causal loop diagrams isolate one or more feedback loops, which makes them easier to follow. This is shown for the four most complex feedback loops in Figure 12.10.

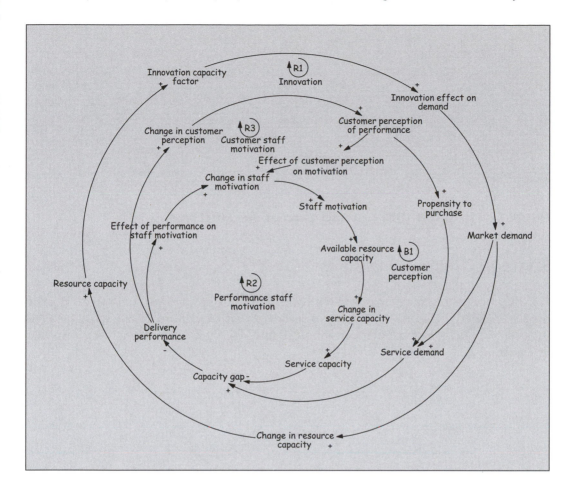

Figure 12.10 JANET (UK) key feedback loops

Causal Trees

Causal trees contain essentially the same information as loop diagrams but trace the cause and effect threads in a more familiar tree form. This presentation is particularly valuable for defining and quantifying the linkage between deliverables, drivers and benefits covered under the next IMPACT phase. A causal tree for the customer perception theme is as shown in Figure 12.11. Items in brackets, such as (Service demand), denote a complete loop, B1 is shown explicitly in Figure 12.11.

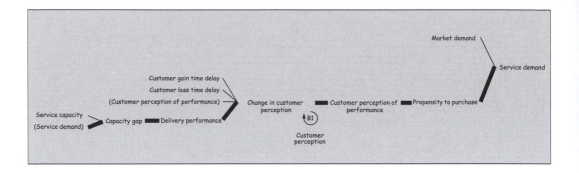

Figure 12.11   JANET (UK) customer perception causal tree

Strategic Themes: Measures

For intention, the strategy map was built with relationships between objectives. For the model phase, themes link underlying measures which are defined by the more detailed dynamics model. The customer perception theme, showing the measure level, is shown in Figure 12.12.

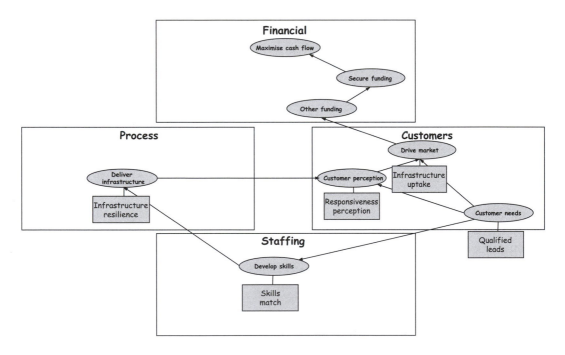

Figure 12.12   JANET (UK) customer perception theme measures

Building Certainty: Deliverables–Measures Mapping

This step is to ensure that deliverables target measures precisely. Deliverables are now mapped against specific measures which contribute to objectives in the strategy map. The deliverables–measures mapping for the customer perception theme is shown in Figure 12.13.

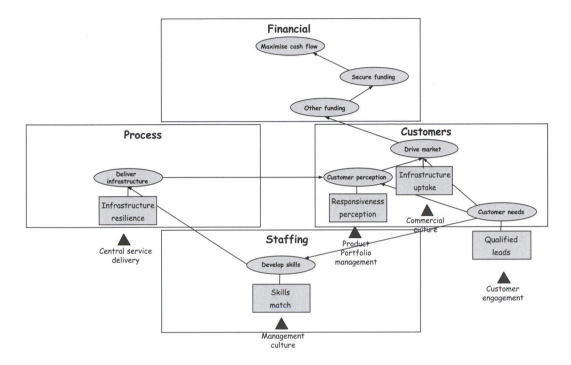

Figure 12.13   JANET (UK) deliverables–measures mapping

Programme

Key outputs from this phase were an outline programme structure and a cause and effect linkage comprising causal connections between deliverables, drivers and financial benefits. The context within IMPACT is shown in Figure 12.14.

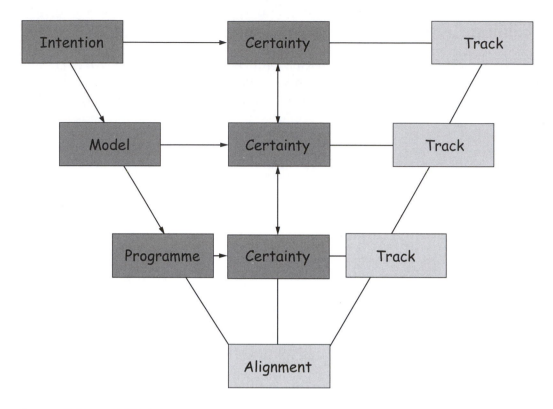

Figure 12.14   IMPACT context – programme

Cause and Effect Linkage

A cause and effect linkage was developed comprising threads connecting deliverables to drivers and benefits. The threads read as storylines derived from the causal trees defined in the model phase. Examples of the causal storylines, relating to the customer perception theme, are shown diagrammatically in Figure 12.15 and summarised in Table 12.1 (calculations are not shown).

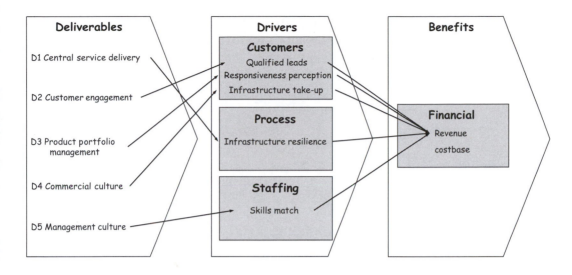

Figure 12.15   JANET (UK) cause and effect linkage

Table 12.1   JANET (UK) cause and effect linkage storylines

Deliverable	Deliverable – driver causation	Driver	Driver – benefit causation	Benefit
Central service delivery	Greater control of network infrastructure enables higher resilience	Infrastructure Resilience	Improved resilience increases demand	Revenue
Customer engagement	JANET (UK) better at identifying and following through on leads	Qualified leads	Greater number of leads increases demand	Revenue
Product portfolio management	Better product management results in increased uptake	Responsiveness Perception	Customer perception of improved service increases demand	Revenue
Commercial culture	JANET (UK) staff promoting and valuing JANET (UK) brand into the commercial sector	Infrastructure Uptake	Increases connections	Revenue
Management culture	Empowered management at all levels leads to better use of HR	Skills match	Increased capability improves service and increases demand	Revenue

The cause and effect map also contained costbase benefits, which are not shown above.

Initial Programme Structure

An initial programme structure was developed comprising a work package breakdown structure and high-level programme plan, as shown in Figure 12.16. At this stage the structure was kept as simple as possible with one-to-one relationships between the deliverables, work packages and programme phases. Later, in alignment, we optimised the structure with the aim of improving the return on investment. Benefits were attributed to each deliverable as quantified through the cause and effect linkage. Development and support costs were attributed to each programme phase.

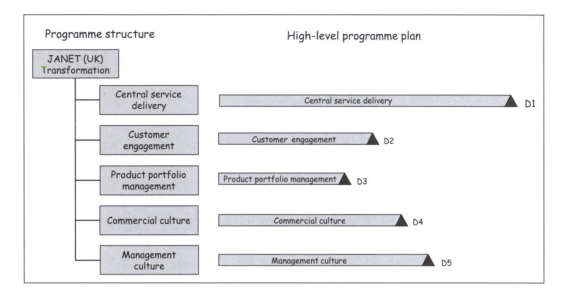

Figure 12.16   JANET (UK) outline programme structure

Programme Value Linkage

Benefits were then attributed to programme phases, in this case on a one-to-one basis, and the programme plan linked dynamically to a DCF output as shown in Figure 12.17.

Alignment

The key output from this phase was an implementation strategy comprising a programme plan optimised to deliver maximum benefits for least cost and risk and within the shortest time. The context within IMPACT is shown in Figure 12.18.

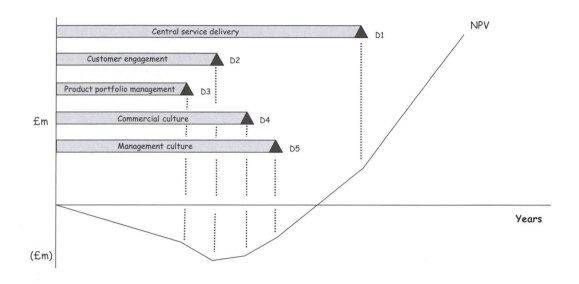

Figure 12.17   JANET (UK) programme value linkage

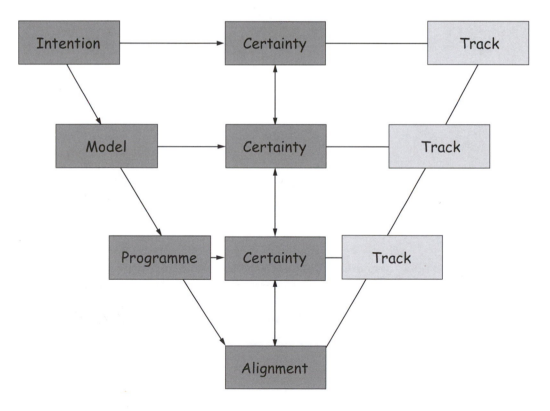

Figure 12.18   IMPACT context – alignment

Benefits Analysis

An important output from the cause and effect linkage was a database enabling us to determine how benefits were attributed across components, such as stakeholders, drivers, deliverables and programme phases. An example profile which mapped financial benefits against deliverables is shown in Figure 12.19.

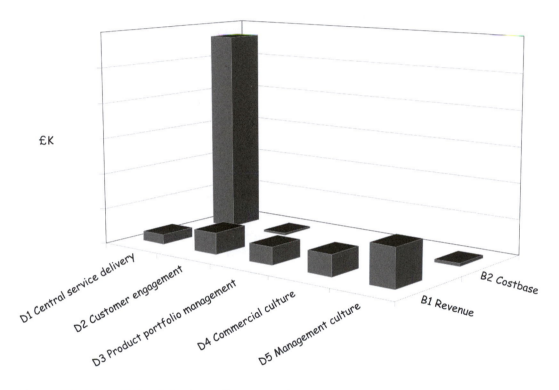

Figure 12.19   JANET (UK) benefits analysis

Implementation Strategy

These 'bangs per buck' benefit profiles directed a restructuring of the programme into an implementation strategy which optimised overall value whilst minimising risk. The strategy comprised three implementation phases each contributing a proportion of the maximum annual benefits attributable to the deliverables, as shown in Figure 12.20.

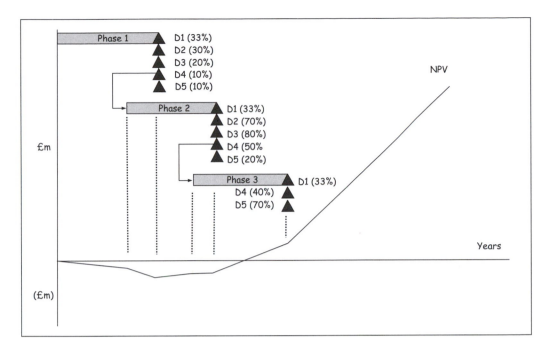

Figure 12.20   JANET (UK) implementation strategy

The implementation strategy had a similar six-year NPV to the initial programme plan. However, by delivering positive returns much earlier, this strategy had a higher IRR and lower risk.

Certainty

The key output from this phase was a risk-assessed baseline business case. Certainty was assured by subjecting the aligned implementation strategy to destruction testing. The context within IMPACT is shown in Figure 12.21.

Destruction Testing

Destruction testing was conducted by subjecting the financial business case to extremes. Resulting NPV J-curves for scenarios against which the baseline DCF was subjected, as listed below, are shown for JANET (UK) in Figure 12.22:

- Double all programme development and support costs
- Halve annual benefits
- Slip the end of phase 1 by a year
- Exclude the deliverable to which the highest annual benefits were attributable

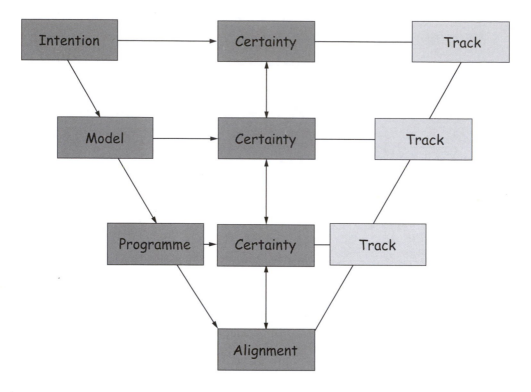

Figure 12.21   IMPACT context – certainty

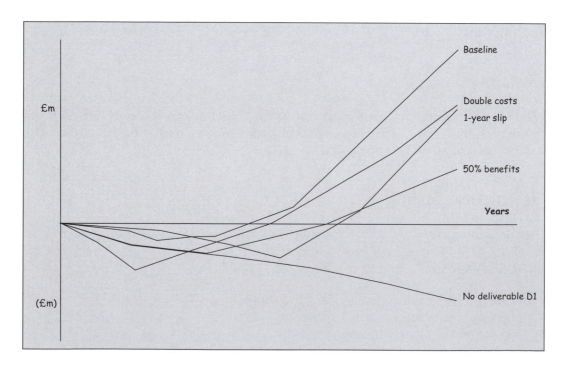

Figure 12.22   JANET (UK) transformation programme DCF destruction testing

We were more interested in patterns rather than decimal point accuracy, that is the comparative shapes of the resulting NPV J-curves. The JANET (UK) case study displayed patterns which we see consistently in this type of strategic transformation programme, characterised by large early costs and lagging benefits.

First, timing is more critical than programme costs; in this case a one-year slip is equivalent to doubling of costs for the six-year NPV at 10 per cent discount factor. Secondly, the NPV is also very sensitive to under-delivery of annual benefits; a 50 per cent general reduction in benefits is far more destructive than doubling of programme costs. Finally, the 80–20 rule or Pareto law is at work. Deliverable D1, central service delivery, accounts for 88 per cent of the maximum annual benefits. Consequently, any deterioration or total loss, as shown, in benefits attributable to this deliverable, can completely destroy the financial viability of the entire programme.

Track

The key output from this phase was a value realisation plan comprising deliverables, benefits and programme value tracking. The context within IMPACT is shown in Figure 12.23, noting that the lateral relationships are now two-way to close the double-loop control in the V-model structure.

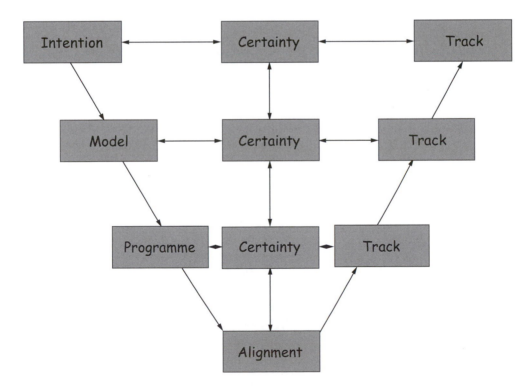

Figure 12.23   IMPACT context – track

Deliverables Tracking

Deliverables tracking is concerned with sound project management, ensuring that deliverables are output fully compliant against specification, on time and budget. The focus was delivering the new business capability through which stakeholder benefits are realised.

Benefits Tracking

However, deliverables tracking is not enough to assure that intended value is delivered. Two further levels of tracking are needed. The first is benefits tracking, which traces the change in value of key drivers linked causally through themes to benefits. The projected change in driver measures was tracked against actuals. A Balanced Scorecard was used for benefits tracking. An example of the trending screen, in this case for perspective level customers, is shown is shown in Figure 12.24.

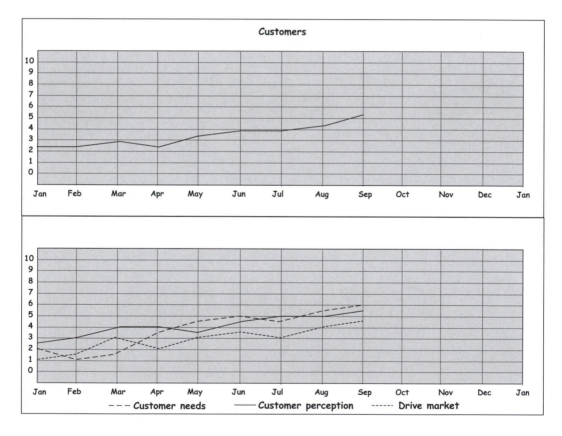

Figure 12.24   JANET (UK) transformation programme benefits tracking

Value Tracking

The final level is value tracking which plots changes against the baseline NPV J-curve, as shown in Figure 12.25.

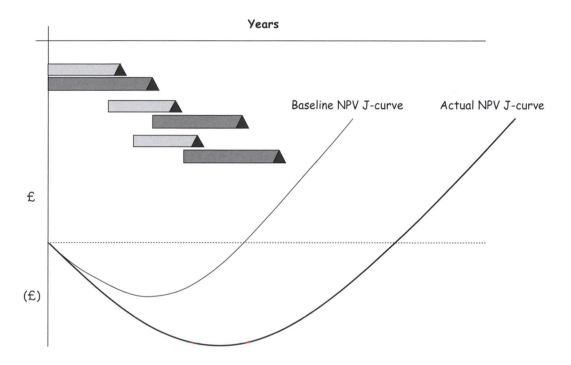

Figure 12.25   JANET (UK) value tracking

Appendices: Precision – Advanced Techniques and Tools

The first three parts of this book set out the purpose, principles and process for Value Management. The aim was to provide sufficient background and real examples to enable the reader to apply the approach immediately and gain rapid results. To this end, nearly all the techniques can be applied using either paper or PC-based spreadsheets, drawing tools and so on.

However, the power, speed and cost-effectiveness of the approach are greatly enhanced with the use of specialist techniques and associated support tools. These Appendices are for readers who wish to consider these advanced areas, the most important of which are discussed from a Value Management perspective.

We take a journey which explores two diametrically opposite tools, dynamics modelling and Business Intelligence (BI), which when combined enable us to create a truly agile enterprise through dynamic performance management. Finally, we introduce the Value Management Toolset™, an ensemble of capabilities designed specifically to support the IMPACT framework.

Appendix A: Dynamics Modelling

What is Dynamics Modelling?

Dynamics modelling refers to the simulation of how entities in which we are interested change over time. In Value Management, we are interested in entities related to the business which when changed have an impact on performance. These entities can be physical items, such as people, inventory and infrastructure or non-physical, such as knowledge, intellectual capital or trust.

Why is Dynamics Important for Value Management?

Dynamics modelling represents an investment it itself, so we need to be clear as to why it is justified. Consider a visit to the tyre fitters to buy a new set of tyres for the car. Time is money for these guys so they work fast. After fitting each new tyre, the wheel must be rebalanced. If we were only going to drive slowly this would be unnecessary. However, when travelling at speed even small variances in weight distribution are accentuated and result in uncomfortable, potentially dangerous, vibration. The solution is simple, involving the attachment of small lead counterweights to the rim. However, the dilemma for the fitters is to pinpoint where there are imbalances and how much lead to attach. They could do this *statically* by placing the wheel on a scale which is sensitive enough to show weight inconsistencies. In practice, however, this would be difficult because something that appears to work statically may perform very differently when in motion. So, each wheel is placed on a *dynamic* balancer, which spins the hub/tyre assembly and directs the fitter to the exact point on the wheel and the size of counterweight to use. All it takes is a few seconds for each wheel.

This is an example in which measuring something while things are in motion, that is dynamically, gives us a more precise answer, more quickly. We have a similar challenge in business. When change was relatively slow and predictable, we could model our businesses using static organisation charts and process diagrams. However, these models prove inadequate when the pace of change exceeds what we can model statically. The limitations of static models are compounded when there are complex internal relationships between functions, as well as processes and external interactions in the form of constant shifts in economics and competition. In today's business we experience all these; pace, complexity and global competition, and dynamics modelling provides a means to direct, drive and deliver value in this environment.

In Chapter 6, we identified four reasons for modelling: to expose and define problems and opportunities, direct value-creating solutions, define criteria for success, measure twice cut once. Dynamics modelling offers four further advantages:

1. Exposing problems and opportunities, not made visible by static, qualitative or linear models, and directing solutions with which to address issues most effectively.
2. Quantifying the capacity needed to deliver intended stakeholder outcomes, together with opportunities for eliminating waste as a means to provide more capacity at no extra cost.
3. Quantifying leverage and the relative importance of performance drivers in generating value, directing action to gain the greatest and fastest positive effect for least effort and risk.
4. Defining the most critical measures for a performance management framework, for example Balanced Scorecard, with greater precision and certainty.

Mental Model Limitations Revisited

In explaining how dynamics is critical in our quest to create business value, we need to revisit the limitations of mental models, first discussed in Chapter 3. As human beings, we are pretty good at dealing with stable objects, and relatively adept at predicting how things change when this is linear, that is in a single direction and at a constant rate. For example, we all get on quite well on a clear motorway when everyone is travelling at high speed, if following the rules. However, we tend to overestimate our ability to predict non-linear behaviour, even when presented with apparently simple problems displaying obvious behaviours. This limitation becomes more apparent when the behaviour we are trying to predict is the result of numerous, interconnected things working together; in other words, systems. For example, we collide with each other through the new contra-flow road works, even though we are only travelling at a snail's pace, because of our difficulty in dealing with unpredictable starting and stopping.

There is a paradox here. We are usually ready to accept our limitations when faced with obviously complex systems, such as the economy, and tend to assume that they are unpredictable. Consequently, we tend to underestimate our ability to predict dangerous outcomes, even when they are staring us in the face. The housing market, dot.com boom and bust and credit crunch are good examples. From a systems thinking perspective these are all examples of the limits to growth pattern, or archetype, characterised in overheating, fanned by unjustified trust that collapses once the truth is rumbled. We can overcome much of our mental limitations by simply shifting our attention from *events*, which tend to reflect *effects*, to *patterns* which reveal the underlying *causes*. However, this shift also requires us to surrender our need for *absolute* decimal point accuracy in exchange for *relative* patterns of key measures over time.

> *Great hardships could be avoided, or value created, if we learn to look behind surface events and see the underlying causal dynamic patterns.*

Conversely, we overestimate our ability to predict the behaviour of seemingly simple systems. Nowhere is this tendency more obvious in business than in supply chains. During my early career, I constructed many investment appraisals for factory automation programmes, such as robotics, for which I gained a reputation and treated myself to a feeling of pride. The financial cases were presented as detailed DCF analyses, often based on labour saving resulting from higher utilisation enabled by automation of manual work. Then one day I was given a copy of Eli Goldratt's *The Goal*,[1] which introduced the Theory of Constraints (TOC). TOC shows that the primary driver of output is bottlenecks, created from the interaction of statistical fluctuations and logical dependencies. This is a manifestation of the law of redundancy which we defined in Chapter 6. Bottlenecks are exacerbated, not improved, by increasing utilisation. In fact, the way to go out of business in batch manufacturing, Goldratt argues, is to match supply and demand before removing asynchronous flows. So automation can actually make things worse. I was not pleased, and neither was my ego; it meant that much of my work was flawed. What seemed like a simple no-brainer had much greater ramifications, which my sophisticated linear calculations had missed.

> *We underestimate the potential to foresee complex system behaviour and overestimate our ability to predict how simple systems behave.*

As we stated in Chapter 6, we need to combine more effective thinking in order to counter these limitations, with tools that support the corresponding new mental models needed for the job. Fortunately, such tools exist, are mature and relatively inexpensive. We will be exploring the most important for Value Management, but first we discuss the foundation for all dynamics modelling, state transition.

State Transition

Modelling is concerned with representing the real world sufficiently closely to enable us to learn from the past, manage the present and prepare for the future. Most fundamentally, we need a way of defining real-world entities, together with the manner in which they change over time, either by themselves or by interacting with other entities. The concept that most effectively models real-world entities is state transition, in which entities are represented in terms of their defined states at given points *in* time, and change, that is transition, between these states *over* time. Entities are defined by attributes, the values of which determine the specific state of an entity at a given time. Transitions refer to changes in attributes over time. States are photographs and transitions the films which show what happened between each still.

Dynamics modelling can be viewed as a form of state transition. The concept of entities having states and capacity to move between states is the basis of Object Orientation (OO) in modern software engineering. It is no coincidence that the first OO language, Simula, was designed for simulation. Object Orientation comes with a number of rather imposing terms referring to principles which account for the power of the discipline. Fortunately, whilst we exploit these principles, it is not necessary to know about them for our purposes and we keep the language as jargon free as possible.

The best way to introduce both the principle and importance of state transition is by considering a business level example, as shown in Figure A.1.

---

1   Goldratt, E., Cox, J. 1989. *The Goal*. Revised Edition. Aldershot: Gower.

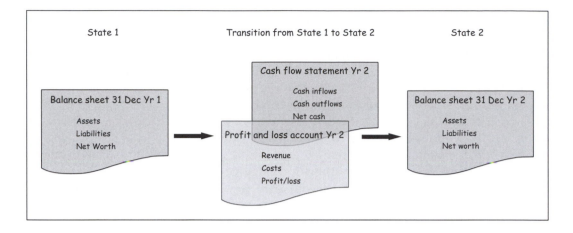

Figure A.1   State transition for a business

The three primary financial accounting documents for a business are the balance sheet, profit and loss account and cash flow statement. Balance sheets define the *state* of a business at the end of each accounting period, for example a year end, in terms of three key attributes: assets, liabilities and net worth. Profit and loss accounts and cash flow statements are different views of the *transition* between each year end, which explain what accounted for changes in the balance sheet.

Now consider state transition as a programme of change intended to transform the business from one state to another, as shown in Figure A.2. In this case, the states are represented by measure values and scores in the Balanced Scorecard which define the As-is and To-be performance of the business. For example, changes in the annual accounts, as described above, will be reflected in the financial perspective. The transition is accomplished through the value realisation stage of Value Management for the change programme, when deliverables become operational and influence drivers to create benefits.

The transition from the As-is state to the To-be state involves thousands of transitions in the many entities engaged in the business, across all Balanced Scorecard perspectives. For example, staff are recruited, gain capabilities and leave. Capital assets deteriorate, are maintained and replaced. Processes convert raw materials into products. Customers are acquired, refer other customers and churn. The key point is that all these business as usual occurrences, which account for the overall growth or decline in the business, can be modelled as state transitions.

The problem is that there are far too many items to keep track of, even with the latest IT. Also, the way in which the transition operates varies between different types of entity and circumstances. Consequently, we need to home in on those specific entities, and associated attributes, that are most relevant for managing performance, and use the appropriate dynamics modelling tool for deriving knowledge that can be applied to create value. A key skill in dynamics modelling is to define an entity using the minimum number, and simplest type, of attributes which enable us to achieve intended outcomes through the modelling. To this end, we consider state transition for the key business entity, customers, in terms of their maturity and value, as shown in Figure A.3.

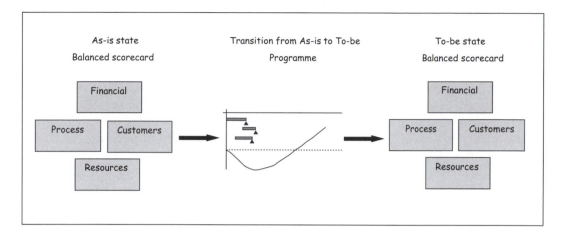

Figure A.2 State transition for a programme

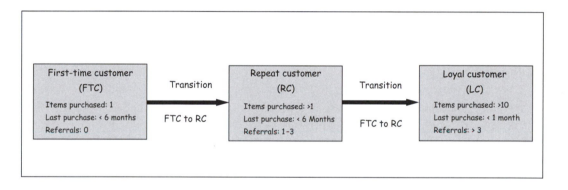

Figure A.3 State transition for customer maturity

In this simplified example, we model customer maturity as the transition of the entity through three key states: First-time customer (FTC), Repeat customer (RC) and Loyal customer (LC). As customers transcend through each state, their value to the business increases as they are likely to purchase more products, buy more frequently, and be more likely to refer other new customers. To reflect this, each state is defined by the same three attributes, that is number of items purchased, time from the last purchase and number of referrals. The values assigned to these attributes determine the state. For example, in this case, a customer is designated RC if they have purchased at least two products and becomes a LC when they have purchased ten. We could also build more sophisticated rules using the other two attributes.

Types of Dynamics Modelling

Of the many types of dynamics modelling techniques and tools, we are most concerned with those which help us manage business *performance*. In Value Management, great emphasis is placed on the need to quantify key cause and effect relationships within the business as a prerequisite for effective performance management. As Barry Richmond put it 'When improving performance is your aim, causation must be your game.'[2] Therefore, we use tools that enable us to model true cause and effect related to performance. There are three techniques most relevant to achieving this purpose:

1. system dynamics
2. discrete event simulation
3. agent-based modelling

Rather than define underlying theoretical bases, it is more useful to discuss how the techniques apply state transition principles for practical application in complementary ways. Consequently, in the next three sections we illustrate how the different tools can be applied for Value Management by extending the customer maturity model in Figure A.3.

System Dynamics

In system dynamics, causal structure is represented by levels, also called stocks, which can change through flows into, out of and between them, as shown in Figure A.4 in which we have expanded the customer maturity model. Levels are *states* because they represent the status of an object at a particular point in time. For example, the number of customers in a defined state, such as first-time customers, can be defined by a level. Flows are *transitions* which enable changes in the entity from one state to another over time, for example, the number of customers migrating from first time to repeat, in a month. The rate of transition is determined by settings in the flows, which can be controlled by levels, flows or other variables in the model. These flows can be activated by specific *triggers*, which cause an almost instantaneous step change, or factors which result in a constant or non-linear rate of change over a duration of time. The opposing triangles are flow controls and the clouds represent the boundary between the scope of the model and the rest of the world.

After some time in each state, a proportion of customers will be lost whilst another percentage will move on to the next state. This combination of time and proportion dictates the rate of transition. For example, it may be deemed that a first-time customer either becomes a repeat customer, or is lost, depending on whether they make at least one other purchase within six months of the customer acquisition. The relative levels in customer states, indicated by the dark grey, reflect the familiar 'funnel' pattern in CRM, whereby there are more first-time customers but a higher proportion churn, and so on through the cycle.

---

2   Richmond, B. 2004. *An Introduction to Systems Thinking with iThink*. Lebanon, USA: isee systems, inc.

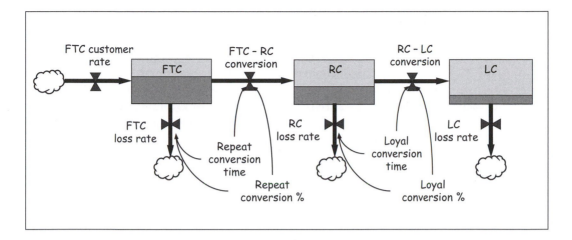

Figure A.4 System dynamics

This basic simulation can be made more sophisticated with the use of multiple, interactive models and/or dimensions. For example, we could replicate the customer maturity model using identical structures to represent specific customer segments, each demonstrating different behavioural and buying characteristics. In addition to customer dynamics, we use this same basic structure for applications as diverse as staff trust and capital asset management. Large models can be constructed from a number of modules, or views, which render complex models far easier to build, test, communicate and use. In the case study at the end of this chapter, we illustrate how modules and the relationships between them have been used to mirror objectives and themes defined in a strategy map.

It should be noted that the Achilles' heel in constructing models is the temptation to include too much detail in order to mimic the real world. In the world of the model, 'less is more'. We must be ruthless in excluding all but the essential model structures, otherwise the model becomes too complex to be of practical use and dangerous because it is too complex to fully test and de-bug.

Relationship with Systems Thinking

One of the most powerful aspects of system dynamics is that it mirrors systems thinking, a primary basis for modelling cause and effect in Value Management. In Chapter 12, we illustrated how a cause and effect map, comprising several interwoven causal loop diagrams, can be converted into a system dynamics model. Experienced system dynamics modellers often omit producing causal loop diagrams, instead incorporating them into the model directly. However, the step is deemed important in Value Management because causal loop maps provide a key role in the verification and validation process discussed in Chapter 11. As system dynamics so closely relates to systems thinking, it is used most frequently in Value Management and all case study examples in this book use this type of model.

Causal Loop Diagrams and Causal Tracing

System dynamics models support causal loops and causal tracing, both essential tools for deriving the most critical performance drivers, which we discussed in Chapter 6. Some system dynamics support tools can produce these loop and tree representations semi-automatically, which greatly enhances their value. For example, both iThink® and Vensim®, packages used for case studies in this book, can define causal loops automatically; Vensim® can produce tree representations using the Causal Tracing™ tool.

Discrete Event Simulation

Expanding on the customer maturity model, suppose that the channel for developing our customer base and sales growth is a call centre. A common tool for sizing call centres is the Erlang algorithm, which enables us to calculate the number of agents needed to provide a defined level of service for a given call rate and duration. Erlang tools can be sold as Excel add-ins and can give very accurate results; if all calls are of similar nature and length, and can be handled by just one type of sales agent. Under these circumstances we could also use system dynamics very quickly and effectively.

However, suppose that many of the calls vary wildly in both subject and duration, and must be routed to subject specific specialists. We can still use, and have used, Erlang or system dynamics, but as the variety increases, the models can become very large and unwieldy. The key distinction in this case is that each primary entity, that is sales call, is fundamentally unique and needs to be modelled individually. We would face a similar challenge for parts in batch manufacturing, patients in hospitals and complex supply chains or distribution networks. The ideal tool for these situations is Discrete Event Simulation (DES) as shown in Figure A.5.

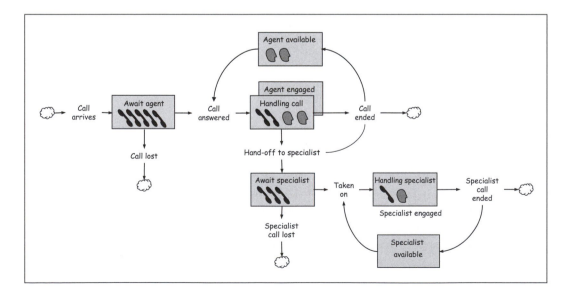

Figure A.5   Discrete Event Simulation

DES models the world by focusing on the *events* that occur to entities and determine the start and finish of transitions between states. There are essentially two kinds of event, conditional and bound. Conditional events, such as Call answered and Taken on, are *conditional* because they are dependent on one or more conditions being true. For example, the event Call answered is only triggered if there is a call waiting and an agent available to take it. Bound events happen after a predetermined time. For example, the event Call ended will happen at the end of the call duration. Because each call can have a different duration, the call time is set from a distribution. Modern DES tools provide a plethora of distributions with which to accommodate statistical fluctuations. In DES, the state transition constructs for the various types of entity, that is call, agent and specialist, are called activity cycle diagrams or entity cycle diagrams.

The routing is also call specific. For example, some calls may be relatively simple and can be handled by the agent, whilst others are more involved and need to be handed over to a specialist. Data are held on each *instance* of an object so that every specific item can be studied, as well as their group behaviour. In this way, it is much easier to spot bottlenecks and their causes; this is the principle underlying Goldratt's Theory of Constraints, which we cited earlier.

A great strength of DES is that it is highly visual and modern tools make it easy and quick to build what would otherwise be difficult models, using animated, even 3-D graphics. Also, much of the pre-model diagramming and distinction between different event types is rendered unnecessary, because these are built into the drag and drop construction process within the tools. However, for Value Management, we work from first principles in order to define the underlying causality which drives the model and for verification and validation purposes.

Agent-based Modelling

In system dynamics and DES, entities follow paths determined by the model structure. For example, customers follow a defined maturity path and calls are routed through the call centre depending on the type of call. There can be interaction between entities which may be significant, for instance, repeat and loyal customers refer new customers to the company, and there are usually some relationships between customer segments. Nevertheless, the behavioural dynamics of the entities is determined mainly by the structure.

However, as the world grows more global and interconnected, there is increasing interest in behaviours which develop primarily from the interaction between large numbers of entities, responding to each others' behaviour using *rules*, in the context of their environment. These *emergent* behaviours are characteristic of Complex Adaptive Systems (CAS). As the name implies, CAS are highly complex, chaotic systems which find their own order through the law of self-organisation, defined in Chapter 6. Natural examples of CAS are flocks of birds and shoals of fish, which display ordered patterns from small, apparently chaotic movements. How do they do it? The answer is that they respond by making often minute adjustments in relation to each other using very simple rules. In the business world, people, markets and entire economies operate as CAS. For example, the stock market is driven by sentiment and patterns of behaviour between traders, as well as rational analysis of individual shares. CAS is also important in social sciences, where much of the work on CAS has been aimed to date.

Extending our customer maturity model still further, suppose we want to model how the market is likely to segment within a social media environment. A combination of Internet and social websites, such as Facebook and Twitter, have transformed the way in which many products and services take off or flop, in what is now sometimes referred to as the *truth economy*. This means that buyer behaviour can be far more influenced by what other customers say, than claims made by suppliers through advertisement.

In *The Tipping Point*, Malcolm Gladwell[3] contends that just a few people, of three types, determine whether something tips or disappears into obscurity. These types are connectors, mavens and salespeople. Connectors are supreme networkers. Mavens must have the latest and best things at bargain prices, and inform as many other people about them as possible. Salespeople possess extraordinary powers of persuasion operating at a subconscious level. Also critical is the 'stickiness' of the message in any communication and the context within which the message is received. A powerful tool for modelling this kind of challenge is Agent-based Modelling (ABM), sometimes referred to as intelligent agents, as shown in Figure A.6.

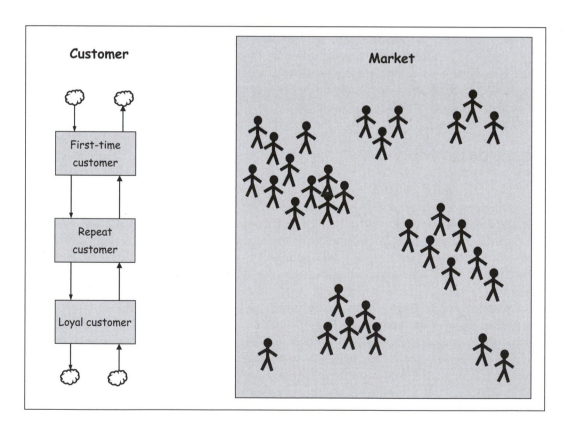

Figure A.6   Agent-based modelling

---

3   Gladwell, M. 2000. *The Tipping Point: How Little Things can Make a Big Difference*. London: Abacus.

In ABM, the state transition representation of each entity, in this example being a customer, is called a state chart, which also has triggers which invoke transitions. In Figure A.6, each customer may posses the same three states that we used in the system dynamics example, first time, repeat and loyal. There are various ways through which transitions between these states can be triggered. For example, through social networking certain groups of customers with similar ages, interests and tastes could be brought together through Facebook, and form a closely interactive segment. With this knowledge, we could target specific value propositions to customers in this segment, invite feedback which provides even more precise knowledge about their wants, and ask 'permission' to offer them new products for up- and cross-selling opportunities. Amazon excels at this targeted permission selling. They worked out pretty quickly that I am a total sucker for books on complexity theory, and email me with offers that I would need therapy to refuse.

Integration of Modelling Tools

It must be stressed that the examples demonstrate general concepts and potential applications. In reality, there is considerable overlap between the various tools. For example, system dynamics can model tipping point behaviour very effectively. DES can simulate high-level process flows, as well as individual items at a micro level. ABM can be used for detailed design, such as underground station exits, by studying how crowds would react when confronted with a terrorist bomb or fire and need to escape through confined areas. The important point is not to pigeonhole each tool for a single application or purpose. In recognition of the value in combining the approaches, in the latest generation of dynamics modelling tools, some tool suppliers provide the means of integrating the techniques into a single model. It is also important to recognise that emergent behaviours are non-deterministic. So, whereas process models using system dynamics and DES can provide reasonably accurate and repeatable predictions, CAS models using ABM will indicate patterns, which often provide insights upon which effective action can be directed, but not absolute outcomes.

The Dynamics of Capacity

In Chapter 6, we introduced the critical role of capacity in relation to performance management. Now we expand this theme and explore how dynamics modelling is used to quantify real capacity requirements, determine ways to increase capacity, often for little or no extra cost, by eliminating waste and managing available capacity more effectively and efficiently.

Value Added versus Non-value Added

Capacity refers to the resources, that is inputs, needed to generate value. In Value Management, we are most interested in capacity required to deliver intended outcomes. More specifically, required capacity is defined as the resources necessary to deliver a defined level of intended stakeholder outcomes. However, as we have stressed, capacity is consumed in generating outputs which may or may not deliver stakeholder outcomes. This brings us to the question of value added versus non-value added consumption.

During our Value Management workshops, attendees are asked, without prompting of any particular response, 'What proportion of your effort is waste?' The answer is almost universally consistent, between 15 and 20 per cent. It is as if this figure feels about right. Then we ask another question, 'What proportion of your effort is actually spent directly contributing to your primary purpose, such as making sales or delivering value?' The answer is typically also 15 to 20 per cent. What accounts for the 60 to 70 per cent discrepancy? One answer is that they are either unaware of, or are not owning up to, the real figures. This is not our experience: the level of honesty from people is generally quite extraordinary, considering the sensitivity of the subject. The explanation lies in the distinction between three categories of resource consumption, which hold the key to capacity:

1. waste
2. essential redundancy
3. right first time

WASTE

Waste is non-value added consumption. Waste refers to the consumption of resources needed to cover *avoidable* effort, of which there are essentially three types, nugatory, correction and duplication. Nugatory work refers to consumption that makes no contribution to value, the most obvious example being *deliberate* abuses, such as false expense claims, jollies and non-jobs. These require sound leadership, management, political will and procedures to address, and should clearly be eradicated first. However, much less obvious forms of nugatory effort relate to *non-deliberate* waste, such as terminated programmes that would not have been started if they had been subjected to a rigorous business case, or development work conducted against an ill-conceived specification, and then thrown away.

Correction, or rework, includes fixing things that were not done properly in the first place. In our call centre examples, repeat calls from customers who do not get satisfactory outcomes from their initial contact are examples of rework. Duplication is where consumption to achieve the same result is conducted more than once, or by more than one resource unnecessarily. Poor reuse, resulting from inadequate standardisation or a desire to reinvent the wheel, a fault we engineers often exhibit, is also an example of duplication.

Waste tends to create even more waste, which takes two forms. First, knock-on nugatory, corrective and duplicated consumption, and secondly the management overhead to coordinate increased complexity, introduced by waste, that should not be there in the first place. For example, a pattern that we see frequently is where the most capable resources are engaged in either fixing problems or managing other people fixing them, instead of creating value.

ESSENTIAL REDUNDANCY

Non-essential redundancy is a form of duplication and therefore waste. Essential redundancy is also non-value added but is critical because it relates to the spare capacity needed to ensure that intended outcomes are achieved, taking into account *unavoidable* variations in activities, process dependencies and levels of uncertainty, that is risk. For example, in order to ensure acceptable service levels, a typical call centre handling similar types of call, operates at around 80–85 per cent utilisation. This figure decreases dramatically as the size of the call centre decreases and/or the call duration increases. This apparently low utilisation is because of the unavoidable lost time from the queuing effect between calls, over which management has limited or no control. After this we need to add in comfort, lunch and tea breaks, normal sickness, learning time and training and so on. This can often increase the number of agents needed to maintain a defined customer service level quite significantly.

Despite this seemingly obvious logic, essential redundancy is often ignored. Some years ago we were working on a sizing programme for a social housing call centre, in one of the largest and most diverse London boroughs. The council's initial design was based on a simple calculation: Required Agents = Peak number of calls per hour/Call handling rate per agent. This gave a figure of around 42 seats. Our calculations, using Erlang combined with other allowances, increased the number to 84 seats, which was not accepted. The simple mental model was so entrenched despite copious evidence based on their existing facilities. The new call centre eventually ended up with 86 agents. It should be noted that often the predicted results from models will not be initially accepted because they differ widely from the expectation driven by mental models, so we need to be prepared for this resistance.

RIGHT FIRST TIME

Right first time (RFT) is the only real value added type of consumption. RFT is required to produce outputs which contribute to the attainment of intended outcomes, with a given capability of resources, with no waste or redundancy. There are only two types of value added activities: decisions which direct value creating actions (doing the right things) and acting upon effective decisions to create value (doing things right).

Removing Non-value Added Consumption

A corollary from the above analysis is that for improvements to be optimal, the categories of consumption must be tackled in order; waste followed by redundancy then right first time. This is because although waste and essential redundancy are both non-value added the removal of each has profoundly different results. In a climate of cuts, it is particularly important that government agencies and commercial businesses alike understand the impact of this difference. If waste is removed there is a double benefit, costs are reduced and resources are freed up to add greater value. For example, eliminating errors not only reduces costs, but also potentially results in less customer churn, greater trust and increased sales. Conversely, if essential redundancy is removed, before the removal of the waste that necessitates the redundancy, stakeholder outcomes will suffer in the form of reduced service levels. For example if, the number of agents covering sickness are reduced *before* management have corrected excessive absenteeism, customers will wait longer, and their issues are likely to be dealt with less effectively, because remaining agents cut corners to get through the workload.

There is also great scope for improving RFT, for example through advanced technology, but we must take great care not automate the wrong things. Following Michael Hammer's seminal 1990 paper 'Reengineering work: don't automate, obliterate',[4] and the subsequent flurry of Business Process Re-engineering (BPR), there was a greater awareness of the need to emulate the Japanese mastery of process improvement. However, there is still a tendency to use technology to automate non-value added work. For example, inspection is often treated as a value-adding activity. It may well be essential for a given level of process capability, but it is *not* value added. It is a consequence of imperfect process. The problem with confusing value and non-value added activities is that it can result in suboptimal solutions. By treating inspection as value added for example, we automate inspection rather than eliminate the causes that necessitate inspection, such as poor quality.

Modelling Capacity Dynamically

We now need to consider how dynamics modelling enables us to quantify and design for capacity, which is often more effectively modelled dynamically because the key drivers, such as bottlenecks, change over time and often are not visible using static models. In Value Management, capacity relates to the resources needed to deliver intended outcomes as defined by the value equation expressed in quotient form as defined in Part I:

$$Value\ for\ Money = (Outcomes/Outputs) \times (Outputs/Inputs)$$

$$Value\ for\ Money = Effectiveness \times Efficiency$$

Therefore, capacity needs to reflect both the ability to deliver outputs *and* intended stakeholder outcomes, that is benefits, enabled by the outputs. Considering the call centre example, capacity is defined as sales per unit time, for example hours, days, months and so on, and comprises three prerequisites:

1. Agents (inputs that consume resources and incur cost)
2. Agent capability (conversion rate per call, that is outcomes/outputs)
3. Agent productivity (volume of calls per agent per unit time, that is outputs/inputs)

$$Capacity = Number\ of\ Agents \times Agent\ Capability \times Agent\ Productivity$$

$$Capacity = Agents \times Value\ per\ Agent$$

or

4   Hammer, M. 1990. Reengineering work: don't automate, obliterate. *Harvard Business Review*, July–August, 68(4): 104–112.

$$Capacity = Agents \times Value\ for\ Money$$

or

$$Capacity = Agents \times Effectiveness \times Efficiency$$

We could go further and include the sales value per converted call, potential overall customer value and so on. The important point is that capacity must include effectiveness. This is a critically important conclusion from a performance management perspective. Although it may appear obvious to include effectiveness, most performance regimes measure only productivity. For example, performance in many call centres is still focused on call rate, that is how many calls an agent can close per hour. This has important implications on behaviour and value creation, and is often self-defeating; by rushing calls, customers become dissatisfied and sales opportunities are lost.

Dynamics modelling provides a powerful means to quantify capacity requirements and determine processes and policies to increase capacity for little or no extra cost. This is achieved by simulating the interaction of the entire system dynamically, and including non-value added items explicitly. For example, consider the call centre customer satisfaction model shown in Figure A.7 (simplified for clarity).

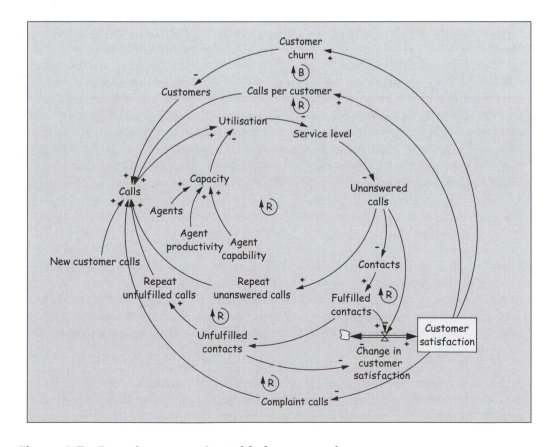

Figure A.7 Exposing non-value added consumption

In this model there are several sources of call. First, general enquiry calls arrive from existing customers and new customers. Service level depends on the capacity to deal with the calls, reflected in utilisation. As utilisation increases beyond the point at which service levels can be maintained, the number of unanswered calls and/or answered calls ending in unsatisfactory customer outcomes increases, which results in repeat calls. In turn, these create vicious reinforcing loops that cause service levels to deteriorate further. This situation gets worse until either management takes action or, as in this model, the universe solves the problem for you by reducing the number of customers through churn. This kind of pattern is observed frequently and, if not addressed, the waste can quickly account for a greater consumption of resources than value-added work, even if it is not recognised or measured. Although the call centre example may seem specific, it should be noted that most agencies and businesses that we have worked with exhibit similar archetypes in various parts of their transaction/event-processing organisations.

Dynamics Modelling of Performance

The National Grid Metering Story

National Grid Metering (NGM) supplies gas meters to domestic, commercial and industrial end consumers within the UK. Operating as a separate company within the parent organisation, National Grid (NG), NGM's customers are the domestic and commercial gas suppliers who contract NGM to fit and maintain meters in end consumer homes and business premises. NGM meters vary depending on the type and preference of the end user, but all domestic meters are 'dumb', meaning that they simply measure usage and require a visual reading for billing purposes. In the domestic sector, NGM generates revenue from meter rental and requests from gas suppliers and end users for changes. All maintenance and customer request work is undertaken by third-party service providers under contract to NGM. Gas supplier and end consumer requests and issues are handled by internal call centres and process teams within customer operations.

The domestic market is undergoing a transformation to SMART metering. SMART meters feed data back to operators, who can then provide advice to end consumers concerning the most cost-effective and green tariffs to suit their needs. SMART meters also have intelligent capability, enabling remote control of the supply to agreed tariffs and appropriate responses to changed circumstances. Over the next ten years, government policy intends that all dumb meters are replaced by SMART devices. As National Grid have not fully clarified the group approach to options surrounding how they intend to supply the SMART market, NGM is potentially facing a declining asset base, reaching zero in 2020, and certainly an extremely volatile period of change.

This presents significant challenges for NGM. Providing an essential and safety-critical function, the company will need to maintain safety and service levels with dwindling revenue streams. As the meter population declines three things will happen. Rental and customer request revenue will reduce. The geographic density becomes sparser making the distance between each visit greater and more costly. There are less economies of scale with which to attract favourable contracts with third-party service providers, justify investment, motivate staff and assign internal costs.

In addition, the pattern of meter base reduction is an unknown. The population profile will be driven by the rate at which customers decide to switch dumb for SMART meters. Customer behaviour may be influenced by factors under NGM control, such as service levels, reputation and pricing, or factors outside NGM influence, for example government incentives and/or pressure, and customer strategies and policies. Consequently, during a period of reduced funding and investment, NGM must also be sufficiently agile to manage any pattern of asset population, ensuring that the business continues under strong strategic direction, delivering a first rate service.

Sponsored by the Chief Operating Officer, a partnership was formed by the business architecture manager, Janet Jordan, and management reporting manager, Abby Cardall, to derive a set of KPIs which will not only enable the company to manage a declining market, but improve the value that NGM delivers. Abby and Janet supported the development of a dynamics model for this purpose, which evolved through a series of executive workshops.

This case study is particularly interesting because NGM is a private sector company with the same challenge facing many parts of the public sector; delivering greater essential stakeholder outcomes with less income and fewer resources. The study is also intriguing because it clearly demonstrates the power of dynamics modelling in the context of performance management.

Causal Hypothesis

The starting point for any modelling exercise is to define the purpose of the model. For this we need to answer the question, 'What value will we be able to create as a result of the model that we could not achieve without it?' It is useful to sketch one or more simple plots over time to represent the dynamic behaviour that we are intending to model. This step is called causal hypothesis and is an invaluable way of testing our grasp of the problem. The causal hypothesis for NGM is shown in Figure A.8.

The fundamental challenge for NGM is to model various profiles of a declining asset base over the next 10 years, 2012 being a key date for the expected switch to SMART metering. It is important to note that the graph represents possible market developments rather than a definite future. The power of the model lies in the capability to simulate, and direct solutions in response to, the high level of uncertainty in the metering sector.

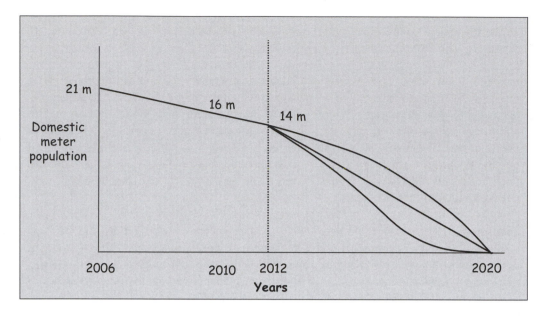

Figure A.8   NGM causal hypothesis

Modelling Scenarios

The executive workshops were also used to define scenarios which the model was required to simulate, together with the answers needed from the simulations. Scenarios are potential future situations relating to the causal hypothesis, including extreme cases, within which we need to model business behaviour. Scenario modelling is the means by which we test how the business will operate under a wide span of possible circumstances and provide the scope, specification and acceptance criteria for the model. In this case, the executive team defined 18 scenarios connecting strategic and operational levels. Examples listed below illustrate the wide range of interconnected issues:

- commercial impact of SMART roll-out
- impact of weather on service delivery workload
- commercial impact of proactive maintenance
- sensitivity of meter population to pricing
- impact on service delivery from accurate asset information

Storytelling

The NGM strategy map and dynamics model were constructed through four half-day workshops, one for each Balanced Scorecard perspective and integrated through a review with the entire executive team. The most effective way to build a strategy map, together with the more precise cause and effect map from which the dynamics model is derived, is through storytelling. In this case, the process involved each perspective owner and team answering precisely structured questions designed to identify key problems, define the deep underlying causes and derive solutions, together with the resources needed to deliver them. Finally, the owners were asked to specify precise lead measures, to be certain that the solutions were being achieved, and lag measures to be certain when solutions were actually achieved. This final question returned candidate KPIs which were subsequently refined using the dynamics model.

Dynamics Model

The dynamics model was then constructed in iThink®, using a top-down approach, to mirror the strategy map developed during the workshops, as shown in Figure A.9.

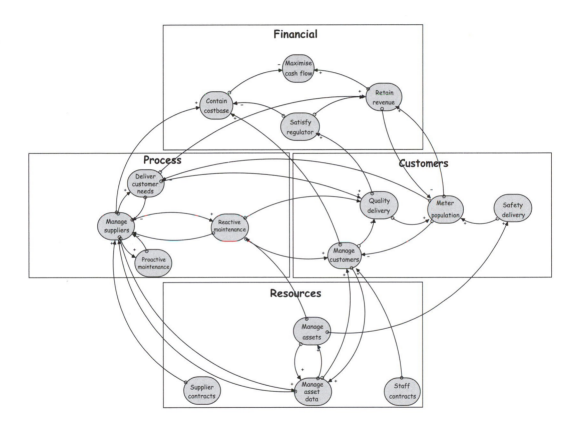

Figure A.9   NGM dynamics model high-level structure

The dynamics model comprised a number of modules, one for each Balanced Scorecard objective. Designing the architecture to reflect the strategy map made the transition to a quantitative model much easier. The model was also exhaustively reviewed by the executive team and operational managers. Each module contained the underlying causal dynamics from which both the KPIs and underlying drivers were defined. Feedback loops were shown explicitly between modules. Controls were added with which to vary the leading drivers, and output graphs to capture the dynamic profile of the lagging KPIs.

In addition to defining and quantifying the relative importance of the KPIs, the primary objective, it was intended to apply the model for several other functions:

- development of strategies and solutions by cross-functional teams
- calibration of business plans
- approval of business cases

Essence

- The primary purpose of dynamics modelling in Value Management is to define causal measures, through which the greatest stakeholder value can be created with least cost most quickly; providing the basis for BI solutions, scorecards and dynamics models
- Dynamics is the analysis of change on a base of time, and dynamics modelling refers to the quantitative simulation of changes in entities, which we call objects, over time
- Modelling tools need to redress the limitations of our mental models
- Dynamics modelling is founded on the principle of state transition
- Three types of modelling are used for Value Management: system dynamics, discrete event simulation and agent-based modelling
- System dynamics mirrors systems thinking, upon which the causal linkages are founded
- Discrete event simulation is particularly well suited to model complex processes and supply chains
- Agent-base modelling can simulate emergent behaviors observed in social groups and market segments
- Dynamics modelling is particularly suited to modelling capacity and exposing waste; the result of avoidable nugatory work, corrections and duplication
- Waste must not be confused with essential redundancy, which is the spare capacity needed to deal with unavoidable variations and dependencies in order to ensure delivery of intended stakeholder outcomes
- Dynamic models can be structured to mirror strategy maps and synchronised with Balanced Scorecards

Useful Websites

isee systems, inc. *iThink*. www.iseesystems.com
Ventana Systems, inc. *Vensim*. www.vensim.com
Ventana Systems UK Ltd. *Vensim*. www.ventanasystems.co.uk
SIMUL8 Corporation *SIMUL8*. www.simul8.com
XJ Technologies. *AnyLogic*. www.xjtek.com
Powersim Software AS. *PowerSim*. www.powersim.com
NetLogo. http://ccl.northwestern.edu/netlogo/

Appendix B:
Business Intelligence

The Importance of Business Intelligence

Business intelligence (BI) solutions are the repositories of an organisation's essential data and, more importantly, provide the means to transform this data into time-critical information and knowledge upon which to act and create value. Consequently, BI is becoming increasing critical for business and this is reflected in spending, which continues to increase year on year. The primary market demands on today's business, increasing regulation, competitive impact of globalisation and dynamism of the economic environment, are reflected in the three key drivers of BI:

- Risk and compliance: enabling traceable and fully auditable information to demonstrate control and accountability to regulatory bodies.
- Customer value: realising greater value for and from customers by matching propositions precisely to their needs, and targeting specific customers who will release the potential value.
- Performance management: supporting value-generating initiatives and providing agility to respond to the pace of global competition and fiscal constraints.

Data, Information and Knowledge

BI is concerned with managing large volumes of *data* to produce *information* which can be used to apply *knowledge*. Therefore, it is important to recognise the distinction between these three terms:

1. Data: raw facts, for example, number of hits on a webpage.
2. Information: combination of data into a structure or report, from which problems can be diagnosed and decisions made more effectively; for example, which specific customers accessed specific web pages in a given order.
3. Knowledge: using information to derive a superior level of intelligence that provides high-leverage opportunities to create value; for example, the preferences and buying behaviour of precise market segments and specific customers.

Purpose and Definition of Business Intelligence

The purpose of BI is to enable effective decision making through the timely presentation, interpretation of and action upon information.

The following are two complementary definitions of BI:

1. BI concerns transformation of operational data into decision relevant knowledge
2. BI provides perspective and insight, based on the access to and analysis of quantitative data sources

BI refers to computer systems that manage the organisation's data to support decision making by structuring the data optimally for analysis and reporting.

BI transforms data into information optimal for value creating decision making.

The strength of a good BI solution can be measured by simply asking, 'Is it delivering the right information at the right time and place to the right person to allow them to take the right action?' The value of the information that BI delivers can be measured by the improvement in business outcomes that have been achieved as a result of having the information available. Other important terms in relation to BI achieving its purpose are:

• data quality
• master data management

Data quality is the largest Achilles' heel for BI solutions. All businesses have a diverse range of transactional applications. Each application will hold data that is appropriate to support its own local processing needs. The quality of data within particular applications will vary, in that some applications tolerate a high level of missing, inaccurate and/or inconsistent data because this is acceptable within the objectives of that application. Other business applications require far higher levels of data quality. Many transactional computer systems in the same company will hold different answers to the same question; for example, a simple metric 'How many 5mm type 23 screws were sold by shop x this year?' can be represented in three different transactional applications as:

1. Computer system A: answer 4328.
2. Computer system B: answer 3752. This number is different because system B works on a financial year whereas system A works on a calendar year.
3. Computer system C: answer 2547. System C only counts the direct retail sales; it knows nothing of the sales made to business accounts.

Each of the above systems holds data that is accurate for its own purpose. The data quality issues arise when businesses need to integrate data from several existing systems, such as when a BI solution takes data from each system to build a holistic view of performance. In this case, the BI system must accurately identify differences in data and apply a sophisticated suite of business rules to translate each system's unique view of the world into an aligned holistic view, which is often called the *single source of truth*.

Master Data Management (MDM) has similar issues to data quality, but it relates specifically to non-transactional (often called reference data) that is a *shared* resource, used by many computer systems across the organisation. For example, customer data is maintained in a central place and used by several different applications in processing specific transactions, such as billing, payments and so on. Managing this kind of shared data can involve complex business rules for seemingly trivial situations. For example, consider the business rules needed to determine whether four customers at the same address are really one, two or three people. Mr Joe Bloggs and Mr J. Bloggs seem obvious because they have the same date of birth, but could Mr J. S. Bloggs be their son, or did somebody mistype the third digit of the year in his date of birth? Is Ms J. Bloggs the wife or mother who happens to have the same date of birth as Mr J. Bloggs, or is the title incorrect and it is really Joe again? MDM has the objective of providing processes for collecting, aggregating, matching, consolidating and de-duplicating such data, so that all computer systems can reference the single source of truth. Usually, MDM functions are set up and assigned responsibility for defining and managing non-transactional data entities of an organisation.

Single Source of Truth

As we saw earlier in the discussion on data quality and MDM, the greatest power of BI is also the greatest challenge; the creation, maintenance and application of information which is correct, consistent and complete. This is referred to as the *single source of truth*. The key to successful delivery of value from programmes is precise, responsive feedback and correction, for which only the truth will do. Consequently, the single source of truth is critical for Value Management because it provides precisely the raw material for both building a robust baseline business case and subsequent value realisation. Two things are fundamental in realising this single source of truth. First, initial *design* of BI architecture and the business rules/algorithms need to conform and align the data and to populate derived information. Secondly, proper ongoing *governance* of changes is essential so that the BI solution adapts to reflect faithfully changes in the real business environment.

Governance of Business Intelligence

Another major challenge is ownership of BI. It is quite possible, and often the case, to manipulate data from BI used in reports to spin a particular story. This is a reason that good BI solutions allow 'read only' access to their data, to prevent pollution of the single source of truth. However, it is also necessary to impose a 'kite mark' approach, to identify the formal reports that have been generated using the raw data and derived fields that have been read from the BI solution under proper governance. This practice exposes manipulated data reports, even though they are usually generated using exactly the same tools as the formal BI reports and so would otherwise look the same and could cause confusion to business users.

Types of Business Intelligence Solution

The vast majority of the computer systems that are used by organisations, whether commercial businesses or public service authorities, will fall into one of three broad types:

1. Online Transaction Processing (OLTP) systems: these are designed to handle business transactions in near-real time. They can be large and highly complex, but they are typically tightly focused and departmental; for example, a telephone company's call billing system or a Social Security payments processing system.
2. Real-time processing engines: these are generally built to process massive numbers of workstreams in parallel, and to complete each stream's processing in a sub-second; for example, a road traffic light control system, a bank's transaction authorisation system.
3. Enterprise Resource Planning (ERP) systems: these typically comprise an integrated set of modules that form a single solution to take care of the entire organisation's back-office functions, such as finance, accounting, manufacturing, sales and customer service.

Although on the face of it these types of solution seem to be very different, they are similar in that they all hold transactional data in order to carry out their own processing and they will all offer some form of stand-alone (silo) reporting capability. Although extremely rich in raw data, all of the above types of capability provide little in the way of meaningful management information. By combining transactional data and reference data, for example customer details, that is taken from all of these systems, plus other sources, such as external market trends, a BI solution tracks meaningful management information in a way that reflects a more holistic view of the business; people, customers, suppliers and products.

Who needs this? Surely, everyone who cares about achieving their organisation's objectives. BI solutions provide executive teams with timely and accurate information which allows them to track their current level of performance against plans, compare this with the past and pinpoint areas which have over or under performed. Examples include the following:

- discover the profile of customer behaviour, then track changes
- measure changes in the competitive performance of products/brands over time
- model the impact of changes of operating costs on profitability
- integrate management reporting to track changes after mergers/acquisitions

BI Architecture

It is useful to consider the main elements within a BI solution in the context of their importance to enable a business to generate value. BI architecture comprises four key parts as shown in Figure B.1.

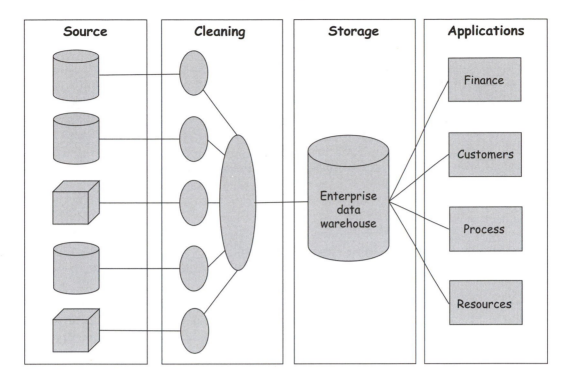

Figure B.1   High-level Business Intelligence architecture

SOURCE

Data is provided from various sources within the business. These sources are usually diverse, spanning corporate ERP systems to local spreadsheet applications. In this form, the data is inevitably incorrect, incomplete and/or inconsistent. Consequently, it is difficult for business leaders and managers to use information derived from the data either confidently or effectively. Looking back at the previous data quality example, imagine three executives at a global sales performance meeting debating how many 5mm type 23 screws were sold by all regional shops this year. These kinds of debate, concerning inconsistent data, waste valuable time, cloud understanding of real performance and lead to mistrust between executives who need to operate as a united force. This dangerous scenario is summarised by Elaine Fletcher, a Partner at IBM's Business Analytics and Optimisation Group, 'a man with a watch knows the time, but a man with two watches is never sure'; she finds that most of her client's executive teams typically juggle four or more watches when trying to track a single key metric.

Paradoxically, some people thrive in this environment. For them, lack of clarity is power because they can manipulate information which they control to suit their own agendas. Because there is no single data baseline, this game-playing may be suspected but cannot be proved, so it continues and gets worse as lies are used to cover lies. We see this pattern, even after some BI solutions are in place, unless there is sufficient governance.

CLEANING

In order to make source data value creating, it must be cleaned. This is achieved using *business rules*. The sheer quantity and diversity of data and reporting needs in a typical business means that the business rules can become immensely complex. Modern BI tools provide automation for defining and implementing business rules through the process of Extraction, Transformation and Loading (ETL). Extraction refers to the capture of data from multiple sources within the business. Typically, the core data needed to build the BI will come from formally managed business application databases. However, sometimes departmental spreadsheets and a number of other sources, which have evolved over time, are used where they are the only option to source crucial data. Transformation is the conversion of this data into a consistent, single source of truth. A major challenge is removing inconsistencies between data items; illustrated by the data quality and MDM examples above. Loading involves organising the data into a form that is suitable for a *data warehouse*, where data is typically organised in multiple dimensions, for example time, geography and so on, and then physically loading the data into the dimensions of the warehouse or large data subsets used for local applications, called *data marts*.

ETL is the least sexy, and often the most poorly executed part and of the BI architecture. This is a mistake. Corners cut here undermine both data quality and data integrity and, typically, 80 per cent of the effort of building a well-implemented BI solution is consumed in completing ETL.

STORAGE

Clean data can be loaded into an Enterprise Data Warehouse (EDW) or straight into a federated suite of data marts. Both options enable the data to be queried and presented into the most appropriate way for decision making. EDWs give the advantage of storing aligned data in one *schema* for general use across all parts of the business. However, some businesses feel that they do not need to query across the business, so they choose to organise their data as a federated, that is aligned, suite of subject area focused data marts for use by specific departments, for example sales mart, procurement mart. Most businesses would have a combination of EDW plus federated data marts to give flexibility and/or higher query performance/simplicity where needed.

In BI, a schema is the organisation or structure for a database developed through the activity of data modelling. There are many types of schema in common use; the most common are Star Schema, Cube and 3rd Normal Form. Although a detailed description is beyond the scope of this book, the important point is that these data structures have particular strengths which can be matched to business needs. For example, a star schema gives good performance, is flexible to accommodate change and is highly intuitive for business users to access because it holds all facts in one central fact table, and queries these facts via a set of high performance indices which are the dimensions for example time, geography, departmental hierarchies. This allows business users to ask questions like, 'How many call centre agents resigned in Cardiff between 15 February and 8 April, how many for the same period last year and how does this compare with London and Edinburgh?'

Cube architectures deliver very high performance for business user's queries, but are more limited than Star Schemas in the number of dimensions that they can cope with.

Consequently, they tend to be used for more tightly focused subject areas. For example, an environmental agency might have a cube to track the pollution of rivers from heavy industry, another cube to track pollution of the same rivers from agricultural chemicals and another cube to track fishing licenses and so on for those rivers. There is a tendency for cubes to proliferate and careful maintenance is needed to ensure that changes, for example re-categorisation of a river, are applied consistently in all cubes at the same time.

3rd Normal Form does not hold data in conformed dimensions; instead it opts for the highest level of flexibility by holding data at the smallest level of groupings. This flexibility comes at the cost of higher complexity and, consequently, most business users find them too technical and difficult to navigate for ad hoc queries. Solutions using 3rd Normal Form tend to be more dependent on their technical IT department to build new reports and queries. This dependence can cause bottlenecks and delays which impact the business more than would be the case for star schemas and cubes, where typically, business users would generate their own ad hoc queries and reports when they need them.

APPLICATIONS

Applications provide the reports and queries for decision making using derived data from the single source of truth. This is often seen as the sexier part of BI but is often mistaken as the entire solution, with the result that sophisticated reports are produced using poor quality data and are not worth the pixels used to display them. Therefore, it is important to consider some best practice. Typically, the BI solution will store a mixture of raw facts, together with derived information that it calculates at the time that new data is loaded into the BI data schemas, by applying a suite of approved business rules and algorithms. It is best practice to make heavy use of derived information to populate all derived data fields, rather than allow applications and reporting tools to calculate them.

There are two advantages of this approach, the first being *performance*. BI solutions are designed to give high performance in the 'heavy lifting' of data when performing complex queries. They can run highly parallel processing streams (usually overnight) to pre-calculate all derived fields and store them in the EDW and data marts, ready for business users to read. The alternative is for reporting tools and applications to carry out this complex processing on demand, which means that business users must wait for this to be executed before they can see the results of their query.

The second advantage of using derived information is *consistency*. Proper governance of business rules and algorithms can be applied so that the derived information can be trusted to be stable and accurate, and have proper data integrity with other fields. Alternatively, where local applications and reports calculate their own derived fields, there is usually only local governance, and knowledge confined to other data items that are used locally. Consequently, the derived values tend to be less trustworthy. For example, they may not be consistent with derived fields calculated by other departments, or adjust algorithms without all relevant stakeholders being consulted.

Applications and reporting tools should always be used in 'read only' mode so that they do not allow updates to the data held by a BI solution. This ensures that the data, which the whole enterprise relies upon, does not become polluted. The purpose of the applications and reporting tools is to allow business users to slice, dice and drill into the data to answer queries and produce reports to support decision making.

Maturity and Capability

Another major challenge in BI concerns the problem of legacy systems. In almost all cases, data capture, storage and reporting systems have evolved on different, diverse and often incompatible systems. This results in three things. First, it introduces gaps, inconsistency and duplication in the data so the information derived from it can be of poor quality. Secondly, vast manual effort is required to analyse data and compile reports, then to reconcile conflicting information resulting from poor base data. Thirdly, resulting systems are notoriously expensive to maintain from an IT perspective.

The value that can be created as a result of BI is closely related to how it is deployed with the business. It is useful to consider the typical stages of BI, in terms of the business capability that each stage enables. As an example, Figure B.2 shows the Logica Capability/Maturity Model.[1] The first four capabilities are concerned with measuring the business by focusing on the past using the single source of truth. The final three competences apply the single source of truth to align the business and drive future performance.

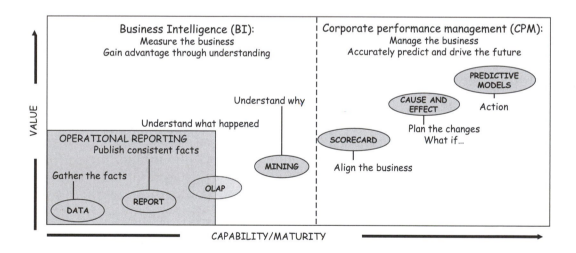

Figure B.2 Logica BI maturity/capability model
© Logica 2008–2011.

DATA: GATHER THE FACTS

The first prerequisite for providing information upon which effective decisions can be directed is to gather the facts and build a single source of truth whereby data is correct,

1   Roekel, H., Linders, J., Raja, K., Reboullet, T., Ommerborn, G. 2009. *The BI Framework: How to Turn Information into a Competitive Asset*. Reading: Logica.

complete and consistent. This stage comprises the ETL of data into a BI solution under the control of business rules. Important aspects include data quality and MDM.

REPORT: PUBLISHING CONSISTENT FACTS

The most pressing outputs from BI are reports that publish the raw facts and derived information in a consistent and timely manner. Reporting includes defined periodic reports and alerts concerning actual or anticipated problems. Automation is an important element of reporting. Without a BI solution, typically 80 per cent of reporting activity is consumed in compiling reports and reconciling data to get to the truth, whilst only 20 per cent or less is spent using the information to create value. A BI solution automates the collection and crunching of data into information, so that business users spend their time acting to create value using the new insights that they have gained as a result of the automated BI information.

ONLINE ANALYTICAL PROCESSING: UNDERSTANDING WHAT HAPPENED

Online Analytical Processing (OLAP) is the capability of slicing, dicing and drilling the data to follow guided lines of enquiry either for ad hoc queries or predefined analyses. OLAP queries are driven by a business user who has a focused ad hoc question and waits for the results. For example, 'How often has supplier X failed to meet their service level agreement during the past six months?' This capability is important in Value Management for diagnosing causes of variances in measures.

MINING: UNDERSTANDING WHY

Data mining is often confused with OLAP, but they are very different functions. Data mining casts the net far more broadly across all available data sets (usually overnight because it makes highly intensive use of computer resources). Mining exploits the power of statistical algorithms and correlation to expose unseen patterns and potential relationships between things or events, when applied to large amounts of data. For example, suppose the transactional behaviour exhibited by eight customers last week indicates that they are likely to be operating as a new fraud ring, because it has several similar traits to behaviours displayed by previous fraud rings, even though only one of the eight customers has previously been suspected of fraudulent activities. The results of automated data mining models are often fed directly into transactional line of business applications (for example call centre screens, transactional authorisation systems), to ensure that timely action is taken to improve business outcomes. Data mining is also used by specialist business analysts and strategic planners to undertake research into the current business, together with potential impacts of future changes, such as market conditions, regulatory frameworks, mergers/acquisitions and so on.

SCORECARD: ALIGN THE BUSINESS AND ASSESS CURRENT PERFORMANCE

A scorecard is an excellent way to present business insights in a top-down manner from the executive board cascading down through senior to middle management teams. A scorecard helps managers to focus on KPIs that track those things that matter most to the organisation's ability to create value against its core objectives. This prevents managers from becoming distracted by day-to-day issues that may have far less bearing on the real objectives. Scorecards can be one of two types:

1. Balanced Scorecard
2. executive dashboard

In a Balanced Scorecard, all measures are expressed as a score, for example between 1 and 10. This is especially useful where executives seek to identify best practice from business areas of different scales; for example, Malaysia may be tiny compared with the USA for a global oil business, but their excellent growth from 6 to 8 in margin score will be clearly highlighted by a Balanced Scorecard.

In an executive dashboard, measures are expressed as their factual numbers, that is actual turnover, rather than a score. This is useful to publish real facts, but due to vast differences in scale, some areas of best practice are completely hidden by larger business areas. In our above example, Malaysia's performance would be completely hidden by that of the USA, and the business would not realise that new best practice procedures had delivered excellence in Malaysia, and could be imported into the USA to achieve stunning uplift in the USA. (This is an example of waste through poor reuse.)

Many businesses are now using a combination of Balanced Scorecard and executive dashboard; the approach adopted in Value Management. This is a useful approach, but careful consideration must be given to alignment between the two views, so as not to cause confusion amongst the management teams. The best way to ensure this alignment is to derive the score from the values mathematically, rather than using disconnected and subjective scores, a practice that is still quite widespread in our experience. Both scorecard and dashboard should both be populated from the BI solution to ensure that they reflect the single source of truth.

CAUSE AND EFFECT: PREDICT THE FUTURE

Cause and effect models identify the most significant drivers of business performance. They help the executive teams to understand how the current performance is the shape that it is. For example, 'How did my change initiative deliver great uplift for the first seven months but then settle back into steady state despite increases in resource?' Causal models also allow executive teams to predict the likely future outcomes of change, for example 'What if' models to show the impact of regulatory change.

In practice, the greatest results are achieved by using scorecards/dashboards and cause and effect models together. For example, a Balanced Scorecard delivers insight into *past* and *current* performance, and the data used to refresh the cause and effect model shows the likely *future* outcomes of change. We explore this further in Appendix C.

PREDICTIVE MODELS: SHAPE THE FUTURE

Predictive models are a specialist form of data mining. They analyse the detailed behavioural patterns of each customer or citizen to predict their propensity to carry out a particular action. Predictive models are widely used to:

- Predict which customers are the most likely to buy product x at a particular offer price: this is called 'cross-sell and up-sell'. The propensity is calculated based on analysis of the behaviour of each customer who has not yet bought product x and those who did buy product x.
- Identify existing fraudulent activity, and predict which citizens are likely to be in the early stages of future fraudulent activity, so that these can be tracked or stopped before they pose a commercial risk.
- Predict which customers are the most likely to churn (that is, take their business to a competitor). Like cross-sell/up-sell, the churn models carry out a deep analysis of each customer's behaviour, to identify which events and actions led past customers to churn, and to identify current customers who are at the highest risk of churning. The models will also identify the special offers or actions most likely at this point in time to change the customer's mind and prevent churn.

The three most advanced stages of BI maturity – scorecard, cause and effect and predictive models – operate most effectively if integrated.

Business Intelligence and Dynamics Modelling Integration

The eAnalytics Story

Imagine that you are running a high street fashion shop. You have a photographic memory and can remember every customer by name, what they looked at, what they tried on, with what accessories, and what they bought. Every time they pull a garment out of a rack, you note it, when they put it back you note it, when they try something on you note it, and if they leave your shop without purchasing anything you note the last thing that they looked at. You keep track of every significant action your customers take, and after a time build up a complete picture of their needs, preferences, dislikes, shopping and buying patterns.

As a consequence of this intimate customer knowledge, you are able to stock more precisely what people want, and when customers return to your store you direct them to those items which are most likely to produce a sale. You ask whether they would like to receive special offers from you, based on your knowledge of what they are likely to want, and offer special deals which include additional, higher-value items. This results in more repeat and loyal customers, who not only buy more of the same sort of product, but allow you to cross-sell related accessories and up-sell higher value garments. Loyalty cards achieve this capability and as a consequence have proved very successful.

Now relate this story to an online business. In this case you cannot watch your customers in person or physically swipe a loyalty card, but you have something potentially even more powerful, the ability to keep track of every web page they look at on your site, over time building a precise log of everything they have ever done via your site. This is not just counting the hits on each page, which is of very limited value because it builds only a vague, general picture of customer behaviour. Instead, you filter out all irrelevant data and end up with a trace of which pages a customer looked at, for how long, in what order, and what actions they took as a result of viewing the page content. This is called true path analysis and is key differentiator in an advanced form of on line customer analysis, called eAnalytics, made possible by BI.

eAnalytics was pioneered over 10 years ago. Although superseded by advances in BI since that time, the essential principles remain unchanged and provide a real example of the power of integrating BI and dynamics modelling.

Causal Hypothesis

The causal hypothesis for eAnalytics in the context of customer value is shown in Figure B.3:

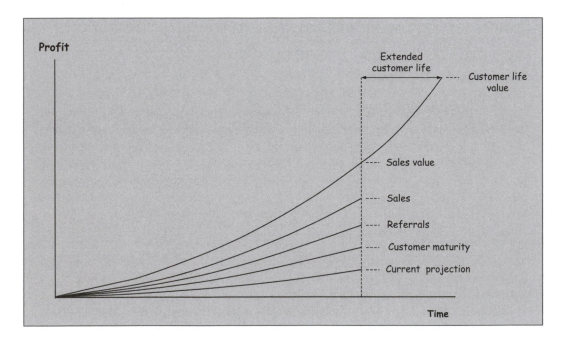

Figure B.3 Causal hypothesis for eAnalytics

In this example, the online business is already successful and is anticipating steady, compound growth in revenue as indicated by the current projection. However, by adopting eAnalytics, the business is now able to leverage three new capabilities enabled as a result of acquiring superior customer knowledge. First, the business is able to target the development of value propositions to profitable segments and individual customers; noting that sales only add value to a business if they generate profit. Secondly, the website can be designed to optimise the manner in which the value propositions are promoted to both prospective and existing customers. Thirdly, through permission marketing, value propositions can be promoted precisely to targeted customers and segments.

Taken together, these new capabilities result on several compound effects and described below:

- Customer maturity: the rate at which customers transcend to repeat and loyal states increases, so the level of sales associated with each maturity level is achieved earlier.
- Referrals: referrals, leading to more first-time customers, increases as existing customers reach higher value states, where they are more likely recommend your products, more quickly; this is even more critical in the world of social media.
- Sales: the level of sales relating to each maturity level also increases as customers buy more of the same or similar product.
- Sales value: the value per sale and overall value of purchases, sometimes referred to as share of wallet, increases as the business is able to sell related and/or higher value products, that is cross-sell and up-sell.
- Customer life value: customer life is extended so the additional revenue continues for longer.

Dynamics Model

A dynamics model for the causal hypothesis, simplified in order to make it easier to follow the essential causal logic, is shown in Figure B.4.

Although at first viewing Figure B.4 appears to be very complex, it is actually remarkably simple. In essence, we have overlaid the effect of customer knowledge onto the customer maturity model covered in Appendix A, Figure A.4. There are two main state transitions. The first is customer maturity which models the transition through key states: first-time customers (FTC), repeat customers (RC) and loyal customers (LC). (Customer loss flows from FTC and RC would also be included in the full model.)

The second main transition tracks the knowledge associated with customers in each state, that is FTC knowledge, RC knowledge and LC knowledge, which can be regarded as data relating to each of these states held in a BI data warehouse. In the full model, there would be logical connections between the two chains in order to keep them in step with one another. For example, as a RC becomes a LC, knowledge relating to that customer undergoing the transition will follow them. We could have consolidated all customer knowledge into a single stock but this would have reduced the precision.

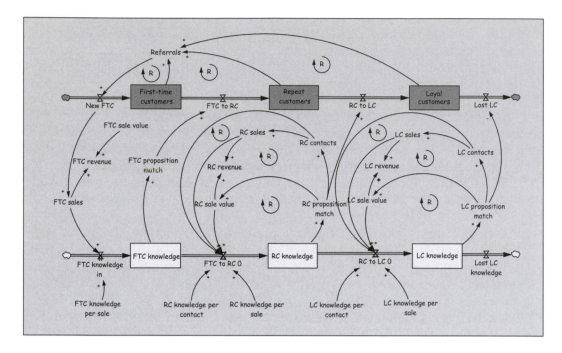

Figure B.4   Dynamics model for eAnalytics

CUSTOMER MATURITY

Each FTC makes a single purchase, and the knowledge relating to the sale, together with much relevant information about the new customer, is captured in the stock FTC knowledge. The level of this knowledge, and the degree to which it is used to match other value propositions to these customers, influences the rate at which FTCs become RCs, or are lost (not shown for brevity purposes). The faster the rate at which customers mature to higher value states, the earlier the sales associated with these states are realised.

REFERRALS

The volume of FTC is determined by their exposure to your products through advertising or enquiry, and as a result of referrals from existing customers. Referrals can be word of mouth, emails, social media sites and so on. The important distinction for referrals is that they are independent recommendations, which tend to result in a higher conversion rate than advertising. Referrals from customers increase with maturity. For example, an FTC who enjoys a good initial experience may refer new FTC. Then as they become RC, they generate more referrals and finally, as LC, they become your unofficial sales force.

SALES

Whilst maturing through the higher value states, customers increase their propensity to buy more of the same products. For example, consider a business supplying stationery to individuals and other businesses on line. A FTC buys some economy pads and pens. Satisfied with the product, price and free next day delivery service, the FTC purchases more of the same pads and pens next time they are needed. Customer intelligence is not only gained when a sale is made, but during every customer contact. Every contact is treated as an opportunity to gain information that enables more precise targeting of customers and value propositions.

In the full model we would have added two earlier states for an online business, first-time visitor and repeat visitor, during which intelligence is gathered concerning *potential* customers, leading to more rapid and valuable new customer acquisition with less churn.

SALES VALUE

So pleased is the now RC that you are able to *cross-sell* them related items, such as a desk pen holder and some storage boxes for filing, and *up-sell* some premium branded paper and pens. Cross- and up-sold items are generally higher value. When the RC transcends to LC, they buy all their office needs from you, including furniture and computer equipment. The key to winning LC is *trust*. Loyal customers actively seek your advice, want you to sell to them and need to believe that you will not shaft them.

CUSTOMER LIFE VALUE

Continued satisfaction results in more repeat customers becoming loyal. Whereas repeat customers can still churn (not shown) quite early, as soon as they see a better deal or have a one-off adverse experience, loyal customers are generally far more sticky; as long as you treat them properly. One of the key insights that these models provide is the leverage on value of building a loyal customer base, over focusing on acquiring new customers at great expense, who buy little and have a high churn rate. The effect of extending the customer life is to increase the overall customer value.

We have built many customer maturity models to work in combination with BI for both online and brick and mortar businesses, spanning a wide variety of sectors. Whilst the specific results and solutions to which they direct us are business-specific, the patterns are remarkably similar and share one central truth; the key to success in modern business is ownership of the customer through precise intelligence. This brings us to the BI solution.

Business Intelligence Solution

The dynamics model demonstrates that the key to growth is the rate at which customer intelligence can be collected and applied to target specific customers with well-matched value propositions. The rate at which customer information is gathered is represented in the model through the knowledge per contact and sale feeds. Again, these are different for each customer maturity level. For example, for a first-time sale, the information about the new customer may be basic, such as name, address, contact details and nature of sale. As the customer becomes a RC, there are increased opportunities to gather more valuable information concerning their age, profession and personal circumstances. Loyal customers trust you to give sound advice and fair deals and are quite prepared to share more intimate details which enable you to cement the relationship further. Amazon offers a prime example of the supreme power of customer intelligence, evidenced by the precision with which they are able to target offers.

Essence

The principal learning from this appendix is summarised below:

- BI manages and makes sense of large volumes of data which can be rolled up to the present the big picture or drilled down and across to interrogate the detail
- A primary purpose of BI is to provide a single source of truth comprising data with which the business can generate value; data quality and strong governance are critical
- BI solution architectures comprise essentially four key parts: source, cleaning, storage and applications
- Source refers to multiple, diverse raw data origins, often across many locations
- Cleaning involves making the data complete, correct and consistent by extracting, transforming and loading (ETL)
- Storage concerns organising clean data into multidimensional schemas which facilitates rapid access
- Applications slice, dice and drill the data into value creating information
- Business success is increasingly dependent on two prerequisites, managing large volumes of detailed data and simplifying causal complexity; which can be achieved through BI and dynamics modelling respectively
- BI and dynamics modelling can be integrated to provide high-leverage opportunities to create value where these two approaches meet

Appendix C:
Dynamic Performance Management

What is Dynamic Performance Management?

At the twentieth anniversary of the Gartner Symposium/ITxpo 2010,[1] analysts highlighted the top 10 technologies and trends that will be strategic for most organisations in 2011. Included on this list was next generation analytics. Quoting from their findings:

> *Increasing capabilities of computers, including mobile devices along with improving connectivity, are enabling a shift in how businesses support operational decisions. It is becoming possible to run simulations or models to predict the future outcome, rather than to simply provide backward-looking data about past interactions, and to do these predictions in real time to support each individual business action. Whilst this may require significant changes to existing operational and business intelligence infrastructure, the potential exists to unlock significant improvements in business results and other success rates.*

Dynamic performance management enables this advance through the integration of historical measurement using a single source of truth, provided by Business Intelligence (BI), and future predictive performance, based on dynamic cause and effect relationships, enabled by dynamics modelling.

> *Dynamic performance management provides both rear view mirror and windscreen views of the business.*

So far in the Appendices, we have added precision to the Value Management approach in two complementary ways. First, in Appendix A, we explored how qualitative cause and effect maps can be translated into quantitative dynamics models, which enable us to determine the relative leverage of possible actions. Secondly, in Appendix B, we introduced BI to acquire value creating knowledge, by analysing and summarising large volumes of clean, detailed data, the single source of truth. We then integrated dynamics modelling with BI to form powerful solutions, which combine predictive capability with complete, correct and consistent data. We now extend the integration of dynamics modelling and BI to provide dynamic performance management.

---

1   Gartner. 2010. Gartner Symposium/ITxpo, 17–21 October, Orlando, Florida. Available at: http://www.gartner.com/it/page.jsp?id=1454221, accessed 9 December 2010.

Correlation and Causation

Essentially there are two ways in which we can model causation, whether mentally or using analytical tools:

1. correlation: deriving cause by comparing data
2. causality: deriving cause by defining relationships

CORRELATION

Correlation involves observing apparent relationships between things or events to determine *potential* relationships between them. The strength of the relationship is called *significance*, and can be derived at a basic level using a spreadsheet or in a highly sophisticated way across massive datasets, using data mining algorithms. Correlation is powerful where there are adequate data to provide statistical significance, and a reliable premise with which to corroborate the link causally. For example, cholera was traced to water rather than air, as was originally believed, through statistical correlation of incidence of the disease with location. The analysis was influenced by the observation that the disease was most prevalent near the River Thames, which shifted the analysis. However, correlation can give the wrong answer if used blindly. For another example, there is strong statistical significance between the consumption of ice cream and increased levels of street crime, but banning ice cream sales will not make any difference to street crime. These kinds of correlation are co-incidental (in this instance they share the same driver, hot weather, so will appear together), but their relationship is not causal.

Correlation indicates potential causal links between factors through statistical significance.

The most powerful industry strength tool for a correlation approach is BI, using a single source of truth with data mining to identify the patterns, correlations and hidden relationships between diverse data sets. BI provides the means to add precision to value models through the analysis of large volumes of data. Taken to an extreme, BI can provide highly reliable predictive models. For example, predictive analytics can enable businesses which are particularly reliant on the relative size of user base, such as mobile network operators, to anticipate when an individual customer is likely to churn and, most importantly, offer the customer a precisely targeted proposition that is likely to keep them. Conversely, the technology will also lead the business to opportunities for cross- and up-selling services, for example to persuade customers to upgrade their handset and use applications (Apps), which are more profitable to the operator than voice or text messaging.

The effectiveness and value of BI is closely related to the degree to which underlying data are complete, correct and consistent. Data mining can provide very impressive results. For an apocryphal example, we need only consider how mining techniques in supermarket retailing revealed a correlation between the purchase of disposable nappies and beer on certain days, by a specific segment of customers. The cause was traced to fathers nipping in to buy nappies after work, and grabbing some cans of beer into the bargain. The practical response to this event-based marketing was to place nappies near the beer and the checkout, following the same principle as children and chocolate.

Although data mining can expose unexpected insights, BI is generally far more effective if analyses can be directed through robust causal hypotheses. This brings us to causality.

CAUSALITY

Causality, as we apply it in Value Management, is the reverse of correlation; defining the cause and effect relationships between factors from first principles. The causal approach is powerful where there is limited data but relationships between the data can be defined with reasonable precision. In this case, actual experience becomes invaluable. In causality, we are looking for broad patterns with which results can be reliably predicted.

The most powerful tools for a causal approach can be grouped under dynamics modelling, that is computer simulation, which we explored in Appendix A. There is much debate and contention about the superiority of BI or dynamics modelling. This is wasted energy, which serves only to obscure the massive value creating opportunity by integrating them; it is not an 'or' but an 'and' argument. In Value Management, we combine and complement the power of BI and dynamics modelling to reach that hitherto elusive goal, dynamic performance management.

Causality focuses on the precise definition of cause and effect relationships from first principles.

Causal Interrogation: What? And How?

Causal interrogation refers to the diagnosis and direction for corrective action of a problem and can be of value to the business in two, fundamental ways. First, it can diagnose true operational causes behind variances exposed in financial and other performance reports precisely and quickly, enabling rapid corrective action to avoid repeating the problem and further cost escalation. Secondly, it exposes repeating patterns, their underlying causes and the ineffectiveness of typical responses. Long-term solutions can be implemented, which not only prevent the problems from recurring, but release critical resources to focus on value adding activities, rather than fire fighting. When analysing any problem there are essentially two things we need to know:

1. What? The effect of the problem
2. How? The cause of the problem

BI works from bottom-up and top-down, as shown in Figure C.1. Working from the bottom, operational level data are summarised to provide the big picture; this is called *rolling up*. BI uses two mechanisms in this process, aggregation and consolidation. Aggregation is the mathematical summation of data through increasingly higher levels. For example, material costs are rolled up from operations, often through an Enterprise Resource Planning (ERP) solution, into summary accounts through management and executive levels. Consolidation is more complex, and involves introducing and/or eliminating data through the hierarchical levels. For example, a profit and loss report may include certain cost categories, such as depreciation, to satisfy particular accounting rules, which is not included in a cash flow report. These mechanisms are controlled through defined business rules.

Working from the top, BI enables *drilling down* from summary information to increasingly more detailed data, from which the high level data are derived. BI can analyse effects, i.e. *what?* using summary level data, and point to likely causes, i.e. *how?* by drilling down into more detailed data. In this way, BI can be used to pinpoint problems, diagnose them and direct activity to the most effective solution. For example, a summary level report would typically include revenues from all the sales territories, which might show underperformance in one or more areas. Drill down would then be used to interrogate how the adverse variances are made up and home into the specific sales functions that require corrective action, as shown by the drill path in Figure C.1. This same approach can be used to identify budget overspends.

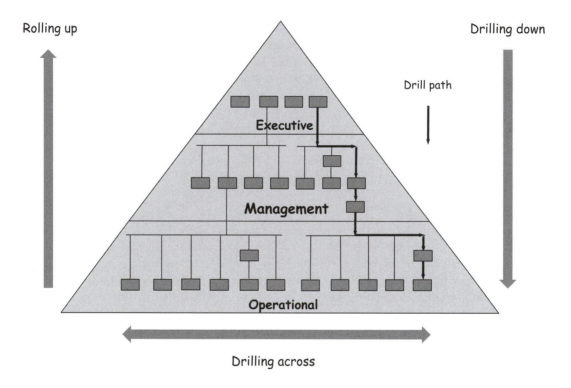

Figure C.1 Vertical drill paths

Most BI solutions *only* perform vertical interrogation by drilling down and across into increasingly more detailed levels of data to determine *what* specific area, product or person and so on is accountable for the parent-level value. From a causal point of view, this works well when the *what* points directly to the *how*, as in the above example. In other words, where there is only one causal thread and the subject of interrogation is the origin of the problem, vertical interrogation can infer operational causality, by narrowing the source of a given value to the point at which the cause can be found and resolved.

Vertical interrogation can also work for more complex operational problems. For example, in a manufacturing plant if scrap can be traced to a specific machine tool and operator, the likely cause, such as human error or incorrect tooling calibration, can be isolated and fixed. However, in many business situations the source of a problem will be remote from the subject of interrogation, as dictated by law of separation defined in Chapter 6, and multiple possible threads may need to be explored to determine the root cause. In these cases, detail does not necessarily indicate causation. In order to determine the cause, it will be necessary to drill *across* one or more data paths.

In real BI solutions, a myriad of potential drill paths can exist, too many to investigate all, so executives must guess at which would, in their experience, be most likely to be relevant. Often, the causes of complex problems are counter-intuitive and may lie in a department outside the knowledge of the enquiring executive, and therefore be overlooked. The following example, shown in Figure C.2, illustrates how causal drill across can complement standard BI vertical and horizontal drills to diagnose causes.

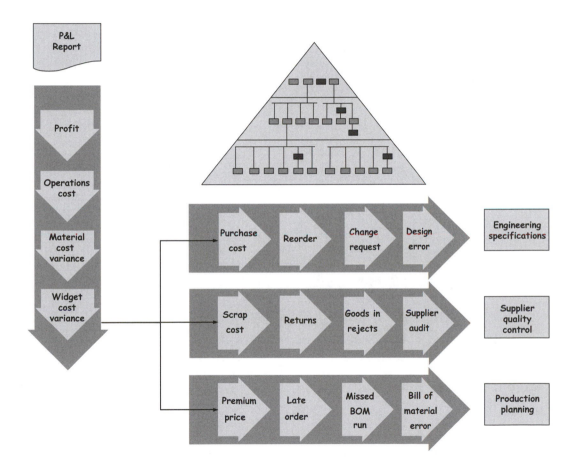

Figure C.2   Causal analysis

Suppose that we are investigating excessively high factory-cost variance. The specific elements contributing to the variance can be isolated by the assembly manager, using vertical drill-down and comparisons with best practice using horizontal drill-across. However, this does not necessarily explain *how* the higher than expected costs were caused operationally, at the *point of power* where a solution can be most effectively targeted. For instance, possible causes include over-purchase, premium prices or vendor issues, all of which are originated by a different department, and may neither be recognised nor addressed by the assembly manager, despite being the root cause of his problem. Over-purchase and premium prices could be due to poor scheduling in production planning. Vendor issues may be due to incorrect specification from engineering or quality of incoming goods.

Designing Business Intelligence for Causal Analysis

When designing a traditional BI solution, the linear drill paths (vertical drill-down/up and horizontal drill-across) are often designed into the star schemas. This is shown by the light grey cells in Figure C.3, in which we interrogate the procurement thread described in the previous example:

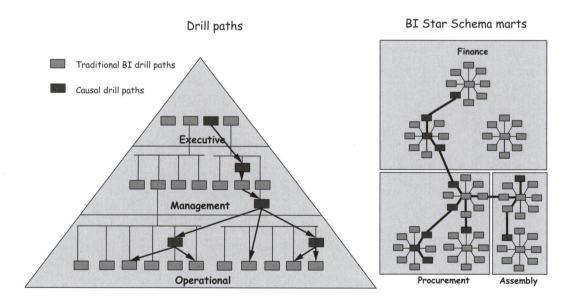

Figure C.3   Causal drill paths

For causal analysis, it is crucial to provide drills *between* data relating to entities across different, often apparently unconnected, business functions. Consequently, when designing for causal BI, a more flexible approach is necessary because causal cells may appear elsewhere in the hierarchies and may need to cross between other star schemas, as shown by the dark-grey cells in Figure C.3. This is achieved by linking dimensions in the stars which are at compatible levels, in which case the stars are said to be *federated*. This process is part of the Logical Data Model (LDM) design.

Relationship between Causal Interrogation and the Balanced Scorecard

BI provides the industry strength solution for populating a Balanced Scorecard through frequent, ideally real time, data refreshes derived from the single source of truth. In Chapter 8, in the context of business alignment, we advocated a causal cascade structure for the Balanced Scorecard, developed around themes. This means that data for the Balanced Scorecard must be sourced from across the entire organisation and, because of the dynamism of today's business environment, significant flexibility is needed to restructure themes. Therefore, it follows that the underlying BI solution must possess the flexibility to accommodate these changes, and this adaptability is provided by a BI solution designed for causal analysis, as described above.

Governance Cycle: Past, Present and Future

Under dynamic performance management, the business as usual governance cycle is transformed by executive teams combining a BI driven Balanced Scorecard with dynamics modelling, as shown in Figure C.4.

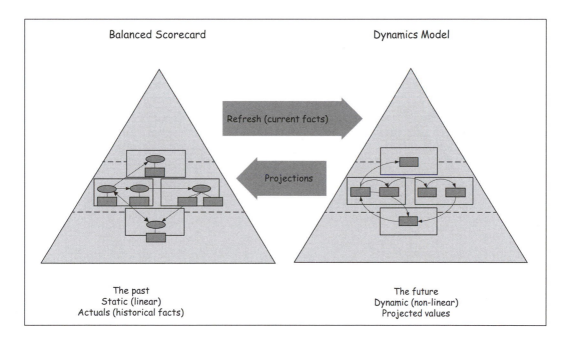

Figure C.4   Dynamic performance management

The monthly board meeting starts with a review of business performance using the Balanced Scorecard, which has been populated by the BI solution and is, therefore, demonstrably accurate. From the scorecard, they can readily see where performance is on target and identify any issues. They can slice, dice and drill from the scorecard into the underlying BI solution, including causal drills, quickly identifying those areas that are causing the issues.

They then use the dynamics model, which has been automatically or semi-automatically populated from the BI solution, in conjunction with the Balanced Scorecard. The model allows them to explore underlying causes of issues dynamically, and to simulate the outcomes of various initiatives that board members submit for review. This is a very effective approach, because all board members, together in one room, can see the short-, medium- and long-term impact of proposed initiatives, across all parts of their business.

Where board members agree to a proposed initiative, the programme will be formally sanctioned and its projected driver and outcome values, derived from the dynamics model, duly linked back into the Balanced Scorecard to reflect the changes. It is important to reiterate that programmes relate to all initiatives, spanning operational improvements to major capital investments. In future months, the board uses the Balanced Scorecard to *track* the steady state business performance, and compare the results with and without the initiative, in order to evaluate how successful this initiative is as it rolls out.

To summarise, the board uses the Balanced Scorecard to evaluate the past (using drills into the detailed BI solution where appropriate, for example compared with the past five years) and to highlight current issues. They then use the dynamics model to gain deeper causal insight about the issues, and run hypothetical 'what if' scenarios to identify the best course of remedial action. In future months, they will use the Balanced Scorecard and BI solution to track whether the remedial action has set them back on target, viewing performance both with and without the remedial initiative to quantify its effectiveness.

The integrated BI and dynamics modelling approach is new and innovative, but so far, the feedback from the clients who have implemented this is strongly positive. They feel that it has made a vast improvement to their business outcomes, largely because of an increased level of coherence between board members, as they jointly explore the impact that issues and proposed remedial actions will have across all aspects of their business, not just their own departments. They also report new confidence in making bigger changes, because outcomes from smaller changes have proved to be as predicted by their 'what if' scenarios. So, having initially eaten the 'low-hanging fruit' to optimise their business, they have then felt confident to make the more strategic changes that are necessary to achieve a step change in performance.

Proof of Concept

Finally, it is appropriate to discuss the most successful approach for implementing dynamic performance management quickly and with containable risk. Large and complex businesses, with vast amounts of operational data, will require industrial-strength BI solutions, with strong governance to ensure data integrity. Typically, detailed operational data are provided through Enterprise Resource Planning (ERP), stored in an enterprise data warehouse, incorporating business rules for aggregating and consolidating the data, from which it is processed into information through reporting and other applications. These components may be provided by different software vendors and system integrated through industry standards, or supplied by a single vendor.

The design and implementation of a BI solution requires very significant investment and the resulting applications are not tolerant of changes. Consequently, great effort must be devoted to defining requirements and design phases, in order to avoid expensive and time-consuming modifications. Conversely, it can be difficult to anticipate all queries and reports that may be needed. This is where dynamics modelling comes in. BI and dynamics modelling operate in diametrically opposite ways. Whereas BI creates information and determines knowledgeable insights through manipulation of detailed data with simple hierarchical links, dynamics modelling works with minimal data but using precise causal relationships.

This difference is mirrored in the ease of development and change. Once the techniques outlined in this book are mastered, dynamics models can be developed very quickly, sometimes within a few hours, and even during interactive workshops. Because the models are constructed using graphical elements, the design is more transparent and changes that represent major structural changes in BI can be made very easily and quickly.

The important point is that dynamics modelling is a powerful tool for developing requirements for industry-strength BI solutions. The emphasis is rapid, time-boxed development of models against clear modelling outcomes, such as definition of KPIs to be used in a corporate Balanced Scorecard. We refer to this approach as Proof of Concept (PoC). Whilst PoC models contain limited detail, logical and mathematical integrity is *never* compromised and models are tested exhaustively, that is to destruction, in order to ensure that results can be relied upon.

PoC models have not only been highly valuable in supporting the BI business requirements definition stage, but have also saved effort, time and cost in the BI architecture design stage, because the requirements have become stable during the PoC modelling stage. Dynamics modelling tools support this transition by providing a range of input controls and results displays. In almost all cases, the PoC model proves so useful that clients request that they be enhanced for operational use, as a 'what if' scenario modelling tool. For example, a major retail client continued to use a PoC Balanced Scorecard for over two years as the key business performance solution in monthly board reviews. The key to an effective PoC is using tools that support precise simplicity.

Essence

- BI excels in correlation which indicates potential causal relationships between factors through statistical significance in large historical data sets
- The capacity for BI to reveal value creating insights is greatly enhanced if analytic interrogation is directed through validated causal hypotheses
- Dynamics modelling promotes the precise definition of cause and effect from first principles and provides validation by calibrating against known historical outcomes and simulating multiple future scenarios
- Dynamic performance management enables delivery of business value through the integration of historical measurement, using a single source of truth and predictive analytics facilitated through BI, and future predicted performance based on validated causal relationships provided by dynamics modelling

- The most cost effective approach to getting fast, low-risk results from dynamic performance management is to use a Proof of Concept (PoC) implementation which delivers early returns and hones the requirements for an industry-strength solution
- Key to effective PoC implementations is the use of tools which support the causal approach and enable dynamic 'what-if' modelling in which the effects of changes are quantified dynamically

This brings us to the Value Management Toolset™.

Value Management Toolset™

Traditionally, business case development is a time-consuming and costly exercise, often taking several months to complete. Apart from the time and cost, our experience is that the resulting analyses are often very superficial, relying on vague and optimistic assumptions, and against which it is difficult to track the realisation of programme value.

The approach to Value Management described in this book seeks to reverse this pattern by providing the means to build baseline business cases very quickly, supported by precise, simple and transparent quantification, thereby being fully auditable for subsequent value realisation. The Value Management Toolset™ (Toolset) is a PC-based application, built in Microsoft Excel and Project, designed to fulfil this imperative, and is particularly suited to building Proof of Concept (PoC) solutions, as described in Appendix C.

The Toolset provides a dynamic linkage between the programme plan and the DCF analysis, allowing 'what if' modelling of any number of scenarios, involving both magnitude and timing changes of programme benefits and costs. The Toolset comprises five modules, as shown in Figure T1 and outlined below.

Value Management Toolset™

1. Components module: the central repository containing elements used to build the benefits in the business case including: deliverables, drivers and benefits, together with stakeholders and beneficiaries. This module is linked to the Balanced Scorecard, another toolset within the Value Suite for PoC fast starts, in order to ensure consistency in developing the baseline business case and subsequent value realisation. For example, the drivers defined in the Balanced Scorecard are used for deriving the causal connection between phases and net present value (NPV) in the Toolset.
2. Programme module (top window): contains the high level plan comprising key phases of the programme.
3. Programme benefits module: attributes changes in drivers and benefits to programme phases through the cause and effect linkage process.
4. Programme costs module: attributes development and support costs to programme phases.
5. Results module: combines programme benefits and costs to derive the NPV. This module includes a certainty analysis screen in which any number or variables can be flexed, either individually or in combination, to facilitate 'what if' modelling and destruction testing.

The programme phases are linked dynamically to both programme benefits and costs so that the effects on value of changes are calculated automatically. For example, in Figure T2, the first phase of the JANET (UK) transformation programme is extended by 1 year resulting in a 29 per cent reduction in the NPV against the baseline, shown in the graph. Numerous magnitude and timing changes can be modelled using the certainty analysis screen. (Values in the figure have been modified for confidentiality purposes.)

Certainty Analysis using the Value Management Toolset™

The Toolset provides support throughout the IMPACT framework described in this book. Due to its simplicity of use, the Toolset can be populated and applied interactively during value breakthrough workshops, during which the potential value of prospective strategies and delivery programmes can be modelled immediately. Keys to success in the workshops are business knowledge, high energy and speed. For example, the initial business case and implementation strategy for the JANET business transformation programme were both completed in four hours of intensive workshop with the Operations Director.

The Toolset is used in parallel and interactively with the Balanced Scorecard, first to derive the baseline business case, and then through the subsequent value realisation stage, during which actual outcomes are tracked, compared and corrected against the baseline. The impact of changes can be assessed and corrective action targeted, timed and aligned most effectively. The Toolset has been used successfully at all levels, spanning tactical projects and business as usual improvement initiatives, strategic programmes and enterprise portfolios.

Website

Impact Dynamics Limited. *Value Management Toolset™* www.impactdynamics.co.uk.

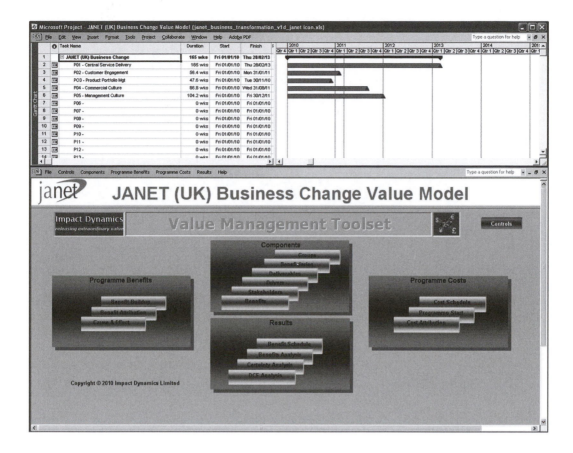

Figure T1   The Value Management Toolset™

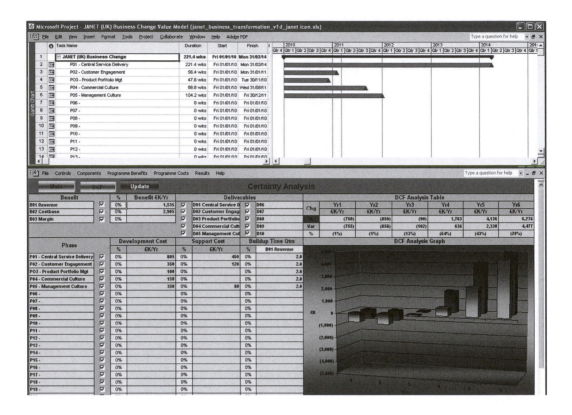

Figure T2   Certainty analysis using the Value Management Toolset™

Glossary of Terms

Term, (abbreviation), aliases	Definition	Elaboration/application
Activity	A task or piece of work	Activities can be part of a process, project or programme
Activity-Based Cost Management (ABC/M)	Method of costing using drivers to assign costs using activities and the means to influence the drivers	ABC/M principles are used to provide precise causal linkage between programme deliverables, drivers and benefits
Balanced scorecard (BSC)	A performance management framework built around stakeholder views, called perspectives	This is divided into four perspectives, also called quadrants: financial, customers, process, resources; process and resources are also called internal and learning and growth respectively
Baseline	Approved intended measure of performance	Datum against which actual performance is compared to ensure that the intended change is achieved
Baseline business case	Approved business case with a defined baseline	Key output from, and name of, the first stage of the IMPACT Value Management framework
Beneficiaries *driver owners*	People who will experience a measurable change in a driver	Beneficiaries are at the point of power, where a change in drivers enabled by programme deliverables takes place; drivers are owned by beneficiaries
Benefit *outcome lag indicator, lag measure*	A measurable outcome as perceived by a stakeholder	Although intentionally positive, benefits can be negative, for example a reduced service level to customers as a result of cost-cutting; benefits are owned by stakeholders, who are generally represented by key people within the business
Benefits profile *bangs per buck*	Attribution of benefits across one or more dimensions, for example deliverables, drivers, stakeholders and so on	Most effectively presented as multidimensional charts which provide an instant clear picture of the relative contributions to benefits
Business *organisation*	Organisation which converts inputs into outputs intended to be of positive benefit to stakeholders	Used generically to include commercial, public sector and not-for-profit organisations
Business as usual (BAU) *operations*	Day-to-day operations of an organisation	BAU processes and activities are the point of power where benefits are caused and sustained by changes in drivers

Term, (abbreviation), aliases	Definition	Elaboration/application
Business case	Document used to justify investment in change	Includes an implementation strategy with explicit linkage between programme phases and a financial DCF analysis
Business Intelligence (BI)	BI concerns transformation of operational data into decision relevant knowledge	BI is important for Value Management by providing a single source of truth from which to measure and direct performance and predictive analytics
Business model	Essential means by which a business is sustained by delivering value to stakeholders	A useful starting point for defining a business model is the value chain
Business scope	Degree to which capabilities, enabled by each deliverable, are implemented within the business, in terms of value	For example, full functionality is implemented within selected business departments
Capability scope	Degree to which capabilities, enabled by each deliverable, are implemented, in terms of value	For example, partial functionality is implemented across the entire business
Capacity	Measure of ability to deliver intended stakeholder outcomes	It is important to relate capacity not only to outputs but also to outcomes, that is benefits, that the outputs are intended to deliver
Causal loop diagrams	Diagrammatic representation of one or more feedback loops, and their interaction	Valuable for isolating specific feedback loops in a complex map or model; also for validation and testing purposes
Causal trees	Causal loop diagrams presented in tree format	Often easier for people to follow, and used to select key drivers for the cause and effect linkage and trace themes in the strategy map
Causation	Explicit cause and effect relationship between objects	Derived from a precise definition of the relationship between objects, which represents true causation and can be non-linear
Cause and effect linkage	Explicit, quantified relationships between deliverables, drivers and benefits	Most importantly, quantifies benefits attributable to each deliverable
Cause and effect map	Qualitative definition of true casual relationships between drivers and benefits	Usually structured using Balanced Scorecard perspectives and includes feedback loops
Certainty	Probability that intended value will be delivered	Used to address the question, 'What would we have to do to be certain that intended value is delivered?
Certainty management	Mindset and process of ensuring that intended outcomes are delivered	Used in combination with risk management to provide a 'failure is not an option' focus on delivering value

Term, (abbreviation), *aliases*	Definition	Elaboration/application
Complex adaptive systems (CAS)	Groups whose behaviour is governed by complexity, in particular self-organisation	Important for modelling highly interactive behaviour such as customers in a social media environment
Complexity theory	Set of concepts that attempts to explain complex phenomenon not explainable by traditional (deterministic) theories	Encompasses still developing new systemic sciences which, while being non-deterministic, can provide useful insights and applications in business, if used with great caution
Compliance matrix	A document used to ensure that all requirements have been included and met	Usually a table which maps the means by which requirements are met in the design (verification) and the means by which they are proved to be met through testing (validation)
Correlation	Implied cause and effect relationship between objects	Derived from statistical significance between object behaviours, which may or may not be true causation
Customer relationship management (CRM)	Strategy for managing a company's interactions with customers, clients and sales prospects	The overall goals are to find, attract, and win new clients, nurture and retain those the company already has, entice former clients back into the fold, and reduce the costs of marketing and client service
Deliverable *new business capability, programme product*	High-level programme product which enables new, or releases latent, business capability that causes a change in one or more drivers	Deliverables can cause changes in drivers, either directly or by enabling other deliverables; in which case they are reflected as dependencies between programme phases
Dependence: functional dependence	Operational order in which phases are naturally done	For example, the wall of a house must be completed before fitting the roof
Dependence: value dependence	Structure and sequence of phases which result in the greatest value	For example, high-value houses on a building plot could be finished first, in order to release an early revenue stream; whilst respecting functional dependence, for example completing the drains servicing those houses
Discounted cash flow (DCF)	Investment appraisal technique which takes into account the time value of money	There are essentially two DCF approaches: net present value (NPV) and internal rate of return (IRR) or yield
Double-loop control	Process by which both purpose and means to achieve the purpose are ensured	In Value Management, purpose is concerned with benefits (outcomes) and the means relates to new business capabilities enabled through the deliverables
Driver *performance driver, lead indicator, lead measure*	Measurable factor in the business which, when changed, may cause benefits	Drivers can cause benefits either directly, or by causing changes in other drivers in a cause and effect chain that results in benefits; in practice drivers will include outputs, factors that link inputs to outputs and factors that link outputs to outcomes

Term, (abbreviation), *aliases*	Definition	Elaboration/application
Dynamic performance management	Highly responsive diagnosis, prognosis and corrective action, ideally in real time	Two prerequisites are single source of truth and predictive dynamics modelling, providing both rear view mirror and windscreen views of performance
Feedback loop	Circular causal chain in which outputs become inputs	There are two types of feedback loop: reinforcing and balancing
Feedback loop: balancing	Feedback loop in which at least one item works in the opposite direction	Results in correction or overcorrection towards an intended or system-driven goal, often through oscillation; important for control
Feedback loop: reinforcing	Feedback loop in which all items work in the same direction	Results in either virtuous or vicious circles; important for growth
Governance	Relates to decisions that define expectations, grant power, or verify performance	A key aspect of governance for Value Management is ownership of deliverables, drivers and benefits, together with partnership between the respective owners
Implementation strategy	Programme design in which the structure and sequence of phases are optimised in order to maximise overall value	Programme value alignment is the process used to develop an implementation strategy and comprises two parts: magnitude value alignment and timing value alignment
Input, *resource, cost*	Resource consumed in or enabling the conversion of inputs into outputs, measured as cost	Inputs may or may not result in intended outputs; strictly speaking cost and resources are not the same thing, but this simplification holds for most practical purposes
Key performance indicator (KPI)	Measures in the Balanced Scorecard with most strategic significance	KPIs comprise both lead indicators and lag indicators that have a clear causal link to the business vision
Leverage	Large effects from small causes	Critically important in developing solutions that deliver more for less
Linear thinking	Thinking in straight lines and proportional cause and effect	Representation of reality in which causality operates in one direction and effects are directly proportional to causes
Measure	Specific factor against which a value can be assigned	In the Balanced Scorecard, measure values are used to derive measure scores and rolled up into objective scores; measures can be lead or lag indicators
Mental model	Worldview held by an individual or group	A mental model is an internal representation of reality filtered by distortions, generalisations and deletions
Mission	Purpose for the business being in existence	Mission defines the why?
Objective	What must be achieved in order to realise the vision	Expressed in an action context in the Balanced Scorecard, for example innovate premium products, scored from underlying measures, rolled up into perspectives and linked into themes

Term, (abbreviation), *aliases*	Definition	Elaboration/application
Output	The product or service from a business, process or programme	Outputs may or may not result in intended stakeholder outcomes, that is benefits, and can be undesirable, for example emissions from a factory
Point of power	Function and/or person within the business at which benefits are caused	Normally refers to the function at which drivers are changed, as a result of deliverables, and cause benefits
Portfolio	Totality of initiatives within the business	Managed as a coherent whole, in order to optimise overall value, usually under a programme support office (PSO)
Predictive modelling	Techniques enabling prediction of future outcomes	This is most important and challenging when the past cannot be relied upon to determine the future
Programme	Combination of initiatives focusing on value delivery to stakeholders	Programmes focus on benefits, enabled by deliverables, and normally comprise multiple projects with interdependencies between them; spanning operational improvements to major capital investments
Programme risk dynamics	Analysis of the impact of changes on programme NPV	Effects on NPV result from magnitude and timing changes in programme costs and benefits
Programme support office (PSO)	Organisation providing support services for managing a programme or portfolio	Often, the PSO maintains the Balanced Scorecard, for example collating input data, particularly during implementation
Project	Initiative with a start, do something and finish	Projects tend to focus on outputs, but can have a business case in their own right
Redundancy, Essential	Spare capacity needed to account for variations, whilst ensuring delivery of intended outcomes	Removal of essential redundancy will reduce delivery of intended outcomes; it must not be confused with waste
Risk	Exposure of intended value to threats	Risk is quantified by the product of the probability that a defined threat will materialise and the impact if it does
Risk management	Process of avoiding and preparing for threats to delivery of value	Risk management involves anticipating, assessing, mitigating against and dealing with manifestation of risk
Risk register, *causal risk register*	Document for defining and monitoring the most significant programme risks	Exposure is calculated as the product of probability that a risk will happen and the impact if it does, ideally quantified as real measures determined through modelling
Single source of truth	Complete, correct and consistent data	Enables a true picture, from which past and present performance can be derived
Stakeholder, *benefit owner*	Individual or group that has an interest in or is affected by the outcomes of the business	Stakeholders are recipients and owners of benefits; in practice external stakeholders, such as customers, are represented by accountable people within the business

Term, (abbreviation), *aliases*	Definition	Elaboration/application
State transition	Representation of a real-world object in terms of its state, at any point in time, and its transition from one state to another	A generic representation which is important for dynamics modelling
Storyline	Cause and effect linkage between a deliverable, driver and benefit	Reads as a story and includes a calculation used for developing the cause and effect linkage
Strategy map	Balanced scorecard view in which objectives are linked in chains of cause and effect	Used to develop business strategy and forms the basis for selecting the most critical measures for inclusion in the Balanced Scorecard to achieve the vision
Systems thinking	Thinking in causal loops which produce effects that can be disproportionate with causes	Value Management uses the deterministic representation, in which causality operates in feedback loops, and small causes can have large effects
Target operating model (TOM), *blueprint*	Precise definition of the intended business architecture, deemed necessary for achievement of the vision	Comprises three levels: business, operational and technology, which must be integrated to be effective
Theme, *strategic theme*	Chain of cause and effect linking objectives to financial outcomes in the Balanced Scorecard	For dynamics modelling, also used to link measures underlying the objectives using causal relationships derived from the cause and effect map
Validation	Ensuring that the outputs operate as intended; doing the right things	Involves test scripts, which exercises each requirement against specification; in Value Management, validation is extended to encompass outcomes
Value	Degree to which benefits exceed the costs from a specific stakeholder perception	This definition provides a foundation for the value and value for money equations
Value assurance	Process of ensuring that intended value is delivered	Integrates risk and certainty management
Value chain	Sequence of essential high-level activities through which the business creates value	The value chain provides a foundation for building a strategy map
Value equation	Value = benefits − costs Value = outcomes − inputs	This provides an absolute measure of value
Value for money (VfM) *value quotient*	VfM = benefits/costs VfM = outcomes/inputs VfM = effectiveness × efficiency	This presents the value equation as a ratio of benefits in relation to costs, and is useful for public sector and not-for-profit businesses which do not have revenue streams
Value magnitude alignment	Targets the greatest size of programme benefits in relation to programme costs	Comprises two dimensions, capability scope and business scope

Term, (abbreviation), *aliases*	Definition	Elaboration/application
Value realisation plan, *benefits realisation plan*	Principal control document for ensuring that intended value is delivered during and post implementation of the programme	Includes three parts: deliverables tracking, benefits tracking and value tracking
Value testing	Testing the value of a programme to destruction	Comprises four types of analyses, all of which exercise programme value to extremes: sensitivity, risk, scenario and user, to determine bounds of certainty
Value timing alignment	Optimises the structure and sequence of programme Phases to maximise value	Comprises two dimensions: phase structure and phase sequence
Verification	Ensuring that requirements are incorporated within the programme; doing things right	Involves a compliance matrix which maps how requirements are implemented in the design and tested; in Value Management, verification is extended to encompass outcomes
Vision	Intended destination of the business, and timescale for achieving it	Vision defines the where? and when?
Waste	Capacity engaged in nugatory, duplicated or corrected work, together with managing this waste	Waste consumes resources and if removed results in both reduced cost and increased delivery of intended outcomes; must not be confused with essential redundancy

Bibliography

Business Performance Management: Balanced Scorecard, Strategy Maps, Business Design

Bourne, M., Bourne, P. 2000. *Understanding the Balanced Scorecard in a Week*. London: Hodder & Stoughton.

Coveney, M., Ganster, D., Hartlen, B., King, D. 2003. *The Strategy Gap: Levering Technology to Execute Winning Strategies*. Hoboken, USA: Wiley.

Drucker, P. 1993. *The Effective Executive: The Definitive Guide to Getting the Right Things Done*. New York, USA: HarperBusiness Essentials.

Hope, T., Hope, J. 1996. *Transforming the Bottom Line. Managing Performance with the Real Numbers*. London: Nicholas Brealey.

Kaplan, R., Norton, D. 1996. *The Balanced Scorecard: Translating Strategy into Action*. Boston, USA: HBS Press.

Kaplan, R., Norton, D. 2001. *The Strategy Focused Organisation: How Balanced Scorecard Companies Thrive in the New Business Environment*. Boston, USA: HBS Press.

Kaplan, R., Norton, D. 2004. *Strategy Maps: Converting Intangible Assets into Tangible Outcomes*. Boston, USA: HBS Press.

Kaplan, R., Norton, D. 2006. *Alignment: Using the Balanced Scorecard to Create Corporate Synergies*. Boston, USA: HBS Press.

Kaplan, R., Norton, D. 2008. *The Execution Premium: Linking Strategy to Operations for Competitive Advantages*. Boston, USA: HBS Press.

Meyer, M. 2009. *Rethinking Performance Measurement: Beyond the Balanced Scorecard*. New York, USA: Cambridge University Press.

Neely, A.. 1998. *Measuring Business Performance: Why, What and How*. London: Profile Books.

Niven, P. 2002. *Balanced Scorecard Step-by-step: Maximizing Performance and Maintaining Results*. New York, USA: Wiley.

Olve, N., Roy, J., Wetter, M. 1999. *Performance Drivers: A Practical Guide to the Balanced Scorecard*. Chichester: Wiley.

Person, R. 2009. *Balanced Scorecards and Operational Dashboards with Microsoft® Excel®*. Indianapolis, USA: Wiley.

Phelps, B. 2004. *Smart Business Metrics: Measure what Really Counts and Manage what Makes the Difference*. Harlow: Pearson.

Schumacher, E. 1973. *Small is Beautiful: A Study of Economics as if People Mattered*. London: Blond and Briggs.

Slywotzky, A. 2002. *The Art of Profitability*. New York, USA: Warner.

Slywotzky, A., Morrison, D. 1997. *The Profit Zone: How Strategic Business Design will Lead You to Tomorrow's Profits*. Chichester: Wiley.

Slywotzky, A., Morrison, D. 1999. *Profit Patterns: 30 Ways to Anticipate and Profit from Strategic Forces Reshaping Your Business*. Chichester: Wiley.

Slywotzky, A., Wise, R. 2003. *How to Grow When Markets Don't*. New York, USA: Warner.

Treacy, M., Wiersema, F. 1995. *The Discipline of Market Leaders*. London: HarperCollins.

Financial Management: Investment Appraisal, Activity-Based Costing, Shareholder Value

Arnold, J., Turley, S. 1996. *Accounting for Management Decisions*. Third Edition. Hemel Hempstead: Prentice Hall.

Bennett, S. G. 1991. *The Quest for Value*. New York, USA: HarperCollins.

Black, A., Wright, P., Davies, J. 2001. *In Search of Shareholder Value*. Harlow: Pearson.

Botzel, S., Schwilling, A. 1999. *Managing for Value*. Oxford: Capstone.

Cokins, G. 2001. *Activity-Based Cost Management: An Executives Guide*. New York, USA: Wiley.

Cokins, G., Stratton, A., Helbling, J. 1992. *An ABC Managers Primer*. Montvale, USA: Institute of Management Accountants.

Cox, D. 2005. *Business Accounts*. Third Edition. Worcester: Osbourne.

Drury, C. 1995. *Management and Cost Accounting*. Third Edition. London: Chapman & Hall.

Kaplan, R., Norton, D. 1998. *Cost and Effect: Using Integrated Cost Systems to Drive Profitability and Performance*. Boston, USA: HBS Press.

Mabberley, J. 1993. *Activity-Based Costing in Financial Institutions*. London: Pitman.

Moore, G. 2000. *Living on the Fault Line: Managing for Shareholder Value in the Age of the Internet*. New York, USA: HarperCollins.

Rice, A. 2003. *Accounts Demystified*. Fourth Edition. Harlow: Pearson.

Rutterford, J. 1998. *Financial Strategy: Adding Shareholder Value*. Chichester: Wiley.

Sizer, J. 1978. *An Insight Into Management Accounting*. London: Penguin.

Smith, T. 1996. *Accounting for Growth*. Second Edition. London: Century.

Thuesen, H., Fabrycky, W., Thuesen, G. 1971. *Engineering Economy*. Fourth Edition. Englewood Cliffs, USA: Prentice-Hall.

Turney, P. 1992. *Common Cents: The ABC Performance Breakthrough*. Portland, USA: Cost Technology.

Wileman, A. 2010. *Driving Down Cost: How to Manage and Cut Costs – Intelligently*. London: Nicholas Brealey.

Walsh, C. 2003. *Key Management Ratios*. Third Edition. Harlow: Pearson.

Warner, A. 1993. *The Bottom Line: Practical Financial Knowledge for Managers*. Aldershot: Gower.

Yunus, M. 2007. *Creating a World Without Poverty: Social Business and the Future of Capitalism*. Philadelphia, USA: Perseus Books.

Delivering Value through Process: Process Re-engineering, Quality and Waste

Bank, J. 1992. *The Essence of Total Quality Management*. Hemel Hempstead: Prentice Hall.

Brown, S. 2000. *Manufacturing the Future: Strategic Resonance for Enlightened Manufacturing*. Harlow: Pearson.

Champy, J. 1995. *Reengineering Management: The Mandate for New Leadership*. London: HarperCollins.

Craig, D. 2005. *Rip-Off! The Scandalous Inside Story of the Management Consultancy Money Machine*. London: Original Book Company.

Craig, D. 2008. *Squandered: How Gordon Brown is Wasting Over One Trillion Pounds of our Money*. London: Constable.

Craig, D. 2006. *Plundering the Public Sector: How New Labour are Letting Consultants Run off with £70 Billion of our Money*. London: Constable.

Dutta, S., Manzoni, J., INSEAD.1999. *Process Re-engineering, Organisational Change and Performance Improvement*. Maidenhead: McGraw-Hill.

Elliott, M., Rotherham, L. 2007. *The Bumper Book of Government Waste: Brown's Squandered Millions*. Petersfield: Harriman House.

Hammer, M. 1990. Reengineering work: don't automate, obliterate. *Harvard Business Review*, July–August, 68(4): 104–112.

Hammer, M., Champy, J. 1993. *Reengineering the Corporation: A Manifesto for Business Revolution*. London: Nicholas Brealey.

Harrington, H. J. 1991. *Business Process Improvement*. New York, USA: McGraw-Hill.

Howe, R., Gaeddert, D., Howe, M. 1993. *Quality on Trial*. Maidenhead: McGraw-Hill.

Goldratt, E., Cox, J. 1989. *The Goal*. Revised Edition. Aldershot: Gower.

Lepore, D., Cohen, O. 1999. *Deming and Goldratt: The Theory of Constraints and the System of Profound Knowledge*. Great Barrington, USA: North River Press.

Lewis, W. 2004. *The Power of Productivity: Wealth, Poverty and the Threat to Global Stability*. Chicago, USA: University of Chicago Press.

Oakland, J. 1990. *Total Quality Management*. Oxford: Heinemann.

Pande, P., Neuman, R., Cavanagh, R. 2000. *The Six Sigma Way*. New York, USA: McGraw-Hill.

Porter, M. 1985. *Competitive Advantage: Creating and Sustaining Superior Performance*. New York, USA: Free Press.

Scheinkopf, L. 1999. *Thinking for a Change: Putting the TOC Thinking Processes to Use*. Boca Raton, USA: CRC Press LLC.

Schroeder, R. 1993. *Operations Management: Decision Making in the Operation Function*. Fourth Edition. New York, USA: McGraw-Hill.

Spenley, P. 1992. *World Class Performance Through Total Quality: A Practical Guide to Implementation*. London: Chapman & Hall.

Zinkgraf, S. 2006. *Six Sigma: The First 90 Days*. Upper Saddle River, USA: Pearson.

Delivering Value through Programmes: Programme Management, Benefits and Risk Management, Value of Information Technology

Benko, C., McFarlan, F. 2003. *Connecting the Dots: Aligning Projects with Objectives in Unpredictable Times*. Boston, USA: HBS Press.

Bradley, G. 2010. *Benefit Realisation Management: A Practical Guide to Achieving Benefits Through Change*. Second Edition. Farnham: Gower.

Curley, M. 2007. *Managing Information Technology for Business Value*. Hillsboro, USA: Intel Press.

Fowler, A., Lock, D. 2006. *Accelerating Business and IT Change: Transforming Project Delivery*. Aldershot: Gower.

Jenner, S. 2009. *Realising Benefits from Government ICT Investment: A Fool's Errand?* Reading: Academic Publishing International.

Jenner, S. 2010. *Transforming Government and Public Services: Realising Benefits through Project Portfolio Management*. Farnham: Gower.

OGC. 2007. *Managing Successful Programmes MSP™*. Norwich: The Stationery Office.

OGC. 2008. *Portfolio, Programme and Project Offices P3O®*. Norwich: The Stationery Office.

OGC. 2009. *Managing Successful Projects with PRINCE 2™ Manual*. 2009 Edition. Norwich: The Stationery Office.

OGC. 2010. *Management of Value MoV™*. Norwich: The Stationery Office.

OGC. 2010. *Management of Risk M_o_R®: Guidance for Practitioners Book*. Third Edition. Norwich: The Stationery Office.

Remenyi, D. 1999. *IT Investment: Making a Business Case*. Oxford: Butterworth-Heinemann.

Sessions, R. 2009. Cost of IT failure: what does IT failure cost us annually? Available at http://simplearchitectures.blogspot.com/2009/09/cost-of-it-failure.html. Accessed 20 December 2010.

Strassmann, P. 1990. *The Business Value of Computers: An Executives Guide*. New Canaan, USA: Information Economics Press.

Strassmann, P. 1997. *The Squandered Computer: Evaluating the Business Alignment of Information Technologies*. New Canaan, USA: Information Economics Press.

Strassmann, P. 2001. Technology and the bottom line – making the connection. Butler Group conference and exhibition, Marriott Hotel, Heathrow, 20–21 June 2001, conference paper.

Strassmann, P. 2005. IT spending as a measure of organizational disorder. Available at http://www.archive.org/details/I.t.SpendingAsAMeasureOfOrganizationalDisorder. Accessed 25 November 2010.

Thiry, M. 2010. *Program Management: Fundamentals of Project Management*. Farnham: Gower.

Thorp, J. 2003. *The Information Paradox: Realizing the Business Benefits of Information Technology*. Whitby, Canada: McGraw-Hill.

The Stationery Office. 2010. *The Green Book: Appraisal and Evaluation in Central Government*. Available at http://www.hm-treasury.gov.uk/d/green_book_complete.pdf. Accessed 31 December 2010.

Uyttewaal, E. 2005. *Dynamic Scheduling with Microsoft Office Project 2003*. Boca Raton, USA: J. Ross Publishing.

Ward, J., Daniel, E. 2006. *Benefits Management: Delivering Value from IS and IT Investments*. Chichester: Wiley.

Webb, A. 2003. *Using Earned Value: A Project Manager's Guide*. Aldershot: Gower.

Willcocks, L., Graeser, V. 2001. *Delivering IT and e-Business Value*. Oxford: Butterworth-Heinemann.

Williams, D., Parr, T. 2004. *Enterprise Programme Management: Delivering Value*. Basingstoke: Palgrave Macmillan.

Winston, W. 1995. *Simulation Modelling Using @RISK*. Belmont, USA: Duxbury Press.

Cause and Effect: Complexity and Chaos, Economic Shifts, Systems Thinking

Ashby, R. 1976. *Introduction to Cybernetics*. London: University Paperbacks.

Axelrod, R. 1990. *The Evolution of Co-operation*. London: Penguin.

Axelrod, R. 1997. *The Complexity of Cooperation: Agent-Based Models of Competition and Collaboration*. Princeton, USA: Princeton University Press.

Casti, J. 1994. *Compelxification: Explaining a Paradoxical World Through the Science of Surprise*. New York, USA: HarperCollins.

Checkland, P. 1999. *Systems Thinking, Systems Practice*. Chichester: Wiley.

Flood, R. 2006. *Rethinking the Fifth Discipline: Learning within the Unknowable*. Abingdon: Routledge.

Gladwell, M. 2000. *The Tipping Point: How Little Things can Make a Big Difference*. London: Abacus.

Gleick, J. 1997. *Chaos: The Amazing Science of the Unpredictable*. London: Random House.

Gribbin, J. 2005. *Deep Simplicity: Chaos, Complexity and the Emergence of Life*. London: Penguin.

Johnson, N. 2009. *Simply Complexity: A Clear Guide to Complexity Theory*. Oxford: Oneworld.

Lewin, R. 1993. *Complexity: Life at the Edge of Chaos*. London: Dent.

Kelly, S., Allison, M. 1999. *The Complexity Advantage: How the Science of Complexity Can Help Your Business Achieve Peak Performance*. New York, USA: McGraw-Hill.

Koch, R. 2000a. *The 80/20 Principle: The Secret of Achieving More with Less*. London: Nicholas Brealey.

Koch, R. 2000b. *The Power Laws: The Science of Success*. London: Nicholas Brealey.

Levitt, S., Dubner, S. 2005. *Freakonomics: A Rogue Economist Explores the Hidden Side of Everything*. London: Penguin.

Meadows, D.H., Meadows, D.L., Randers, J., Behrens, W. 1974. *Limits to Growth: A Report for the Club of Rome's Project on the Predicament of Mankind*. London: Pan Books.

Miller, J., Page, S. 2007. *Complex Adaptive Systems*. Princeton, USA: Princeton University Press.

Mitchell, M. 2009. *Complexity: A Guided Tour*. New York, USA: Oxford University Press.

Morgan, G. 1997. *Images of Organisation*. Thousand Oaks, USA: Sage.

Mulgan, G. 1997. *Connexity: How to Live in a Connected World*. London: Random House.

Obolensky, N. 2010. *Complex Adaptive Leadership: Embracing Paradox and Uncertainty*. Farnham: Gower.

Ohmae, K. 1995. *The End of the Nation State: The Rise of Regional Economies*. London: HarperCollins.

Ormerod, P. 1994. *The Death of Economics*. London: Faber and Faber.

Ormerod, P. 1998. *Butterfly Economics*. London: Faber and Faber.

Penrose, R. 2005. *The Road to Reality: A Complete Guide to the Laws of the Universe*. London: Vintage.

Richmond, B. 2004. *An Introduction to Systems Thinking with iThink*. Lebanon, USA: isee systems, inc.

Prigogine, L. 1996. *The End of Certainty: Time, Chaos and the New Laws of Nature*. New York, USA: Free Press.

Prigogine, L., Stengers, I. 1984. *Order Out of Chaos: Man's New Dialogue with Nature*. New York, USA: Bantam.

Senge, P. 1990. *The Fifth Discipline: The Art and Practice of The Learning Organisation*. London: Century.

Senge, P., Kleiner, A., Roberts., C., Ross, R., Smith, B. 1998. *The Fifth Discipline Fieldbook: Strategies and Tools for Building a Learning Organisation*. London: Century.

Smith, L. 2007. *Chaos: A Very Short Introduction*. Oxford: Oxford University Press.

Talab, N. 2004. *Fooled by Randomness: The Hidden Role of Chance in Life and in the Markets*. London: Penguin.

Talab, N. 2008. *The Black Swan: The Impact of the Highly Improbable*. London: Penguin.

Wheatley, M. 1994. *Leadership and the New Science: Learning about Organisation from an Orderly Universe*. San Francisco, USA: Berrett-Koehler.

Mental Acuity: Learning and Innovation, Transformational Change, Neuro-Linguistic Programming

Alder, A. 2010. *Pattern Making, Pattern Breaking: Using Past Experience and New Behaviour in Training, Education and Change Management*. Farnham: Gower.

Argyris, M. and Schön, D. 1974. *Theory in Practice. Increasing Professional Effectiveness*. San Francisco, USA: Jossey-Bass.

Bandler, R., Grindler, J. 1975. *The Structure of magic*. Palo Alto, USA: Science and Behavior Books. Bandler, R., Grindler, J. 1982. *Reframing: Neuro Linguistic Programming and Transformation of Meaning*. Moab, USA: Real People Press.

Barrett, R. 1998. *Liberating the Corporate Soul: Building a Visionary Organisation*. Woburn, USA: Butterworth-Heinemann.

Beck, D., Cowen, C. 2006. *Spiral Dynamics: Mastering Values, Leadership, and Change*. Malden, USA: Blackwell.

Bridges, W. 1992. *The Character of Organisations: Using Jungian Type in Organisational Development*. Palo Alto, USA: Consulting Psychologists Press.

Cooper, R., Sawaf, A. 1997. *Executive EQ: Emotional Intelligence in Business*. London: Orion.

Davenport, T. 1999. *Human Capital: What it is and Why People Invent it*. San Francisco, USA: Jossey-Bass.

Frankl, V. 1984. *Man's Search for Meaning*. Revised and Updated. New York, USA: Washington Square Press.

Gibson, J. 1986. *The Ecological Approach to Visual Perception*. Hillsdale, USA: Lawrence Erlbaum Associates.

Gladwell, M. 2005. *Blink: The Power of Thinking without Thinking*. London: Penguin.

Goleman, D. 1996. *Emotional Intelligence: Why it can Matter More Than IQ*. London: Bloomsbury.

Knight, S. 2002. *NLP at Work: The Difference that Makes a Difference in Business*. Second Edition. London: Nicholas Brealey.

Kline, N. 2006. *Time to Think: Listening to Ignite the Human Mind*. London: Cassell.

Lawley, J., Tompkins, P. 2005. *Metaphors in Mind: Transformation Through Symbolic Modelling*. Lisburn, Northern Ireland: The Developing Company Press.

Lewis, B., Pucelik, F. 1990. *Magic of NLP Demystified: A Pragmatic Guide to Communication and Change*. Portland, USA: Metamorphous Press.

Mark, M., Pearson, C. 2001. *The Hero and the Outlaw: Building Extraordinary Brands through the Power of Archetypes*. New York, USA: McGraw-Hill.

McCarthy, B., McCarthy, D. 2006. *Teaching Around the 4MAT® Cycle: Designing Instruction for Diverse Learners with Diverse Learning Styles*. Thousand Oaks, USA: Corwin Press.

McGill, I., Brockbank, A. 2004. *The Action Learning Handbook*. Abingdon: RoutledgeFalmer.

Moore, G. 2006. *Dealing with Darwin: How Great Companies Innovate at Every Phase of their Evolution*. Chichester: Capstone.

Nonaka, I., Takeuchi, H. 1995. *The Knowledge-Creating Company: How Japanese Companies Create the Dynamics of Innovation*. New York, USA: Oxford University Press.

O'Brien, R. 2001. *Trust: Releasing the Energy to Succeed*. Chichester: Wiley.

O'Connor, J., McDermott, I. 2001. *Way of NLP*. London: Thorsons.

O'Connor, J., McDermott, I. 1996. *Principles of NLP*. London: Thorsons.

O'Connor, J., McDermott, I. 1997. *The Art of Systems Thinking: Essential Skills for Creativity and Problem Solving*. London: Thorsons.

O'Connor, J., Seymour, J. 1993. *Introducing NLP: Psychological Skills for Understanding and Influencing People*. London: Aquarian Press.

Pedler, M. 2008. *Action Learning for Managers*. Aldershot: Gower.

Pink, D. 2010. Drive: The strange truth about what motivates us. Available at http://www.goodreads.com/videos/list_author/96150.Daniel_H_Pink. Accessed 9 December 2010.

Reed, A. 2003. *Capitalism is Dead: Peoplism Rules: Creating Success Out of Corporate Chaos*. Maidenhead: McGraw-Hill.

Schon, D. 1991. *The Reflective Practitioner: How Professionals Think in Action*. Aldershot: Ashgate.

Scott, S. 2002. *Fierce Conversations: Achieving Success in Work and in Life, One Conversation at a Time*. London: Piatkus.

Revens, R. 1998. *ABC of Action Learning: Developing People and Organizations*. London: Mike Pedler Library.

Revens, R. 1971. *Developing Effective Managers*. London: Longman.

Sloane, P. 2004. *The Leader's Guide to Lateral Thinking Skills*. London: Kogan Page.

Stewart, T. 1998. *Intellectual Capital: The New Wealth of Organisations*. London: Nicholas Brealey.

Talbot, M. 1996. *The Holographic Universe*. London: HarperCollins.

Thomson, K.1998. *Emotional Capital: Capturing Hearts and Minds to Create Lasting Business Success*. Oxford: Capstone.

Tushman, M., O'Reilly, C. 1997. *Winning Through Innovation: A Practical Guide to Leading Organisational Change and Renewal*. Boston, USA: HBS Press.

Watzlawick, P., Weakland, C. E., Fisch, R. 1974. *Change: Principles of Problem Formulation and Problem Resolution*. New York, USA: Norton.

Dynamics Modelling: Scenario Modelling, Simulation, Causal Mapping

Bryson, J., Ackermann, F., Eden, C., Finn, C. 2004. *Visible Thinking: Unlocking Causal Mapping for Practical Business Results*. Chichester: Wiley.

Flood, R., Jackson, M. 1999. *Creative Problem Solving: Total Systems Intervention*. Chichester: Wiley.

French, W., Bell, C. 1995. *Organization Development: Behavioral Science Intervention for Organization Improvement*. Englewood Cliffs, USA: Prentice-Hall.

Gharajedaghi, J. 2006. *Systems Thinking: Managing Chaos and Complexity A Platform for Designing Business Architecture*. Second Edition. Burlington, USA: Butterworth Heinemann.

Gilbert, N. 2008. *Agent-based Models*. Thousand Oaks, USA: Sage Publications.

Hauge, J., Paige, K. 2004. *Learning SIMUL8: The Complete Guide*. Second Edition. Bellingham, USA: PlainVu.

Meadows, D. 2009. *Thinking in Systems: A Primer*. London: Earthscan.

Morecroft, J. 2008. *Strategic Modelling and Business Dynamics: A Feedback Systems Approach*. Chichester: Wiley.

Richmond, B. 2004. *An Introduction to Systems Thinking with iThink*. Lebanon, USA: isee systems, inc.

Rieley, J. 2001. *Gaming the System: Stop Playing the Organisational Game Start Playing the Competitive Game*. Harlow: Pearson.

Robinson, S. 2004. *Simulation: The Practice of Model Development and Use*. Chichester: Wiley.

Schrage, M. 2000. *Serious Play: How the World's Best Companies Simulate to Innovate*. Boston, USA: HBS Press.

Seddon, J. 2008. *Systems Thinking in the Public Sector: The Failure of the Reform Regime and a Manifesto for a Better Way*. Axminster: Triarchy Press.

Sherwood, D. 2003. *Seeing the Forest for the Trees: A Manager's Guide to Applying Systems Thinking*. London: Nicholas Brealey.

Sterman, J. 2000. *Business Dynamics: Systems Thinking and Modelling for a Complex World*. Boston, USA: McGraw-Hill.

Van der Heijden, K. 1998. *Scenarios: The Art of Strategic Conversation*. Chichester: Wiley.

Vennix, J. 1996. *Group Model Building: Facilitating Team Learning Using System Dynamics*. Chichester: Wiley.

Warren, K. 2005. *The Critical Path: Building Strategic Performance Through Time*. London: Viola Press.

Warren, K. 2003. *Competitive Strategy Dynamics*. Chichester: Wiley.

Analytics: Business Intelligence, Analytics, Business Architecture

Barlow, J. 2005. *Excel Models for Business and Operations Management*. Second Edition. Chichester: Wiley.

Brown, Mark. 2007. *Beyond the Balanced Scorecard: Improving Business Intelligence with Analytics*. New York, USA: Productivity Press.

Cokins, G. 2009. *Performance Management: Integrating Strategy Execution, Methodologies, Risk, and Analytics*. Hoboken, USA: Wiley.

Connelly, R., McNeill, R., Mosimann, R. 1997. *The Multi-Dimensional Manager: 24 Ways to Impact your Bottom Line in 90 Days*. Ottawa, Canada: Cognos Inc.

Connelly, R., Mosimann, R. *The Multi-Dimensional Organisation: How to Deliver the 24 Ways*. Ottawa, Canada: Cognos Inc.

Connolly, T., Begg, C., Strachan, A. 1999. *Database Systems: A Practical Approach to Design, Implementation and Management*. Second Edition. Harlow: Addison Wesley.

Gartner. 2010. Gartner Symposium/ITxpo, 17–21 October, Orlando. Available at http://www.gartner.com/it/page.jsp?id=1454221. Accessed 9 December 2010.

Keogh, J., Giannini, M. 2004. *OOP Demystified: A Self-Teaching Guide*. Emeryville, USA: McGraw-Hill/Osborne.

Kimball, R., Ross, M. 2002. *The Data Warehouse Toolkit: The Complete Guide to Dimensional Modelling*. Second Edition. New York, USA: Wiley.

Murphy, C. 2005. *Competitive Intelligence: Gathering, Analysing and Putting it to Work*. Aldershot: Gower.

Roekel, H., Linders, J., Raja, K., Reboullet, T., Ommerborn, G. 2009. *The BI Framework: How to Turn Information into a Competitive Asset*. Reading: Logica.

Simon, J. 2005. *Excel Data Analysis*. Second Edition. Hoboken, USA: Wiley.

Taylor, D. 1990. *Object Oriented Technology: A Manager's Guide*. Reading, USA: Addison-Wesley.

Taylor, D. 1995. *Business Engineering with Object Technology*. New York, USA: Wiley.

Winston, W. 1998. *Financial Models Using Simulation and Optimization*. Second Edition. Newfield, USA: Palisade.

Index

NEW PROGRAMMERS START HERE

New Programmers Start Here
An Introduction to Computer Programming Using JavaScript

Copyright © 2016 Jonathan Bartlett all rights reserved.

Published in the United States by BP Learning in Broken Arrow, Oklahoma.

This book is part of a BP Learning series of books, *The Programmer's Toolbox*.

Library of Congress Control Number: 2015902481

ISBN: 978-0-9752838-8-2

For author inquiries please send email to info@bplearning.net.

Bookstore bulk order discounts available. Please contact info@bplearning.net for more information.

For more information, please see www.bplearning.net.

1st printing

New Programmers Start Here

An Introduction to Computer Programming
Using JavaScript

By
Jonathan
Bartlett

Most good programmers do programming not because they expect to get paid or get adulation by the public, but because it is fun to program.

—Linus Torvalds

Contents

Acknowledgements

I want to take a moment and thank everyone who helped me write this book. First, I want to thank those who read and appreciated my first programming book, *Programming from the Ground Up*. The encouragement I received from that book has given me the encouragement to continue writing and educating throughout the years.

Next, I want to thank my homeschool summer co-op class for being guinea pigs for this material. Your questions, your successes, and your difficulties all informed the writing of this book. You were both my motivation to write in the first place, and the first proving ground for the material.

A lot of thanks goes to the cover artists—both Branko Balšić for the cover layout and Christopher Doehling for the robot illustration. I also want to thank my editor, Heather Zeiger. My family and friends are constantly subject to my bad writing habits, but, thanks to Heather, the readers of this book benefit only from the good points of my style.

I would also like to thank my family, my friends, and my church, all of whom are essential parts of my life. Thanks especially to my wife who puts up with me when I am too focused on my writing to notice what the kids have been up to or to put a stop to whatever trouble they have found themselves in!

Chapter 1

Introduction

The modern world is filled with computers. Computers run our phones, our cars, and even our refrigerators. Computers manage our businesses, our calendars, and our social lives. With the world relying on computers for so many functions, it is important to know how these devices work. Even if you never need to program a computer yourself, chances are that at some point in your life, you will be involved with software development. You may be an accountant who needs to tell a computer programmer how you want your purchasing system setup. You may be an engineer who needs to describe your engineering process so that a programmer can automate it. In all such tasks as these, it is important to know something *about* how computers are programmed, even if you are not personally writing the software.

1.1   What You Will Learn

When programming computers, a programmer uses a **programming language** to tell the computer how to do something. Because computers are not intelligent beings, they can't understand ordinary human languages. Computers understand a type of language called **machine language**, which will be discussed further in Chapter 5. Machine languages are very different from the kind of languages ordinary people use. Therefore, programming languages were developed to meet programmers halfway—they are more human-like than machine language, and more machine-like than human language.

Numerous programming languages have been developed over the years. Some that you may

have heard of include JavaScript, Ruby, Python, C, Lisp, Smalltalk, ActionScript, and Swift. Although each language looks different, they are all trying to do the same task of helping you to interface with the machine in a way that is friendlier and easier to manage than machine language. In fact, most programming languages are geared around very similar concepts, and some of them even look similar. Therefore, learning any programming language will help you more easily learn any other programming language. I have rarely hired people for my development team who already knew the programming language that my team uses. If someone learns one programming language and practices until they are good at it, then the effort to learn a new language is fairly minimal.

You may wonder why, if the languages are so similar, there are so many programming languages to choose from. The fact is, when engineering anything, trade-offs have to be made. Sometimes in order to make one type of task easier, another type of task has to be made harder. In my kitchen I have both a mixer and a blender. Both of them operate on the same basic principles—you put food into the main container area, an electric motor turns, and some attachment combines the food together. While these tasks are very similar and operate on the same principles, there are many types of food in the world and many ways that they need to be mixed. Similarly, with programming languages, some of them are better suited to different tasks. Also, the choice of programming language is dependent on the programmer. Just as different types of cars suit the preferences and tendencies of different types of drivers, so do different programming languages suit the preferences and tendencies of different types of programmers. Because of these reasons, there are numerous programming languages available for nearly any task you might want to perform.

The programming language covered in this book is called JavaScript. I like to teach JavaScript as a first language for several reasons. First of all, JavaScript was developed to be a first language. One of the goals of the language was to make it easy for new programmers to get started quickly. Even though JavaScript was designed to make programming easier for new programmers, it is not any less powerful as a language. Second, JavaScript has become the *de facto* programming language for website interfaces. If you use a website that does anything besides link to other web pages, JavaScript is probably involved. Therefore, learning JavaScript will have immediate practical benefits in learning how the web operates. Third, the tools for programming JavaScript are available on every computer. You don't need to download any special tools to program JavaScript. If you have a computer with a web browser, you can program JavaScript! Finally, JavaScript is very similar to other popular programming languages, such as C#, Java, ActionScript, and Swift. Therefore, knowing JavaScript will not only be immediately beneficial for programming websites, it is also a language that makes it easy to transition to other popular systems.

This book is for the first-time programmer. No prior programming experience is assumed. This book does assume that you have a basic understanding of how to use your computer and browse the Internet. That is all that you need!

You will learn not only the basics of computer programming, but also a more general knowledge of how computers and data work. You will learn where computers came from, how they work, how computers work with data, how data is transmitted, and how web pages work. This book will not go in-depth in these subjects, but it will give you a basic working framework that will help you better understand the computerized age we live in.

1.2 How to Use This Book

This book follows several conventions to help you along your programming journey. First, this book will introduce you to new terminology. In order to highlight the important words, terms will be printed in **bold print** the first time that they are used. You can find a complete list of terms in Chapter 17. These terms are important, and you should memorize their meanings.

When this book lists out computer programs, parts of computer programs, or anything that should be typed in directly (and precisely), it will be offset from the text and written in a special font to help you see that it is a computer program. Computer programs will look like this:

Figure 1.1: How Computer Programs Will be Displayed in the Book

```
window.alert("This is an example of a computer program.");
```

When discussing smaller pieces of code within a paragraph, code that is under discussion will `look like this`.

Now, there are many different types of computers, each with different operating systems and software loaded on them, with each of those having different versions. There are also numerous different web browsers, each with different features available and slightly different ways of working. This book attempts to walk you through setting everything up on each operating system. If there is anything in this book that depends on the specific operating

system or browser that you are using, Appendix A has the steps for several different systems, including Windows and Mac operating systems. This book will refer you to the appropriate section of the Appendix when needed. Though this book works with any modern web browser (basically anything released after 2008), I recommend that you use Google Chrome. As of the time of this writing, Google Chrome is the easiest browser to work with as a programmer. That being said, you should be just fine with any web browser, including Internet Explorer, Firefox, Safari, Chrome, or Opera.

This book contains several practice questions and practice activities. The goal of these questions and activities is to provide you with a hands-on way of understanding the material. By doing the questions and activities, the text will become much more meaningful and understandable. More importantly, they might show you the places where you did not fully understand the text. Many people have a tendency to skip over things if they don't understand them well. Practice questions and activities give you a chance to slow down and make sure you know which parts you understood and which parts you need to read again and spend time thinking about. Practice questions build on each other, so by doing them all in the order given you can see exactly where you are having problems.

At the end of every chapter is a review section which covers the most important concepts of each chapter. After that is a section to help you practice applying your knowledge to problems. These questions require you to further engage your brain and really think about what you learned in that chapter and what it means.

Chapter 17 contains an extended glossary of terms used in this book, plus others you are likely to encounter when reading about programming. This chapter will help you find your bearings as you read and talk with other people about programming. I would suggest that, concurrent with your readings, you also take the time to look through the glossary for words that you may have heard but did not understand at the time.

Also, if you run into problems when writing code, Section A.7 has several suggestions for getting you back on the right track.

1.3   Using the Website

In addition to the book, a website has been created with some supplementary material: www.npshbook.com. The website contains a forum for questions, additional resources, and video walk-throughs of some of the exercises. The exercises in Chapter 5 may be particularly

helpful to watch on video before attempting them yourself. The website also allows you to sign up for the mailing list so that you can be notified as new titles in this series are released.

1.4 For Younger Students

This book is geared for high school and college students, for people who are coming to computer programming as a new career, or for people who have been programming but want to come back and revisit their foundations. However, it can also be used for middle school students with some modification. Middle school students, generally, are not cognitively ready for the material following Chapter 10. For middle school classes, the instructor should skip to Chapter 13, and possibly add Chapter 15 at the end.

All right, are you ready? Let's get started!

Part I

Computers, Data, and Communication

The purpose of this part is to help you understand how computers work on the inside. While it is possible to learn programming without learning how your computer works, in the long term, knowing what is going on inside the computer will help you write better programs. This part covers the basics of how computers communicate, how they store data, and how computer programming works at the lowest level.

Chapter 2

A Short History of Computers

The history of computers is weird and wonderful. What started as an abstract philosophical quest ended up setting the course for society for over a century, and continues to be one of the most profound parts of modern life. The goal of this chapter is to trace an outline of where computing started, where it has been, and where it is now.

2.1 The Prehistory of Computers

Humans have always had tools. Humans have built fires, made spears, and built houses from the beginning. At first, however, technology was limited to standing structures, or tools that were extensions of yourself—like knives or bows and arrows. Very little early technology was powered and free-functioning. It was manually powered by human effort. Therefore, since the power of a machine was limited to what humans could drive, only small machines could be devised.

The ability to power a machine led to huge advances in technology. The earliest power source was probably water, where water could turn a wheel to grind wheat or operate a sawmill. These water-based power sources, however, were fairly limited in the types of devices they could drive. Such technology was mostly limited to standing wheel-based inventions.

This was essentially the state of technology from about 300 B.C. to the early 1700s A.D. At this point in history, technology had two main limiting factors. The first was limitations

11

of power availability, and the second was the need for customized parts. The industrial revolution solved both of these problems. The steam engine allowed the creation of powered machines anywhere. Powered machines were no longer tied to being near streams, but could now go anywhere, since the power could be generated from fire and water. Eventually this even allowed the creation of trains, since the power could move with the vehicle.

The other invention of the industrial revolution was interchangeable parts. This allowed a standardization and maintenance of equipment that was previously unattainable. Instead of having each part be a unique piece, the parts became standardized and the machine became unique. It is one of the more curious paradoxes of technology that as the *pieces* of technology become less unique, the more advanced and unique the systems created from those parts can become. Standardization allows for users of technology to stop having to think about all of the low-level decisions and focus on the larger, more meaningful decisions. This also allows for better communication *about* systems, because the parts can be more readily described. If I can give you a schematic that lists pre-made parts, it is much easier to design and communicate that design than if I also had to describe how each individual part was supposed to be made.

So the introduction of available powered machinery and standardized parts in the industrial revolution led to an explosion of specialized machines. We then had machines to perform any number of tasks that a person could want to do. The next step was the introduction of machines which were directed not by people directly controlling the machine, but by coded instructions. The earliest of these machines was the Jacquard Loom, which used punched cards to signify a pattern woven into a fabric. The cards had punched holes to signify to the machine the raising or lowering of the particular thread causing it to be visible or hidden in the pattern. Thus, the loom could be programmed to make a pattern by specifying at each point whether each thread should be raised or lowered.

Later inventions applied this concept to mathematics. Calculating machines had been around for a long time, with Blaise Pascal's mechanical calculator having been invented in the mid-1600s. However, this required the power of physical manipulation to actually accomplish the addition. Most mathematical tasks are not single-step like addition, but require a process of several steps, sometimes repeating steps, before finding an answer. Charles Babbage invented a more advanced machine to perform navigational calculations. In this machine, the user entered the input, and then the machine used that input to run a series of steps which eventually yielded results. Babbage eventually designed a machine that could take a list of arbitrary instructions much like a modern computer, but he was never able to build that design.

Once humans had the ability to power a machine, create a machine that operated on external instructions, and use those instructions to perform mathematical functions, they had all of the pieces in place to create a computer. However, the revolution in computing took place not from an invention, but from a problem in philosophy.

2.2   The Idea of a Computer

What separates modern computers from the calculating machines of the past is that modern computers are **general-purpose computers**. That is, they are not limited to a specific set of predesigned features. I can load new features onto a computer by inputting the right program. How did we get the idea of creating such a general-purpose machine?

It turns out that a question in philosophy led to the creation of general-purpose machines. The question was this—was there a way to create an unambiguous procedure for checking mathematical proofs? This seems like an odd question, but it was a big question in the 19th century. There had been many "proofs" where it was unclear if the proof actually proved its subject. Thus, philosophers of mathematics tried to find out if there was a way to devise what was then called an "effective procedure" for checking the validity of a mathematical proof. But that leads to another question—what counts as an "effective procedure" anyway? If I list out the steps of a procedure, how do I know that I've given you enough details that you can accomplish this procedure exactly as I have described it? How can I tell that my instructions are clear enough to know that the procedure that I have listed can be unambiguously accomplished?

Alan Turing and Alonzo Church both tackled this problem in the 1930s. The results showed that one could define unambiguous procedures with the help of machines. By describing a machine that could perform the operation, one can be certain that the operation of the procedure would be unambiguous. In addition, Turing described a set of operations which could be used to mimic any other set of operations given the right input. That is, Turing defined the minimum set of features needed for a computing system to become truly programmable— where the programmer had an open-ended ability to write whatever software he wanted. Machines and programming languages that are at least as powerful as Turing's set of features are known as **Turing-complete** or **Universal** programming languages. Nearly every modern programming language in common usage is Turing-complete.

It is interesting to note that the creation of computing came from a question in philosophy. Many are eager to dismiss the role of philosophy in academics as being impractical or unim-

portant. But, as we see here, like all truths, philosophical truths have a way of leading to things of deep practical importance.

And what happened to the original question—can you develop an effective procedure for checking proofs? The answer is, strangely, no. It turns out that there are true facts that cannot be proved via mechanical means. But to learn that answer, we had to develop computers first. Of course, that leads to another interesting intersection between computers and philosophy. If there are true facts that cannot be mechanically proved, how could we know that? The only way must be because our minds cannot be represented mechanically. This puts a limit on the potential capabilities of artificial intelligence, and shows that even though computer programmers have developed some very clever means of pretending to be human, the human mind is simply outside the realm of mechanism or mechanistic simulations.

2.3   The Age of the Computer

Shortly after Turing described the necessary feature set for computers, they began to be built. Probably the first Turing-complete machine was Konrad Zuse's Z3 computer, built in 1941. Although the Z3's operating principles were somewhat similar to modern computers, the Z3 was still largely a mechanical device. The first general-purpose, digital electronic computer was the ENIAC in 1946, and was about a thousand times faster than its mechanical predecessors. It should be noted that the ENIAC was the size of a very large room, but it had roughly the same processing power as a scientific calculator. Its main jobs included performing calculations for the production of the hydrogen bomb and calculating tables for firing artillery.

The next generation of computers introduced what is normally termed the **von Neumann architecture**, which means that the computer had a single memory area which held both programs and data. This is based on the fact that both a program and the values that the program generates can both be represented by numbers. Therefore, the same memory can be used both for the program that tells the computer what to do and for the data that the program generates and operates on. This makes the computers much easier to program and use, which led to the ability to sell computers commercially. The first commercially-available computer to implement this idea was the Manchester Mark 1. The first mass-produced computer was the UNIVAC I, followed shortly after by IBM's 650. These computers were still massive in size, but contained less memory storage space than a single graphic on a modern computer. The UNIVAC I was the first computer to have an external tape storage,

and external disk storage (similar to modern hard drives) followed soon after.

The next move for computer hardware was towards miniaturization. The original computers used large devices called vacuum tubes to perform data processing (see Figure 2.1, left column). These vacuum tubes would allow or not allow current to flow based on whether other wires had current flowing through them or not. Combinations of many of these tubes could allow for data to be stored as current flow, for mathematical operations to be performed on such data, and for the data to be moved around.

After the vacuum tube came the invention of the transistor (see Figure 2.1, middle column). Transistors generally have three wires, where the middle wire controls whether the electricity can flow between the other two wires. As with vacuum tubes, transistors can be wired together to create digital computer memory, digital computer logic operations , and digital information pathways. Transistors, while they performed the same basic functions as the vacuum tube, was able to do so in a much smaller package and operating on a lot less power. Transistors allowed much smaller devices to be built which also required almost 1,000 times less power. The Metrovick 950, released in 1956, was the first commercial computer that operated on this principle.

Miniaturization continued with the advent of **integrated circuits**, or what are often called **microchips** or just **chips** (see Figure 2.1, right column). An integrated circuit basically allows for miniaturized transistors to be stored on a small, single plate of silicon. When integrated circuits were first introduced, they only had a few transistors. Today, integrated circuits come in a variety of sizes, and the ones used for desktop computing can hold billions of transistor equivalents on a two-inch square chip. Integrated circuits basically brought computers as we know them into the world. However, so far, they were primarily used by very large businesses.

In the 1960s, Douglas Engelbart led a research team to look at the future of computing. In 1968, Engelbart presented what has been termed "the mother of all demos," which predicted and demonstrated all aspects of modern personal computing, including graphical interfaces, networking, email, video conferencing, collaborative document editing, and the web. This served as an inspiration for a number of companies to start pushing to make this vision of computing a reality. Engelbart had accomplished it in a lab, but others were needed to make it a commercial reality.

The first recreational personal computer was the Altair, and the first commercial personal computer was the Apple I which came out in 1976, after which a flood of personal computers entered the market. IBM eventually entered the market, with Microsoft providing the

Figure 2.1: Advancements in Computer Hardware Miniaturization

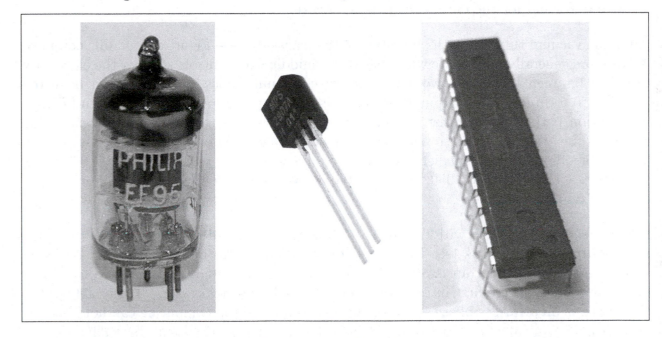

The picture on the left is of a vacuum tube (photo courtesy of Tvezymer on Wikimedia). Vacuum tubes are still around today, primarily for audio applications. The picture in the middle is of a transistor. Transistors were much smaller, required fewer materials to produce, and used much less power, but still did largely the same job as vacuum tubes. The picture on the right is a modern microchip used in appliances (photo courtesy of Vahid alpha on Wikimedia). Such a microchip contains the equivalent of a few hundred thousand transistors.

software for the computer. The interfaces for these computers were usually text-only. However, eventually Apple released the Macintosh, which inaugurated the age of graphical user interfaces. Shortly after, Microsoft released Windows, which brought the graphical interface to the IBM side of the personal computer world.

2.4   Computers in the Age of Networks

Thus far, computers had been largely isolated machines. You could share files through disks, but, by and large, computers operated alone. When you link together two or more computers, it is called a **network**. Though networking technology had been around for quite a while, it had not been cheap enough or popular enough to make an impact for most personal computer users.

For most users, networking started with office file sharing systems, usually using a type of local networking called **Ethernet** which runs networking services over specialized networking cables. People would use applications that were installed on their own computers, but store the files on a **server** so that the other members of the office could access it. A server is a computer on the network that provides one or more services to other computers and users on a network. A software program that accesses a server is often called a **client**. Many office networks eventually added **groupware** services to their networks—local email and calendar sharing systems that allowed the office to work together more efficiently. While smaller organizations were focused on local services such as file sharing and groupware, larger institutions were also at work linking networks together. This allowed organizations to share information and data between each other more easily.

At the same time, a few home computer users started reaching out to each other through the phone system. A device called a **modem** allowed a computer to access another computer over standard telephone lines. Services called **bulletin-board systems** (known as a BBS) started popping up which allowed people to use their computers to access a remote computer and leave messages and files for other users.

These developments laid the groundwork for the idea of the **Internet**. At the time it was developed, there were many different, incompatible networking technologies. Organizations wanted to connect their networks to other organizations' networks, but were finding it problematic since everyone used different types of networks. In the 1970s and 1980s, DARPA, the Defense Advanced Research Projects Agency, developed a way to unify different types of networks from different organizations under a single system so that they could all communicate.

This network, known as ARPANET, became very popular. Other large, multi-organizational groups started using the design of ARPANET to create their own network. Since these networks all used the same basic design, they were eventually joined together to become the Internet in the late 1980s.

The 1990s witnessed the rise of Internet Service Providers, or ISPs, which provided a way for computer users to use the modems that they used to use for bulletin-board systems to connect their computers to the Internet. Instead of using a modem to connect to a single computer, like they did with bulletin-board systems, the ISP allowed a user to use their modem to connect to a whole network. This began the mass public adoption of the Internet by both individuals and organizations of all stripes.

In the early days of the Internet, the speed of the network was very slow, and only text could be transmitted quickly. Eventually, modems were replaced with more advanced (and faster) ways of connecting to the Internet, such as DSL, cable, and fiber. This allowed more and more complex content to be transmitted over the Internet. Also, because these technologies do not tie up a phone line, they can be used continuously, rather than intermittently. In addition, wireless technologies, such as **WiFi** and cellular-based networking, allowed users to connect to the Internet without being tied down by cables. These developments together led to the near-ubiquitous availability of the Internet that we have today.

So, today, nearly all computer software is built with the network in mind. In fact, much of the software that people use on a daily basis operates not on an individuals computer, but over a network. This allows for users to access software programs no matter where they are or what computer they are using. It has also changed software development so that the focus of computer software is no longer on individuals and individual tasks, but on organizing groups of people.

Review

In this chapter we covered the basic history of computers. We have learned:

- Humans have used tools to accomplish tasks from the beginning.

- Early tools were limited by available power options.

- Advances in power technology allowed for the improvements and industrialization of tools.

- Standardization of parts allows for more complex machines to be built and serviced.

- Electricity allowed for the movement of power to any needed location.

- The ability to control a machine via instructions, such as the Jacquard Loom, allowed for the creation of more general-purpose tools which could be specialized by providing the right sets of instructions.

- Alan Turing and Alonzo Church identified the logical requirements for making general-purpose computations.

- Several early computers were built around the idea of a general purpose calculating machine.

- Advances in electronics allowed for storage of millions of transistors onto a single microchip.

- The availability of microchips led to the era of personal computing.

- The increased usage of computers in organizations eventually led to the need to have better means of communication between computers.

- Networks were invented to allow computers to be hooked together to share file and messages.

- The isolated networks around the world were eventually unified into a single internetwork, known as the Internet.

- The growth of the Internet combined with the ability to access the Internet wirelessly has made the Internet a primary factor in computer usage.

- The ubiquity of the Internet has led programmers to start designing applications with the network in mind first, rather than as an afterthought.

Apply What You Have Learned

1. Take some time to think about the history of technology and the Internet. What do you think is next on the horizon for technology?

2. The pace of technology appears to have been accelerating over the past century. What do you think has caused this acceleration?

3. Pick your favorite piece of technology mentioned in this short history and research it. What inspired the person who developed it? What other inventions came after it? Was it successful? Write a few paragraphs describing the technology you have chosen, how it functioned, and how it impacted the future of technology.

Chapter 3

How Computers Communicate

Before we start our study of computer programming, we are going to begin by studying the way that computers communicate. The Internet is basically a giant communication system. Communication systems operate using **protocols**. A protocol is a predefined sequence of steps used to ensure proper communication. We actually use protocols every day. Think about what happens when you answer the phone. What do you say and why do you say it? The first thing most people say when answering the phone is "hello." This signals to the person calling us that we have picked up the phone and we are ready to start talking. If we didn't say "hello" the person might think that we accidentally accepted the call without knowing it, or that we are not quite ready to talk yet. Then, at the end of the call, we usually say something like, "Thanks for calling! Goodbye!" This signals to the other person that we are done with the conversation. If we didn't tell them goodbye, they might think that we are still on the line and continue talking. If they heard silence, they may presume that either we were not speaking because we were upset, or that there was a technical problem. Therefore, we end our conversations with a "goodbye" to let the person we are talking to know that the conversation is over.

This is the essence of a protocol. A communication protocol is a sequence of steps or possible steps that enable two parties to communicate or interact and know the status of the communication or interaction. Because computers cannot think or feel, computers rely on very rigid and exact protocols to allow them to communicate with each other. In fact, computers use hundreds of different protocols to communicate different types of data in different ways. Most of the time, there are actually multiple protocols happening at once.

Figure 3.1: Even Answering the Phone has a Protocol

Think about writing a letter. When you write a letter, there is a basic protocol that governs the form of a letter—at minimum it should have a date, a greeting, and a closing. However, if you decide to mail the letter, you have to send it through the mail service, which has its own protocol. To send the letter through the mail, you need to take the letter, fold it up, and put it in an envelope. What you write on the envelope is governed by another protocol designed by the U.S. Postal Service. Their protocol requires a return address on the top left corner of the envelope, a destination address in the middle of the envelope, and a stamp in the top right corner. Now you have two protocols happening simultaneously—the letter-writing protocol and the envelope-addressing protocol. These protocols are *layered*, which means that one of the protocols runs fully inside of the other protocol. In computer jargon, we would say that the envelop protocol *encapsulates* the letter protocol. The envelop protocol takes the results of the letter protocol, packages it up, and puts its own protocol on top.

3.1 The Layers of Internet Communication

On the Internet, there is a similar layering of protocols occurring. The difference is that on the Internet, there are many more layers interacting at once, and they all have funny names like HTTP, SSL, TCP, IP, IEEE 802.3, SMTP, and FTP. The International Standards Organization developed a way to help you think of these layers called the **OSI Model**, which identifies seven different layers of protocols that may need to be active when communicating on a computer network. To understand what these layers are doing, let's look at the questions that have to be answered in order for one computer to talk to another.

Let's say that we have a chat application that sends messages to another computer. What must happen to get that message to another computer?

1. The computers must be physically connected to the Internet. "Physical" can include both wired connections and wireless connections. This is called the **physical layer**.

2. The computers must know how to move data on those physical connections. It is not enough for the wires to be connected, they must also know the protocols for sending messages. Each computer has to be able to identify other physically-connected computers, be able to signal to them that they are sending data, and know which computer they are sending it to, among other details. This is called the **data link layer**.

3. Once the computers know how to talk to the other computers they are physically connected to, they need to be able to talk to computers which they are only indirectly connected to. For instance, most locations get their Internet connection by connecting a **router** to their DSL or cable line, and then the other devices in the home connect to that router. The devices in the home are all connected physically and communicate using the data link layer. However, only the router is physically connected to the Internet Service Provider (ISP). The other computers must adopt a protocol in order to tell the router to relay their messages on to the rest of the network. The rest of the network, likewise, must be able to follow the same protocol. In addition, in order to speak to other computers on the network, you must be able to identify them, so it also includes at least some sort of naming or numbering system for the computers on the network. This layer, which interconnects computers which are only indirectly connected to each other, is called the **network layer**.

4. Now that we can move data across the Internet, there is another issue. Other networks might not be as reliable as we want them to be. Since we have no control over how reliable the other networks are, we must adopt a protocol for making sure all of the data arrives at the other side of the network safely and allows us to retransmit any missing data that did not make it to the other side. This layer is called the **transport layer**.

5. Once we know how to reliably move data through the network. We need to be able to signal to a computer that we want to start talking to it, and let it know when we are finished with our communication. This is called the **session layer**.

6. Now that we have a connection to a remote computer, and the remote computer is accepting data, sometimes we need to adjust or rework some aspect of that communication. This is called the **presentation layer**. For instance, oftentimes we want encrypted communication between computers. The message, when it is sent, goes through a layer of encryption. The encryption and decryption of the message happens at the presentation layer. Other times (though this is rare), two computers have different ways of representing data, and, therefore, the message has to be translated between the computers. This would also happen at the presentation layer.

7. Finally, now our application can reliably send data to a similar application on the other computer. Of course, for our applications to speak to each other, they must both use their own protocol. This layer of communication between applications is called the **application layer**.

As you can see, there is a lot going on when you send a message from one computer to another

Figure 3.2: Overview of the OSI Model

	Layer	What it Does	Example
7	Application Layer	the main content of the message	HTTP
6	Presentation Layer	handles encodings and encryption	SSL
5	Session Layer	controls the conversation flow	TCP
4	Transport Layer	ensures reliable sending in a noisy network	TCP
3	Network Layer	provides a logical addressing mechanism and bridges different physical configurations	IP
2	Data Link Layer	low-level communication protocol for the physical medium	Ethernet
1	Physical Layer	how the machines are physically connected	Category 5 Cable

through the Internet! Thankfully, since this is built in layers, we rarely have to think about all of the things that are going on at the different layers. For instance, when you mail a letter to a friend, you never have to think about the different mail sorting facilities, postal routes, or delivery times of the post office. That is a system that is already in place, and you must simply drop your letter in the mailbox and let the system do the rest. That is the same with communication on the Internet. However, it is good to know what is happening behind the scenes, both so you can better understand the capabilities of the system you are using, and so you can better identify issues when something goes wrong!

Computers haven't always been connected through the Internet, and the OSI Model was developed when the Internet was not the primary means of communication. In fact, at the time, nearly all communication was on private networks. Since its development, certain technologies have become fairly standard in each layer.

For the physical layer and data link layer, the two primary technologies are **Ethernet** for wired connections and **WiFi** for wireless connections. In addition, your connection to the Internet, whether it is through cable, DSL, or fiber, also uses its own physical and data link layers. The network layer is handled by the **Internet Protocol**, usually abbreviated as **IP**. The number that identifies each computer on the Internet is known as the computer's **IP address**. On the Internet, the transport and session layers are usually combined and

handled through a protocol called the **Transmission Control Protocol**, abbreviated as
TCP. Because TCP and IP are almost always seen together, they are often collectively
labeled **TCP/IP**. The only common presentation-layer protocol is the **Secure Sockets
Layer**, usually abbreviated as **SSL**. SSL handles the job of encrypting and decrypting data
on a secure connection, to prevent other people from being able to listen in on your communication.

Thankfully, however, we rarely need to know much about these layers. In fact, this is one
of the main reasons such layers were invented—so that all an application programmer really
needs to interact with is the application layer. It is still good to know that these other layers
exist, as occasionally you might interact with them. In addition, knowing the basics of how
the network works is part of being a programmer.

The layer that most computer programmers deal with directly is the application layer. There
are several application-layer protocols that operate on the Internet. The Internet is best
known for **HTTP**, which is the protocol used to access websites. Second to HTTP is
probably **SMTP**, which is the protocol used to send email. **POP** and **IMAP** are two
protocols often used to *receive* emails if you use a separate email program. These protocols
make up a large majority of people's use of the Internet.

3.2   Communicating Using HTTP

As mentioned earlier, when you access a website, the protocol you are using is HTTP, which
stands for "HyperText Transfer Protocol." Web pages are considered "hypertext," and the
file format that web pages use is called the "HyperText Markup Language," or HTML. We
will dive further into the details of HTML in Chapter 6. For now, we will just consider the
protocol used to access HTML documents and not concern ourselves with the contents.

The first thing to know about HTTP is that it is fundamentally about *documents*. Websites
might look fancy, but really they are a collection of interactive documents. Therefore, when
you go to a website, your browser connects to the remote computer (called the **server**), and
requests a document. When you click on a link, what usually happens is that the link tells
your browser the location of a new document to fetch. Your browser then retrieves that new
document and shows it to you. These documents are identified and located by a piece of
text called a "Universal Resource Locator," or **URL**.

A typical URL looks something like this:

Figure 3.3: Typical URL Structure

Each URL has three main parts—the protocol, the hostname (the server's name), and the document path. Optionally, there is also a fourth and fifth part, the query string and the anchor, but these aren't covered in this book. (See the glossary entries for these terms in Chapter 17 for more information.) In a URL, the protocol is the everything up until the colon. In this case, it is "http," which is the normal protocol used on the Internet. If the connection is an encrypted connection, the protocol would be "https." The two slashes after the protocol indicate that the next piece of the URL is the **hostname**. In this case, the hostname is `www.npshbook.com`. We will discuss hostnames in more depth in Section 3.3. The slash after the hostname is the beginning of the path. The path includes the starting slash, and is essentially the rest of the URL. Sometimes the path is extremely short. For instance, when you first go to a website, the path is usually just `/`. It can also be very long, like `/orders/123/products/5`. The way to think about a path is that each piece of the path is like a folder on your computer, and the path is the list of folders someone has to go through to find a document. That isn't exactly what is happening on the server, but it is a helpful way of thinking about it.

For an example, open up your browser. Find the location bar in your browser. (For more information on finding the location bar in your browser, see Section A.1.) Put `http://www.npshbook.com/example/` into the location bar and press the enter key. This will bring up an example website that I built for this book. Depending on your browser, it might show you the whole URL, or it might remove the protocol from the URL to make it easier to read. Now, click on the link titled "About." Once the page finishes loading, take another look at your browser's location bar. The location bar should now read `http://www.npshbook.com/example/about.html`. That URL is used to find the server, tell the server what document it should give you, and communicate back to you what document it just retrieved.

Now we will look at how the browser actually retrieves the document. Data transmission on the Internet is not quite as mysterious as it may seem.

The main steps are as follows:

1. Establish a connection with the server

2. Tell the server what the path to the document is

3. Tell the server any additional information about the communication

4. Send a blank line

5. Receive the file

Once the connection with the server is established, here is what the protocol looks like to request the "about" page:

Figure 3.4: An Example HTTP Request for the About Page

```
GET /example/about.html HTTP/1.1
Host: www.npshbook.com
Connection: close
```

The first line, called the request line, does most of the work. It has three components. The first component is called the **HTTP verb**. This tells the server what action you are trying to do. You are retrieving the document, so you use the GET verb. Other verbs include DELETE for remotely destroying documents and POST for sending data to a document on the server. The next component is the path, which tells the server how to find the document. The last component is the protocol version—you are using HTTP version 1.1.

The next few lines are called the request headers. They are a list of options that you send to the server to clarify in more detail what you want and how you want it delivered. The first request header line that we send tells the server what hostname you are looking for. This may seem redundant, since we already connected to the server that we want. However, modern web servers are actually built to serve requests for any number of hostnames. Therefore, even though you are connected to the server for www.npshbook.com, you still have to tell it what site you were really looking for. The next header line is optional, but it tells the server to close the connection after it gives you the document. Otherwise, it will sit and wait for you to request something else. Then, to signal that we are at the end of our request headers, we send a blank line. There is also an optional request *message* that we can send at this

point, but that is beyond the scope of our discussion. The requests we will be discussing in this book will not have a request message.

When the server receives the blank line, it knows that you are done asking for your document, and it attempts to process your request. It then responds with something that looks like this:

Figure 3.5: General Server HTTP Response

```
HTTP/1.1 200 OK
...Possibly other data here...
Content-Type: text/html; charset=UTF-8
...Possibly more data here...

....Document Gets Put Here....
```

The response is very similar in format to the request. The first line is the response line. It lists the protocol version that the server is responding with, followed by a status code and status message. 200 is the status code that means everything went just fine and there is a document coming. Other common status codes include 404 which means that the document could not be found, 500 which means that the server ran into an error, 301 and 302 which mean that the document has moved locations, and 400 which means that the request did not follow the proper protocol. After the response line is a series of response headers. These communicate additional information about the server and the response. The headers shown here are just an example—most servers give back several more headers as well, and in various orders. The two headers shown tell us the type of document we have retrieved (in this case an HTML file, which is what `Content-Type: text/html` means), and the way that it is going to send the file back to us (in this case, in chunks). The server then sends a blank line telling us that it is done sending the headers, and the rest of the communication will be the document we asked for. The document we get back is an HTML file. It may look strange, but that is exactly what the browser receives from the server. It includes all of the data that the browser needs to display as well as the instructions for how to display it on the screen and how you can interact with it.

Now it is time for you to do the HTTP communication yourself. For this, you will need to go to the command line of your computer. For information about what the command line is and how to get to it for your computer, see Section A.2. We will be using the `telnet`

command to directly talk to servers without using our browser so we can see exactly what is taking place under the hood. Once you are on the command line, type:

Figure 3.6: Connecting to a Remote Server Using Telnet

```
telnet www.npshbook.com 80
```

When it says you are connected, you are now talking *directly* to the server yourself! Now you just need to follow the HTTP protocol to get what you need. Type in the request that we mentioned earlier (note that the request ends with a blank line):

Figure 3.7: HTTP Request Example

```
GET /example/about.html HTTP/1.1
Host: www.npshbook.com
Connection: close
```

The server will then respond with its response line, response headers, and response message as outlined above. The response message, since it is the document itself, will be fairly lengthy.[1] You may be wondering what the "80" was in our telnet command. This is the "port" to connect to on the server. A port is merely a number that the server uses to know where to direct your request. Port 80 is usually the port that is used to handle HTTP requests. You can typically assume that any HTTP request will be using port 80.

You have now communicated directly with a server using the HTTP protocol. You have spoken your first bit of computer-ese!

---

[1]If you already know HTML, you might notice that there are a few extra letters and numbers in the response that aren't in the HTML file itself. This is due to the transfer encoding, which sometimes sends the HTML in chunks. Those numbers and letters tell the browser how much data is coming in the next "chunk." However, since we haven't covered HTML yet, you probably didn't notice the extra numbers and letters in the response. In any case, for our purposes they can be ignored.

3.3 How Computers Are Located on the Internet

One thing that we haven't talked about yet is how computers are located on the Internet. We mentioned earlier that the URL contains a hostname that names the computer. You might wonder, how is a server found if you just have its hostname? It turns out that there is a lot involved in that process!

We talked in Section 3.1 about the different protocol layers in the Internet. Layer 3 is the network layer, and on the Internet, the network layer is handled by the Internet Protocol (IP). The Internet Protocol mandates that each computer on the Internet is identified by a series of numbers, known as the computer's **IP Address**. However, we don't normally refer to computers by that series of numbers for two reasons. The first reason is that humans aren't good at remembering numbers. It's much easier to remember google.com than it is to remember 64.233.160.138. The second reason is that it is good to separate out *physical issues* from *logical issues*. In other words, the IP Address tells the network what location on the Internet you want to go to. However, the user doesn't care where that is. The user just wants to go to Google's website. Therefore, by creating a *name* for Google's website (i.e., google.com), the user can access the site even if its location on the network changes. The IP Address is similar to a phone number, and the hostname is like the name of the person you want to reach.

However, when you want to connect to a server for a website, the computer must know the destination IP Address to make the connection. How does the computer know what the IP Address is for the website you want to visit?

The computer finds the destination IP Address through the **Domain Name System** (DNS). DNS is a system that translates hostnames to IP Addresses, kind of like the way a phone book translates a person's name into a phone number. However, DNS is a *distributed* system, so, rather than just one big phone book, there are millions of them organized into a hierarchy. Each server (i.e., "phone book") in this system is called a nameserver. So, when you tell your browser you want to go to `http://www.npshbook.com/example/about.html`, before it makes a connection to the server, it must first figure out *where* `www.npshbook.com` is located. In order to do that, it breaks the hostname down into pieces, separated by a dot. In our case, there are three pieces—`www`, `npshbook`, and `com`. The browser starts with the rightmost piece, called the top-level domain name (TLD). Each browser is preprogrammed with a set of "root" nameservers. The browser begins by asking the root nameservers if they know who maintains the DNS records (i.e., who handles the phone book) for `.com` domains. The root nameserver responds with the IP address of the nameserver or nameservers that

handle requests for those domains. Next, the browser goes to the `.com` nameserver and asks it who maintains the DNS records for the `npshbook.com` domain. The `.com` nameserver will point to yet another server who handles the `npshbook.com` domain. Finally, the browser will go to the `npshbook.com` nameserver and ask it if it knows what the IP address of `www.npshbook.com` is. The `npshbook.com` nameserver will respond with the IP Address of `www.npshbook.com`, and with that IP Address your computer will be able to establish a connection to the `www.npshbook.com` server.

This usually happens in a fraction of a second, so we don't notice that the computer is doing all of this work behind-the-scenes. In addition, the computer usually skips the steps that it has performed recently, and just remembers what results it got back last time so that it doesn't have to do the same query over and over again.

Review

In this chapter we covered the basics of Internet communication. We have learned:

- Protocols define how communication happens.

- The Internet is built on a layering of many protocols, each with a specific function or set of functions.

- HTTP is an application-level protocol, used for transmitting interactive documents to users browsing the web.

- A URL is a piece of text that gives the browser all of the information it needs to locate a document on the Internet.

- A URL is composed of a protocol (usually HTTP), a hostname, and a path.

- The hostname on the URL is translated into an IP Address using DNS nameservers.

- The path of the URL is sent to the server to identify the document being requested.

Apply What You Have Learned

1. Go to your favorite website. Click through the different pages. Pay attention to how the URL changes on each page. Does every click change the URL? Which ones change the URL and which ones don't?

2. Some websites have very structured, easy-to-understand URL paths, and some of them don't. When a website uses structured URLs, it is often easy to predict what the URL will be for something you are looking for. Go to Wikipedia.org and click around. Look at what the URLs look like. Now, try to guess what the URL to the Wikipedia entry on JavaScript will be. Put it into your browser and see if you are correct.

3. Go to Amazon.com and click around. Are the URLs as predictable and easy to understand as those on Wikipedia? Do you think you could guess the URL of a book the same way you could guess the URL for JavaScript in Wikipedia?

4. Go to the command line and try to retrieve the web page for JavaScript from Wikipedia directly using the HTTP protocol.

Chapter 4

How a Computer Looks at Data

Chapter 3 covered the basics of how computers transmit data to each other over the Internet. This chapter expands on that, covering how documents are stored within the computer. Much of the information in this chapter, like the last one, is more background information than practical knowledge. The JavaScript programming language automates a lot of the data handling for you, so you don't have to worry about it. Nonetheless, it is important to know what the computer is doing for you!

We think of computers as systems which are capable of anything, but in reality computers are very limited. In many areas of engineering, engineers achieve the most powerful results by *limiting* the possibilities, which makes the remaining available possibilities more potent. Engines are made by taking the energy from combustion reactions and channeling them in a specified direction to operate the engines. Instead of letting the energy go in every direction (which is what it normally does), it is only allowed to go in specific directions. The driver of the car can go anywhere he or she wants to, but only because the combustion within the engine is directed to a very limited number of directions. Computers are powerful precisely because they are similarly limited.

Computers, at their core, perform two functions—they process numbers and they transmit numbers. This may seem counterintuitive. After all, when you type on your keyboard, doesn't it produce letters on the screen? Doesn't your computer do graphics and sound? In reality, all of these things are controlled by numbers. The color of each pixel on your screen is a number. Each letter you type has a corresponding number. Each sound is a long sequence of numbers. The computer may *look* like it is doing lots of different things, but it

is really doing only two things—processing numbers and transmitting numbers.

The first part of this chapter will cover how data is stored on a computer using numbers. The second part of this chapter will cover how those numbers can be arranged into a **file format** which can be read by software applications like web browsers.

4.1   What Computer Memory Looks Like

To understand how the computer views memory, imagine a room filled with numbered lockers that are all the same size. These lockers are similar to computer memory in that each are numbered sequences of fixed-size storage locations. For example, if you have 2 gigabytes of computer memory, that means that your computer contains roughly 2 billion fixed-size storage locations. Or, to use our analogy, 2 billion lockers. Each location has a number, and each location has the same fixed-length size. The difference between a locker and computer memory is that you can store different kinds of things in a locker, but you can only store a single number in a computer memory storage location.

On modern computers, each storage location can store a single number between 0 and 255. Such a number is called a **byte**. You may be wondering why computers use the range between 0 and 255, and not something more natural, like 100 or 1000. The reason is that the range of 0 to 255 *is* natural to a computer. In math, we usually represent numbers using the decimal system which has ten digits—zero through nine. Computers, however, use the binary system which only has two digits—zero and one. Each digit is called a **bit**, which is short for *binary digit*. If you write down numbers, when you get to ten you have run out of digits, so you add another digit to keep counting, making a two-digit number. In binary, you run out of digits at two.

Here are the numbers zero through eleven in decimal and in binary:

Figure 4.1: Numbers Displayed in Decimal and Binary

Decimal	Binary	
0	0	The first two numbers look the same
1	1	
2	10	Since we only have two digits in binary, we have to add another place.
3	11	Just like in decimal, the digit on the right will increase again.
4	100	However, we already have to go to yet another place!
5	101	
6	110	
7	111	
8	1000	
9	1001	
10	1010	Since the decimal numbers have ten digits, it is only when we get to ten that we need another place.
11	1011	

If you carry this out, you will find that the number 255 is the maximum number that you can get with 8 bits. It looks like `11111111` in binary. In short, the reason why a computer byte stores numbers between 0 and 255 is because a byte is made up of 8 bits.

It is important to note that the numbers in the left column and right column are the *same numbers*, just represented differently. The reason we use decimal numbers is probably due to the fact that our culture started counting with its fingers. A few cultures, such as the Yuki, started counting using the spaces between their fingers, and only have eight digits in their system. The numbers are not different—only the way they are displayed!

Two other systems that are regularly encountered in computer programming are the **octal** system and the **hexadecimal** system. The octal system uses only the digits 0–7, but the hexadecimal system actually *adds* digits to our current ones. Hexadecimal uses letters to add additional digits. So, in hexadecimal, the letters A–F represent the decimal numbers 10–15, and 10 in hexadecimal is the same as the number 16 in decimal.

Here is a combined list of the numbers 0–16 in decimal, binary, octal, and hexadecimal:

Figure 4.2: Numbers 0–16 in Decimal, Binary, Octal, and Hexadecimal

Decimal	Binary	Octal	Hexadecimal
0	0	0	0
1	1	1	1
2	10	2	2
3	11	3	3
4	100	4	4
5	101	5	5
6	110	6	6
7	111	7	7
8	1000	10	8
9	1001	11	9
10	1010	12	A
11	1011	13	B
12	1100	14	C
13	1101	15	D
14	1110	16	E
15	1111	17	F
16	10000	20	10

The reason why octal and hexadecimal are often used in computing is that a single octal digit represents exactly three bits, and a single hexadecimal digit represents exactly four bits. Two hexadecimal numbers together represent one byte. Therefore, octal and hexadecimal are essentially used as a shorthand for writing binary numbers. An example of this is in screen colors. Each dot on your screen is represented by 3 bytes—one byte for the red component, one byte for the green component, and one byte for the blue component. In many tools, these are all smashed together as a six-digit hexadecimal number. For instance, red is represented by FF0000, green is represented by 00FF00, blue is represented by 0000FF, a greenish blue would be 00FFFF, and a darker shade of greenish blue would be 009999.

In any case, computer memory is a long sequence of millions or billions of bytes, one after another. Each byte has an address, which is basically like a locker number, so you can refer to specific memory locations on the computer. We won't be accessing bytes by their memory addresses ourselves, but that is how the computer works at the lowest level.

Now, it might seem very limiting to only be able to deal with numbers that are between 0 and 255. The reason this is not a problem is because this is only how the machine works at the lowest level. Programming languages group several of these bytes together to represent much larger numbers, or other kinds of data altogether. Representing numbers that have a decimal point is a harder problem, but it is usually done by designating some number of bytes to be the number, and some number of bytes to be the location of the decimal point. Even though you won't have to deal with these details in JavaScript, it is good to keep in mind that, at the lowest level, everything you deal with is just a sequence of numbers between 0 and 255.

Going forward, we will assume that the computer can handle whatever size number we throw at it. This isn't entirely true, but it is true enough for our purposes.

☞ Practice Questions

- How do you write the decimal number 12 in binary?

- How many bits are represented by a single hexadecimal digit?

- Since black is the absence of color, how do you think you would represent black in the hexadecimal system discussed in this section?

- What about white, which is the mix of all colors?

4.2 Using Numbers to Represent Data

So, if all we have to work with are numbers, how do we store other types of data? The answer is that we must convert our information into a series of numbers. Let's say we want to describe a person. What information might we want to store? We might want to store:

- height

- weight

- hair color (black, blonde, brown, red, white, etc.)

- eye color (blue, green, hazel, etc.)

Some of these values are actually numbers, like height and weight. We just have to decide what units we are using. Let's use inches for height and pounds for weight. Hair color and eye color are not numbers, but computers only have numbers to work with. So, what do we do? We choose numbers to represent the possible values. We might say that, for hair color, black is 0, blonde is 1, brown is 2, red is 3, and white is 4. There doesn't have to be any reason that a color gets a particular value. The important thing is to make sure that whatever number we assign, we consistently use that same number to represent that hair color. Next, we can choose numbers to represent eye color. For eyes, we can say blue is 0, green is 1, and hazel is 2. It doesn't matter that our numbers overlap with the same numbers we used for hair color, as long as we know which one we are dealing with.

We can now represent a person with a sequence of four numbers - their height, weight, hair color, and eye color. Using this system, I would be 72, 275, 2, 2. Someone identical to me, but with blue eyes, would be 72, 275, 2, 0. Notice how important the order of the numbers is. If we didn't know what order the numbers were in, we wouldn't be able to understand the data. It isn't that the numbers are in order of importance—we could just as easily have arranged it as weight, eye color, height, hair color—the important thing is that we know what order to expect the numbers, and follow that convention every time we use the data. Otherwise, we might wind up mistaking someone's weight for their height or their eye color for their hair color.

When you have a pre-defined set of data to describe something, it is called a **data format**. It might not seem like a data format is that big of a deal. However, when communicating with other programs, they may have their data in a different pattern than you do with yours. Imagine another program which stored the same data, but used feet instead of inches for the height. Or, let's say that it had five numbers for each person, with the fifth being their age. In each of these cases, if you loaded data from this other format, you would have to convert the data from the data format you are given to the data format you need for your own program. This may include transforming certain pieces of data (e.g., feet to inches), ignoring certain pieces of data (since our format doesn't include an age), calculating data (if one program needs an age or another program sends the date of birth), or any other number of possibilities. These are called **data transformations** and account for a very large portion of programming tasks.

☞ **Practice Questions**

---

1. Describe yourself using the data format described in this section.

2. Write out in plain language what someone with the following numbers looks like:
   `69, 150, 0, 1`

4.3   Sequences in Data

The data format we explored in Section 4.2 is only helpful if we have a fixed number of things to store. Because each piece of data is identified by its position in the sequence, if we changed the number of items in the data, we would also change what they meant. Let's say you wanted to store the ages of a person's children. The problem is that we don't know how many children a person might have. They might have none or twenty. One way to solve the problem is to have a count of the number of children first, then the children's ages. This way we would know when the children's ages stopped. For instance, we could modify our format to be height, weight, number of children, age of child 1, age of child 2, etc., hair color, and eye color. By storing the number of children *before* the list of children, even though each record would be slightly different, we would still know where we were in the record because we know how many children we need to be looking for.

Let's say that our friend Fred has three children, ages 12, 10, and 5. His record might look like this: `70, 200, 3, 12, 10, 5, 1, 1`. The number 3 tells you that the next three records will be children's ages. After that, you go on to the rest of the record.

Another way of storing repeated values is to use what is called a **sentinel** value. A sentinel is a value that tells you that you are at the end of a list. Therefore, rather than storing the number of children, we could decide that we are going to use a sentinel value. Since no children have a negative age, we could use a −1 to indicate that we are at the end of the list, rather than having a count. Under this scheme, Fred's record would look like this: `70, 200, 12, 10, 5, -1, 1, 1`.

Such sequences of data are commonly referred to as **arrays**. An array is simply a sequence of data that is packaged together into a single set. In this example, the children's ages are treated as an array.

☞   **Practice Questions**

1. What would Fred's record look like if he had 6 children, aged 21, 19, 14, 12, 10, and 5, using the format that counts his children?

2. What would that record look like using the format that has a sentinel value?

3. Why is it important that the sentinel value not be a possible data value?

4.4   Using Numbers to Represent Letters

Now that we know a little about how computers represent data using numbers, we can now talk about one of the most common things for computers to store—text. One thing that was missing from our description of a person in the previous section was the person's *name*. How would you represent a name, or any text, using only numbers?

Before we look at how computers store whole blocks of text, let's start by looking at how a computer might store an individual character. Since computers store everything as numbers, computers do the same thing for letters. Just like we used the number 0 to represent blue eye color, we could come up with a number to represent each letter in the alphabet. However, what we display on the screen is not just the letters of the alphabet. There is also punctuation, upper- and lower-case letters, symbols, and even digits. It might seem odd that a digit needs a representation as a number, but when you mix them in with the list of "characters that need to be typed or displayed," it makes sense. Since there is nothing preventing you from typing a 0 as part of a piece of text, it is something that must be represented along with everything else.

Each character that might be displayed has a corresponding number that represents it. The most common system for representing characters by numbers in a single byte is called the **ASCII** code, which was developed in the 1960s. In ASCII, the decimal numbers 65–90 represent the uppercase letters A–Z, the decimal numbers 97–122 represent the lowercase letters a–z, the decimal numbers 48–57 represent the digits 0–9, and the space is represented by the decimal number 32. A more complete ASCII table is available in Appendix B.

That is how you represent a single character, but how should a whole block of text, like someone's name, be represented? If you think back to the previous section, how did we

represent a sequence of things? We used an array, and a block of text can be thought of as an array of characters. As an array, it can either be represented as a length followed by the list of characters, or as a list of characters with a sentinel value. In ASCII, the decimal number 0 is a special character called the **null** character, which is used as a sentinel for a list of characters. An array of characters is often referred to as a **string**, and a string that is represented using a null for its sentinel value is sometimes called a **null-terminated string**.

Let's go back to our person data format before we added the children. Let's say we wanted to store the name of the person to the record. The record would store the name, height, weight, hair color, eye color. We can use a null-terminated string for the name. Therefore, my name, "Jon," would be encoded as 74, 111, 110, 0. Then, my whole record would be:

74, 111, 110, 0, 72, 275, 2, 0

You can tell where my name ends and the rest of the record begins by the sentinel.

Now, let's add children, using -1 for the sentinel value. We'll pretend I have two children, Jim and Bob. In the next record, we will use the format name, height, weight, hair color eye color, name of child 1, age of child 1, ..., -1. It looks like this:

74, 111, 110, 0, 72, 275, 2, 0, 74, 105, 109, 0, 14, 66, 111, 98, 0, 12, -1

☞ **Practice Questions**

- Look at the record above. Based on the format, what is Jim's age?

- Create a new record for Jim if he had another child named Mary Ann, aged 6.

As you can see, in order to process data, computers have to be very exact about what kind of data goes where, how long it is, and whether it repeats. In order for two programs to communicate, or even for two functions within the same program to communicate, they must both agree on the format of the data. Now, in modern programming languages such as JavaScript, the representation is much nicer than a string of numbers. JavaScript, for instance, allows you to say "Jim" instead of 74, 105, 109, 0, but underneath it actually does the same thing. "Jim" is a string of characters. In most programming languages, putting quotations around a string of characters indicates that those characters should be

treated as a string of text. Generally, if you see 234 in a program it means the *number* 234, but "234" means the string of characters 2, 3, 4 (which would be represented by the numbers 67, 68, 69 in ASCII).

Modern programming languages and programs use an encoding called **UTF-8** instead of ASCII, but for most purposes, when using the English language, they are equivalent. For more information about character encodings and UTF-8, see Appendix B.

4.5   What Is a File Format?

So far, we have discussed how computers store things in memory using data formats. Data formats are used because everything is represented by numbers, so we need a format to know what the numbers *mean*. A *file format* is exactly like a data format, except that it is stored on a disk rather than in memory.

Have you ever tried to open up a document in the wrong application? What happened? Usually, if you open up a document in the wrong application, it either gives you an error, or it gives you a lot of junk. As we have seen, since programs are just dealing with numbers, they have to know what the data format is to make sense of the data. Without knowing that format, the file is gibberish.

Computers often distinguish between different file types by the name of the file. Most files have a **filename extension** which tells you the type of file it is. For instance, Adobe Portable Document Format files usually end in .pdf. There are many different graphics formats, each with their own extension, such as .jpg, .png, or .gif. MP3 audio files have the extension .mp3.

However, on the Internet, the URL does not always contain an extension, and for various technical reasons sometimes even contains a *different* extension from the type of file it is sending you. In addition, sometimes there is more than one format with the same extension. Therefore, to remove ambiguity, the Internet signals a file format differently, using **content types**, also called MIME types. If you remember back to communicating with a server using HTTP in Chapter 3, after we sent our request, it sent back a response line, response headers, and a response document. One of the response headers that gets sent back from the webserver is the `Content-Type` header. In our example, the server gave back a content type of `text/html`. Content types have two parts, a type and a subtype. In this case the type is "text" and the subtype is "html." Since the type is "text," how do you think it stores

its data? All text documents store their data as a long sequence of characters. In a text document, the *only* type of data allowed are characters. Most files that do not have a "text" type are called **binary** files, which only means that it contains data that is not text.

Notice, however, that there is a subtype, "html." This indicates that text files themselves can have formats. That is, we can organize a text file such that it is easy for a computer to locate specific kinds of data. For instance, spreadsheets often use CSV (comma-separated value) files. The CSV file format uses a comma to separate data that go into different columns and a return character to separate data that go into different rows. Below is a sample CSV file with three columns and four rows:

Figure 4.3: An Example CSV File

```
Name , Age , Height
Jon  B , 36 , 72
Fred  F , 44 , 70
Jennifer  Q , 50 , 60
Jim  Z , 22 , 68
```

Since a CSV is a text document, this whole file would be stored as a string of characters. A spreadsheet, when loading the document, might convert columns two and three into numbers, but, on a disk, since it is a text document, it is stored as a string of characters. The format says that when the spreadsheet loads the file, it should split the row into columns based on where the commas occur, and split the file into rows based on where the line breaks are. So, because it is a text format, all of the details of the file are easily viewable and understandable by people, since it is just a string of characters. However, it is in fact a *data format* because the different pieces of the file have significant meanings—in this case the commas and the newline characters.

In Chapter 6 we will look at the HTML file format.

☞   **Practice Questions**

To see the difference between text files and binary files, open up different file types with your text editor. For information on what a text editor is and how to use one, see Section A.3.

1. Open up your text editor according to the instructions in A.3.

2. Open up a file on your computer with one of the following extensions: `.jpg`, `.png`, `.pdf`, `.mp3`, `.doc`, `.xls`. If your computer is not showing you the file extension, Section A.3 describes how to make them visible.

3. Since you are using a text editor, it will attempt to treat each number in the file as if it were a character. This is what makes all of the funny characters—your text editor doesn't know how to deal with the non-text characters.

4. Now open up a file on your computer with one of the following extensions: `.txt`, `.csv`, `.html`, `.rtf`. If you don't have any of these types of files, you can easily create a `.rtf` file using any word processor. Just tell the word processor to export your document in "Rich Text Format," and it will produce an appropriate file with an extension of `.rtf`.

5. Even if you don't *understand* the file, it should at least be viewable—you should recognize the characters that it is using.

6. Note that the extensions themselves don't do anything—they are merely there to help you know what is in the file, what program to use to open the file, and what icon to display for the file. Your operating system keeps a list of default programs to use for various file extensions. If you change a file extension of a file, the computer will likely open up the wrong program for that file!

Review

In this chapter we covered some of the details about how computers look at and process data. We have learned:

- Computers store everything using numbers.

- In order for a computer to understand what those numbers mean, they must be in a pre-defined data format.

- Lists of data are often stored by storing the length before the number of data items, or by using a sentinel value to indicate the end of a list.

- Display characters, including letters, digits, punctuation, and spaces, are stored using numbers to represent each character.

- Blocks of text are stored as sequences of display characters called *strings*.

- Just like other sequences, the size of a string is given either by a length or by a sentinel value at the end, usually the number zero (not the text digit "0"), called the *null* character.

- A file format is just a data format stored on a disk.

- Filenames have a *file extension* to indicate what the format of the data is.

- A text file is a file format where the entire file is stored as one long string.

- Text files often have a specific structure themselves.

- CSV files are an example of a text file with a specific structure—they use the newline character to separate records and commas to separate fields.

- HTML files are text files with their own structure.

Apply What You Have Learned

1. Let's say that we wanted to store data on a computer about a car. What pieces of data might we want to store? How would we want to represent it in the computer using numbers?

2. Write the name of your favorite car using ASCII numbers.

3. Try to create your own CSV-formatted file. Be sure to make the file extension `.csv` when you save it. Now, if you have a spreadsheet program on your computer, try to open up the file with your spreadsheet program. What happens?

4. Take your spreadsheet program and create a spreadsheet. Add colors and styles to the spreadsheet cells. Now, save or export the spreadsheet to a CSV file. Open up the file in the text editor. What does it look like? Open the CSV file again in the spreadsheet. What changed?

5. Write a document in your word processor. Write three or four lines of text, with each line being formatted slightly differently (font size, italic, etc.). Save this file as an RTF (also called "Rich Text Format," extension `.rtf`) file. An RTF file is a text format for word processors. Open up the file with your text editor. What does it look like? Can you find your original text? Can you decipher what those other characters might mean? Now, in the text editor, make a change to some of your original text and open it in the word processor.

Chapter 5

How Computers Work

Now that we know a little bit about where computers come from, how they communicate, and how they store data, we can learn how computers work. Chapter 1 discussed the difference between a machine language, which allows a programmer to give a computer instructions that it directly understands, and a programming language, which is a more human-like way of programming the computer. Programming languages, since they are not native to a computer, eventually have to be translated into machine language instructions. Therefore, because they have to be translatable into a machine language, programming languages have to be more rigid and exact than a human language.

Most programmers never need to use machine language. However, it is good to at least understand conceptually what a machine language looks like, as it will help you understand the exactness required in programming. The biggest problem that new programmers run into is that, when they write programs, they expect the computer to do what they *mean*, which is often different from what they actually told it to do. Knowing how machine language works will give you a feel for the exactness required to program a computer. Therefore, before we begin our study of programming, this chapter will give you a feel for how the computer actually does its processing at the machine language level.

The examples in this chapter may seem tedious. They are. Few people program in machine language anymore because *it is* quite tedious. Don't worry, though—programming languages were invented specifically to remove the tediousness of machine language. The point is to introduce you to the way a machine thinks, so it will help you understand the exactness required, and start thinking in the ways that the computer needs you to think.

5.1   Parts of a Computer

You can conceptually break a computer into four main pieces:

- the **Central Processing Unit** (CPU)

- the computer's **memory** (also known as Random Access Memory, or RAM)

- an **input/output system**

- a **data bus** which moves the data between these different parts

The computer's CPU is where most of the data processing happens. The CPU itself is divided into two components—the **control unit** and the **arithmetic and logic unit** (ALU). The control unit manages the process of computing itself. The control unit maintains a piece of data called the **instruction pointer** which holds the location in memory of the next instruction to perform. The control unit looks at an instruction, determines what is needed to process that instruction, and then manages all of the components needed to make that instruction happen. This might include things like writing and fetching data to and from the memory, reading and writing data to the input/output system, and telling the arithmetic and logic unit to perform computations. The arithmetic and logic unit performs basic calculations, such as add, subtract, multiply, and divide, directly. It also performs logical comparisons, such as comparing if two values are equal or if one value is greater than another. Although some processors have more basic calculation features than others, all of them are computationally equivalent. Even if you only had a processor that could add and subtract, you could write additional code that would use addition and subtraction to be able to multiply and divide. A computer equipped with only minimal instructions can perform any computation necessary—it just takes more work from the programmer. The ALU can also contain temporary storage locations, called registers, which are used to perform the computations.

The computer's memory is where a computer stores data that is being actively used for processing. The computer's memory is *not* the same thing as its hard drive. The hard drive is actually external to the computer and is connected through the input/output system. The hard drive is where data can be permanently stored. Computer memory is where data is stored while it is being used. To conceptualize the difference, if you turn off your computer suddenly, the information stored in RAM is wiped away. In Chapter 4, we discussed how computer memory was laid out. It is divided into billions of storage locations, where each

location can hold a number between 0 and 255. The locations themselves are numbered so that they can be identified and accessed easily.

The input/output system in a computer is tasked with communicating with the outside world. The main computer itself is incapable of interacting with people. Keyboard input, screen output, hard drives, network adapters, and all of the other things that we think of when we interact with our computer, are all actually on the "outside" of the computer, connected through the input/output system. There are several standards for input/output systems, the most common of which is the **Universal Serial Bus** (USB). USB defines a standard way of connecting input/output devices to a computer. This allows USB drives, USB cameras, USB keyboards, and a myriad of other devices to all connect to your computer. Without the input/output system, computers would be impossible to use, as there would be no way for us to give it data or programs or see the output of computation.

The data bus handles moving data between each of these systems. It is an important, but often overlooked, feature of computer systems. For instance, if you have a really fast CPU, and a lot of memory, neither of these do much good if the data bus is slow in moving the memory to the CPU. Buses are connected together by hubs, which direct traffic to and from each device. Many modern computer architectures have two separate hubs. The fastest hub, which connects directly to the CPU, is often called the northbridge. It connects the CPU to the memory and the graphics card. The other hub, often called the southbridge, connects from the northbridge to the rest of the input/output systems.

5.2 A Simplified Paper Machine Simulation

For the rest of this chapter we will be playing with a "paper machine." That is, we will use a pen and paper to simulate what a CPU would be doing when running a program.

The purpose of the machine and machine language introduced here is to help you understand the *concept* of a machine language. The machine language we will cover is not an actual machine language used on any computer but it is very similar, and should help you understand and learn real machine languages should you ever wish to. Because of this, you do not need to memorize anything from here to the end of the chapter. You do, however, need to follow the instructions and do the activities because they will help you understand what it is that the computer is doing.

To perform the simulation, you will need several blank sheets of paper, a pen, and a pencil

with an eraser. You also might want to use a ruler to help you make straight lines. Be sure to use a pencil when it says to, because you will be doing a lot of erasing.

These first steps should be done in pen.

On the top of the first sheet of paper, title the paper "Computer Memory." Now, make an 8x8 grid of squares to fill the whole sheet of paper. Number each square in the top-left corner of the square, starting with 0 and going through 63. These are the addresses of the memory locations. Be sure to leave enough room to write a value in each box. Each memory location can receive a number between 0 and 255. If there is no value written in the square, then the value is assumed to be zero (so right now your memory is all zeroes). This sheet of paper will represent a very tiny computer memory. (Real computer memories would take about half a billion sheets of paper.) As we progress in our simulation, the values in the squares will change.

On the top of the second sheet of paper, title the paper "Control Unit." Now, make an empty box at the top-left of the paper, and label the box "Instruction Pointer." Now make four columns on the rest of the paper, titled "Meaning," "Opcode," "Operand 1," and "Operand 2."

On the top of the third sheet of paper, title the paper "Arithmetic and Logic Unit." Make 16 boxes in this area and label them "Register 0" through "Register 15."

At the end of this process, you should have three sheets of paper that look like Figure 5.1.

In the next section, we will have a machine language program to process, which should be done in pencil. You will copy the program (Figure 5.3) into memory. Then to run the simulation, you will use the steps detailed in Figure 5.2.

In this machine language, each instruction consists of three parts—the **opcode**, operand 1, and operand 2. The opcode is the actual function being performed. This might be loading a value from memory into a register, adding register values together, comparing register values, etc. Operand 1 and operand 2 will behave differently based on what opcode is being used. The description will tell you how to use each one.

The way an operand is used is called a mode. Sometimes an operand will specify a register number (called *register mode*). This means that the number in the operand refers to a register in the Arithmetic and Logic Unit. If the operand was 6, using register mode would mean that the operand was referring to register 6. Sometimes an operand will specify a memory location (called *memory mode*). This means that the number in the operand refers

Figure 5.1: Machine Simulation Setup

Figure 5.2: Simulation Steps

These steps should all be done *in pencil*. Before you begin a simulation, be sure to double-check that you copied the memory locations *exactly*.

Before you start the steps below, set the box labeled Instruction Pointer to 0. Then, repeat the steps below until you get to a halt instruction (0, 0, 0). Each time through the steps will allow you to execute one instruction.

1. Take the Control Unit sheet and look at your Instruction Pointer.

2. Look at the Computer Memory sheet at the location indicated by the Instruction Pointer. For instance, if the Instruction Pointer says "0," then you would retrieve the first value in Computer Memory. If the Instruction Pointer says "15," you would get the last value on the second row in Computer Memory.

3. Copy the value from the Computer Memory into the first empty line of the Control Unit sheet under the heading "Opcode."

4. Now, look back at the Computer Memory, and copy the next value into the Operand 1 column of the Control Unit, and the value after that into the Operand 2 column of the Control Unit. So, if the Instruction Pointer said 15, then you would copy the value in memory location 16 to Operand 1 and the value in memory location 17 to Operand 2. The Control Unit now has the full instruction to execute.

5. Add 3 to the value in the Instruction Pointer (erase the old value). If the value was 15, you would erase that and write 18.

6. Look up the value that you wrote in the "Opcode" column in the list of opcodes (these are provided in Section 5.5). Write the name associated with the opcode in the column labeled "Meaning."

7. In the opcode table, there is a description that tells you what to do with each opcode. Perform the task as specified in the description. If it is the "Halt" opcode (0), the simulation is finished.

8. Go back to step 1 and do it again.

to a memory location in Computer Memory. If the operand was 6, using memory mode would mean that the operand was referring to memory location 6. Sometimes an operand will specify a value (called *immediate mode*). This means that the number in the operand is used as the number itself. If the operand was 6, using immediate mode would mean that the operand was just referring to the number 6. Finally, there is a mode called *indirect mode*. In this mode, the operand refers to a register, but the register is used to refer to a memory location. So, if the operand was 6, using indirect mode would mean that the operand was referring to a memory location stored in register 6. If register 6 had the value 23, then in indirect mode memory location 23 would be used as the operand.

As an example, let's say that the instruction was 20, 5, 10. This means that 20 is the opcode, 5 is operand 1, and 10 is operand 2. Now, let's look up opcode 20 in the opcode tables at the end of the chapter (Section 5.5). It says that this opcode means "Load Immediate." In the table, it says that operand 1 uses *register mode* and therefore refers to a register. Since operand 1 is 5, operand 1 is interpreted to mean register 5. The table says that operand 2 uses *immediate mode*, and therefore the number itself is used. Since operand 2 is 10, operand 2 is simply the value 10. In the description, it says that we are supposed to load the value specified by operand 2 into the register specified by operand 1. Therefore, we would pull out the "Arithmetic and Logic Unit" sheet, and erase what is in register 5, and write in the value 10.

In the next section, we will do a full simulation.

☞ Doing the Simulation in a Class Setting

This simulation is easy to do in a class setting, and was actually originally developed for use in a class. To do this, you need to use markerboards or chalkboards rather than sheets of paper. Appoint one student to be the Control Unit. This student is responsible for performing the steps outlined above, but they cannot leave the control unit area or write on another student's board.

Appoint another student to be the Data Bus. This student is responsible for transferring all needed data to and from the Computer Memory. The Control Unit will direct which values the Data Bus needs to fetch or store. The Data Bus only takes instructions from the Control Unit.

Appoint another student to handle the Arithmetic and Logic Unit sheet. They will

perform any computation requested by the Control Unit on its registers, and can give
to the Control Unit any value that has been computed in its registers.

I have found that doing the computations interactively greatly increases the ability of
students to visualize what is happening inside the computer and makes them better
programmers long-term.

5.3   A Short Program: Multiplying by Two

Now we will perform a program to multiply a number by 2. If you look through the opcode
tables at the end of this chapter (Section 5.5), you might notice that there is no opcode for
multiplication. However, basic arithmetic tells us that we can multiply by repeated adding.
Therefore, we will need to fetch a number, add it to itself, and then store the value back to
a register or memory. In our program, memory location 62 will hold the value that we want
to multiply (in this case, the number 12), and, at the end of the program, memory location
63 will hold the value that we calculate.

5.3.1   Setting Up the Simulation

To begin the simulation, the code and the data are both written into memory. Copy the
following values into your Computer Memory sheet:

Figure 5.3: Machine Language Program to Multiply a Number by Two

0	1	2	3	4	5	6	7
22	0	62	21	1	0	133	0
8 1	**9** 25	**10** 63	**11** 0	**12** 0	**13** 0	**14** 0	**15** 0
16 0	**17** 0	**18** 0	**19** 0	**20** 0	**21** 0	**22** 0	**23** 0
24 0	**25** 0	**26** 0	**27** 0	**28** 0	**29** 0	**30** 0	**31** 0
32 0	**33** 0	**34** 0	**35** 0	**36** 0	**37** 0	**38** 0	**39** 0
40 0	**41** 0	**42** 0	**43** 0	**44** 0	**45** 0	**46** 0	**47** 0
48 0	**49** 0	**50** 0	**51** 0	**52** 0	**53** 0	**54** 0	**55** 0
56 0	**57** 0	**58** 0	**59** 0	**60** 0	**61** 0	**62** 12	**63** 0

Before you decide to quit programming altogether, let me remind you that the point of this exercise is not that we would ever actually program this way, but rather to give you a glimpse into how the computer looks at processing. The very reason that computer programming languages were invented was so that we would not have to deal with this stuff on a daily basis. So, to allay your fears, below is what this would look like in JavaScript:

Figure 5.4: Multiply a Number by Two in JavaScript

```
var multiply_by_two = function(x) {
    return x * 2;
};
```

You still may not understand what exactly this does or why it is written that way, but hopefully it gives you hope that it will be more understandable than a bunch of numbers written out.

Now, to run the program, you need to look at the steps in Figure 5.2. We will go through them step-by-step so you know how to do it.

5.3.2   Running the Simulation

Now, let's go through the program step-by-step to see what is happening. This will all be done *in pencil*. Look at Figure 5.2. The first thing it says is to double-check that the memory locations were copied over correctly. Do this now. Next, it says to write a 0 in the box labeled Instruction Pointer. Do so now. Now we can proceed to the numbered steps.

Step 1 says to look at the instruction pointer. It should read 0.

Step 2 says to look at the memory location indicated by the Instruction Pointer. Since ours says 0, we will look at memory location 0.

Step 3 says to copy the value at that memory location to the first line of the Control Unit sheet under the heading Opcode. The value at memory location 0 is 22, so we will write 22 in the first line of the Control Unit sheet in the Opcode column.

Step 4 says to copy the next value in memory to the column labeled Operand 1. The next memory location is memory location 1, and it has the value 0. Therefore, we will write the number 0 to the Operand 1 column. We then copy the next value in memory (memory location 2) to the Operand 2 column. Memory location 2 has the value 62 in it, so write the number 62 in the Operand 2 column. This is our first instruction: 22, 0, 62.

Step 5 says to add 3 to the value in the Instruction Pointer. The instruction pointer currently has a 0 in it, so $3 + 0$ is 3. Erase the 0 and write 3 in the box. This will allow us to read the next instruction the next time we go through the steps.

Step 6 says to look up the value in the Opcode column in the list of opcodes in Section 5.5. The opcode is 22, so go through the list of opcodes to find opcode 22. The opcodes are not listed in numerical order, so you will need to look through all of them until you find the right one. The opcode is "Load Memory." Therefore, write "Load Memory" in the column labeled Meaning.

Step 7 says to perform the steps listed in the opcode table for this opcode. You will notice that the opcode table says that Operand 1 refers to a register and Operand 2 refers to a memory location. Therefore, we will be working with register 0 and memory location 62. The description says to load the value in the memory location specified by Operand 2 into the register specified by Operand 1. Therefore, we will load the value in memory location 62 into register 0. Memory location 62 has the value 12 in it, so we will write 12 in register 0 on the Arithmetic and Logic Unit sheet.

Step 8 says to go back to step 1 and repeat for the next instruction.

Now we are back to step 1. Therefore, we need to look at our Instruction Pointer again. This time it is set to 3. Step 2 says to look at the memory location indicated by the instruction pointer. It is the number 21. Step 3 says to copy that number to the next line on the Control Unit sheet under the Opcode column. Therefore, write the number 21 into the Opcode column. Step 4 says to copy the next two memory locations to the Opcode 1 and Opcode 2 columns. The next two memory locations have the numbers 1 and 0 in them, so write 1 in the Opcode 1 column and 0 in the Opcode 2 column. The instruction we copied is 21, 1, 0.

Step 5 says to add 3 to the Instruction Pointer. Therefore, write 6 in the Instruction Pointer box, erasing the previous value.

Step 6 says to look up the value that is written in the Opcode column in the list of opcodes in Section 5.5 and write the name of the opcode in the Meaning column. Step 7 says to do

what the description of the opcode says to do. The description says to copy the value of the register specified in Operand 2 into the register specified by Operand 1. Operand 1 is 1 and Operand 2 is 0. Therefore, look at register 0. It currently contains the number 12. So write 12 into the box for register 1.

This instruction has given us two copies of the same number—one in register 0 and one in register 1. This is good because multiplication by two is just adding the same number twice. Therefore, what type of instruction do you think will come next? Look through the list of instructions to see which one you think we will do next. Step 8 says to repeat the process for the next instruction, so let's do that now.

If you go through steps 1–4 again, you will have the next instruction copied over, which is 133, 0, 1. Step 5 then tells us to add 3 to the Instruction Pointer, so write a 9 in the Instruction Pointer box. Step 6 says to look up the Opcode (133) in the list of opcodes and write down its meaning. Write "Add" in the Meaning column. Step 7 says to do what the description of the opcode says. It says to add the two registers specified by Operand 1 and Operand 2 and store the result in the register specified by Operand 1. Operand 1 is 0 and Operand 2 is 1. Therefore, we will add the value in register 0 to the value in register 1. Register 0 has 12 in it, and register 1 also has 12 in it. Added together, this makes 24. The instruction says to store the value in register specified by Operand 1. Operand 1 is 0, so we will store the result in register 0. Therefore, erase what is currently in register 0 and write 24 in it.

Register 0 now has the value we want (24 is 12 * 2), but the goal was to get it stored in memory location 63. So what do you think the next instruction might do? Step 8 says to repeat the process to find out.

Following steps 1–4 will give us the next instruction: 25, 63, 0. Step 5 tells us to increase the Instruction Pointer to 12. Step 6 tells us to look up the meaning of opcode 25 in the opcode list and write it down in the Meaning column. This gives us "Store Memory."

Step 7 tells us to perform the instructions associated with the opcode. This says to store the value in the register specified by Operand 2 into the memory location specified by Operand 1. Operand 1 is 63 and Operand 2 is 0. Therefore, we will take the value in register 0 (which is 24) and write it in memory location 63, erasing what is currently there. Therefore, write 24 into memory location 63.

Step 8 says to go back to step 1 and process the next instruction.

Performing steps 1–4 will give us our next instruction—0, 0, 0. Step 5 says to increase the

Instruction Pointer to 15. Step 6 says to look up the opcode, which tells us that opcode 0 is "Halt." Step 7 says that if we reach a Halt instruction, we should end the simulation.

Now we are done! If you remember from the beginning of this section, the goal was to take the value stored in memory location 62, multiply it by 2, and store it in memory location 63. Memory location 62 has a 12 in it, and memory location 63 has a 24 in it. It took a lot of work, but that is exactly what the computer does when it processes instructions. The instructions have to be so simple because computers themselves cannot think; they can only process. Because the instructions are so simple, it takes quite a few of them to perform even simple tasks. However, this simplicity also allows the computer to perform billions of them every second.

5.4   Adding a List of Numbers

Now we are going to do a more complicated program—we are going to add a list of numbers. In order to do this, we need to be able to know when we are at the end of our list of numbers. We will use a sentinel value to indicate that we are at the end of the list of numbers. (See Chapter 4 for more information on sentinel values.) We will use the number 255 as the sentinel to represent the end of the list of numbers.

What the program will do is add up all of the numbers starting in memory location 57 until it hits the sentinel value and then store the result in memory location 56.

Here is the program:

Figure 5.5: Machine Language Program to Add a List of Numbers

0	1	2	3	4	5	6	7
20	0	0	20	3	255	20	1
8: 57	9: 20	10: 5	11: 1	12: 23	13: 2	14: 1	15: 21
16: 4	17: 3	18: 37	19: 4	20: 2	21: 65	22: 33	23: 4
24: 133	25: 0	26: 2	27: 133	28: 1	29: 5	30: 64	31: 12
32: 0	33: 25	34: 56	35: 0	36: 0	37: 0	38: 0	39: 0
40: 0	41: 0	42: 0	43: 0	44: 0	45: 0	46: 0	47: 0
48: 0	49: 0	50: 0	51: 0	52: 0	53: 0	54: 0	55: 0
56: 0	57: 10	58: 12	59: 3	60: 255	61: 8	62: 2	63: 0

Now, before we go through the program step-by-step, let's think about what needs to happen to do this procedure. First, we will need a place (probably a register) to hold the current results of the sum as we go through the numbers. As we go along, we will need to check each number to see if it matches our sentinel value, 255. We need to get the computer to do something *different* if it hits the sentinel value than if it doesn't. Finally, we will need a way to repeat steps, since we don't know how many times we will be doing the calculation.

The way to accomplish all of this is with comparisons and conditional jumps. That is, we will compare two numbers, and, based on the results of that comparison, potentially change the instruction pointer to tell the computer to run different code. Since we look at the instruction pointer to retrieve the next piece of code, if an instruction modifies the instruction pointer, then we will do a *different* task than we would otherwise have.

The other feature we will look at is indirect mode. Since we will be looking at an unknown number of different values, we cannot put the location of the value to load in our code. Therefore, what we will do is use a register to hold the address of the first value, and then use indirect mode to tell the computer to load the value from the address stored in the register. From there, we can add one to the value in the register to have it point to the next location in memory.

So now, let's run through the simulation using the steps in Figure 5.2. Instead of going through each step like we did in the previous program, I am going to assume that you now know how to work the steps. Each paragraph is the entirety of the 8 steps. I will focus on the meaning of each instruction rather than all of the steps to perform it. Performing the steps is your job, but be sure to do all of the steps *in the right order*. Also, in order to make what is happening more understandable, as we go along we will be writing names on our registers so we know what they are doing. The compute doesn't use this—this is entirely for our own purposes so we know what each register is being used for.

The first instruction is 0, 0, 0. This says to load register 0 with the number 0. Register 0 will hold the sum of all of the numbers. You might go ahead and label register 0 as "sum" so you can remember what it is for. Remember, the computer doesn't care what it is for—the computer just does what you tell it. But *you* need to remember what it is for so you can understand the program.

The next instruction is 20, 3, 255. This says to load register 3 with the number 255. This is our sentinel value and will be used for comparison. You might label register 3 with the word "sentinel."

The next instruction is 20, 1, 57. This says to load register 1 with the number 57. This is the beginning of the locations that we will be reading the values from. Note that we are storing the *number* 57 into register 1, not the contents of memory location 57. That will come later. Label register 1 with the word "pointer," since it will point to the location in memory that we are reading values from.

The next instruction is 20, 5, 1. This says to load register 5 with the number 1. This is the number that we will use to increment the memory location pointer. Label register 5 with the word "increment."

Take note of what the instruction pointer currently is. It should be at 12. All of the previous instructions were "setup" instructions that were meant to get the ball rolling. The next instruction will really start the process. You should label memory location 12 with the words "main process start" to remind yourself that this is where the core of the process will happen.

The instruction here at memory location 12 is 23, 2, 1. This says to look in register 1, and use that value as the memory location to look in. Right now, register 1 has the number 57 in it. Therefore, look in memory location 57 and put that value in register 2. Label register 2 with the words "current value." It should have the value 10 in it.

If you think back to what we are trying to do, the next thing we need to do is determine whether or not the current value is our sentinel value or not. Therefore, we have to compare our current value (register 2) with our sentinel value (register 3). However, since in this machine language comparisons overwrites one of the values being compared with the results of the comparison (look at the Compare instruction in the tables), we have to first copy one of the values to a new register so it doesn't get destroyed. Therefore, the next instruction reads 21, 4, 3. This says to copy the contents of register 3 (the sentinel value) to register 4. Label register 4 with the words "sentinel comparison." It should have the value 255 in it.

The next instruction is 37, 4, 2. When you look up that instruction, it says to compare the value in register 2 (the current value) with the value in register 4. If they are equal, it will store the number 0 into register 4. If the value in register 2 is greater than the value in register 4, it will store a 2 in register 4. Finally, if the value in register 4 is greater than the value in register 2, it will store a 1 in register 4. This way, at the end of the comparison, register 4 will contain the result of comparing the current value with the sentinel. Since register 4 had the value 255 and register 2 has the value 10, the value in register 4 should be erased, and, in its place, you should write the number 1 since 255 is greater than 10.

Now that we have the comparison, what do we do with it? The next instruction is 65, 33, 4. This instruction says to look at register 4. If the value is 0, then change the instruction pointer to 33—otherwise, do nothing. This is a conditional jump. Basically, it says if the previous comparison of our current value to the sentinel showed that they were equal (gave the value 0), then go to the end of the program (which is at memory location 33). Since register 4 contains a 1, nothing happens and we go to the next instruction like normal.

The next instruction is 133, 0, 2. This adds the contents of register 2 (the current value) to register 0 (the sum so far), and stores the result in register 2. Since register 0 currently is at 0, it should now be $10 + 0$, or 10.

Now we need to do the same thing to the next value. But how do we get to the next value? Since register 1 holds the pointer to the next value, we just need to increase register 1 by 1, which is stored in register 5 (the increment). The next instruction is 133, 1, 5. This says to add the contents of register 5 (the increment) to register 1 (the pointer) and store the result in register 1.

Now we are all set to do the same computation on the next value. We just need to go back to the right place in our code to do it all over again. The next instruction is 64, 12, 0. The instruction for 64 is an "unconditional branch." This means that we directly modify the instruction pointer to be 12. Therefore, on the next instruction you will go back to memory location 12 to get the next instruction. We labeled this earlier with the words "main process start." Label this location in memory (30) "main process end."

Now, I'm not going to walk you through all of the next steps, as you will just be going back through the same steps repeatedly. However, think about what happens when you do load in the value 255 from memory? At that point, our comparison above will notice that the value in register 4 (sentinel comparison) is equal to the value in register 2 (current value), and will therefore store the value 0 in register 4. Then, the next "Jump if Zero" instruction will actually work—the value in register 4 *will* be zero, so we will modify the instruction pointer to point to the location specified in the instruction (which is 33).

At that point, we will load the instruction at memory location 33, which is 25, 56, 0. This stores the value of register 0 (the current sum, which is now the final sum) into memory location 56. Memory location 56 should now contain the sum of the relevant values (i.e., 25).

The next instruction is 0, 0, 0, which tells the simulation to stop. We are now finished, and memory location 56 holds the value of the sum of memory locations 57, 58, and 59.

Just as before, this is much easier in JavaScript. A similar function in JavaScript would look like this:

Figure 5.6: Add a List of Numbers in JavaScript

```
var add_numbers = function(num_list) {
    var sum = 0;
    for(var i = 0; i < num_list.length; i++) {
        sum = sum + num_list[i];
    }
    return sum;
};
```

Again, I don't expect you to understand what this means yet, but you should at least recognize that this will be much easier than writing out numbers for machine instructions!

Hopefully this exercise has helped you understand the precision with which computers perform their processing and the exactness required from the programmer. If even one of the instructions for the computer programs were written incorrectly, the whole program would fail. While you probably won't ever need to do this again, the goal was to get your brain in line with the way that computers think. This will make thinking about programming much easier in the future.

If you enjoyed this process, a few other machine language programs are available in Appendix C.

5.5 Machine Opcode Tables

This section lists out the different machine opcodes used by the simulated machine in this chapter. The opcodes are ordered by category, not by number, but this shouldn't be too much of a hindrance as there are fewer than twenty of them. While we will not be using all of the listed opcodes, they are included for completeness and also for the examples in Appendix C.

Each opcode is listed along with what types of operands it uses. The operands are the list of values that will be used for processing the instruction. For instance, for an add instruction the operands would be the locations which hold the values to be added together, and where the result should end up. This simulated machine has four types of operands:

- Immediate operands: An immediate operand means that the number represents itself. That is, if we want to load the value 1 somewhere, we would use an immediate-mode operand.

- Register operand: Registers are temporary storage locations within the ALU. Therefore, if an opcode takes a register operand, this operand will refer to the register number.

- Memory operand: A memory operand is a number, called a **memory address**, that refers to a storage location in the computer memory from which to load or store values.

- Indirect operand: an indirect operand uses the value in a register as the memory location that is to be used for this operand. For instance, let's say that an indirect operand had the value 1. That would mean to look at register 1 and use the value in that register as the memory address that the instruction needs to operate on. So, if register 1 has the value 35, then we would read or write to memory address 35.

The first set of instructions we will look at are the load/store instructions. These instructions simply move data around between storage locations. They also make the most use of the different operand types discussed above.

Figure 5.7: Load/Store Instructions

Opcode	Name	Operand 1	Operand 2	Description
20	Load Immediate	Register	Immediate	Loads the value specified in operand 2 into the register specified in operand 1.
21	Load Register	Register	Register	Loads the value contained in the register specified in operand 2 into the register specified in operand 1.
22	Load Memory	Register	Memory	Loads the value contained in the memory location specified in operand 2 into the register specified in operand 1.
23	Load Indirect	Register	Indirect	Takes the value in the register specified in operand 2, and use that as a memory address to load a value from. The value in the memory address is loaded into the register specified in operand 1.
25	Store Memory	Memory	Register	Takes the value in the register specified in operand 2, and stores that in the memory location specified by operand 1.
29	Store Indirect	Indirect	Register	Takes the value in the register specified in operand 2, and stores that in the memory location specified by the register specified by operand 1.

The next set of opcodes are the arithmetic opcodes. These are opcodes that modify values by adding, subtracting, etc. In our simulated machine, there are very few arithmetic opcodes, but most real computers have a fairly large set of them. Nonetheless, even with our limited opcode list, a lot can be done with it using a little creativity. The comparison function may seem unusual, but it is made to fit with the conditional jumps in the next opcode table.

Figure 5.8: Arithmetic Instructions

Opcode	Name	Operand 1	Operand 2	Description
133	Add	Register	Register	Takes the value in the register specified by operand 2 and adds it to the value in the register specified by operand 1, storing the resulting value in the register specified by operand 1.
149	Subtract	Register	Register	Takes the value in the register specified by operand 2 and subtracts it from the value in the register specified by operand 1, storing the resulting value in the register specified by operand 1.
37	Compare	Register	Register	Takes the value in the register specified by operand 2 and compares it to the value in the register specified by operand 1. If the value in the register specified by operand 2 is greater than the value in the register specified by operand 1, it stores the number 2 in the register specified by operand 1. If the value in the register specified by operand 2 is less than the value in the register specified by operand 1, it stores the number 1 in the register specified by operand 1. If the value in the two registers are equal, it stores the number 0 in the register specified by operand 1.

The last list of opcodes are the jump instructions. These instructions cause the instruction pointer to change, usually based on a certain condition. The conditions are made to match the results of the Compare opcode above (i.e., 37). A common pattern is for a Compare instruction to be followed by a conditional Jump instruction based on the result of the Compare. We don't use the indirect versions of the jump instructions in this book, but they are listed here because they are very powerful and important features available in all general-purpose processors.

Figure 5.9: Jump Instructions

Opcode	Name	Operand 1	Operand 2	Description
64	Jump Always	Immediate	0	Changes the instruction pointer to the value in operand 1, causing the next instruction executed to be the one listed at that location. Note that the second operand is *always* 0.
76	Jump Always Indirect	Register	0	Changes the instruction pointer to the value in the register specified in operand 1.
65	Jump if Zero	Immediate	Register	Changes the instruction pointer to the value in operand 1 if the value in the register specified by operand 2 is zero.
77	Jump if Zero Indirect	Register	Register	Same as the previous instruction, but operand 1 specifies a register to use to find the next instruction pointer.
81	Jump if One	Immediate	Register	Change the instruction pointer to the value in operand 1 if the value in the register specified by operand 2 is one.
93	Jump if One Indirect	Register	Register	Same as the previous instruction, but operand 1 specifies a register to use to find the next instruction pointer.
97	Jump if Two	Immediate	Register	Change the instruction pointer to the value in operand 1 if the value in the register specified by operand 2 is two.
109	Jump if Two Indirect	Register	Register	Same as the previous instruction, but operand 1 specifies a register to use to find the next instruction pointer.
0	Halt	Unused	Unused	This instruction ends the computer program.

That's it! That is all that computers are. Even though it may seem confusing, the fact that you can write out all of the rules in a few pages is pretty amazing. Computers really are simple at heart. The confusion most people make is thinking that they are complicated. But really, they do exactly what you tell them. Exactly.

While performing these minute calculations may seem overwhelming to you, to the computer they are rather simple. In fact, it is their simplicity that makes it possible for computers to run quickly. Modern computers can perform around 200,000,000,000 of these types of instructions *every second*. They have to be that fast in order to keep up with the latest software. Every time you move your mouse, the computer has to do very similar operations as the above in order to recalculate the new mouse position and redraw your cursor on the screen. You might have noticed that even with 200,000,000,000 instructions per second, sometimes it is still not enough!

☞ **Opcode Numbering**

You might be thinking that the numbering system for the opcodes is kind of strange. However, the numbering system actually has a very logical ordering, but this plan is only evident if you write out the numbers in binary. Each opcode is a combination of a general instruction type (load, add, jump, etc.) and the types of operands that it takes, with two bits dedicated to each operand. This is often true of computers—what may seem arbitrary or strange oftentimes makes a lot more sense with a little more knowledge.

Don't worry, I don't expect you to go through and convert the opcodes into binary—after all, this is just a toy system to help you understand how these things work. But nonetheless, keep in mind that not only computers, but all of life is filled with things whose logic may not be directly visible, but is knowable if you are willing to look beneath the surface.

Review

In this chapter we covered how machines really work. We have learned:

- The main parts of the computer are the CPU, the computer memory, the input/output system, and the data bus.

- The CPU works by taking instructions one at a time, decoding them, and then running the processes they specify.

- Each instruction on a CPU performs a single, very small task.

- The computer can only do exactly what you tell it to do.

- All steps of a program must be specified exactly in order for the computer to perform it correctly.

Apply What You Have Learned

1. Think about what would happen if one instruction in the program was changed. How would a missing or faulty instruction affect the result?

2. Did you notice that the code and the data were both in the same memory? By storing everything as numbers, both code and data can be stored using the same system. What problems might you run into if you accidentally overwrote an instruction with a data value?

Part II

Basic Ingredients for Web Programming

JavaScript is primarily a language for making websites more interactive. This part introduces the basics of the technologies that make web pages work—HTML, CSS, and JavaScript. This part does not go into any depth for any of these topics, but should give enough background to help you understand how they work together to make a web page.

Chapter 6

The HTML File Format

In Chapter 4 we took a look at how computers format data. In this chapter, we are going to look at the data format used on the Internet for displaying web pages. That format is HTML—the HyperText Markup Language. This book is not a book on HTML, but it is needed to really understand how JavaScript works. The introduction to HTML in this chapter will not go into great depth, but should give you a functional understanding of how HTML works.

6.1 A Quick Introduction to HTML

HTML has many features that has made it popular, and it has become the official format of the web. First of all, it is a hypertext format. That means that each file contains **hyperlinks** (or just **links** for short) to other files on the Internet. This is what enables the web-like structure on the Internet. Each document (i.e., web page) contains a number of links to other web pages, which themselves have more links to more web pages. Thus, the file format follows the basic idea of the web—that information is connected to each other, and if we want to know more about something, we can just click the link.

Another great feature of HTML is that it is a **markup language**. The term "markup language" comes from the way manuscripts were edited and laid out before computers. Writing by hand is a little different than making a print book. When you make a book, you need to know what font you want to use for the text, how big you want the letters,

Figure 6.1: An Example of How Authors Marked Up Documents for a Printer

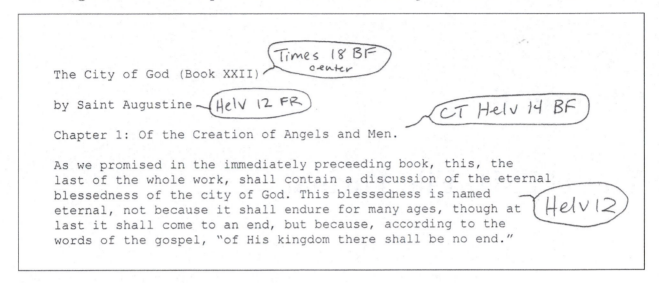

and whether you want some of them bold, etc. Typewriters and handwritten material don't convey any of this information for a printer. Therefore, when an author wrote a book, they would "mark it up" with annotations telling the printer how he should make the final text look.

Figure 6.1 shows what a marked up document looks like. Since manuscripts were written by hand or using a typewriter, authors couldn't type the document in the font that they wanted, so they put in these markup annotations to tell the printer what to do. "Helv 12" tells the printer to make the font 12-point Helvetica; "BF" means to use a bold-faced font; and "FR" means to flush the text right. These types of instructions tell the printer exactly how to typeset each piece of text. Sometimes that can get tiresome, and, instead, the instructions to the printer tell them what *function* the text serves, and then a separate sheet tells how to typeset that function. In this example, "CT" tells the printer that the marked text is the chapter title, so the printer also knows to put that title into the page header at the top of each page. Sometimes the markup would tell the printer exactly what to do (e.g., "Helv 12" says to use 12 point Helvetica font) and sometimes the markup would tell the printer the function of the text in the document (e.g., "CT" tells the printer that use text is a chapter title). If the author specified the function of the text, they would also supply a separate sheet telling the printer how each type of text piece should be handled. This idea of separating the structure and function of the document from the way that it is displayed is something we will return to in Chapter 7.

HTML is a very similar concept. It is a markup language, meaning that it consists of text, and then additional text telling the computer how that text is to be interpreted. Below is a short bit of HTML to give you the feel of the language:

Figure 6.2: A Simple HTML Document

```
<!DOCTYPE html>
<html>
<head>
<title>This is the title of this document</title>
</head>

<body>

<h1>This is a large heading</h1>
<p>This is a paragraph.</p>

<h2>This is a smaller heading</h2>
<p>This is another paragraph.</p>

</body>
</html>
```

As you can see, an HTML document consists mostly of text with additional codes written around the text to tell the computer what function the text is to play. In HTML lingo, these codes are called **tags**. <p> is a **start tag** that tells the computer to treat that text as a paragraph, and </p> is an **end tag** that tells the computer that this is the end of the paragraph. Similarly, <h1> tells the computer to treat the text as a large heading (i.e., heading level 1), and </h1> tells the computer that this is the end of the large heading. HTML has a predefined set of tags that you can use to make your document. By arranging text and tags in a text file, you can easily build your own web pages!

☞   **Practice Activity**

1. Open your text editor, and type in the HTML document above into a new file.

2. Save the file so that it has a `.html` extension.

3. Open up your browser. Rather than typing in a URL, go to the "File" menu and choose "Open." Open up the file you just saved.

4. Observe how the browser displays each piece of tagged text.

5. Also observe the location bar of your browser. If it tells you the protocol, notice that it is *not* an HTTP URL, but rather a `file:` URL. This is because it is getting the file from your hard drive and not from a web server.

6. Go back to your text editor and add a new heading and a new paragraph of text and save it.

7. Click the refresh button on your browser to see your changes.

8. Add extra spaces between words and before and after tags. Save the file and reload the browser. Did anything change? Other than separating text into words, blank space (termed **whitespace**) is not used in HTML. If you need to alter spacing, you have to use tags to tell the computer what you want to do.

6.2   The Parts of an HTML Document

Now that you've seen what an HTML document looks like, it is time to dig deeper into the format. The first thing to know are the basic rules of tagging. These are important, so pay special attention.

1. All tags are enclosed in angled brackets (i.e., `<` and `>`).

2. For nearly every tag, there is a start tag and an end tag. For the paragraph tag, the start tag is `<p>` and the end tag is `</p>`. The only difference between them is that the end tag has a forward slash (/) before the tag name. If you forget the end tag, many browsers won't complain, but you may get strange results.

3. Pairs of start and end tags must be fully within other pairs of start and end tags. For instance `<p>hello <i>there</p></i>` is not allowed, but `<p>hello <i>there</i></p>` is allowed. In the first example, the `<p>` tag starts *before* the `<i>` tag, but the end tag `</p>` occurs before the end tag `</i>`. Therefore, the `<i>` `</i>` pair is not fully within the `<p>` `</p>` pair.

4. For the few tags that do not have an end tag, you combine the start and end tag together. `<br>` does not have an end tag, so it is written `<br />`. This is called a self-closing tag.

5. The combination of a start tag, end tag, and their enclosed content and tags is called an **element**. `<p>` is a tag but `<p>hello</p>` is an element.

6. Blank space (called whitespace) is used to separate words, but is not used for anything else. HTML ignores all extra spacing before, between, and after words. This includes line breaks and spaces for alignment. All of these things are controlled by tags, not by trying to do the spacing yourself.

From here on out, I will only refer to a tag by its start tag. You should always assume that the start tag requires an end tag unless we explicitly say otherwise.

Now, you may have noticed that in our original HTML example, there were several tags that didn't seem to do anything—namely `<html>`, `<head>`, and `<body>`. The `<html>` tag is known as the document root tag. It is the tag that contains all other tags and is required to be there. In this book, if you see an example that doesn't have an `<html>` tag, then it is only showing you a fragment of the document—the rest is assumed to be there, but we are only showing the important parts to make the example clearer. The first tag of every document should be an `<html>` tag, and every document should end with an `</html>` end tag. The `<head>` tag includes tags that tell the browser *about* the document, but which are not displayed within the document itself. In the example given, the `<head>` tag contained a `<title>` tag, which told the browser what the title of the document was. The browser probably displayed this title in the top of the window, and would also use it if you bookmarked the page. The `<body>` tag tells the browser that we are starting the portion of the document which should be displayed.

Some basic tags that you will encounter in most HTML documents include:

`<html>` This is the main container of all other tags within a document.

`<head>` This tag contains tags which give information to the browser *about* the page instead of the page content itself.

`<title>` This tag tells the browser the title of your page.

`<body>` This tag contains the actual page content.

`<h1>` This tag is used for the largest heading on the page.

`<h2>` This tag is for a subheading in the page. HTML has additional subheading sizes down to `<h6>`.

`<p>` This is the paragraph tag. Browsers usually give a blank line between any two paragraphs.

`<br>` This is a line break. This tag self-closes, and is used to force a line break anywhere in the document.

`<b>` This tag tells the browser to use a bold font.

`<i>` This tag tells the browser to use an italic font.

`<u>` This tag tells the browser to underline its contents.

`<div>` This is a general-purpose tag used for grouping blocks of content together.

`<span>` This is a general-purpose tag used for grouping letters or words together within a paragraph or other block of text.

Also notice that we began our file with `<!DOCTYPE html>`. This is called the **doctype declaration** and tells the browser that, yes, this really is an HTML document.

☞ **Practice Questions**

1. If `<h4>` is a start tag, what is its end tag?

2. Which of the following HTML fragments use tags in an invalid way? Why?

   (a) `<h1>My Heading</h1>`
   `<p>This is a <i>great</i> section.`
   `<b>Don't you think?</b></p>`

   (b) `<h1>My Heading</h1>`
   `<p>This is a <i>great</i> section.`
   `<b>Don't you think?</p></b>`

   (c) `<h1>My Heading</h1>`
   `<p>This is a <i>great</i> section.</p>`
   `<p><b>Don't you think?</b></p>`

3. Open up any web page on the Internet. View the HTML source of the web page (see Section A.4 for instructions on doing this). Try to identify tags from the list above.

4. In a previous practice activity, you created an HTML file. Modify your HTML file using some of the tags in the list above.

6.3   Adding Attributes to Tags

HTML tags can also have what are called **attributes**. An attribute modifies or specializes an HTML tag. For instance, most tags take a `width` attribute, which tells the browser how wide to make the tag's content. An attribute looks like this:

Figure 6.3: Tag Attributes Example

```
<div width="100">
    This block is only 100 pixels wide,
    no matter how much text I put into it.
</div>
```

As you can see, the attribute is placed *inside* the start tag. It has the format *attribute-name="value"*. The value should always be surrounded by quotes, though you may choose either single quotes or double quotes. The allowable values inside the quotes depends on the particular tag you are using. You can also specify multiple attributes on the same tag. If you specify multiple attributes, just separate your attributes by a space (*not* a comma), and you can add as many attributes as you want.

I should note that setting a width in this manner is actually frowned upon in HTML. I only present it here because it illustrates the concept of attributes.

6.4   Tags that Refer to Other Documents

As mentioned previously, one of the things that makes HyperText valuable is its ability to refer to other documents. HTML pages refer to other documents either to include them into the current page or to link to them for when a user performs an action. The tags that you will run into most often are:

`<img>` This tag is used to include an image into the page at the location where the tag is placed. The `src` attribute tells the browser where to find the image. Note that `<img>` is a self-closing tag.

<a> This tag is used to link to another document when the text inside the tag is clicked. The href attribute (i.e., hypertext reference) tells the browser what URL to go to next.

<link> This tag is used to connect stylesheets to your HTML page. We will cover more about stylesheets in Chapter 7. Note that <link> is a self-closing tag.

<script> This tag is used to connect JavaScript programs to your HTML page. We will start covering JavaScript in Chapter 8.

Here is an example of a few of these tags in a document:

Figure 6.4: Example Document Showing Tags Referencing Other Documents

```
<!DOCTYPE html>
<html>
<body>
<h1>This document refers to other documents</h1>
<p>
    Click on
    <a href="http://www.youversion.com/">this link</a>
    to access the Bible online.
</p>
<p>
    Below is an image of a cat:
</p>

<img src="http://placekitten.com.s3.amazonaws.com/homepage-
    samples/408/287.jpg" />

</body>
</html>
```

As you can see in this example, the <a> tag creates a link to another document. The document to link to goes in the href attribute, and the text to link to goes between the start and end tags. Then, at the end, the <img> tag refers to an image file at a specified URL and includes that within the page.

☞   **Practice Questions**

- Create a new HTML file using the example document in this section. View it in your browser to make sure you entered everything correctly.

- Modify this HTML file. Add links for all of your favorite places to go on the web.

- Find an image on the web that you like. Find out its URL (see Section A.5). Add that image to your web page.

When a document refers to another document, it is not always necessary to refer to the full URL of the destination document. In addition, if you ever have to move a set of documents, it is difficult to modify the links in all of the web pages to point to the new URL. For instance, let's say that you owned the website *www.example.com*. But then, someone offered you a large sum of money so that they could own the domain name. So now you have to move your stuff to be under a different domain. However, if all of your links refer to `http://www.example.com/whatever`, you now have to modify each one to point to the new domain! In a more practical scenario, think about if you were building a new version of your website. While you are still building it, the current website needs to stay where it is, so you put your test version on another site. Wouldn't it be great if all of the links just worked when you moved it over? That doesn't work with complete URLs because they refer to the exact location on the Internet. Once we move locations, the URL is now wrong.

In order to solve this, URLs can be rewritten to be *relative* to the location of the current document. Let's say that I have one file at `http://www.example.com/fruit/oranges.html` and another at `http://www.example.com/fruit/apples.html` but they each link to the other. Under the scheme demonstrated so far, we would have the first file have a link that looks like this: `<a href="http://www.example.com/fruit/apples.html">See the Apples</a>`. The second file will have a link back to the first file that looks something like this: `<a href="http://www.example.com/fruit/oranges.html">I prefer oranges</a>`. This is rather tedious, especially since they are in the same directory (i.e., `/fruit`).

The HTML standard gives us three choices of what to do. The regular URL, also called the **fully-qualified URL** or **absolute URL**, that we have been using contains all of the data necessary to connect. The **relative URL** takes most of its connection information from the *current* URL, which, for linking purposes, is also called the **base URL**. So, in the previous example, if we were already looking at `http://www.example.com/fruit/apples.html`, we

could link to the other file just by referring to `oranges.html` like this:

Figure 6.5: Example of a Relative Link

```
<a href="oranges.html">See the Oranges Page</a>
```

Using relative URLs not only gives us less typing, but it also makes it easier to move groups of documents. As long as `apples.html` and `oranges.html` stayed in the same directory together, you could move them around to be under a different site or to a different directory on your site, and their links would still work. In short, relative URLs use the current URL, up to and including the current directory, as the starting point. The relative URL just tells how to get to the document *from where you already are*. You can tell a relative URL from a fully-qualified URL by the fact that it doesn't include a protocol and it doesn't start with a slash.

There are two other kinds of URLs which are hybrids between absolute and relative URLs. The first is the **absolute path**. The absolute path tells the browser to use the current protocol and server, but replace the path entirely with the one specified. In our example, the absolute path to `apples.html` is `/fruit/apples.html`. Note that absolute paths *always* begin with a slash. If it does not begin with a slash, it is considered a relative URL.

The final type of URL is the **network path**. This URL uses the protocol of the current page, but you specify everything else. So, the network path of `oranges.html` is `//www.example.com/fruit/oranges.html`. Network paths are rarely necessary, but it is good to know what they mean in case you see them.

☞ **Practice Questions**

1. Create another simple web page in the same directory as your other web pages.

2. Create a link from your new page to one of your other pages. Remember to use relative links!

3. Create another link to some other page on the Internet.

4. Save the page, and open it up in your browser.

5. Test out your links. Did they work? If not, check the URL in your browser to see where the browser thought you were asking it to go.

6.5   Relative URLs

Relative URLs have a lot of features that make them helpful both when building a website and when using a book like this. For instance, since the files we create will be on your hard drive instead of a webserver, it is much easier to use relative URLs rather than the extremely long `file:` URLs that specify where on your hard drive it is. In addition, by using relative URLs, it means that the web pages you create will still work if you hand them in to a teacher or parent. If you use `file:` URLs, then all of the URLs would be wrong when your parent or teacher loads them on their computer, because they would be in a different location on their computer than they were on yours. If, instead, you use relative URLs, then, as long as you deliver all of the files together, the URLs will still work in their new destination. For the purposes of this book, every time you reference a file that you create or that you store on your hard drive, you should use a relative URL, but when you reference a file stored somewhere else on the web, you should use absolute URLs.

Another feature of relative URLs is that you can use them to refer to subdirectories. Let's say that you want the page at `http://www.example.com/fruit/apples.html` to link to the file `http://www.example.com/fruit/exotic/rambutan.html`. You will notice that they share a lot of their URLs between them. The relative URL tells you how to get to the document from the current directory. From `http://www.example.com/fruit/` I only have to say that I want to go to `exotic/rambutan.html`. Therefore, I can link to this page like this:

Figure 6.6: A Relative URL with a Subdirectory

```
<a href="exotic/rambutan.html">See information about the
   rambutan fruit</a>
```

Now, let's say that I am writing the page on rambutans, and I want to see my page on apples. How does that work with relative URLs? There is a special di-

rectory name that refers to the enclosing directory (also called the **parent direc-tory**). This is referred to with two periods (i.e., ..). If you are writing the page http://www.example.com/fruit/exotic/rambutan.html and you want to link to http://www.example.com/fruit/oranges.html you can write the link like this:

Figure 6.7: A Relative URL with a Parent Directory

```
<a href="../oranges.html">See information about oranges</a>
```

You can include as many directories as necessary in your URL. For example, if you were writing the page http://www.example.com/fruit/exotic/rambutan.html and wanted to link to the page http://www.example.com/fruit/poisonous/snowberry.html, you would write:

Figure 6.8: A Relative URL with Multiple Directory References

```
<a href="../poisonous/snowberry.html">Don't eat snowberry
    fruit!</a>
```

One other important special directory name is the . directory. While the two periods (..) refer to the parent directory, the single period (.) refers to the current directory. This is rarely used in HTML, but you will see it on occasion.

6.6 Other HTML Features

HTML has many other great features. The goal of this book is to get you just enough HTML to get started and to understand what you read about HTML on the Internet. There are many tags which do many different things. In this section we will cover a few of the more popular tags and simple features, but this is not meant to be exhaustive.

6.6.1   Entities

Because HTML uses the < and > characters to signify that the given text is a tag, how would you then actually write those characters? HTML provides **entities** to refer to characters that either have a special use by the HTML format or are hard to type (i.e., characters from other languages). An HTML entity starts with an ampersand (&) and ends with a semicolon (;). Common entities include:

> >

< <

& &

" "

' '

   a "non-breaking" space—a space that doesn't allow a line break at that point

© ©

6.6.2   Lists

Lists are great ways of organizing things in HTML. A list can either be unordered (i.e., a bulleted list), or ordered (i.e., a numbered list). The tag that encloses the whole list is <ul> for an unordered list, or <ol> for an ordered list. Then, each list item is enclosed in an <li> tag for both kinds.

Here is a short HTML fragment that illustrates how these are used:

Figure 6.9: Simple Lists

```
<h1>An Unordered List of Plants in my Garden</h1>
<ul>
    <li> Tomatoes </li>
    <li> Peas </li>
    <li> Beans </li>
</ul>

<h1>An Ordered List of my Favorite Books by G. K.
    Chesterton</h1>
<ol>
    <li> <i>The Everlasting Man</i> </li>
    <li> <i>Manalive</i> </li>
    <li> <i>Heretics</i> </li>
</ol>
```

The first list will display as a bulleted list, while the second list will be numbered.

6.6.3 Table Tags

In addition to paragraphs, headings, and lists, people often need to represent tables of data on web pages. HTML has a set of tags specialized for displaying tables of data. Let's say we wanted to make a list of our friends, with their name, their email, and their phone number. We would want the first row to be the headings (such as "Name," "Email," and "Phone"), and the other rows to be the data. For that, we will need several tags:

<table> This tag wraps around the whole table.

<tr> This tag wraps around a row of data.

<td> This tag wraps around the contents of a single data cell.

<th> This is just like the <td> tag, but it is used for headings (i.e., by making the content bold).

<thead> This tag is not strictly necessary, but it is often used to wrap around the row(s) of your table heading.

<tbody> This tag is also not strictly necessary, but it is often used to wrap around rows of data in your table.

<tfoot> Just like the <thead> tag, but used for footers of tables.

We can put them together to make the following web page fragment:

Figure 6.10: An Example Use of Table Tags

```
<table >
    <thead >
        <tr >
            <th >Name </th >
            <th >Email </th >
            <th >Phone </th >
        </tr >
    </thead >
    <tbody >
        <tr >
            <td >Jeff </td >
            <td >jeff@example.com</td >
            <td >555 -555 -1234 </td >
        </tr >
        <tr >
            <td >Melissa </td >
            <td >melissa@example.com</td >
            <td >555 -555 -6789 </td >
        </tr >
    </tbody >
</table >
```

This will display something like this:

Name	Email	Phone
Jeff	jeff@example.com	555-555-1234
Melissa	melissa@example.com	555-555-6789

6.6.4   Form Tags

A lot of web pages allow you to enter data. Data entry web pages are commonly referred to as "forms." These tags allow the user to enter in their own values. They won't be useful until we know how to process them, but we will list some of those tags for future use. Notice that the `<input>` tag can actually be several different input elements. The element that is displayed on the page is chosen based on the `type` attribute. The `<input>` tag should also be written as a self-closing tag.

`<form>` This tag normally encloses other form tags. If the form is supposed to submit data to a server, that destination is usually put in the `action` attribute.

`<input type="text">` This is a basic, single-line data entry field.

`<input type="checkbox">` This is a single box that can be checked on or off.

`<textarea>` This is a multi-line data entry field.

`<select>` This is a drop-down list. Each option is specified inside this tag using the `<option>` tag.

`<button>` This is a basic pushbutton. The enclosed text is the text of the button.

Most of these tags also have a `name` attribute that you can use to specify what the field is for (this will be important later), and a `value` attribute to give the field an initial value, or, in the case of check boxes, to give the value that this box represents.

Here is an example HTML fragment for a form (note that this doesn't do anything, it just lets the user interact with it):

Figure 6.11: Form Element Demonstration

```
<form>
    Here is an input field: <input type="text" /> <br />
    Here is a checkbox: <input type="checkbox" /> <br />
    Here is a multi-line input field:
        <textarea></textarea> <br />
    Here is a drop-down list:
        <select>
            <option>Option 1</option>
            <option>Option 2</option>
        </select>
        <br />
    Here is a button: <button>Click Me</button>
</form>
```

6.6.5 Comments, Declarations, Processing Instructions, and CDATA Blocks

When we talk about the structure of a language, we are talking about its **syntax**. The syntax includes what sorts of letters, symbols, and features are allowed in what places. For instance, the tag is an integral part of HTML's syntax. To get a good example of what syntax is, perhaps an example of a violation of that syntax will help. We have seen tags like this: `<p><i>This is an italicized paragraph</i></p>`. This is perfectly legitimate. Imagine, however, that instead of starting with `<p><i>` we accidentally typed `<p <i>`. That would be a *syntax error*, meaning that we didn't properly follow the structure of HTML. Syntaxes are important because that is how the computer knows what we are attempting to do.

The two primary units of HTML syntax we have discussed so far are tags and entities. There are several other syntactical units that are important to know, but they will rarely be used in this book.

The most common syntactical unit is the HTML **comment**. For writing any kind of code, most programming and markup languages allow for developers to add comments to their code. Comments are notes that the programmer writes to himself or any other developer looking at the code. It basically says something like, "I did it this way because I had trouble getting some other way to work," or "here are the reasons the code looks this way." It holds important information that is not immediately obvious to someone looking at the code, but which is ignored by the browser.

In HTML, like most other computer languages, comments are essentially ignored by the browser. This feature allows for another use of comments—temporarily disabling parts of your code. Let's say that you have built a large web page, and you want to see what it looks like without a big chunk of your code. Rather than deleting that code and having to re-type it later, you can just wrap it in a comment, and the browser will ignore it. This is called *commenting out* code, because you are taking the code out of the document or program using comments.

So what does a comment look like? Comments are simple. They start with <!- and they end with ->. Here is a short HTML fragment with a few comments:

Figure 6.12: A Comment Example

```
<h1>Web Page with Comments</h1>
<!-- Here is an unordered list -->
<ul>
    <li>Here is a list item</li>
    <!--
        <li>This list item is not visible because it has been
            commented out</li>
    -->
    <li>Another list item</li>
</ul>
```

Another feature of HTML is the declaration. Declarations are used to identify, and possibly extend, the list of valid tags, attributes, and entities. Usually, the only declaration you will see is the HTML *doctype* declaration, which tells the computer the basic type of document you are working with so it knows what tags are valid and what they mean. HTML doctype

declaration tells the computer that, yes, you are really looking at an HTML document. In its basic form it looks like this: `<!DOCTYPE html>`. It is always placed *before* the first `<html>` tag. There are other, fancier ways of writing it, but the meaning is basically the same—yes, computer, you are looking at an HTML document.

Another feature is the processing instruction. These are used to give document processors (such as browsers) special information on how to handle your document. However, with the exception of a single processing instruction, this feature is almost entirely unused. The processing instruction looks like a start tag and can include attributes, but it has a question mark before the processing instruction name and before the right angled-bracket, like this:

Figure 6.13: The Structure of a Processing Instruction

```
<?processing-instruction-name attribute1="value1"
   attribute2="value2" ?>
```

The only processing instruction you are likely to see is this one, known as the XML declaration:

Figure 6.14: The XML Declaration Processing Instruction

```
<?xml version="1.0" encoding="UTF-8" ?>
```

If used, this goes at the beginning of the document, before the doctype declaration, and even before any blank lines or whitespace. It tells the browser to use special, more strict rules when processing the HTML document.

One last feature that is sometimes seen is CDATA sections. A CDATA section is most often used when you have a lot of angled brackets to write in the document itself, but don't want to have to write entities for each one. A CDATA section tells the browser to just treat the text as literal text, and don't try to find tags, comments, or entities. CDATA sections start with `<![CDATA[` and end with `]]>`.

Here is a short example:

Figure 6.15: A CDATA Example

```
<h1>A CDATA Example</h1>
<p>
    This is me writing a tag name that I want displayed
        without CDATA: &lt;p&gt;
</p>
<p>
    <![CDATA[
        This is me writing a tag name to display with CDATA:
            <p>
    ]]>
</p>
```

Many browsers don't fully support CDATA sections in all circumstances, so it is best not to use them, but it is good to know what they are in case you see one.

Review

In this chapter we covered the basics of HTML, what it is, and how to write it. We have learned:

- A markup language is a text document that uses tags (which are also text) to specify the structure and function of the different pieces of the document.

- HTML is the markup language that is used on the Internet for web pages.

- In HTML, spacing is essentially ignored—tags are used instead to mark locations of paragraphs and line-breaks.

- URLs specify the location of documents on the Internet.

- An HTML document can reference another document on the Internet using URLs.

- A relative URL can be used to reference other related files on the same website.

- Relative URLs make it easy to keep document links working even when the files are moved, as long as they are moved together.

- HTML has a number of tags for many different situations.

Apply What You Have Learned

1. Create a new HTML file. Place an image in the same directory (one with a .jpg or .png extension). Can you figure out how to write an `<img>` tag to include the image into your web page using a relative URL?

2. Create a sequence of three web pages that relate to each other on the same subject. At the top of the web page, put links to each of the other pages in the group. Test it out and make sure that you can navigate between them on your browser.

3. Go through the list of tags in this chapter. Modify your pages so that each page has one or more headings, and your sequence of pages has at least one table, one list, and one entity.

4. Go to several of your favorite websites, and view the HTML of several of the pages on that site (see Section A.4). Identify which tags you know and which tags you don't know. Look up on the Internet at least two tags that you aren't familiar with. The official list of elements in the current version of HTML is available at `http://www.w3.org/TR/html-markup/elements.html`.

5. As you go through different websites, make note of how their sites are organized and laid out. What types of content are common to all of the websites? Are there common ways of laying out the website? The basic structure of the web pages themselves, and their organization on the site is known as the site's **information architecture**, also known as IA. Can you sketch the basic layout of the web page—where they put their menus, where they put their images, where they put their content, etc.? Can you draw a map of how you move from page to page on the site?

Chapter 7

Introduction to Cascading Style Sheets

7.1   The Origin of Cascading Style Sheets

When HTML was first developed, it was entirely used for communicating information. HTML was originally built as an easy way to browse and view documents. Therefore, HTML documents were never pretty, but were very functional. In addition, there was a direct match between the tag used and the purpose that the tagged text served in the document. For instance <h1> tags meant that the given text was a main heading. If you were looking at the HTML code itself, you would know precisely what it meant if you found text with that tag. In fact, if you knew the tags, you could almost just as easily read the document source with the tags as you could read it rendered in the browser.

However, as more and more people started using the web, HTML started serving more purposes than purely informational ones. The modern web is much more user-focused, and incorporates many other types of media and functionality, including navigation, entertainment, advertising, and branding. In the early days, in order to accommodate for these new uses, HTML's tag and attribute set expanded and expanded. The problem was, however, that the initial beauty and simplicity of HTML was lost. Web pages became complicated messes of undecipherable tags. In addition, different browsers rendered the tags slightly differently. Therefore, in order to write a web page, you had to know not only what each tag *did*, but how the tag would *look* in every browser, and how to get them all to work together to produce a good-looking web page.

The organizations that control the standards for the web recognized this problem, and decided to move HTML back closer to its roots. In order to achieve this, they attempted to separate **content** from **presentation**. Content refers to the data that the web page is intended to communicate. Presentation refers to how that page will look to the user. Headings, paragraphs, figures, etc. are all part of the content. The background, formatting, layout, colors, fonts, and decorations are all part of the presentation.

In order to do this, they removed styling from HTML, and created a new language, called **Cascading Style Sheets** (CSS for short), to tell browsers how the HTML should look. In this new paradigm the structure and content of the document is written in HTML. How that content should be laid out, formatted, and presented is written in CSS. The advanced interactions between the user and the content is written in JavaScript. This separation is not perfect, but it is a huge improvement.

☞   The Progression of Technology

It is interesting to note the way that technology progresses. The way HTML progressed is very similar to many other technologies. The first version was very simple and direct. It accomplished the needs of its users very well.

However, its success led to many problems. Because everyone was using it, new people, with different needs than the original users, were also using it. In order to accommodate this, they simply added a bunch of features to HTML. However, it quickly became apparent that simply adding features was making a mess of things. It did expand the capabilities of HTML, but at the cost of making all HTML work more complicated (and expensive).

The next step in the progress of HTML was to re-evaluate the different aspects of how HTML worked and the different needs they served. As it turned out, there were several needs that were plainly distinct. There was the need to handle content, the need to display content in a visually-pleasing manner, and the need to make the content interactive.

Because these needs were distinguishable, they were then **refactored** into entirely separate pieces. HTML would handle the content, CSS would handle the presentation, and JavaScript would handle the interactivity. HTML was a great content language, but a bad styling language. So this new setup allowed HTML to do what it did best and left

styling and interaction to other technologies which were better suited for the task.

Refactoring is a common occurrence in the progress of technology. The word "refactoring" is based on the idea of factoring in mathematics. In math, factoring refers to taking a number and separating it out into its prime components. The number 15 has the prime factors 5 and 3. In technology, refactoring is similar. It is re-evaluating the technology you have and looking for components which are more basic that the technology can be divided into. This usually happens when the growth of a technology causes it to become overly complex. At that point, it needs to be re-evaluated to find if there are *simpler* components that the technology can be divided into.

Refactoring is not a panacea and must be used judiciously. If refactoring is done prematurely, all of the different components may not be clearly seen, and it may be refactored in ways that make progress more difficult rather than less. However, for the most part, refactoring tends to give new life to old technology as it increases both flexibility and understandability.

7.2 The Structure of a CSS Document

The best way to understand the basic operation of CSS is to see it in action. To start with, create a file called `basic.css` with the following content (as usual, be sure to enter it *exactly* as shown):

Figure 7.1: A Simple CSS Document

```
h1 {
    font-size: 20pt;
    color: blue;
}

p {
    font-size: 12pt;
    color: black;
}
```

What this document says is that:

- All text inside `<h1>` tags should be shown as blue text in a 20-point font (a **point** is a unit of measurement in typography—1 point is $\frac{1}{72}$ of an inch).

- All text inside `<p>` tags should be shown as black text in a 12-point font.

Now, create a document called `basic.html` in the same directory as `basic.css` with the following contents:

Figure 7.2: A Web Page Using CSS

```
<!DOCTYPE html>
<html>
<head>
<title>Stylesheet Test</title>
<link rel="stylesheet" href="basic.css" />
</head>
<body>
<h1>This is a Heading</h1>
<p>This is a paragraph.</p>
</body>
</html>
```

The part of the file that links together these two files is the `<link>` tag. The `<link>` tag can be used to specify all sorts of related documents (what it is linking is specified by the `rel` attribute), but its most important usage is to specify the stylesheet to use for a web page. The document that the `<link>` tag refers to is listed in the `href` attribute. So, in short, the `<link>` tag in the document above says to use the file `basic.css` as its stylesheet.

If you open this file with your browser, you will find that, indeed, it renders the document as we specified. If it doesn't, go back through and try to find your mistake.

The CSS file format is fairly simple and straightforward. It consists of two major parts: selectors and properties. CSS properties list out the styles to be used, and CSS selectors

tell which pieces of HTML those styles are to be used on. So, in the file we were looking at, h2 and p were the selectors. The selector was followed by a property list wrapped in curly braces({ and }). The property list tells what styles to use on the text.

The two properties we use in the file in Figure 7.1 are color, which defines the color to make the text, and font-size, which tells what size font to use for the text. CSS2 defines 98 different properties to use, and CSS3 defines even more. However, there aren't that many properties that you need to know to get started. This chapter will only cover the most important ones, but you can see a full list at http://www.w3.org/TR/CSS2/propidx.html.

7.3   Understanding Selectors

The CSS selectors used in the previous section listed the tag name that was to be styled. However, such a selector has limited use, and will not give us the kind of flexibility needed to produce really nice documents.

Let's say, for instance, that you have different types of paragraphs that you wanted to lay out in different ways. You want one paragraph to be red text on a blue background and another paragraph to be green text on a black background. In order to do this, the CSS file will have to be able to distinguish between these two different types of paragraphs, but HTML only provides one paragraph (<p>) tag. To accomplish this, CSS can also use attributes to choose which tags that a set of properties applies to. In order to facilitate this process, HTML defines a class property available on *all* HTML tags, which can be used for whatever purpose the writer wants. Usually, they are used to make distinctions between tags for CSS to process.

Let's look at how this works.

Create the following HTML file, called `classes.html`:

Figure 7.3: An HTML File Using Classes

```
<!DOCTYPE html>
<html>
<head>
<title>Testing HTML Classes</title>
<link rel="stylesheet" href="classes.css" />
</head>
<body>

<div class="section1">
<h1>A Title</h1>
<p class="style1">My paragraph 1.</p>
<p class="style2">My paragraph 2.</p>

</div>

<div class="section2">
<h1>Another Title</h1>
<p>Another paragraph.</p>
</div>

</body>
</html>
```

This document uses `<div>` tags to group the document into two sections, where each section has a title and one or more paragraphs. The sections are differentiated from each other by the `class` attribute. In the first section, the paragraphs are differentiated from each other by the same way.

CSS allows us to use HTML attributes to supply specific styles for different uses of the same tag.

To see this in action, create a file called `classes.css` in the same directory as the previous file with the following content:

Figure 7.4: A CSS File Styling Classes

```
p {
    font-size: 10pt;
}

p[class=style1] {
    color: red;
    background-color: blue;
}

p[class=style2] {
    font-size: 12pt;
    color: green;
    background-color: black;
}
```

After typing both the HTML and CSS files, open the `classes.html` file and see what the results look like.

The first selector is just like before—it is a tag name followed by styling properties. It says that paragraph tags should have a font size of 10 points.

The next selector, however, is different. This selector says `p[class=style1]`, which means that it applies *only* to `<p>` tags that have the `class` attribute set to the value `style1`. The properties for this say that paragraphs with the `style1` class should be red text on a blue background. Note that a `<p>` tag with the `style1` class would *also* match the first selector, since the first selector applies to *all* `<p>` tags. Therefore, any attribute set in the original selector would be still be applied, so it uses a 10 point font as well.

The final selector is just like the previous one, except that it is set to match paragraphs with a class of `style2`. It displays the paragraph with green text on a black background. It also sets the size of the font to 12 points. This is in conflict with the setting that was set in the first group of CSS properties, which set all `<p>` tag sizes to 10 points. However, because the

selector for these properties is more specific, its properties supercede the ones from the more general selector.

Now, you can select HTML elements by any attribute you want. However, selecting by the `class` attribute is very common. In fact, it is so common that there is a special simplified notation for selecting by class. Instead of writing `p[class=style1]` for a selector, I can just write `p.style1`.

Therefore, if I were to rewrite my `classes.css` file using this simplified notation, it would look like this:

Figure 7.5: A CSS File Using Simplified Notation for Classes

```
p {
    font-size:  10pt;
}

p.style1 {
    color:  red;
    background-color:  blue;
}

p.style2 {
    font-size:  12pt;
    color:  green;
    background-color:  black;
}
```

Not only is that easier to write, it is easier to read!

CSS has a rich supply of selectors that allow you to style documents in a very dynamic way. You can have selectors that indicate tags that are within other tags, tags that are preceded by some other tag, and a number of other ways of selecting HTML elements for styling. This book only covers the very basic elements of CSS that you will need on your way to understanding how to program web pages.

Figure 7.6: The CSS Box Model

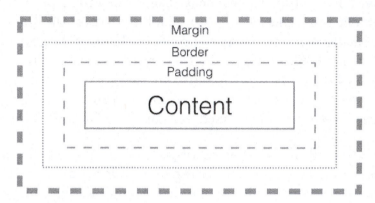

7.4   The CSS Box Model

In order to understand how styling works, it is important to understand how CSS looks at the content on a web page. This is known as the CSS "box model," because CSS thinks about web pages in terms of boxes. There are four main ways that CSS looks at content—either as lines of text (known as *inline* style), as a rectangular box (known as *block* style), as a table, or as a list. This chapter will only look at inline and block styles since table and list styles have a lot of complexities that we don't need to deal with.

Most tags we have dealt with, such as `<div>`, `<p>`, `<h1>`, `<h2>`, etc., are all block style tags by default. This means that when the content is generated, the browser will put the given element into a rectangular box. Unless otherwise specified, this box will be as wide as possible (i.e. the size of its container) and as tall as required to hold all of the content. Inline tags, such as the `<a>` and `<span>` tags, are primarily for text within a paragraph. Therefore, these are not strictly rectangular boxes, since you could have text that started in the middle of one line and wrapped onto the next line, producing an irregular shape. So, block tags are for styling paragraphs, groups of paragraphs, and other blocky content, and inline tags are used for styling text *within* a paragraph. You can also change an HTML element from inline to block and vice-versa using the `display` property. By setting the property using `display: block;` or `display: inline;` you can force HTML elements to behave in a different way than their default.

The general box model is presented in Figure 7.6.

Every box that CSS makes is a block of content surrounded by padding, a border, and a margin. If a width is specified for the element (using the `width` property), then the width is applied to the content box. The height is normally based on the content within the box, but it can be set manually using the `height` property. The padding is the area surrounding the content. If there is a background set, the background extends through the content. The border is a (usually) solid line that surrounds the padding. The margin is the minimum amount of space between one element and the next. Margins of two elements next to each other collapse together so that the combined margin is the largest of the two box margins.

Oftentimes you don't see all of these pieces (especially the border) because they are zero-width. However, you can, using CSS, set the size and other properties of each one of these. Inline content, because of its irregular shape, can have padding and a border but not a margin.

If you go back to the HTML from Figure 7.3, we can modify the CSS stylesheet (`classes.css`) to show how the box model works. The HTML is divided into two sections by `<div>` tags. We will set each `<div>` tag with a border, a background, a padding, and an internal width. Here is the code to use:

Figure 7.7: CSS Example for the Box Model

```
div.section1 {
   border: 1px solid black;
   padding: 20px;
   margin: 10px;
}
div.section2 {
   border: 1px solid red;
   background-color: green;
   width: 50%;
   padding: 50px;
   margin: 10px;
}
p {
   border: 1px solid blue;
}
```

This gives us two large boxes, one for each section, and several smaller boxes. Note that, unless otherwise constrained, the boxes take up as much width as they can. The top box takes up the width of the page (minus the margin around itself). The boxes within that box also take up as much width as they can, but they are constrained by the margin, border, and padding of the box around them.

The second box does not go all the way across the screen because we set the width of that box to be 50%. Therefore, it only goes halfway across the page. Likewise, the boxes within that box are constrained to this new size.

So far, we have seen several different units for the sizes of things in CSS. CSS has several units of measure available, but the most common are `pt` for points, `px` for pixels, `in` for inches, and `%` for percentage width.

7.5 Other Capabilities of CSS

We have only scratched the surface of CSS in this chapter, but hopefully you have a taste for what it can do and how it works. In addition to the capabilities we have discussed so far, CSS also has the ability to move boxes around, put data into tables, put numbers on lists, generate small amounts of content, use images for backgrounds, show and hide elements, and even more. On the box model, the top, right, bottom, and left sides of each part of the box can be set separately (i.e., `margin-right`, `margin-left`, etc.).

Also, CSS can adjust your layout based on the screen size. So, for instance, if you have a lot of content on your page but only want to show a small part of it if you are looking at it on a small screen (like a phone), CSS will let you hide different elements based on the screen size.

There are a number of different extensions to CSS that have been developed over the years which allow lots of additional features such as animations, some 3D manipulation, gradient backgrounds (where one color slowly transitions to another color), and more. These extensions are not all supported across every browser, but every year more features become available for developers to use.

In any case, CSS is a great tool for adding style to your web pages. To see the amazing flexibility of CSS, you should check out CSS Zen Garden, which is at `http://www.csszengarden.com`. This is a collection of styles which all display *the same*

web page, with the only difference being the CSS used. It is almost unbelievable the amount of creativity that can be achieved in this fashion. It should also be noted that this is possible precisely because HTML was refactored into separate content and design components. Thus, you really can change the design of an entire website just by switching out the stylesheet. Before the advent of CSS, such changes required rewriting the entire website. Now it only requires rewriting the stylesheet.

Review

This chapter covered the basics of Cascading Style Sheets. We have learned:

- Technology often develops by refactoring an old technology into distinct concepts.

- Cascading Style Sheets (CSS) developed when HTML was refactored into separate content, presentation, and interactive components.

- CSS files are meant to handle the presentation of content written in HTML.

- CSS allows HTML to hold the content of a web page without regard to how it will be displayed.

- CSS works by having a list of style properties applied to HTML elements designated by selectors.

- CSS selectors are often based on the names of tags and the values of attributes.

- CSS lays out a page on the basis of the CSS box model, in which each HTML element is assigned a rectangular box on the page and has its own padding, border, and margin.

- The variety of layouts possible for HTML content simply by changing stylesheets is quite dramatic.

- Because the styling for a page or set of pages lives in an external file, CSS allows the look of an entire website to be changed by updating only the shared CSS file.

Apply What You Have Learned

1. Take the HTML file from Figure 7.3 and write a new stylesheet for it. Put the headings in a 16-point font and the paragraph text in a 12-point font. Put a 12-point gap between the paragraphs.

2. Create a new HTML file with a new CSS file. Create 4 rectangles on the screen with different widths, heights, and background colors.

3. Come up with your own design for the content in Figure 7.3. First, draw on a sheet of paper how you might want to lay it out—be creative! Then, try to see what parts of that design you can replicate with your current knowledge of CSS. Don't worry if your imagination is more than what you know how to do. Just do what you can! Feel free to also look on the web for additional CSS properties you can use to make your design come to life. Sites like `w3schools.com` have a wealth of information on CSS creation.

4. Find your favorite design on CSS Zen Garden (`csszengarden.com`). Somewhere on the page is a link that says "View This Design's CSS." Click on it and see if you can decipher what the CSS file is doing. Don't worry if there are a lot of things you don't understand. Focus on the things that you *do* understand.

Chapter 8

Your First JavaScript Program

In part II we covered the basics of how web pages worked using HTML and CSS. As we noted, HTML is a *markup language*, which is used to tell the computer about the structure of text. CSS is HTML's counterpart, acting as a *styling language* to tell the computer how you want the HTML to look. These are both, limited, special-purpose document languages. They tell the computer about the static structure of a document, or set of documents, but not how to perform any function or computation. Neither HTML nor CSS is truly a general purpose **programming language**. Therefore, in order to add interaction and computation to our web pages, we will need to use the JavaScript programming language.

This chapter covers one, short, simple program. However, it is important to read it in detail because we cover a lot of the terminology that we will use when talking about how programs and programming languages work.

8.1   A Short History of JavaScript

JavaScript was created by Brendan Eich in 1995, while he was working for Netscape (Netscape is now known as Mozilla). JavaScript was a revolution in the way that the web worked because it moved the web from being primarily a group of interlinked documents to being a truly immersive and interactive environment. Many developers (including myself) were initially skeptical of the usefulness of JavaScript when it first came out. Over the years, however, it has proved its usefulness. When it was first released, several other vendors tried

to compete with JavaScript by having their own scripting language. The biggest of these was VBScript, implemented by Microsoft starting in version 3 of Internet Explorer 3. However, in Internet Explorer 11, VBScript support has been more-or-less officially removed.

There are other technologies that also make web pages more dynamic, such as Java, Flash, Silverlight, ActiveX, and other plug-ins, but these are not nearly as integrated into HTML documents as JavaScript. These other technologies usually work by taking a specific area of your web page away from the browser, and handling it itself. JavaScript, on the other hand, works within the web page itself. These other technologies were developed to augment areas where JavaScript fell short, such as animation, video, and integration with other parts of your computer (such as your camera) which are not normally part of the browsing process. JavaScript, however, has been slowly taking over these tasks as well, though you will still see a lot of places where these other technologies are useful.

One confusing thing about JavaScript is the name. As mentioned in the previous paragraph, there is another, *much different* web programming language called Java. These are not the same thing, nor are they even very similar. It is important to always refer to JavaScript by its full name, because it works and acts very differently from Java.

Over the years, support and standardization of JavaScript has increased dramatically. In the early days of JavaScript, each browser handled JavaScript very differently, and it was difficult to write JavaScript that worked everywhere. Now, twenty years later, the situation is much improved. JavaScript was standardized by the ECMA, under the name ECMAScript. Though it is standardized under a different name, this is the same language as JavaScript.

JavaScript is now by far the most standard way of developing interactive web pages. It is installed on every major browser, and most of the inconsistencies between the versions have been worked out. It is also supported by numerous third-party developers who write programming **libraries** (add-in functional modules) that provide JavaScript programmers with the ability to do just about anything imaginable.

☞ **Technology Becomes Politicized**

Many great companies eventually wind up as shadows of their former selves. Tech giants who made great leaps forward and set the standards of innovation sometimes deteriorate into soulless, self-centered, self-important clubs, focusing more on themselves than on using their technology to improve the world.

It is sad that a pioneering company such as Netscape, who basically invented the modern browser more than once, is now, instead of inventing the next generation of web technologies, engaged in petty politically-correct inquisitions. The creator of JavaScript, Brendan Eich, has been responsible for much of Netscape and Mozilla's development both in their technology and as a company. However, he was kicked out of Mozilla in 2014 because of a small contribution he made to an unpopular political organization. This matches with the general shift in technological leadership from Mozilla to Google Chrome over the last several years. The priorities of Mozilla have obviously shifted from being about making the best technology to placating the powerful.

Mozilla, once the great underdog of the Internet who pushed the envelope and challenged the status quo time and again, is now just a club for self-important technologists.

8.2 A Simple JavaScript Program

Instead of describing what JavaScript looks like and how it works, we will begin our study of JavaScript by just entering in an example program, and *afterwards* describing how it works.

Type the following program into your text editor and save it as an HTML file:

Figure 8.1: A Simple Web Page with a JavaScript Program

```
<html>
<body>
<h1>Simple JavaScript program</h1>

<script type="text/javascript">

// This is a program in JavaScript

var person_age_string;
var person_age_number;
var age_in_twenty_years;

person_age_string = prompt("What is your age?");
person_age_number = parseInt(person_age_string);
age_in_twenty_years = person_age_number + 20;

alert("In 20 years you will be " + age_in_twenty_years +
    " years old");

</script>
</body>
</html>
```

After entering this program, load it in your browser. It will open up a dialog box asking you what your age is. It will then open up another dialog box telling you what your age will be in twenty years. Pretty simple, right? If your browser did not do these things, double-check to make sure you entered the code in *exactly* the same way it is listed. If it still doesn't work, see Section A.7.

So let's look at what this code does.

The first thing to notice is the <script> tag. This tag tells the browser that what occurs between the <script> start and end tags is JavaScript code. The browser will start running

this code as soon as it comes across the end tag, even before it finishes loading the page. There are two possible attributes to the `<script>` tag. The one used here is the `type` attribute, which tells the browser what language the script will be in. This should always be `text/javascript`. The `<script>` tag can take another attribute, `src`, which tells the browser to look in another file (designated by the value of `src`) for the JavaScript code instead of it being in the web page itself.

After the `<script>` tag, there is a JavaScript single-line comment.

Figure 8.2: A Single-Line JavaScript Comment

```
// This is a program in JavaScript
```

Whenever JavaScript code has two slashes together, from that point to the end of the line is considered a comment and ignored by the browser (see Section 6.6.5 for more information about comments). Another type of comment you will see in JavaScript starts with `/*` and ends with `*/`, and is intended for multi-line comments.

The first set of programming statements start with the word `var`:

Figure 8.3: Variable Declarations in JavaScript

```
var person_age_string;
var person_age_number;
var age_in_twenty_years;
```

`var` tells JavaScript that we need a temporary storage space, called a **variable**, to hold some data and gives that temporary storage space a name. Therefore, `var person_age_string` says that `person_age_string` is going to be the name of a temporary storage space which we will use to hold data. The way programmers state this is that `var person_age_string` creates a variable called `person_age_string`. This is also referred to as *defining* or **declaring** a variable. When we refer to `person_age_string` later, it will refer to this variable.

After this is a semicolon (;). In JavaScript, semicolons are used to separate statements from each other. So when we see a semicolon, we known we have come to the end of a statement.

The next two statements are just like the first, defining the variables `person_age_number` and `age_in_twenty_years`. Notice that we are using underscores (_) within the names of our variables. This allows us as programmers to see the words spelled out, but it makes sure that the computer knows that they are all one word. For instance, if I said "I am going to the bus stop," you know that "bus stop" is really one word. However, computers are not that smart. Therefore, if you were talking to a computer, you would need to say, "I am going to the bus_stop" (notice the underscore), so that the computer knows that bus_stop should be treated as one word.

The next statement has a lot more action in it. Here is the code:

Figure 8.4: Prompting the User for Input

```
person_age_string = prompt("What is your age?");
```

There are several important things going on. First of all, notice the equal sign (=). In most programming languages (including JavaScript), the equal sign is a *command* that says to put whatever value is on the right side of the equal sign into the variable on the left hand side. It does not say that these two things are equal already; it says to *assign* the right-hand value to the left-hand variable. This is known as an **assignment statement**.

The left-hand side of this statement is one of the variables we just defined. This statement says that we should put a new value into that variable. The right-hand side of this statement tells what the value should be.

The right-hand side is where things get interesting. `prompt("What is your age?")` tells the computer to put up a dialog box, ask the given question, and then give back the value the user entered. This is called a **function** because it accesses functionality that is defined somewhere else. Functions in JavaScript start with the name of the function (`prompt` in this case), then an opening parenthesis (( ), then the function **parameters**, and then a closing parenthesis ( )). A *parameter* (also referred to as an **argument**) is a set of values that alters how a function performs its task. In this case, the function has one parameter, `"What is your age?"`. This is a character string, like we discussed in Section 4.4. In JavaScript, a string is enclosed

in either double-quotes (") or single-quotes (') and is treated as a single value, although you can also access the characters individually if you need to. We say that the parameter is *passed to the function* because the function will receive whatever value we put here. The `prompt` function can take either one or two parameters. The first parameter is the text you want to display to the user in front of the input box. The second parameter (which we are not using here) gives a default value to the user. If a function takes more than one parameter, each parameter is separated by a comma (,). So, if we wanted to give the user a default age, we would write it like this: `prompt("What is your age?", "25")` Remember that `prompt` is working with character strings, not numbers, which is why we put our default value in quotes. The code does not continue until the function is finished, which, in this case, means that the user has typed in a value and clicked "OK." When the user does type something, that value is then used as the value of the function. We say that the function *returns* that value.

Therefore, to use the terminology we have discussed so far, we say that the code `prompt("What is your age?")` calls the function `prompt` with a parameter `"What is your age?"` and returns whatever the user types as the value of that function.

Then, since the `prompt` function returns whatever the user types, the value that the user types gets stored into the variable `person_age_string`. Now, why did we call the variable `person_age_string`? Since we have no control over what the user types, we are getting what he types back as a string. We want the user to type in a number, but in reality he can type anything he wants. Therefore, the `prompt` function always returns a string. Hopefully, the user did what we asked and typed in a number. But no matter what, `prompt` returned a string. We named the variable `person_age_string` so we remember that it is holding a string, not a number.

Now the program needs to add 20 years to whatever age the user typed. That isn't currently possible, because we are holding the *string* that the user typed in, but we need a *number*. The next line, `person_age_number = parseInt(person_age_string)`, does the conversion we need. `parseInt` is a built-in function that takes a string and **parses** it into a number. *Parsing* is the process of taking a string and converting it into a more computerized representation that is easier for computer programs to manipulate. In this case, we are taking a string and converting (parsing) it into a number. `parseInt` is short for "parse integer," where an **integer** is a whole number (i.e., 1, 2, 3, 4, etc.). If you wanted a number with decimals in it, you would used `parseFloat`, which is short for "parse a floating-point number," with a **floating-point number** being a number with a decimal point in it (i.e., 31.25, 0.002, 23.12, etc.).

We then take the value from the `parseInt` function and store it into the `person_age_number` variable. Now we have the value we need in a variable as a number! Since it is a number, we can perform computations with it!

`age_in_twenty_years = person_age_number + 20` tells the computer to add 20 to the value in the variable `person_age_number`, and then store the result in `age_in_twenty_years`. In JavaScript, `+` and `=` are considered **operators**, and the values that they operate on are called **operands**. Operators are special built-in operations in the language. They differ from functions because, as we will learn, you can write your own function, but the operators of a language are essentially fixed. Operators are used to do special tasks (such as assignment) or in places where making a function call would look funny. In math, for example, it is more natural to write `2 + 3` than it is to write something like `add(2, 3)`.

Now we now have the value we are looking for; all we need is to display it. The next line of code displays the value.

Figure 8.5: Displaying Results

```
alert("In 20 years you will be " + age_in_twenty_years +
" years old");
```

This piece of code has several strange features. First of all, it uses the plus sign (+) with strings. How would you add strings? Well, in JavaScript, when the plus sign is used with strings, it no longer means addition, but rather **concatenation**. Concatenation means joining two things together. In this case, we are joining strings end-to-end. There is one problem—`age_in_twenty_years` is not a string but a number! JavaScript handles this automatically by converting anything that is added to a string into a string before the addition takes place. So, the plus sign indicates addition if it has numbers on both sides but concatenation if there is a string on either side of it. In addition, concatenation will convert the other value into a string if it isn't one already.

Another thing to note is that, in JavaScript, strings have to be one line only. Therefore, if you need to break a statement into more than one line, never do it in the middle of a string.

Another interesting feature of this code is that it combines several operations. It concatenates

three items together and then passes the resulting string to the **alert** function. In most programming languages (including JavaScript), you can combine as many operations and functions together as you want to give you the final value.

Finally, this code introduces the **alert** function, which displays a popup to the user. The **alert** function returns when the user clicks on the "OK" button.

☞ **Practice Questions**

1. What is a variable and how do you declare it in JavaScript?

2. What are the two different functions of the plus sign in JavaScript?

3. What do the **prompt** and **alert** functions do?

☞ **Practice Activity**

In this activity we will try to modify the program in this section. Be sure that the program is working before you begin the activity. Test your program after each step to make sure it is still working. If you wait until the end, and it doesn't work, you won't know where you made the mistake.

1. Add an alert before your prompt that simply says "hello."

2. Change the number of years added to 25. Be sure to change the final alert as well so it says the right thing!

3. Can you figure out how to combine the lines with the **prompt** and **parseInt** into one another so that the output of **prompt** becomes the input of **parseInt**? What variable is no longer needed in this case?

8.3   Moving the JavaScript to Its Own File

Just like CSS, JavaScript can either be embedded within your HTML file or stored in a separate file. My recommendation is to always keep your JavaScript in a separate file unless you have a specific reason to include it in your page because sometimes the interaction between JavaScript and HTML can lead to unexpected results. For instance, the browser can confuse some parts of JavaScript for HTML tags. By keeping JavaScript in a separate file, these issues are avoided.

In order to put your JavaScript into a separate file, all you need to do is copy the code between the `<script>` start and end tags and paste them in a new text document with the extension `.js`. Then, modify your `<script>` tag to have a `src` attribute (keep the `type` attribute the way it is) with the relative URL of your new JavaScript file. If we named our JavaScript file `application.js` and put it in the same folder as our HTML file, the HTML would look like this:

Figure 8.6: HTML File Referencing External JavaScript

```
<!DOCTYPE html>
<html>
<body>
<h1>Simple JavaScript program</h1>

<script type="text/javascript"
   src="application.js"></script>

</body>
</html>
```

The `application.js` file would look like this:

Figure 8.7: Short JavaScript File Referenced from HTML

```javascript
// This is a program in JavaScript

var person_age_string;
var person_age_number;
var age_in_twenty_years;

person_age_string = prompt("What is your age?");
person_age_number = parseInt(person_age_string);
age_in_twenty_years = person_age_number + 20;

alert("In 20 years you will be " + age_in_twenty_years +
    " years old");
```

Keeping your JavaScript in a separate file has other advantages too. First of all, it makes your HTML pages easier to read because they only have one language in them—HTML. By keeping your languages separated in their own files, you keep more of your sanity intact. Another reason is that it allows you to share JavaScript programs and JavaScript program pieces between multiple web pages. Therefore, you don't have to write the same code over and over again. This also means that if you change your code in one place, you don't have to search for and make the same change on every other page, a process which is both tedious and error-prone. If you have a large JavaScript application, separating your JavaScript can actually make your pages load faster because your browser only has to load your JavaScript once rather than have it take up space implanted in the middle of each file.

Review

In this chapter we covered the absolute basics of how to write a JavaScript program. We have learned:

- JavaScript is a general-purpose programming language that allows us to create dynamic web pages.

- ECMAScript is the name for the language used by the group which standardized it, but it is usually still referred to as JavaScript.

- JavaScript can either be included on a page or stored in a separate file.

- JavaScript is designated in web pages using the `<script>` tag.

- Variables are temporary storage locations for values and are declared using the `var` keyword.

- The = operator is used for assigning a value to a variable.

- Functions are named processes that are defined elsewhere.

- Functions can be given values, called parameters (or arguments).

- Multiple function parameters are separated by commas.

- When functions complete, the value they give back is called the *return value*.

- JavaScript uses quotes (' or ") to signify character strings.

- `prompt` is a function that brings up a dialog box for the user type in a character string and returns that character string.

- `parseInt` is a function that converts a string to a number.

- `alert` is a function that brings up a dialog box with a message.

- The + operator either adds (in the case of numbers) or concatenates (in the case of strings).

Apply What You Have Learned

1. Create a new JavaScript program that asks the user for *two* values. Add these values together and display the result.

2. Try to rewrite the program you just created so that it doesn't use variables. Hint: make the return value of your functions be the parameter to other functions. It also might help to combine code a piece at a time, eliminating a single variable each time.

Part III

JavaScript Fundamentals

This part covers many of the the basic principles of programming needed to start programming in JavaScript.

Chapter 9

Basic JavaScript Syntax

All languages, whether human or computer, have what is called a **syntax**. The syntax of a language are the ways in which words and symbols are allowed to go together. For instance, consider the English sentence "I ate the the apple." That sentence has a *syntax error*—I put two "the"s in a row. That's simply not allowed (and non-sensical) in English.

But syntax has a larger role than simply telling you how not to form sentences. It also tells you what a sentence *means*. For instance, if I say, "I have a yellow banana and a red apple," you know that the word "yellow" describes my banana, and the word "red" describes my apple. You know that because English syntax tells you what it means for an adjective to be in front of a word—it means that the adjective describes the word.

The syntax of a programming language is very similar. As usual, what makes programming languages different from human ones is that the syntax is stricter and more exact. The computer will never understand what you *mean*, only what you tell it. If I tell you, "I have a banana yellow," you might figure out what I mean. The computer, in most cases, will not.

Note that in order to run the programs in this chapter, you must create an HTML wrapper for them just like you created in Section 8.3. It is recommended that you keep the JavaScript in a separate file and merely reference it through the `src` attribute of the `<script>` tag.

9.1   Elements of Syntax

While every programming language has its own syntax, there are certain types of syntactical units (i.e., pieces of syntax) which are common to nearly all programming languages. For instance, nearly every programming language has a statement separator—a symbol which tells the programming language that you have ended a statement. In JavaScript (and many other languages), the semicolon (;) performs this function. Because programming languages need to know where statements begin and end, most of them include a syntactical unit in the language which says that we are done with a statement.

Standard elements of syntax which are included in JavaScript include:

Literals A **literal** is how you write a specific value in the language. For instance, in JavaScript, 2 is a literal meaning the number 2, and "2" is a literal meaning the string that has one character, which is the "2" digit. We will discuss how to write different types of literals as we learn what they are. For now, numbers and character strings are the main types of literals we are concerned with.

Identifiers An **identifier** is a programmer-defined name. The names of variables, for instance, are identifiers. Each programming language has rules as to how identifiers should be named, usually restricting you to only using certain characters for names.

Keywords A **keyword** looks like an identifier, but is defined by the programming language. var is a keyword that we have seen so far, which indicates that the next identifier will be the name of a new variable. Many syntactical units are indicated by certain keywords. In JavaScript, keywords are also **reserved words**, which means that you are *not allowed* to have an identifier with the same name as a keyword.

Operators An **operator** is something (usually a symbol like + or -) that performs a task that would be inconvenient or unnatural to write as a function. The values that an operator uses to perform a function are called **operands**. So, for 2 + 3, + is the operator, and 2 and 3 are the operands.

Functions A **function** is a way of grouping code together to perform as a unit. We will discuss functions in more detail in Chapter 10.

Expressions An **expression** is a combination of functions, keywords, operators, identifiers, and literals which work together to produce a value. For example, 5 + 2 + 3 is an expression that produces the value 10.

Control Structures A **control structure** (also called a **flow control statement**) is
used to modify the flow of a computer program from its normal, sequential nature. For
instance, if you wanted to only perform a task if someone checked a certain checkbox,
you would need to use a control structure to make sure that it only ran when it was
supposed to.

Keep in mind that the goal of this book is to provide you with a practical introduction, not
a comprehensive list. There will be aspects of the syntax that we skip over, briefly mention,
or oversimplify. In fact, I can guarantee you that if I gave you all of the details, you would
put the book down and find something else to do! This is not a hindrance, however. It
is actually very rare for a programmer to know all of the details of a syntax. Some of the
details cover situations that the programmer would never think to do, but are included by
the person who created the language for the sake of completeness. So, in any language, you
are almost always a student and rarely a master. The few who are masters are usually the
ones writing the languages themselves. What is in this book should serve you well for a long
time, but keep in mind that there is always more to learn.

9.2 Assignment Statements

In Chapter 8 we covered assignment statements quite a bit. Assignment statements are the
foundation of most programming languages.

An example assignment statement is below:

Figure 9.1: A Simple Assignment Statement

```
x = 2 + 3;
```

Assignment statements have two sides—the left-hand side and the right-hand side. The
left-hand side is either a variable, or, as we will see in Chapter 13, some other reference to
a location that can hold a value. For this chapter, the left-hand side of an assignment will
be a variable.

The right-hand side of an assignment statement is an *expression*. As already mentioned, an expression is a combination of operators, functions, literals, and identifiers that yield a value. In this case, 2 + 3 yields the value 5. Therefore, the value of the right-hand side is 5. The value that is generated on the right-hand side then gets stored in the left-hand side.

Expressions can be simple—you can just have a literal value (i.e., 2). You can use variables in expressions, too. In fact, you can use the same variable in the expression that receives the assignment. Take a look at the following code:

Figure 9.2: A Left-Hand Side Variable Being Used in the Right-Hand Side

```
var x;
x = 10;   // x currently has the value 10
x = x + 13; // x now has the value 23
```

If you look at the last statement, the expression is x + 13. Since the value of x is currently 10 (the value that was assigned in the previous line), then the value of the expression is 10 + 13, or 23. Since this is an assignment statement, the value of the expression on the right-hand side (23) is now assigned to the variable on the left-hand side (x). Now, the value of x is 23.

Expressions can also be grouped together using parentheses in order to tell the programming language which operations you want to have happen first. For instance, look at the following code:

Figure 9.3: Expressions with Groupings

```
var x;
x = (2 + 10) * 3;
```

Here, 2 + 10 is evaluated first, which gives the value 12, and then 12 * 3 gets evaluated, giving 36. This number (36) is then stored in the variable x.

You can also include functions in your expressions. For instance, we can do the following:

Figure 9.4: A Function in an Expression

```
var x;
x = "123";   // This is the string "123", not the number 123
var y;
y = parseInt(x) + 12;
```

The last line of this code combines a function call with the + operator. The function call takes the value in x and returns its integer value, and then that value is added to 12, yielding 135.

Expressions can also be contained within a function's arguments. Take a look at the following code:

Figure 9.5: A Function Argument as an Expression

```
var x;
x = parseInt("12" + "3");
```

Here we have "12" + "3" as an expression which yields the value "123" (because "12" and "3" are both strings). This then gets passed into the **parseInt** function, which then yields the *number* 123, which is then stored in x.

9.3   Control Structures

Control structures modify the flow of your program. Normally, you think of your program as going step-by-step, one statement to the next. Control structures are syntactical units which cause the flow of your program to be altered in some way. The two basic control structures

that every programming language has to modify that flow are *conditional branching*, which causes the computer to either perform one section of code or another, and *looping*, which causes the computer to perform a section of code repeatedly.

9.3.1   The `if` Statement

The `if` statement is the primary way that JavaScript programmers do conditional branching. The `if` statement has the following basic form:

Figure 9.6: The Structure of the If Statement

```
if(some_condition) {
   // Put the code to perform if some_condition is true here
} else {
   // Put the code to perform if some_condition is not true
      here
}
```

First notice the use of curly braces (`{` and `}`). In JavaScript, curly braces are used to group statements together into **blocks**. The `if` statement potentially has two blocks—one to perform if the condition is true, and one to perform if the condition is false. You can put any number of statements inside the blocks.

The second thing to notice is the `some_condition` after the `if` statement. `if` statements use **conditional expressions** to decide which block to perform. A conditional expression is just like any other expression, except, rather than the value of the expression being a number or a string, it is a **boolean** value. A boolean value is simply a value that is either `true` or `false`. Boolean expressions usually compare two values to determine if they are equal or if one is greater than the other, or some similar operation that can be true or false.

To make it more clear, here is a program that uses an if statement:

Figure 9.7: An Example if Statement

```
var my_age;

// Prompt for an age and convert it into an integer
my_age = parseInt(prompt("What is your age?"));

if(my_age > 17) {
    alert("You are old enough to vote!");
} else {
    var years_to_vote;
    years_to_vote = 18 - my_age;
    alert("You have " + years_to_vote +
        " years left before you can vote.");
}
```

Here, the conditional expression is `my_age < 17`. What this does is look at the variable `my_age`, and if the value of `my_age` is greater than 17, then the value of the expression is true. If the value of `my_age` is not greater than 17, then the value of the expression is false. The > operator works just like the math operators, except that the value it gives is a boolean (true/false) value rather than a number value.

Notice what happens in the code. If you your age is over 17, then it just gives an alert. However, if your age is 17 or under, it then performs multiple tasks—first, it performs a calculation to see how many years you have left before you can vote, and after that it displays the answer.

Common boolean operators (operators which yield `true` or `false`) include:

Operator	Meaning	Examples
==	Equality	2 == 2 yields `true`; 2 == 3 yields `false`
!=	Inequality	2 != 2 yields `false`; 2 != 3 yields `true`
<	Less-Than	2 < 2 yields `false`; 1 < 2 yields `true`
>	Greater-Than	2 > 2 yields `false`; 3 > 2 yields `true`
>=	Greater-Than-Or-Equal-To	2 >= 2 yields `true`; 1 >= 2 yields `false`
<=	Less-Than-Or-Equal-To	2 <= 2 yields `true`; 3 <= 2 yields `false`

Oftentimes, conditions need to be combined. Let's say that we want to know if *both* of these are true—you are exactly 18 years old and your name is Fred. You could do this in one of two ways. The first way is to embed one `if` statement inside another one, like this:

Figure 9.8: An `if` Statement Embedded in an `if` Statement

```
var my_age;
var my_name;

my_name = prompt("What is your name?");
my_age = parseInt(prompt("What is your age?"));

if(my_age == 18) {
    if(my_name == "Fred") {
        alert("Your name is Fred and you are 18!");
    }
}
```

Note that, first, I don't have an `else` branch on these `if` statements. The `else` branch is actually optional. If the condition is false, and there is no `else` branch, it will just skip it and go on to the next statement. The other thing to note is that we can have an `if` statement within a code block on a condition. In JavaScript, *any* code can go within these blocks.

However, this takes a lot of typing. It would be nicer if we could combine the two `if` statements into a single statement. We can do this by combining the boolean expressions. Boolean expressions can be combined with two operators, `&&` (which is pronounced "and")

and || (which is pronounced as "or"). && yields a true value if *both* of its operands are true, and || yields a true value if *either* of its operands are true. We can therefore combine these statements into a single if statement using &&:

Figure 9.9: Combining Conditions

```
var my_age;
var my_name;

my_name = prompt("What is your name?");
my_age = parseInt(prompt("What is your age?"));

if(my_age == 18 && my_name == "Fred") {
    alert("Your name is Fred and you are 18!");
}
```

The one other boolean operator that we need to cover is the ! (pronounced "not") operator. The ! operator, instead of having two operands, only has one, which appears on the right side of the operator. This operator returns the *opposite* of whatever boolean value is on its right. It is also best to use the ! operator with parentheses so it is obvious to you, to the computer, and to other people reading your code, what expression you are applying it to.

So, for instance, if I wanted to find out if the variable my_value is not between 3 and 10, I can write !(my_value >= 3 && my_value <= 10). The expression in parentheses will yield true if the value is within range, and then the ! operator will cause it to return the opposite.

9.3.2   The while Statement

Now that we've looked at conditional statements with the if statement, it is now time to look at looping statements. Loops are used to repeat a section of code a certain number of times or until a certain condition is reached. Let's say you have a quiz game, and you want someone to keep trying answers until they got the right one. You would use a loop because you would want the code to keep asking them the question and reading answers until they reach the right answer.

The most basic looping structure in JavaScript is the `while` statement. The while statement's overall structure looks like this:

Figure 9.10: Basic Structure of a While Statement

```
while(some_condition) {
    // Perform tasks here
}
```

The `while` statement tells JavaScript to repeat the code in the given block until `some_condition` is false. It checks `some_condition` before each time it runs the block of code, and, if the condition is true, it runs the loop. If the condition is false, then it considers the loop completed and moves on to the next part of the code.

Here is an example program with a `while` loop that will repeat until the user enters the right value:

Figure 9.11: A While Loop Example

```
var answer;

while(answer != "Genesis") {
    answer = prompt("What is the first book in the Bible?");
}
alert("You got the answer right!");
```

What this will do is start out by creating a variable called **answer**. By default, variables in JavaScript, before they are given a value, are given an empty value that is called `undefined`. After defining the variables, the code starts the `while` loop. When it first starts, it evaluates its condition, known as the **loop condition**. The condition is `answer != "Genesis"`. This checks to see if the variable **answer** is different from the character string `"Genesis"`. Indeed, `undefined` is different from `"Genesis"`, so the condition is true. This means that we can proceed with the loop.

After the loop condition comes a block of statements wrapped in curly braces known as the **loop body**. These statements are executed if the loop condition is true. Within this loop, there is only one statement, which asks the user to answer a question, and stores the result in the `answer` variable. When the computer is done executing the body of the loop, it re-evaluates the loop condition again to see if we should run the loop again or if we are done.

Let's say that the user had erroneously answered the question by typing in "Exodus." What would happen? `answer` would have the value `"Exodus"`. When it evaluates the loop condition, `answer != "Genesis"` would still returns true. Therefore, it would run the loop body again.

Now let's say that this time they type in "Genesis" as they should. What happens now? Well, `"Genesis"` gets put into `answer`. Now the loop body is complete again, so it re-evaluates the loop condition. This time, the condition `answer != "Genesis"` is false! When the loop condition is false, it transfers control to the first instruction after the loop body. In this case, that instruction tells the user that they entered the right value.

One thing to be careful of when writing loops is to make sure that the loop condition can, eventually, evaluate to false. Otherwise, what will happen? It will loop forever! In computer terms, this is known as an **infinite loop**. You should always double-check to make sure that your loops will eventually terminate. We will cover infinite loops more in the next section.

9.3.3 The `for` Statement

One common reason for a loop is to perform a computation a specified number of times. Let's say that we wanted to write a program that added up all of the numbers between 1 and 6. This can be easily accomplished through a loop.

Here is how we would accomplish that with a `while` loop:

Figure 9.12: Adding Up the Numbers 1 through 6 with a `while` Loop

```
var num = 1; // This holds the next number to add
var sum = 0; // This holds the sum total so far

while(num <= 6) {  // Check if we are done
    // Add the next number to the sum
    sum = sum + num;

    // Go to the next number
    num = num + 1;
}

alert("The sum of the numbers 1 through 6 is " + sum);
```

The way that this works is that it begins by putting starting values in each variable. This is known as **initializing** the variables. Oftentimes a program succeeds or fails based on whether or not the variables were initialized to the right values. In this case, num is set to the first number we want to add in our sum. The variable sum is set to zero. It is set to zero because that is the state of a sum before anything gets added to it—a sum of nothing is zero.

Next the loop condition is evaluated. Yes, num is less than or equal to 6 since its value is 1. Next, that number is added to sum and assigned back into sum, which is now 1. The next part is the most important part—you add 1 to num and store it back into num to move it to the next number. The value of num is now 2. Notice that even though it is still less than or equal to 6, it is a step closer to terminating the loop. Now we repeat the loop condition and loop body again. At the end of the next iteration through the loop, the value of num is, again, a step closer to terminating the loop.

After running the loop body 6 times, the value of num is 7, which will terminate the loop and give the answer.

Now take a minute to think—what would happen if we accidentally left off the code which added 1 to num at the end of the loop? num would never increase, and so it would *always* be

1, and therefore `num <= 6` would *always* be true and the loop would never, ever finish. A loop that never finishes is known as an **infinite loop**. An infinite loop could lock up your browser, or, even worse, your whole computer.

When you have a simple loop like this, where there is a single variable which is used to manage whether or not the loop repeats, that variable is called the **loop control variable**. However, the problem is that while loops separate out the loop condition from the location where we increment the loop control variable. Yet another location to manage is the place where the loop control variable gets initialized. Having these important parts of the loop in different places can be dangerous as we can easily forget important steps. However, another flow control statement is available which, for simple loops, keeps all of the steps for managing the control variable in one spot. This statement is the `for` statement.

The structure of the `for` statement is like this:

Figure 9.13: Basic Structure of the `for` Statement

```
for(loop_control_variable_initialization; loop_condition;
    loop_control_variable_modification) {
    // Loop Body
}
```

The three places where we used the control variable are now all packaged together in the `for` statement. This makes the process of writing simple loops much less error-prone.

So, if we rewrite our previous program using a `for` statement, it looks like this:

Figure 9.14: Add Numbers 1 through 6 Using a `for` Statement

```
var sum;
var num;

sum = 0;
for(num = 1; num <= 6; num = num + 1) {
    sum = sum + num;
}
```

As you can see, everything we do with our loop control variable is contained. One other thing that the JavaScript syntax allows us to do is to combine our variable declarations and initializations into one line. Therefore, we can rewrite this same code as:

Figure 9.15: Example of Combining Variable Declarations and Initializations

```
var sum = 0;
for(var num = 1; num <= 6; num = num + 1) {
    sum = sum + num;
}
alert("The sum of the numbers 1 through 6 is " + sum);
```

And there you have it! This syntax allows you to better manage your loop control variables by keeping all of the management code in one place. It also makes the code easier to read. `while` statements are still very important, especially for more complicated loops. But most of the time you can get away with using a `for` loop.

Review

In this chapter we covered the basics of JavaScript syntax. We have learned:

- Syntax is the way that the structure of a program or sentence indicates its meaning.

- Every language has its own, unique syntax.

- Types of syntactical units which are common to many programming languages include literals, identifiers, keywords, operators, functions, expressions, and control structures.

- An expression is a sequence of literals, identifiers, operators, and functions which combine to yield a value.

- JavaScript assignment statements have a right-hand side, which contains an expression which gives the value to be assigned, and a left-hand side that says where (i.e., in what variable) the value should be placed.

- The two most common ways for a control structure to modify the flow of your program are by conditional branching and looping.

- The `if` statement is the primary method of conditional branching in JavaScript.

- Most looping in JavaScript is accomplished through either `while` statements or `for` statements.

- The basic structure of a loop are the loop initializers, the loop condition, and the loop body.

- Simple loops are focused around a single loop control variable, which is used in all three parts of the loop's structure.

- The `for` loop allows the programmer to collect all of the manipulation of the loop control variable into a single location, which is easier for the programmer to do correctly and easier for others to read and understand.

- Multiple statements can be placed in the body of a conditional branching statement or a looping statement. The curly braces denote which statements belong in the body of the control structure.

- Conditional branching statements and loop statements can be placed inside of other branching and looping statements as well for more complex processing.

- The `var` statement can also be combined with an assignment statement to provide an initial value for the variable.

Apply What You Have Learned

1. Enter the code for the quiz game in Section 9.3.2. Be sure to create an HTML file that loads the JavaScript code. Verify that the game works.

2. Create your own quiz game with at least three questions.

3. Add additional code to this game to give someone hints if they answer a question incorrectly. If this is your first time programming, this may be harder than you think. Think through exactly how the program is running, and what you would need to do to get it to give hints in the right place. Depending on how you decide to do it, you may need to embed an `if` statement within the body of your loop.

4. Enter the code for adding up the numbers 1 through 6 in Section 9.3.3. Be sure to create an HTML file that loads the JavaScript code. Verify that it works.

5. Modify the code so that you ask the user what number range they want to use for the additions. Don't forget to use `parseInt`!

6. In the previous example, it might be possible for someone to enter an invalid range (i.e., the start of the number range is greater than the end of the number range). Add `if` statements to account for this, either by alerting the user or just fixing the problem.

Chapter 10

Introducing Functions and Scope

In the previous chapter we learned about the nuts and bolts of how programming works, with assignments statements, conditional branching, and loops. For small programs, this is all you need. In fact, you can do any possible computation you might need to do with only these features. However, as your programs get larger—even just a little bit larger—you will need tools that will enable you to get more work done with each line of code and to organize your code into logical blocks. Imagine, for instance, if your program was 10,000 lines long. If you needed to change a line, it might be hard to find!

Likewise, let's say there was a task that you had to do over and over again. If you had to type out the code for it each time, that would be a lot of wasted effort! In addition, let's say that you found an error (known as a **bug**) in your code that you had been copying. If you had 20 copies of the code, you would have to find each copy and fix it. This is tedious, wasteful, and error-prone.

What we need to do is to take sections of code and package them up into a unit. Doing this will make our code both better organized and reusable. The JavaScript language uses **functions** to organize and reuse sections of code.

10.1 Your First Function

You already have some experience with functions. Remember `parseInt`, `prompt`, and `alert`? These are known as **built-in** functions because they are part of JavaScript itself. However, you can define your own functions that you can call in the same way.

To begin our discussion of functions, let me show you a program that illustrates how functions work. Remember to wrap this and the other programs in this chapter in an HTML file like we described in Section 8.3. Here is the program:

Figure 10.1: An Example of Using Functions

```
var square_a_number = function(num) {
   var value = num * num;
   return value;
};

alert("The square of 3 is " + square_a_number(3));
alert("The square of 4 is " + square_a_number(4));
```

What this program does is define a function which takes a single value and returns that value squared (i.e., multiplied by itself). It then uses that function twice, giving it different numbers to square. The function is defined using the `function` keyword.

After the `function` keyword comes a parameter list—a list in parentheses of all of the parameters that the function can take. The function we are defining takes a single parameter, which we have named `num`. This means that the value that is sent to the function gets stored into `num` for the duration of the function, so we have a name to call it by. Since it is in the parameter list, we do not use the `var` keyword to define it. So, in short, `function(num)` tells JavaScript to define a function that takes a single parameter, and name that parameter `num`. When we use `num` within the function, we will be working with whatever value was sent when the program was called.

We could have used any valid name instead of `num`, but `num` seemed like an appropriate name for a number. Then, within the curly braces, is the block of code that defines what the

function will do. In this case, we are creating a new variable called `value`, multiplying `num` by itself, and then storing it into `value`. Then, the `return` statement tells JavaScript what to give back to the code that called our function. In this program, the return statement says that the result currently in `value` should be given as the result for the function.

The `function` operator defines a function. However, we need to be able to call the function from our code. It therefore needs a name. How do we name something in JavaScript? We store it in a variable. Therefore, the code `var square_a_number = function(num) { /* code goes here */ };` defines a function with a single parameter, and then stores that function into the newly-created variable `square_a_number`. As usual, don't forget the semicolon (;) at the end of the assignment statement, or JavaScript might get confused.

Now that we have the variable `square_a_number` which contains our function, we can call it exactly like we called other functions like `parseInt`. `square_a_number(5)` will yield 25, and `square_a_number(6)` will yield 36.

☞ **Practice Questions**

1. In the same file as the `square_a_number` function, define another function called `cube_a_number` that returns the cube of a number (i.e., the number times itself and times itself again).

2. Call the `alert` function a few times giving it the results of the `cube_a_number` function, like we did for `square_a_number`.

3. The body of the `square_a_number` function creates a variable called `value` to store the temporary result of the calculation. However, because the calculation is so simple, we don't really need this variable. Can you rewrite `square_a_number` so that it doesn't use a variable?

4. Remove the existing calls to `alert` from the program. Now, ask the user to type in a number, then call `square_a_number`, and then show the result to the user.

5. Take the program you've just written and put the interactions with the user in a `for` loop that runs three times so that it will ask the user for a number and give the result three times.

10.2   More Function Examples

To make sure that you grasp the concept of a function, let's do another example. Let's say that we wanted to have a function that summed up a range of numbers, like all of the numbers between 2 and 12. This would be similar to the code we wrote in Section 9.3.3, but it would take the start and end values as parameters. How would we write that? Well, we would need a function, but that function would also need to have a loop inside of it to loop through all of the numbers from the start to the finish. The code would look like this:

Figure 10.2: A Function with an Embedded `while` Loop

```
var sum_range = function(range_start, range_end) {
    var sum = 0;
    for(var num = range_start; num <= range_end; num = num +
        1) {
        sum = sum + num;
    }
    return sum;
};

var start_val = parseInt(prompt("Enter the first number"));
var end_val = parseInt(prompt("Enter the last number"));
var result = sum_range(start_val, end_val);
alert("The sum of all of the numbers between " + start_val
    + " and " + end_val + " is " + result);
```

This function has a few differences from our previous function. First of all, it has two parameters instead of one—`range_start` and `range_end`. Functions can have as many parameters as you want. It can even have zero, which would be indicated by writing `function()`. In this case, we need two values because we need both a start and an end value for the range. In JavaScript, parameters are *positional*, which means that the order that you define them with the `function` keyword is the same order as the values that you have to give when the function is called. In other words, since `range_start` is the first parameter, the first value in the function call gets placed here. Since `range_end` is the second parameter, the second value that is sent to the function call gets placed here. So, calling `sum_range(start_val, end_val)` tells

JavaScript to run the function `sum_range`, put the value of `start_val` into `range_start`, and put the value of `end_val` into `range_end`. It then runs the function and returns the value, which, in this case, is placed in the variable `result`. Next, we have a `for` loop embedded in the function. Just like any block of code in JavaScript, we can embed any type of statement or operator within a function.

For this small program, since we only use the `sum_range` program once, it doesn't save us a lot of typing. But can you see how, if we needed it in several different parts of the program and used it over and over again, putting that code into a function will save a lot of typing and headaches in the future? Even though this example doesn't save us any typing, using functions still has a distinct advantage—it separates out different components of our application. In this program, we have both user interaction (prompting, receiving input, and displaying output) as well as computation (summing all of the numbers in a range). By putting the computation in a function, we have made both parts clearer.

Imagine if we had simply stuck all of the code together without a function. It might be difficult to even understand what the program was trying to do. Instead, by separating out a piece into a function with an easy-to-understand name (i.e., `sum_range`), then we make it clearer what the whole program is doing. You can look at it and say, "Oh yes, this piece of code with the name `sum_rage` sums up numbers within a range. And look! Over here we use the function with the two inputs from the user."

Again, this is not as big of an issue with small programs, but when you write programs with many thousands of lines of code, having the code broken up into manageable, understandable components, each with a small, well-defined task makes the code much easier to understand and modify.

☞ **Practice Questions**

1. Create a function that takes three parameters and returns the largest of the three parameters. You will have to use several `if` statements to accomplish this.

2. Create a function called `multiply` which will take two parameters and perform the same function as the * operator. However, don't use the * operator in your code. Instead, perform the task by repeated adding of the first parameter. Be sure to include code to run the function and display the result so that you know whether you did it correctly!

10.3 Functions Calling Functions

Functions can also call other functions. For instance, we can create a new function called `sum_squares_for_range` that is similar to the `sum_range` function, but, instead of summing up the numbers in the range, it calls `square_a_number` on each number to sum up the squares of the numbers in the range. Before looking at the code below, think about how you might implement such a function.

Figure 10.3: A Function Calling Another Function

```
var square_a_number = function(num) {
    var value = num * num;
    return value;
};

var sum_squares_for_range = function(range_start,
    range_end) {
    var sum = 0;
    for(var num = range_start; num <= range_end; num = num +
        1) {
        sum = sum + square_a_number(num);
    }
    return sum;
};
alert("The sum of squares between 2 and 5 is " +
    sum_squares_for_range(2, 5));
```

As you can see, just as we can call a function from anywhere else in our program, we can call a function from within a function as well. Using this feature, we can make functions that are more and more complex. We can take several small functions that we often use together and write a larger function that combines them in an interesting and useful way. Likewise, if we have a large function that is difficult to understand, we can try to break the function up into well-defined pieces and create individual functions for those pieces.

10.4 Variable Scopes

Now that we know how functions work in JavaScript, we need to talk about **variable scope**. The scope of a variable refers to the locations within a program where the variable is created, is active and available for use, and where it is destroyed. In some of the earliest programming languages, all variables had **global** scope—meaning that the variable always existed throughout the whole program and was accessible everywhere within the program. However, this quickly led to problems. We have created temporary variables several times already to hold intermediate values, such as the `sum` variable in the `sum_range` function. If all of your variables have global scope, when you call one function from another function, if both of them use the same name for a temporary variable, then your temporary result will be overwritten by the other function!

If all variables had global scope, the only way to avoid this situation is to make sure that each variable had a unique name. This would be tedious and time-consuming, both to keep track of the variable names and to write the inevitably excessively long names that would result. Programming languages quickly adopted new scoping policies that allowed programmers more freedom.

The type of scoping that JavaScript does is called **function scope**. This means that in addition to the global scope, each function has a unique, separate scope. If we declare a variable `var myvar` outside of a function, that variable exists within the global scope, and is called a **global variable**. Since it is global, I can access `myvar` from *anywhere in my program*. If we instead declared `var myvar` from *inside* a function, then `myvar` would only be available *within that function*. Such variables are often called **local variables**. Parameters to functions also act as if they were local variables in the function's scope.

To illustrate this, take a look at the following program in which we modify a global variable inside the function:

Figure 10.4: Modifying Global Variables

```
var myvar = 3; // Global variable

var my_function = function () {
   myvar = 5; // Writing to a global variable
};

alert("myvar = " + myvar);
my_function();
alert("After calling my_function, myvar = " + myvar);
```

In this code, when it starts, it creates `myvar` as a global variable (it is defined outside of any function), and sets it to 3. Then, it calls `my_function()`. This function sets `myvar` to 5 and then returns. Now, when we show the variable again, it has the value 5.

Contrast that to what happens in the next program:

Figure 10.5: Global and Local Variables

```
var myvar = 3; // Global variable

var my_function = function () {
   var myvar = 5; // This version of myvar is now *local*
};

alert("myvar = " + myvar);
my_function();
alert("After calling my_function, myvar = " + myvar);
```

In this example, because `myvar` has the `var` keyword in front of it in the function, it creates

a local variable that is specific to that function. It exists nowhere else. Even though there is a `myvar` that exists in the global scope, during the function `myvar` will refer to the local variable with the same name. Therefore, setting the local variable `myvar` from inside the function has no effect on the global scope. Both alerts will give the same value because the modification happened to a local variable.

Additionally, if there was another function that also had a locally-scoped `myvar`, it would be a different variable than either the globally-scoped `myvar` or the `myvar` that is locally scoped to this function. Each function's local variables belongs to that function and cannot even be referenced outside of that function.

Having local scopes allows functions to work as "black boxes," meaning that the person who writes the code that calls a function doesn't have to care about the details of how that function is implemented. If we only had the global scope, then, before I called a function, I would need to go and look up all of the variables it was using to make sure I wasn't also using the same variable. However, if a function writer only uses local variables, then if I used that function in my program, I wouldn't have to worry that it might accidentally overwrite a variable I am using. This is true in larger programs even if there is only one programmer. You will not remember the names of every variable you use in your functions. But, if you make sure that you only use local variables and parameters within your functions, you won't need to remember all of the variable names since they will all be within the scope of the given function.

Occasionally, you will need to use the global scope. In fact, this is what we are doing with our function names. In JavaScript, functions are stored in variables just like any other value. Therefore, in order for functions to call each other, they must exist in the global scope.

Review

In this chapter we discussed what a function is and how we can use functions in our code. We have learned:

- The `function` operator creates a function.

- A function takes parameters, which are variables that refer to values passed to the function.

- Function parameters are positional, which means that the order that they are defined using the `function` operator is the same order that the function call must use.

- A function has a function body, which is the code that tells the computer what to do when the function is called.

- Functions are stored in named variables so that they can be called. Without a variable name, there would be no way to call them.

- Functions can call other functions.

- Functions can be used to organize your code into well-defined, understandable units.

- Functions can be used to minimize the amount of code that needs to be written by moving repeated sections of code into a function.

- When repeated code sections are moved into a function, this also makes it easier to fix bugs as they only need to be fixed in one place.

- A variable's scope refers to the period when a variable becomes active and the places from which it can be accessed.

- Variables in the global scope can be accessed from anywhere in your code.

- Variables in a function's local scope can only be accessed from within that function.

- If a function has a local variable with the same name as a global variable, the global variable is hidden from view during that function.

- If two functions have a local variable with the same name, these refer to two *different* variables because they each exist in different scopes.

Apply What You Have Learned

With the knowledge you have learned so far, you can now start making real programs. Remember your tools—if, `while`, `for`, and `function`, and you will be able to make all of the programs listed below.

1. Create a Celsius-to-Fahrenheit converter. It should ask the user for a Celsius temperature and return a Fahrenheit temperature. The conversion from Celsius to Fahrenheit is to multiply the Celsius temperature by 9, divide the result by 5, and add 32. Be sure that the actual conversion is contained within a function.

2. Create a fuel efficiency calculator. It should ask for the number of miles you drove, how many gallons you used, and the price per gallon of fuel. It should then tell you the number of dollars per mile that it cost you to drive. The formula for this is to take the price per gallon, multiply by the gallons, and divide by the number of miles. Be sure that the formula is handled in a function.

3. Implement the factorial function. The factorial function takes a number, and multiplies together every number from 1 to the given number. For instance, the factorial of 6 is `6 * 5 * 4 * 3 * 2 * 1`. The factorial of 3 is `3 * 2 * 1`. Note that since you are repeating an operation, you will need a loop. Be sure that your factorial calculation is written in a function and allow the user to enter the number they want the factorial of.

4. Take any one of these calculators and make it so that the user can enter as many values as they want. You can do this by either asking the user afterwards if they want to keep going, or have a special value that the user types to signal that they are done. In any case, make it so that the user can keep using the application until they are ready to be finished.

Chapter 11

Recursive Functions

In Chapter 10 you learned that functions can be used to package together pieces of code into well-defined units that can be reused over and over again. In this chapter we are going to go into more detail about how JavaScript keeps track of these functions.

11.1   The Program Stack

In the previous chapter we talked about local variables (variables defined within functions) and global variables (variables defined outside of functions). We mentioned that local variables are specific to the function that they are defined in. That is, if we have a global variable called x, and a function has a local variable also called x, these refer to *different* variables. Therefore, the function is able to modify their local x without modifying the global x. One of the many benefits to this is that our functions can be developed without worrying about what someone else working on another part of the program has called their variables. Imagine if you were working with a partner developing a program together. If you both had to agree on every single variable name (to prevent one person from accidentally clobbering the other person's variables), that would get tedious and make the process very slow. With local variables, as long as the variable is defined within a function, it doesn't matter what its name is. You may still have to agree on the names of global variables, but those should be much more rare, especially in large projects.

So, how does JavaScript keep track of local variables? It turns out that nearly every program-

ming language keeps track of local variables in roughly the same way—through a mechanism known as the **program stack**, or just the stack. The stack is the way that the programming language keeps track of what is currently going on in the program. It is, quite literally, a stack of information that the programming language is keeping about what is happening in the program.

For instance, when a program calls a function, it has to remember where to return to after the program is finished. Therefore, it pushes the return location onto the stack so it remembers where to go after the function is finished. If that function calls another function, then it pushes another return location onto the top of the stack. When the second function finishes, it looks at the top of the stack to see where it should return to, pops (removes) the value, and resumes operation at the point indicated. When the original function finishes, its return location is now back at the top of the stack so it knows where it should return to.

Figure 11.1 shows some functions that call each other. It includes comments showing different locations that the program will be executing (marked as "Position 1", "Position 2", etc.) so that we can discuss the flow of the program through the functions.

If you skip the declaration of the variables for the functions, the actual code starts at position 8. For our purposes, we can conceive of the stack being empty when the program starts running.

Figure 11.1: Example of Functions Calling Each Other

```
var function_one = function() {
   // Position 1
   function_two();
   // Position 2
   function_three();
   // Position 3
};

var function_two = function() {
   // Position 4
   function_three();
   // Position 5
};

var function_three = function() {
   // Position 6
   alert("Hello");
   // Position 7
};

// Position 8
function_one();
// Position 9
```

The first thing it does is call the function `function_one`. When `function_one` ends, where should the program continue? It should continue running at position 9. The stack looks like this:

Figure 11.2: Stack After First Function Call

```
Return Location: Position 9
Bottom of Stack
```

Now, look at `function_one`. The code starts running at position 1 and there is an immediate function call to `function_two`. Think about where the code should continue running after `function_two` finishes—it should continue running at position 2. Therefore, that position is pushed to the top of the stack. The stack now looks like this:

Figure 11.3: Stack After Second Function Call

```
Return Location: Position 2
Return Location: Position 9
Bottom of Stack
```

Now, what does `function_two` do? It calls yet another function, `function_three`. Since the next place it should start executing after `function_three` finishes is position 5, that is now pushed onto the stack.

Figure 11.4: Stack After Third Function Call

```
Return Location: Position 5
Return Location: Position 2
Return Location: Position 9
Bottom of Stack
```

Now, `function_three` makes its own function call, but this time to a built-in function. Function calls to built-in functions work exactly like other function calls. So, where should `function_three` resume after `alert` finishes? It should go back to position 7, and the stack will look like this:

Figure 11.5: Stack After Built-in Function Call

```
Return Location: Position 7
Return Location: Position 5
Return Location: Position 2
Return Location: Position 9
Bottom of Stack
```

Now things get interesting. What happens when `alert` finishes? How does it know where to go? It just looks at the top of the stack! The top of the stack says, "When you are done, return to position 7 in the code." JavaScript then removes the top of the stack, and continues operation at position 7. Now the stack looks like it did in Figure 11.4. But then, the only thing left to do at position 7 is to return from the function. Therefore, it performs the procedure again—it looks at the top of the stack to see where it should return to. Now it says to return to position 5, and the stack is back the way it looked in Figure 11.3. Again, the only thing to do in position 5 is to return, and the stack says to return to position 2. We therefore return to position 2 and remove it from the top of the stack. The stack is then back to looking how it did in Figure 11.2.

Now it gets really interesting. What happens at position 2? It calls `function_three` again, but this time with a *different* return location than the previous occasion—position 3. The stack now looks like this:

Figure 11.6: Stack After Second Call to `function_three`

```
Return Location: Position 3
Return Location: Position 9
Bottom of Stack
```

Now when `function_three` runs, it knows to go back to position 3 instead of position 5 like it did when it was called from `function_two`. So, as you can see, the stack keeps track of what is happening in the program and helps the computer know how and where to return from function calls.

Oftentimes, what happens in code is more complicated than this. Since many of our functions have return values, and the functions are actually only part of the statement, the return must send the program to the correct place in the middle of the line of code. This is the same idea as before, only that the positions that the computer keeps track of are more complicated than just line numbers like we had for the example. For instance, take the following code:

Figure 11.7: Complicated Function Call

```
var square_a_number = function(x) {
    return x * x;
};

var y = square_a_number(square_a_number(2) * 4);
```

In this case, we are calling a function several times *in the same line*, and each one returns to a *different place in the line*. Don't worry. JavaScript knows exactly where to return to each time. Its positioning system is much more exact than our crude examples above.

Also, as we will see going forward, JavaScript stores much more information in the stack than just the return location.

11.2   Local Variables in the Stack

The other primary thing that JavaScript keeps in its stack is a list of the local variables used in the current function. To talk about this, let's look at a function that will sum all of the values in a range, which we will call `sum_range`. For instance, if you give it the numbers 3 and 7, `sum_range(3, 7)` will calculate 3 + 4 + 5 + 6 + 7 and give 25.

Let's look at what this looks like in code:

Figure 11.8: Summing All the Values in a Range

```
var sum_range = function(r_start, r_end) {
   var total = 0;
   for(var x = r_start; x <= r_end; x++) {
      total = total + x;
   }

   return total;
};

var result = sum_range(3, 7);
alert("The sum of the numbers 3 through 7 is " + result);
```

In this example, we have local variables—r_start, r_end, x, and total. Remember that local variables are not visible to the global scope. The way that JavaScript does this is by keeping the list of current variables on the stack.

Therefore, when the function is called, not only does the return location get put on the stack, but it also creates a "scope" (list of accessible variables) in memory and links the stack to that scope.

So, when we call sum_range, the stack looks a little more complicated. Figure 11.9 shows how the stack looks when the sum_range function is underway when it first begins its for loop.

Note that there is a big black line around the the current scope and the current location. That is known as the **stack frame**. The stack frame is all of the data that is packaged together on the stack. The scope and the return value go together for each function call, and together they make up a stack frame.

The stack frame points JavaScript to the scope that is currently being used to process variables. The way that the scope works is that when you refer to a variable, say x, in your program, JavaScript first looks on the stack to see where your current scope is. It then looks for that variable in the current scope. If it finds it, that is what it uses for the variable. Do you see the box at the top of the local scope that says "Parent Scope"? Each scope links to a

Figure 11.9: Conceptual Layout of Computer Memory in a Function Call

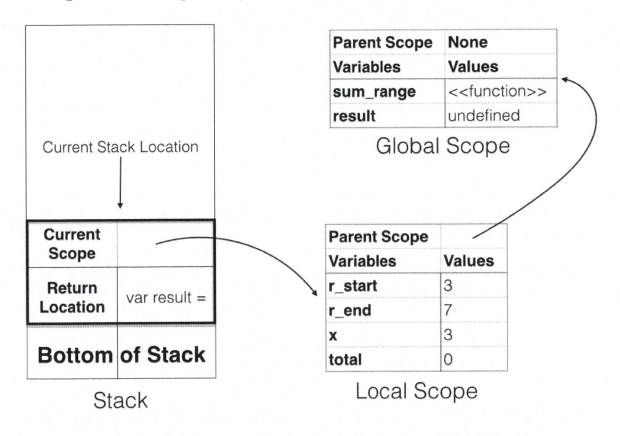

parent scope, which tells JavaScript where to look for variables if they are not in the current scope. In this case, the parent scope is the global scope. In Chapter 12, we will see how we can chain together even more scopes.

So, when a function is called, not only is the return value put onto the stack, but a *brand new* scope is created, and a link to this new scope is also placed on the stack.

Let's look at another, similar program which will declare a function called `sum_squares_of_range`. This works just like `sum_range`, except that it will square each of the numbers in the range. The code for this is below:

Figure 11.10: Summing the Squares of a Range of Numbers

```javascript
var square_number = function(num) {
    var x = num * num;
    return x;
};

var sum_squares_of_range = function(r_start, r_end) {
    var total = 0;
    for(var x = r_start; x <= r_end; x++) {
        total = total + square_number(x);
    }

    return total;
};

var result = sum_squares_of_range(3, 6);
alert("The sum of the squares of the values from 3 to 6: "
    + result);
```

In this program, the stack gets two levels deep. First, it calls `sum_squares_of_range`. This leads to a situation similar to the previous example. Then, to calculate the square of each number, it calls `square_number` on each of them. Figure 11.11 shows the stack layout after the first call to `square_number` just before it returns. Notice that all of the local variables *exist* for both functions, but they are only *reachable* from within their own

Figure 11.11: Stack Frame with Two Functions Active

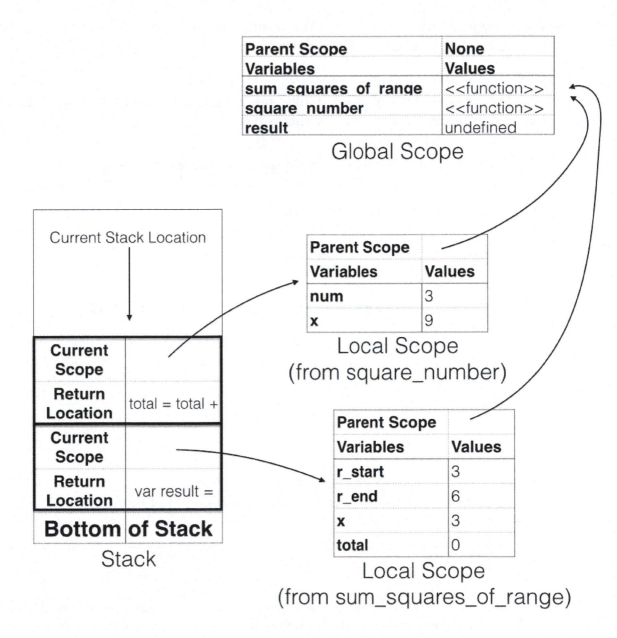

Parent Scope	None
Variables	Values
sum_squares_of_range	<<function>>
square_number	<<function>>
result	undefined

Global Scope

Current Stack Location

Current Scope	
Return Location	total = total +
Current Scope	
Return Location	var result =

Bottom of Stack

Stack

Parent Scope	
Variables	Values
num	3
x	9

Local Scope
(from square_number)

Parent Scope	
Variables	Values
r_start	3
r_end	6
x	3
total	0

Local Scope
(from sum_squares_of_range)

functions. When the `square_number` function is active, the "current scope" points to the local scope for `square_number`, which has its variables plus a link to the global scope.

Therefore, when `square_number` sets the value of x, it only affects its own value for x. The x from `sum_squares_of_range` is not even visible to this function. Therefore, even though we are assigning a value for x, it is only for the *local* copy of x that is specific to this function. When the function returns, it will remove *both* the link to the local scope and return location. When `sum_squares_of_range` starts executing again, its own scope will be at the top of the stack, and it won't see the scope of `square_number` at all.

One additional thing to note is that when a function first starts executing, the local scope *only* has entries for the parent scope and the parameters. JavaScript relies on the `var` keyword to create new variables in its scope. The `var` keyword causes JavaScript to look in the current scope (and *not* any parent scope) to see if the variable exists *in that scope*. If the variable does not exist, JavaScript creates the variable in the current scope. If the variable already exists, JavaScript *does not* create a new copy, but keeps using the one that is already there.

☞ **Practice Activity**

1. Look at the programs you wrote in Chapter 10 that use functions. Pick one of them.

2. Print out your function. Draw lines from any function call to the beginning of the function that is being called. Draw lines from the `return` statements to the place in your program where the program returns.

3. Create a diagram for this program of the stack, local scope(s), and global scope, similar to the one in Figure 11.11, for when at least one function is active.

11.3 Recursive Functions

Now that we know how stack frames and local variables work, it is time to learn about **recursive functions**. A recursive function is a function that is defined in terms of itself. Think about the program back in Figure 11.8 that summed all of the values between two

numbers. In the program, we used a loop to go from one side of the range to the other. But is there another way to think about that problem? Another way to pursue it?

Think about summing all of the numbers from 4 to 10. Is there a smaller, similar problem that works the same way that we might be able to use? Indeed, summing all of the numbers from 4 to 10 is the same thing as adding 4 to the sum of the numbers from 5 to 10. So, sum_range(4, 10) gives us the same answer as 4 + sum_range(5, 10). Likewise, sum_range(5, 10) gives us the same answer as 5 + sum_range(6, 10).

Defining a function in terms of itself is called a recursion. How might we write a program that uses recursion? Below is a partial implementation of what that might look like:

Figure 11.12: Partial Recursive Definition of the sum_range Function

```
var sum_range = function(r_start, r_end) {
    var value = r_start + sum_range(r_start + 1, r_end);
    return value;
};
```

As you can see, the function is defined in terms of itself. However, one problem you would realize if you tried this function is that it never stops! There is nothing in the function that makes it stop when it gets to the end of the range so it will just keep on going.

When writing recursive programs, there are two main situations to code for—the **base case** and the **inductive case**. The inductive case is the one we have already written—it is the case that uses recursion to solve the problem. The inductive case gets its name from inductive proofs in mathematics, which are very similar to recursive functions. The case we are missing is the base case—it is the case that stops the recursion to return an answer. In our program, the base case happens when r_start and r_end are equal. When this happens, we don't need to recurse anymore—we know what the answer is! When the start and end of the range are equal, we just return *that* number.

Therefore, the full definition of our `sum_range` function using recursion looks like this:

Figure 11.13: Full Recursive Implementation of the `sum_range` Function

```
var sum_range = function(r_start, r_end) {
    // Check for the base case
    if(r_start == r_end) {
        // Base Case
        return r_start
    } else {
        // Inductive Case
        return r_start + sum_range(r_start + 1, r_end);
    }
};

var result = sum_range(3, 12);
alert("The sum of the numbers between 3 and 12 is " +
    result);
```

As you can see, there is now an `if` statement that checks for the base case and immediately computes the answer if it is found. Otherwise, it proceeds recursively.

However, you might have noticed something funny. Here we are using local variables, but we are using the same local variables over and over. Wouldn't these variables get clobbered each time we call the function? As a matter of fact, they don't. The reason for this is that JavaScript creates a *new* local variable scope *every time the function is called*. Therefore, each time that `sum_range` is called, there is a new local scope created. So, if you call `sum_range(2, 5)`, it will create 4 local variable scopes, one for each time `sum_range` is called.

After the third call, the stack would look like Figure 11.14. Notice how, after the third call to `sum_range`, there are exactly three copies of the `sum_range` local scope in the drawing, each of them with the global scope as a parent scope, and with it, their own values for `r_start` and `r_end`. This is how the computer makes recursive function calls possible.

In the example so far, there wasn't a reason to use recursion. In fact, with all of the function calls, stack frames, and local scopes generated, our code was actually much slower.

Figure 11.14: Stack Frame for Recursive Function Call

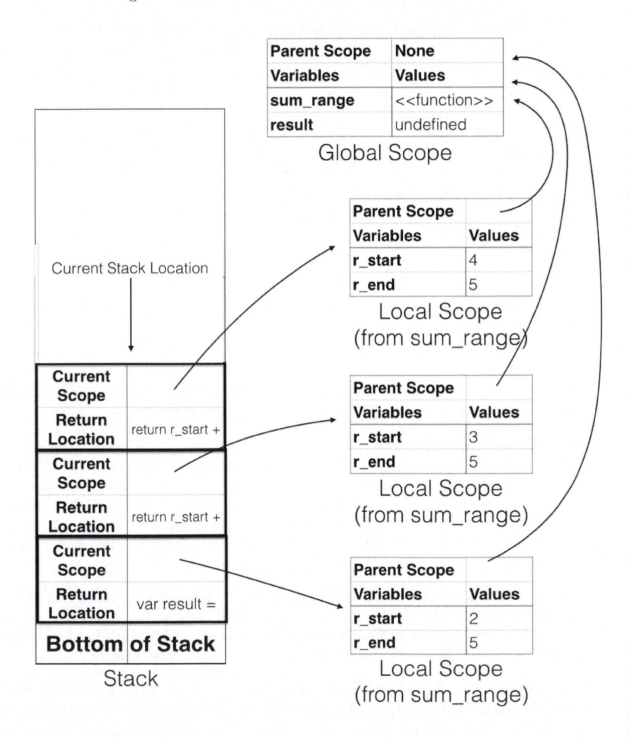

Nonetheless, there are many times when recursion is either the only way to solve a problem, or it is the way that makes the most sense, or it is the easiest to write a program for. Programs today rarely need a lot of optimization. While the speed of the program itself shouldn't be discounted, what usually counts the most is the amount of time the programmer takes to write the program.

Knowing recursion will help you see the solutions to some problems more easily. When you become comfortable with recursion, you begin to see many complicated problems as merely simple problems in disguise. Additionally, knowing recursion will help you better understand other people's code when *they* use recursion. The best time to use recursion is when you can envision the problem as being the same problem over and over again, with each step just being a smaller version of the previous problem.

Review

In this chapter we learned how the JavaScript stack worked and how it enables us to write recursive functions. We have learned:

- JavaScript uses the stack to keep track of what is going on in your program.

- Every time a function is called, JavaScript pushes a bookmark of the return location onto the stack telling it where to go when the function completes.

- Every time a function completes, JavaScript pops a bookmark off of the stack to find out where it should resume processing.

- This stack system allows JavaScript to return to the right spot in your code even if a function is called from more than one location.

- JavaScript keeps a separate list of local variables (the local scope) for every time a function is called even if it is the same function called more than once.

- Every time a function is called, JavaScript pushes a link to the new local scope onto the stack as well so it knows what scope is currently being used. This scope is popped at the end of the function along with the return location.

- When your program references a variable, JavaScript refers to the *current* local scope only and tries to look up your variable there.

- Each JavaScript scope has a link to a parent scope. If the variable you reference cannot be found in the local scope, it tries to look it up in the parent scope.

- Using the `var` keyword causes a new variable to be created in the current local scope. If there is not a current local scope, it creates the variable in the global scope.

- Recursive functions are functions that are defined in terms of themselves.

- Each recursive function needs at least two cases—the inductive case and the base case.

- Recursive functions are best used when each step of a problem is just a reduced form of the larger problem.

- The JavaScript stack is what enables recursive programs to work since the stack keeps a separate local scope for every time the function is called, thus allowing the function a separate copy of each variable for every time the function is invoked.

Apply What You Have Learned

1. Figure 11.14 shows the stack frame for the code in Figure 11.13 at one particular point in its execution. Make similar drawings for what the stack and scopes look like after *every* function call. You should have four drawings at the end.

2. In Section 10.4 we discussed and implemented a factorial function. Try to implement the factorial function as a recursive function. If you get stuck, use the code in Figure 11.13 as a template to help you out.

3. Print out your factorial function. Circle the inductive case and the base case.

4. Expand the program in Figure 11.13 so that a user can enter the start and end of the range.

5. Expand your factorial program so that a user can enter the number that he wants to make a factorial of.

6. Expand either of the two previous programs so that, after the program produces an answer, it asks the user if they want to keep going. Put the program in a loop so that the user can run the calculation as many times as they want and only stop when they want to.

Chapter 12

Manipulating Functions and Scopes

In Chapter 10 we learned about functions and how they create local scopes. Chapter 11 went into further depth about how the JavaScript program stack helps JavaScript keep track of where it is in the program and what local scope to use. In this chapter we are going to go deeper and show how functions can be passed as parameters, returned as values, and how to generate new functions that inherit from a different scope than the global scope.

12.1   Functions As Parameters to Functions

Throughout this book I have tried to emphasize the fact that, in JavaScript, functions are values just like any other value. We have seen that they can be created with the `function` operator and assigned to variables with the = operator. They can also be passed as parameters of functions and returned as the result of functions.

In Chapter 11 (Figure 11.10) we looked at a function called `sum_squares_of_range`, which took a range of numbers, squared each of them, and return the sum of all of them.

The code is repeated below for your reference:

Figure 12.1: Summing the Squares of a Range of Numbers

```
var square_number = function(num) {
    var x = num * num;
    return x;
};

var sum_squares_of_range = function(r_start, r_end) {
    var total = 0;
    for(var x = r_start; x <= r_end; x++) {
        total = total + square_number(x);
    }

    return total;
};

var result = sum_squares_of_range(3, 6);
alert("The sum of the squares of the values from 3 to 6: "
    + result);
```

Let's say that instead of squaring each number, we wanted to cube the number (multiply the number by itself and then by itself again). The function would be identical, but instead of calling the **square_number** function, it would instead call a function called **cube_number**.

The code for that is below:

Figure 12.2: Summing the Cubes of a Range of Numbers

```
var cube_number = function(num) {
    return num * num * num;
};

var sum_cubes_of_range = function(r_start, r_end) {
    var total = 0;
    for(var x = r_start; x <= r_end; x++) {
        total = total + cube_number(x);
    }

    return total;
};

var result = sum_cubes_of_range(3, 6);
alert("The sum of the cubes of the values from 3 to 6: " +
    result);
```

As you can see, the only difference between `sum_squares_of_range` and `sum_cubes_of_range` is that `square_number` is replaced by `cube_number` in the new code. Wouldn't it be nice if we could have just one function for both of them, and then just send up whichever function (we'll call it the *transformation function*) that we want to apply to each number? Well, in fact, you can do just that. What we can do is create a parameter to be used for the transformation function.

The new code looks like this:

Figure 12.3: Summing a Range of Numbers with a Transformation

```
var square_number = function(num) {
   return num * num;
};

var cube_number = function(num) {
   return num * num * num;
};

var sum_range_with_transformation = function(r_start,
   r_end, transformation) {
   var total = 0;
   for(var x = r_start; x <= r_end; x++) {
      total = total + transformation(x);
   }

   return total;
}

var result_squares = sum_range_with_transformation(3, 6,
   square_number);
var result_cubes = sum_range_with_transformation(3, 6,
   cube_number);
alert("The sum of the squares of the values from 3 to 6: "
   + result_squares);
alert("The sum of the cubes of the values from 3 to 6: " +
   result_cubes);
```

As you can see, this is still the exact same code; the only difference is that `square_number` is replaced with `transformation`, which is passed in as a parameter! These types of functions, whose functions are modified by other functions passed in as parameters, are called **higher-order functions**.

☞ **Practice Questions**

1. Modify the program in Figure 12.3 so that you add a function that raises the number to the fourth power and then pass it into `sum_range_with_transformation`.

2. Modify the program again so that it simply sums the numbers from 3 to 6 without any transformation. (Hint—create a function that just returns the number given.)

12.2 Functions That Return Functions

Now that we have seen functions as parameters, we will look at functions that return functions. The first example isn't useful at all, but will illustrate the point:

Figure 12.4: Function That Returns a Function

```
var square_a_number = function(x) {
    return x * x;
};

var get_square_a_number_function = function() {
    return square_a_number;
};

var my_func = get_square_a_number_function();
var result = my_func(5);
alert("The result of calling my_func(5) is " + result);
```

In this program, we have our traditional `square_a_number` function. However, rather than using it directly, we have another function, called `get_square_a_number_function`, which returns that function. Note that the return statement on `get_square_a_number_function` *does not call* `square_a_number`; there are no parentheses after the function name that would indicate a function call. Instead, the function itself is returned from this function.

Then, in the main program, the value returned by `get_square_a_number_function` is stored in `my_func`. What value is this? The `square_a_number` function! Therefore, `my_func` is actually holding the `square_a_number` function itself. Since `my_func` is holding a function, it can be called as a function. This is what is happening with `my_func(5)`—it is calling the function stored in `my_func`, which is the number-squaring function. This will, as expected, return the number 25.

12.3   Functions That Create Functions

Let's say that we wanted to have a function that operated as a counter. That is, every time we called the function, it would give us the next number. The first time we called the function it would return 1, then 2, and so forth. How might we write that function?

Let's start by looking at a way that *does not* work.

Take a moment to see if you can figure out what is wrong with the following program:

Figure 12.5: A Wrong Way to Implement a Counter

```
var next_value = function() {
    var counter = 0;
    counter = counter + 1;
    return counter;
};

var first_value = next_value();
var second_value = next_value();
alert("First value: " + first_value);
alert("Second value: " + second_value);
```

If you haven't figured it out yet, try putting it into a web page and running it. What happens?

The problem with the program is that the definition of `counter` is a local variable. Therefore,

every time the function is run, it will create a brand new variable named **counter** and set it to zero. Because of this, this function will always return the value 1.

One way around this is to make the **counter** variable into a global variable instead of a local one. This code will work a little better:

Figure 12.6: A Counter Function Using a Global Variable

```
var counter = 0;
var next_value = function() {
    counter = counter + 1;
    return counter;
}


var first_value = next_value();
var second_value = next_value();
alert("First value: " + first_value);
alert("Second value: " + second_value);
```

This one actually behaves the way we want it to, but it has two very large drawbacks. The first drawback is that the **counter** variable is a global variable. This means that the person using the **next_value** function has to know about the **counter** variable so they don't use it themselves. It is bad programming practice for the user of a function to have to know so much about how a function is implemented. The second drawback is that this only allows for one counter function in the program. In order to get a second counter function, we would need to recode it. It seems very wasteful to write the exact same code twice, only changing the variable names.

In order to solve these problems, we need a way to make the scope of **counter** isolated from the global scope and to be able to create new instances of the counter function on the fly with each having their own independent **counter** variable. Both of these can be solved by making function-generating-functions.

☞   **Practice Activity**

Draw out the stack diagrams for a call to `next_value` in both of the listings in this section.

In Chapter 10 we learned that the `function` operator creates a new function with the given code. In Chapter 11 we learned that each time the function is called, a new local scope is created for that function. We also looked at how each new local scope has a link to a parent scope, which, so far, has been the global scope. (Go back and look at Figures 11.9 and 11.14 for a refresher.) So how does that parent scope link get created, and can it point to anything other than the global scope?

It turns out that the parent scope points to whatever scope is active at the time that a function is created. So far, when our functions have been created, the active scope has been the global scope. That is why the parent scope on our functions has always been the global scope. If, instead, the function had been created while another function was active, its parent scope would have been the local scope that was active at the time it was created! When such a function is called, it still creates a brand-new local scope for its parameters and all variables declared with the `var` keyword. However, when referring to any variable not defined in its local scope, it will look to its parent scope, which will be the local scope that was active when the function was created. When a computer programming language stores the scope of a function that is newly-created for use as a parent scope, this is known as having **lexical closure**.

An example should help:

Figure 12.7: Example of a Function with a Local Scope as a Parent Scope

```
var create_function = function(x) {
   var new_function = function() {
      return x;
   };

   return new_function;
};

var my_func_a = create_function(12);
var my_func_b = create_function(20);

var my_val_a = my_func_a();
var my_val_b = my_func_b();

alert("The result of calling my_func_a is " + my_val_a);
alert("The result of calling my_func_b is " + my_val_b);
```

This example was kept very short so you could more easily see all of the pieces moving. From a high level, the `create_function` function takes one parameter and creates a function that always returns that value. Note the line that says `var my_func_a = create_function(12);`. This causes `create_function` to build a new function that will always return the value 12 and stores this new function in `my_func_a`.

How does `create_function` do this? Well, let's walk through the code.

The first thing that the `create_function` function does is to create a function. The `function` operator can be used anywhere to create a new function. It then stores this function into `new_function`, which is a local variable for `create_function`. It then returns this newly-created function.

What is so special about this newly-created function? Since it was defined *within* `create_function`, its parent scope is the local scope that was created at the time that `create_function` was invoked. Therefore, each time that `create_function` is run, it will

create a *new version* of the `new_function` function with a *different* parent scope (i.e., the one that was created when the `create_function` function was called). Now, when `create_function` returns, its local scope is no longer active, but it is not destroyed because the function that it returns still refers to it. It will just lie dormant until the created function is called, and then it will become the parent scope of the created function's new local scope.

Therefore, when you call `create_function(12)`, that creates a new local scope with the variable `x`, and `x` is given the value 12 from the parameter list. When the function that will be stored in `new_function` is created, the current local scope (with `x` as a local variable) is linked to the function so that it will be the parent scope of each new local scope created from calling the function. This function is then returned and stored in `my_func_a`. When `my_func_a` is called later on, it creates a new local scope for the function call. However, the parent scope is set to the scope that was active when the function was created—the scope that has `x` set to 12. Therefore, when it runs the code `return x;`, it first looks in its newly-created local scope for `x` and doesn't find it. It then goes to the parent scope and finds `x` defined there. If it did not find `x` in the parent scope, it would move up the chain to the global scope.

Note that `my_func_b` is created in the same way. However, as we've mentioned, every time a function is called, a new local scope is created. Therefore, when `create_function(20)` is called, there is a *new* local scope created, and this scope has `x` set to 20. This scope gets attached as the parent scope for the function that is created and stored in `my_func_b`. When `my_func_a` gets called, the parent scope is the one that has `x` set to 12, but when `my_func_b` gets called, the parent scope is the one that has `x` set to 20.

We now have two different functions that come out of the same code. These functions both work differently because they have *different parent scopes* when they are invoked.

Now, let's get back at the problem of the counter functions. We wanted a function that would create a new counter function for us. So, what we really want is a counter function that can be attached to different parent scopes that each have their own current count.

The code to do this is as follows:

Figure 12.8: A Function to Create Counter Functions

```
var create_counter = function() {
   var current_val = 0;
   var counter_function = function() {
      current_val = current_val + 1;
      return current_val;
   };
   return counter_function;
};

var mycounter_a = create_counter();
var mycounter_b = create_counter();
var mycounter_c = mycounter_a;

alert(mycounter_a()); // 1
alert(mycounter_a()); // 2
alert(mycounter_a()); // 3
alert(mycounter_b()); // 1
alert(mycounter_a()); // 4
alert(mycounter_b()); // 2
alert(mycounter_c()); // 5
```

This code is very similar to the code that just spits out the value from the parent scope. The only difference is that we manipulate the value of `current_val` in the parent scope first (we add one to it) before returning it. This modification is kept because every time you call `mycounter_a`, it pulls that same scope in to be the parent scope. Since `current_val` is *not* declared with a `var` keyword within `counter_function`, it will always refer to `current_val` in its parent scope whether it is reading or writing the value.

Since `mycounter_a` and `mycounter_b` were created from different calls to `create_counter`, they each maintain different parent scopes and therefore independent values for `current_val`. Note, however, that `mycounter_c` continues on just as if `mycounter_a` were called again. Why is that? It is because `mycounter_c` *is not a new function*. It is *the same* function as `mycounter_a` since it was simply assigned.

mycounter_a and mycounter_b were both created by a call to create_counter, but mycounter_c simply gets the same function that was in mycounter_a. Remember that functions are stored in variables just like any other value and can be assigned back and forth to different variables, and these assignments do not change the underlying values. Therefore, mycounter_a and mycounter_c both refer to the exact same function.

12.4 Currying Functions

In Section 12.1 we learned how to take multiple, specific functions, and combine them into a single higher-order function that takes a function as a parameter. In this section we will look at the reverse process—taking a generalized, or higher-order, function and creating new, more specific versions of it by specifying one or more parameters beforehand.

Go back and look at Figures 12.1, 12.2, and 12.3. You will notice that the functionality of both Figures 12.1 and 12.2 are both present in Figure 12.3. You might rightly conclude that the function sum_range_with_transformation that is defined in Figure 12.3 is, therefore, more powerful than the individual sum_cubes_of_range and sum_squares_of_range functions defined in the other programs. However, sometimes calling functions that take another function as a parameter can be confusing. If, for instance, a programmer usually has to sum the squares of a range, but only rarely has to sum another transformation, it might be useful to have sum_squares_of_range as its own function.

Now, we still want to make use of our sum_range_with_transformation function. The reason for this is that if you have code that performs a task, you don't want to have two copies of it lying around. If you find a bug in one copy of the function, you would have to remember to fix it in the other one. If you find a better way of implementing the function, you also have to remember (and take the time) to rewrite the other function to match.

We want to have the ease of calling sum_squares_of_range but maintaining the power of funneling all of the logic through sum_range_with_transformation. The way to do this is with **currying**. Currying a function means that you are taking a general-purpose function and creating a special-purpose function from it by fixing one or more parameters to a constant value.

For instance, if we wanted to build on the program in Figure 12.3 to make a special function called sum_squares_of_range, we could add the code listed in Figure 12.9 to do it.

Figure 12.9: Creating a Special-Purpose Function from a General-Purpose Function

```
var sum_squares_of_range = function(r_start, r_end) {
    return sum_range_with_transformation(r_start, r_end,
        square_number);
};
```

As you can see, instead of writing the **sum_squares_of_range** function from scratch like we did in Figure 12.1, we used **sum_range_with_transformation** as a building block to create our function. This allowed **sum_squares_of_range** to become a simpler way of writing **sum_range_with_transformation** with some of the parameters built in.

We can go a step further to define a function-generating-function where you create a custom summing function based on a transformation function. That sounds a little weird, but perhaps an example might help. The code below can be attached to the end of Figure 12.3 to produce a working program:

Figure 12.10: Creating a Special-Purpose Function Generator

```
var create_summing_function = function(transformation) {
    var summing_function = function(r_start, r_end) {
        return sum_range_with_transformation(r_start, r_end,
            transformation);
    };
    return summing_function;
}

var sum_cubes_of_range =
    create_summing_function(cube_number);

var result_cubes_currying = sum_cubes_of_range(3, 6);
alert("The sum of the cubes (using currying) is " +
    result_cubes_currying);
```

In this example, the `create_summing_function` takes the transformation as its argument and returns a brand new function, which uses that argument as the last parameter to `sum_range_with_transformation`, so that it provides a really easy way to create new transformation functions.

12.5 Anonymous Functions

Functions are just values. As we learned way back in Chapter 8, you often don't even need to create variables to hold each intermediate value. Similarly, we don't always need to store functions in variables either.

Just as typing the number 5 produces the value 5, using the `function` keyword define a new function. Let's look back at the code we wrote in Figure 12.10. Let's say we wanted to create a new summing function, but this time we want to raise the members of the range to the fourth power before summing them. Now, we could create a separate function to raise a number to the fourth power, and then just use the technique in Figure 12.10. However, an easier way would be to skip naming the function altogether and define it when we call `create_summing_function`. The result would look something like this, which would be appended to the program you wrote in Figure 12.10:

Figure 12.11: Using Anonymous Functions

```
var sum_fourth_power_of_range =
   create_summing_function(function(x) {
   return x * x * x * x;
});

var new_result = sum_fourth_power_of_range(3, 6);
alert("The sum of the range raised to the fourth power is "
   + new_result);
```

As you can see, where in Figure 12.10 we used a named function for the transformation, here we are passing in the function directly. The function we are passing in has no name.

It is defined, and rather than being stored in a variable, is simply passed as a parameter to a function. Functions that are defined within the code and not given a name are known as **anonymous functions**.

Review

In this chapter we learned several advanced ways of creating and using functions. We have learned:

- Functions can be passed as parameters to functions.

- When a function takes another function as a parameter, it allows the function's processes to be tweaked.

- When two functions look almost the same except that they each perform a slightly different process, they can often be combined into one function that takes a function as a parameter.

- When a function takes a function as a parameter, it is known as a higher-order function.

- Functions can return other functions as values.

- Functions can create new functions to return as a value.

- When a function is created, it combines and stores both the code to execute and a link to the scope that it was created in.

- The link to the scope will be used as the parent scope when a local scope is created for each function invocation.

- If a computer programming language stores a link to the active scope for use as a parent scope in a function when it is created, it is said that the programming language has lexical closure.

- Currying is a process of defining new, specific functions from more generic or higher-order functions by pre-specifying one or more parameters.

Apply What You Have Learned

1. Modify the counter program in Figure 12.8 so that it takes a starting value, allowing you to start your counter at any value you want.

Part IV

Object-Oriented Programming

JavaScript is an object-oriented language, which means it brings together data and functions into organized units called objects. This part provides an introduction to how to create and manipulate objects in JavaScript.

Chapter 13

Basic Objects and Arrays

So far, while programming, we have basically been dealing with simple values, such as individual numbers and strings. However, when writing computer programs, you usually have to deal with multiple values grouped together. For instance, think about a bank transaction—what values would you need to store? You would need to know when the transaction happened, how much the transaction was for, who sent the money, and who received the money. Therefore, you would need, at minimum, four values—the timestamp of the transaction, the amount, the account number it was coming from, and the account number that it was going to.

Now we could represent this with four separate variables. We could have something like this:

Figure 13.1: Related Variables

```
var transaction_timestamp;
var transaction_amount;
var transaction_from_account;
var transaction_to_account;
```

Then, if we had to pass these variables into a function, we would have to pass them as four separate parameters. Imagine if we then added additional data that went with the

transaction, such as a transfer fee and the currency that the transfer is in. The number of variables we need to move around has now gone up to 6! Not only that, every function that touches the data has to be rewritten to take the extra parameters!

This is not an unusual situation. In many programs, there may be several dozen values that all relate to each other. Passing them around as individual values can quickly get out-of-control.

13.1   A Basic Introduction to Objects

In order to package pieces of data together, JavaScript uses **objects**. An object is simply a collection of named values. It's like packaging up several variables into a single unit.

Going back to our bank transaction example, I could package all of those variables up into a single variable which has named values for each component. Unlike some programming languages, JavaScript does not care how many values you pack into an object, and you don't have to tell JavaScript what they will be ahead of time. You usually start with an empty object and simply stash whatever values you want in there using whatever names you want. That doesn't mean that the names don't matter—it matters a great deal since that is how you will be keeping track of them, but JavaScript itself does not care.

Objects in JavaScript can be generated in a variety of ways. The first way we will look at is using the **new** keyword. To get a blank object, you simply type in **new Object()**.

Figure 13.2: Using the **new** Keyword

```
var my_transaction = new Object();
```

Objects themselves are values, and can be stored in variables and used in expressions just like any other value.

Now, let's look at how we assign values to objects:

Figure 13.3: Assigning Values to Objects

```
var my_transaction = new Object();
my_transaction.timestamp = "2014-02-05";
my_transaction.amount = 1000;
my_transaction.from_account = "12345";
my_transaction.to_account = "54321";
```

JavaScript stores values in objects based on their name. These values are often called **attributes** or **properties** of the object. So, when you type `mytransaction.amount`, that tells JavaScript to look up the **amount** property of the `mytransaction` object.

This is the information we would need for a bank transaction. However, a transaction needs information about the accounts, too. What would a bank *account* object look like? Such an object would need the account number, the name of the person on the account, and their current balance. Therefore, we might have an object that looks like this:

Figure 13.4: A Bank Account Object

```
var my_account = new Object();
my_account.account_number = "12345";
my_account.owner = "Fred Fredston";
my_account.current_balance = 1200;
```

Now let's say that I want to define a function that processes a transaction against an account. What I want it to do is to take `my_transaction` and apply it to `my_account` (i.e., give the money in `my_transaction` to the balance in `my_account`). To do this, I can create a function, which takes the two objects, picks out the values it needs, and processes the transaction. If the account number matches the `from_account` of the transaction, it removes the money from the account, and if it matches the `to_account` of the transaction, it gives the money to the account.

It might look like this:

Figure 13.5: A Function Taking Two Objects

```
var process_transaction = function(account, transaction) {
    if(account.account_number == transaction.from_account) {
        account.current_balance = account.current_balance -
            transaction.amount;
    } else {
        if(account.account_number == transaction.to_account) {
            account.current_balance = account.current_balance
                + transaction.amount;
        } else {
            // Do nothing
        }
    }
};
```

Now I can call this function by typing `process_transaction(my_account, my_transaction);`
Notice that we didn't have to pass in every value; we only had to pass in the objects which
contained the values we needed.

Another important point is that when we passed in objects, we could actually *modify* the
object that we were receiving. Note that, unlike in previous chapters, we didn't return a
value. Instead, we modified the `account` object itself. The result is the modification, not
the return value. This is known as a **mutating function** because it modifies (i.e., mutates)
the objects passed as parameters rather than return a value. Note that this only works with
objects. Basic values (i.e., numbers, strings, etc.) passed directly as parameters cannot be
modified like this.

Note that if a function doesn't have a return value, it returns the special value `undefined`,
which means "no value."

In any case, objects allow functions to manipulate values, not just process them. When
we were just passing in numbers and strings, even if we modified the parameter variable, it
wouldn't modify the value in the sending function. Now that we are using objects we can
modify the properties of any object passed in. However, we cannot replace the whole object

with a new one (though we can modify all of its properties).

☞ **Practice Questions**

1. Find a product catalog (of any kind). Look through the catalog. List out the data items that it has for each catalog item. Pick out two items to use for the rest of this practice.

2. Create a program that builds two objects—one for each item you picked out. It should use the fields you listed in the previous step (feel free to skip fields if they are complex fields, such as an image). Use an **alert** function to show some of the pieces of data you have put in your objects.

3. Create a function that displays all of the information about a single item that takes one parameter—the item to display. It should display each property defined on that object. Then call that function for each item.

4. Create a function that asks the user for the values to be placed in that object and then returns a new object with those values assigned to properties on that object.

13.2 Simplifying Object Creation

Now, because JavaScript programmers create objects using **new Object()** all of the time, JavaScript has a special syntax that allows you to create a new object more quickly and easily: **{}**. This, just like **new Object()**, creates a new, blank object. Therefore, we could have started our code with this instead:

Figure 13.6: Getting a New, Blank Object

```
var my_transaction = {};
my_transaction.timestamp = "2014-02-05";
my_transaction.amount = 1000;
```

However, {} has a few more tricks available. You can actually use it to specify a set of starting attributes at the beginning so you don't have to assign them one-by-one. The syntax looks like this:

Figure 13.7: Getting a New Object with Initial Values

```
var my_transaction = {
    timestamp: "2014-02-05",
    amount: 1000,
    from_account: "12345",
    to_account: "54321"
};
```

As you can see, with this syntax, in between the { and }, there are sets of named values that will be our object properties. Each property name is followed by a colon and the value of the property we are trying to set. This makes initializing objects much faster and cleaner than the long way. Keep in mind that the names of properties should generally be limited to the same types of names that are allowed for variables (i.e., don't put spaces, dashes, or special characters in the property names).

☞ **Practice Questions**

For practice for this section, modify the practice work of the previous section to use the shorter object creation syntax.

13.3   Storing Sequences of Values Using Arrays

So far we have dealt with objects, which are collections of named values. In this section we are going to talk about **arrays**, which are *ordered sequences* of values.

In Section 4.3 we talked about how computers stored sequences of values. In short, it stores the number of things in the sequence, and then it stores the values themselves. Such a

structure in JavaScript is called an array. Arrays in JavaScript aren't quite stored the way that we talked about in Section 4.3, but it is a helpful way to think about them.

Why would we need a sequence of values? Let's say I wanted to store the ages of my children. I *could* do that with an object, but it would be rather awkward. With an object, I could do this:

Figure 13.8: A Bad Way to Store a Sequence of Values

```
var children_ages = {
    first_child: 11,
    second_child: 8,
    third_child: 7
};
```

That somewhat works, but it would be hard to use such a structure. For instance, if I wanted to write out each of their ages, it would be hard to write a loop to go through each child and write out their ages, especially if I didn't know how many children there were ahead of time.

An array, on the other hand, allows us to define ordered sequences of values. So, instead of our awkward object, we could write something more elegant like this:

Figure 13.9: Storing a Sequence of Values in an Array

```
var children_ages = new Array();
children_ages[0] = 11;
children_ages[1] = 8;
children_ages[2] = 7;
```

In this code, `children_ages` is first assigned a blank array—that's what `new Array()` does. This tells JavaScript to make an empty sequence of values and store it in the variable `children_ages`. In the next line, we tell JavaScript that the first value in the sequence

should be 11. The [] notation says that we need to use the number inside the brackets to tell us which element of the array we are referring to and, if it doesn't exist yet, to create it. Therefore [0] says to refer to the first member of the array and the 0 is called the **index** of the array. Normally, we are used to labeling sequences of values starting with a 1, but computers usually label sequences of values starting with a 0. This is known as **zero-based indexing**.

The code `children_ages[0] = 11;` tells JavaScript to look in the `children_ages` array and try to find the first value. Since we initialized the array as being empty, there is no first value yet. There are no values at all. That's all right because JavaScript knows that if the array member doesn't exist, it should create it. Therefore, it will create a space for a new value at index 0. Next, it will look at the right hand side of the equal sign and see what the value of the expression is. In this case, the value is 11 so it stores the number 11 at index 0 of `children_ages`.

The same thing happens with index 1 and 2. At the end of the code, there are three values in `children_ages`—11, 8, and 7.

13.4   Using Arrays in Programs

Now that we have the values in an array, they are much easier to manipulate. When we tried to store the values in an object, we had to know the name of each value (i.e., `first_child`, `second_child`, etc.). If we don't know ahead of time how many children we have, we won't know what to name the variable. By storing them in an array, each value gets a numbered index rather than a property name. These are much easier for a computer to go through sequentially.

Let's say we wanted to go through an array of children's ages, and find the age of the oldest child. How might we do that? Well, when we say we want to "go through an array," that means we want to repeat some code for each element in an array. What sort of programming structure do we use when we want to repeat code? A loop, of course!

The problem is that we have to know when we are finished. That is, we need to know how many values there are in the array so we know when we don't want another value. Arrays, in addition to being able to access its values by index, also works in some ways like an object. It has a few special properties that can be used to find out information about the array. The most important property that an array has is the `length` property. The `length` property

returns the number of values that the array holds. So, in our code, `children_ages.length`
would yield 3 since it holds three values. Notice that, since JavaScript arrays use zero-based
indexing, this is one more than the largest *index*, which is 2.

Let's write a function that takes an array of ages and returns the largest one:

Figure 13.10: Finding the Largest Value in an Array

```
var largest_age = function(age_array) {
    var the_largest = 0;
    for(var i = 0; i < age_array.length; i++) {
        if(age_array[i] > the_largest) {
            the_largest = age_array[i];
        }
    }

    return the_largest;
};
```

In this code, the `for` loop repeated using `i` as the loop counter. `i` starts at zero since the
array indexes start at zero. At the end of every loop, `i` increases by one (`i++` is just a short
way of writing `i = i + 1`). Incrementing the index by one basically means "go to the next
value in the list." The funny part of the `for` statement is the condition. Here, the condition
is `i < age_array.length`. Since the array length is *one greater* than the last index of the
array, this condition says to keep going as long as we have a valid index for the array. When
`i` finally makes it to `age_array.length`, it will no longer point to a valid value, so we should
stop looping.

What do we do inside the loop? We are simply testing each value (`age_array[i]`) to see
if it is greater than the previous value (`the_largest`). If it is greater, we write the current
value into `the_largest`. Otherwise, we ignore it.

Then, after the loop has completed, we return the value of `the_largest` for the result of
the function.

The way that this would be used in a program would be like this:

Figure 13.11: Using the `largest_age` Function

```
var children_ages = new Array();
children_ages[0] = 11;
children_ages[1] = 8;
children_ages[2] = 7;

var largest = largest_age(children_ages);
alert("The oldest child is " + largest + " years old");
```

Just like we were able to simplify object creation with the {} syntax, arrays have a special syntax, too, which makes them easy to create. In JavaScript, you can create an array just by putting in a list of numbers in square brackets ([]). For instance:

Figure 13.12: Using the Simpler Array Syntax

```
// Create an empty array
var empty_array = [];

// Creates the array we had before
var children_ages = [11, 8, 7];

// Gets the largest value in children_ages
var largest = largest_age(children_ages);

// Skip the variable, pass in the array directly
var largest_inline = largest_age([11, 8, 7]);
```

Using this syntax saves us a lot of effort in programming.

☞ **Practice Questions**

---

1. Type out the entire `largest_age` function. Test it by sending it different arrays and making sure it always returns the largest age.

2. Instead of creating the array values yourself, have the user type the values. For the first time around, have the user type in exactly three values. Make sure these values get converted to numbers before storing them in the array!

3. Extend your program so that the user can type in as many values as they want. Remember to include a way that the user can indicate that they are finished either by asking them if they are done after each one or asking the user to type a special sentinel value that indicates that they are done.

13.5 Mixing Objects and Arrays

While objects and arrays are pretty powerful in their own right, you can increase the power of both of them by mixing them together. The values held in object properties don't have to be just numbers and strings—they can be any JavaScript value including other objects or arrays! Likewise, array values don't have to just be numbers, they can be any value that JavaScript supports, including objects and other arrays. Mixing and matching objects and arrays gives you the flexibility to represent just about any real world data set.

For instance, let's say that I wanted to put more information about my children than just their age. I also wanted to include their name and favorite color. In addition, let's say that I really want the list of children to be on a larger record about me, not just sitting by itself in a variable. How would I write that?

Here is how you would write it the long way:

Figure 13.13: Building a Complex Object

```
var my_record = new Object();
my_record.name = "Jon";
my_record.children = new Array();
my_record.children[0] = new Object();
my_record.children[0].name = "Jim";
my_record.children[0].age = 11;
my_record.children[0].favorite_color = "blue";
my_record.children[1] = new Object();
my_record.children[1].name = "Jack";
my_record.children[1].age = 8;
my_record.children[1].favorite_color = "black";
my_record.children[2] = new Object();
my_record.children[2].name = "Joel";
my_record.children[2].age = 7;
my_record.children[2].favorite_color = "orange";
```

As you can see, we start out with a blank object in the variable `my_record`. We then add a name to the object. Next, we add an empty array to the object, and we name the property `children`. Now, to access this array, we have to use `my_record.children`. Since `my_record.children` is an array, we can use indexes on it. Therefore, `my_record.children[0]` refers to the first value in the `my_record.children` array. Since that index doesn't exist yet, it gets created. But what is stored there? It's a new, blank object! Therefore, `my_record.children[0]` now refers to an empty object. What can we do with objects? We can add properties. We can create a `name` property on this new, empty object by doing `my_record.children[0].name = "Jim";`. We then set the age in the same way. At the end of this process, we have an object that has an array of objects.

Now, if we wanted to use our `largest_age` function, we would have to rewrite it. Why? Because now the array is no longer an array of numbers but of objects. Therefore, for each object, we would have to look for the `age` property.

The code would look like this:

Figure 13.14: The `largest_age` Function Using Objects

```
var largest_age = function(child_array) {
   var the_largest = 0;
   for(var i = 0; i < child_array.length; i++) {
      var child = child_array[i];
      if(child.age > the_largest) {
         the_largest = child.age;
      }
   }

   return the_largest;
};
```

What we did in this function is modify our loop so that it stores the object *temporarily* in a variable called `child`. We then use `child.age` to access the child's age. Now, instead of using this extra `child` variable, we could have just done it directly by typing in `child_array[i].age`, but using the extra variable makes for much less typing and much easier reading.

To call this function on our list of children from `my_record`, we would simply write:
`largest_age(my_record.children)`

Figure 13.13 showed the long way to build a complex object. However, just as there is an easier way to write simple objects and arrays, complex objects and arrays can also be built using the simplified syntax.

Below is the exact same object that we built in Figure 13.13, written using the simplified notation:

Figure 13.15: Complex Objects Using the Simplified Notation

```
var my_record = {
    name: "Jon",
    children: [
        {
            name: "Jim",
            age: 11,
            favorite_color: "blue"
        },
        {
            name: "Jack",
            age: 8,
            favorite_color: "black"
        },
        {
            name: "Joel",
            age: 7,
            favorite_color: "orange"
        }
    ]
};
```

As you can see, this takes much less typing and is much easier to read. It takes up more space because of how it is written, but you don't have to do it that way—JavaScript does not care how much or little space is used. You could write that whole complex object on one line if you wanted to, but I think the clarity that comes from having things separated out is worth the extra space it can take up.

Review

In this chapter we covered the basics of composite values—objects and arrays. We have learned:

- Objects hold related pieces of data together in a single, cohesive unit.

- Each value in an object is placed into a property, which is a name that is used to access the value.

- Sequences of data are called arrays.

- Each array holds a sequence of related values.

- Values in an array are accessed through their index.

- Array indexes are zero-based, which means that the first index is always 0, and the last index is always one less than the length of the array.

- If you assign a property to an object or access an array index which does not yet exist, the property or index will be created for you automatically.

- Each array has a `length` property which tells you how large the array is.

- The `length` property can be used in loops to control the number of times the loop occurs.

- Objects and arrays can be embedded within each other—a property can have an array value, and the value at a particular array index can be a full object (which might also have an array).

- Objects and arrays both have special syntax ({} and []) to make typing them easier.

Apply What You Have Learned

1. Create an array of products so that each product is an object that contains a name, a code, a description, and a price.

2. Now create a function that takes two parameters—a product array and a single product code. The function should loop looking for the object that matches the code. When it finds the object, it should return the full object that has a matching code.

3. Now add user interaction. The user should be able to type the product code, and the program will look up information about that product and display it.

4. Extend the program so that the user can look up any number of codes that they want.

Chapter 14

Intermediate Objects

So far we have created objects that just contain data. Objects that just contain data are sometimes known as **records**—they store data, but they don't *do* anything. In Chapter 13, we wrote functions that manipulated these records. If you want to perform an action (such as withdrawing funds from an account), you would call the appropriate function, and it would do what you want. This is a fine programming style and works well for many situations. However, as programs get larger and more complex, it is beneficial to make the functions that operate on the objects more tightly connected to the objects themselves.

In Chapter 13, we grouped together several related variables into a single object. This made several improvements to our code:

1. It used fewer variables since the values were all properties of one variable.

2. It allowed the related values to travel together to functions without having to pass them individually.

3. It made the code more understandable because the related values were packaged into a single unit.

14.1   Attaching Functions to Objects

Packaging together related values into an object like we did in Chapter 13 is known as **encapsulation**. However, encapsulation can be taken further by also adding functions to our objects. Remember, in JavaScript, a function is actually a *value* just like any other value. Functions, since they are values, can also be stored in variables. In addition, because they are values, they can also be stored as *properties* of an object.

It might not be clear at this point why this is beneficial, but hopefully by the end of the chapter you will have a good handle on it. For starters, just like we packaged together related values into an object, we can also package together a related function into an object.

For instance, let's say that we had an object that represented a car. It will have two values—the number of miles traveled and the amount of gas left. Now, let's say we have a function that drives us 10 miles. What needs to happen? Well, that function would increase the number of miles driven and decrease the amount of gas left.

Figure 14.1 has the code for such an object.

As you can see, the `drive_car` function relates several different values—the number of miles traveled, the amount of gas left in the tank, and the car's gas mileage. Since the `drive_car` function is so tightly related to the car abstraction, it makes sense to just attach the function directly to the `my_car` object, like in Figure 14.2.

Figure 14.1: A Simple Car Object

```
var my_car = {
   miles_traveled: 0,
   gas_left: 10,
   miles_per_gallon: 20
};
var drive_car = function(the_car, miles_driven) {
   the_car.miles_traveled = the_car.miles_traveled +
      miles_driven;
   the_car.gas_left = the_car.gas_left - (miles_driven /
      the_car.miles_per_gallon);
   if(the_car.gas_left <= 0) {
      alert("You ran out of gas!");
   }
};

drive_car(my_car, 50);
drive_car(my_car, 100);
drive_car(my_car, 200); // I'm out of gas!
```

Figure 14.2: Attaching a Function to an Object

```
var my_car = {
   miles_traveled: 0,
   gas_left: 10,
   miles_per_gallon: 20,
   drive: function(the_car, miles_driven) {
      the_car.miles_traveled = the_car.miles_traveled +
         miles_driven;
      the_car.gas_left = the_car.gas_left - (miles_driven /
         the_car.miles_per_gallon);
      if(the_car.gas_left <= 0) {
         alert("You ran out of gas!");
      }
   }
};
```

As you can see, we assign the function the same way that we assign the rest of the values. We could have also done it the long way by typing `my_car.drive = function() { ...}`, but this way is simpler.

So how do you call the function now that it is in the object? Well, all function calls that we have made in this book have been made by simply typing the name of the variable which holds the function (usually a global variable) and calling it by adding parentheses and listing the parameters to pass to the function. It is done the same way here. The only difference is that since the function is stored in the object rather than in a global variable, we have to access the function value as a property on the object.

So we would write:

Figure 14.3: Calling a Function Attached to an Object

```
my_car.drive(my_car, 50);
```

What advantages does this give us? Not many yet. However, one important thing that this accomplishes is to have fewer global variables since, so far, we have usually stored functions in global variables. Now the function is only stored *within* the car object. For our simple programs, this might not seem important, but, in large projects, the number of functions can grow to thousands. In those cases, keeping the set of global variables to a minimum is essential for sanity.

Along the same lines, note that when it was a global variable, we named it `drive_car`. We gave it the longer name to prevent **name clashes**—where two functions accidentally get the same name. When you put functions in global variables, you usually have to give them very long names to prevent someone else from accidentally calling another function the same name. This is not the case when the function is stored on the object itself. Additionally, if the function is only attached to the object, we already know that it is operating on a car, because that is where we assigned it. Therefore, we shortened the name of the function to just `drive`, which makes the code clearer and easier to write.

One issue, though, is that the `drive` function looks a bit redundant. The code is calling the `drive` function on the object but is also having to pass in the object as a parameter. It turns out that almost every function you define on an object requires the data of the object to be present. Therefore, if you look up a function on an object using a property (i.e., `car.drive`), JavaScript has a way to automatically send the object (i.e., `car`) to the function without having to make it a parameter. JavaScript has a special variable, always named `this`, which holds the object that was used to look up the function if there was one. It is called `this` because it refers to "*this* current object that we are using."

Therefore, we can remove the parameter `the_car` from the function because it will be automatically passed in through the variable `this`.

Taking advantage of the this variable, our code now becomes:

Figure 14.4: Writing Functions for Objects Using this

```
var my_car = {
   miles_traveled: 0,
   gas_left: 10,
   miles_per_gallon: 20,
   drive: function(miles_driven) {
      this.miles_traveled = this.miles_traveled +
         miles_driven;
      this.gas_left = this.gas_left - (miles_driven /
         this.miles_per_gallon);
      if(this.gas_left <= 0) {
         alert("You ran out of gas!");
      }
   }
};
my_car.drive(50);
my_car.drive(100);
my_car.drive(200); // Out of gas!
```

So, while most parameters to functions are *explicitly* passed to the function because we named them when we defined the function, the this parameter is *implicitly* passed to the function—it is not in the parameter list. Instead, JavaScript handles it automatically.

In object-oriented programming, functions which are defined on objects and make use of the this variable are often referred to as **methods**, or also as **messages**. Unlike other languages, in JavaScript, the distinction between a function and a method is *only* in the way that you use it—if your function makes use of the this variable, it is a method.

You can also think of methods in terms of human language. The object is the subject, the method is the verb or command, and the function parameters are the direct object, adverbs, or other modifiers.

When we see my_car.drive(50), we should read it as "dear my_car, please perform your drive function using 50 as your parameter."

So far, we have seen that using functions attached to objects decreases the number of global variable names, leads to shorter function names, and makes programming a little more English-like.

14.2 Using Objects Productively

There are several reasons to use objects in your code. Because it follows the subject/verb/object pattern of language, it is much easier to understand code written in an object-oriented style. Therefore, by combining functions with their related data, you make your program easier to use and modify because the code is clearer.

Objects also help programmers separate code into clearly-definable parts. This practice is known as **modularization**. By attaching functions to the objects that hold their data, you are not only programming the computer, you are communicating to future programmers (and your future self) where the divisions between ideas within the code are. This allows a programmer to focus their thoughts and actions on relevant functions. If I know where all of the code that relates to `my_car` lives, I can easily find it and modify it. Because all of the functions surrounding `my_car` are defined near each other, when a change needs to be made it is easier to find related functions which also need to be modified in tandem.

When you program larger programs, it is sometimes difficult to keep track of what is happening to the data throughout the program. If you remove a field or change how it is used, how will you know if you modified the rest of the code to use it correctly? By baking all of the code related to an object *into* the object itself, it is easier to find the places where changes need to be made when the code for an object is modified.

Programming is not just about making your programs work. You also must make them understandable and modifiable by both yourself and others. Thinking through what objects you need, what functions they need to work, and what pieces of data they need will help you make better objects which will help you both now and in the future. It will make your code more readable, understandable, and maintainable.

Object-oriented programming has more benefits, though, than just the fact that it makes your code easier to read and understand. Object-oriented programming allows you to use objects, not based on the data they contain, but based on the functions they can perform.

We already have code that allows us to drive a car. Let's say that we invented a new kind

of magic car that is not limited by gasoline at all. It can drive any number of miles that you want. Such a car can be implemented using the following code:

Figure 14.5: A New Object that Implements the Same Interface

```
var magic_car = {
    miles_traveled: 0,
    drive: function(miles_driven) {
        this.miles_traveled = this.miles_traveled +
            miles_driven;
    }
};
```

This object isn't nearly as complicated as our previous object, but that's not what I want to emphasize. Do you notice that this object *also* has a `drive` method? The function operates differently for this new kind of car, but it has the same name and takes the same parameters as the `drive` function on our other object.

This allows us to write functions and methods that take an object as a parameter without having to care exactly what the object is. In other words, if I have a function that needs to use the `drive` method, that function doesn't have to care *which* version of the `drive` method it is using. Whether it is a car or a magic car, as long as my function uses the `drive` method, then I can use the object for the function.

14.3   Constructing Objects

Having a single object with a function attached does not give us a lot of progress. Most programs have lots and lots of similar objects. Building objects with a set pattern is known as constructing objects, and functions that construct objects are known as **constructors**. JavaScript has several different ways of constructing objects. However, since this is an introductory book, we will only look at one—constructor functions.

A constructor function is a function that is called with JavaScript's **new** keyword. Constructor functions, by convention, are named starting with a capital letter so they can be readily

identified as a constructor function. Let's say that I wanted to write a constructor for my car that takes the starting amount of gas in the car.

Such a function might look like this:

Figure 14.6: A Car Constructor

```
var Car = function(starting_gas) {
    this.miles_traveled = 0;
    this.gas_left = starting_gas;
    this.miles_per_gallon = 20;

    this.drive = function(miles_driven) {
        this.miles_traveled = this.miles_traveled +
            miles_driven;
        this.gas_left = this.gas_left - (miles_driven /
            this.miles_per_gallon);
        if(this.gas_left <= 0) {
            alert("You ran out of gas!");
        }
    };
};

var car_with_lots_of_gas = new Car(50);
var car_with_little_gas = new Car(10);

car_with_lots_of_gas.drive(20);
car_with_little_gas.drive(1000000); // Out of gas!
car_with_lots_of_gas.drive(20); // This car still has gas!
```

Notice that we created the car by saying **new Car(50)**. What this did was create a new blank object and set it as the **this** object for the **Car()** function. We then called the **Car** function with 50 as the parameter. The **new** keyword, rather than relying on the function returning a value using the **return** keyword, instead returns the newly-built object that was used in the **this** variable.

In this program, the `Car` function is a constructor. It works together with the `new` keyword to build a new object for use. The function doesn't *have* to start with a capital letter, but most JavaScript programmers follow this convention to make sure that it is clear which functions are supposed to be used as constructors.

In some programming languages, `Car` would be considered a **type** or a **class**. A class gives a programmer an expectation of what the object can do—what properties it will have, what functions it will have, and how they work together. This is somewhat similar to a constructor in JavaScript because the constructor sets up the initial properties and functions on an object. This means that most objects that are made by a constructor will have similar properties and functions.

Review

In this chapter we covered the basics of how to attach functions to objects. We have learned:

- Since functions are values, functions can be stored as attributes of objects just like other values.

- Attaching functions to objects reduces the clutter of the global namespace.

- If a function is called through an object, the object that the function was stored on is passed implicitly through the **this** parameter.

- Structuring code in this way makes software more readable because it follows the typical English subject-verb-object sentence structure.

- Functions that create and initialize new objects are called constructors.

- Constructors are typically stored in variables starting with uppercase letters to distinguish them from other functions.

- Constructors are usually named according to the type of object they are creating.

- Constructors are called using the **new** keyword.

- Using a constructor allows you to create a lot of similar objects with very little code.

Apply What You Have Learned

1. Create a constructor `Rectangle` which creates an object with base and height attributes.

2. Extend your `Rectangle` constructor to also have two methods: `find_area()` and `find_perimeter()` that give you the relevant answers. These should not have any parameters and only use the implicit **this** parameter. If you have forgotten your geometry, for rectangles, *area = base·height* and *perimeter = 2·(base + height)*. Be sure to test them to make sure they work.

3. Create a new constructor for a `Circle` that takes a radius as a parameter. It should also have `find_area()` and `find_perimeter()` methods. If you have forgotten your geometry, $area = \pi \cdot radius^2$ and $perimeter = 2 \cdot \pi \cdot radius$. Be sure to test them to make sure they work.

4. Create a function called `biggest_area` that takes an array of `Rectangle` objects and tells the user what the biggest area was in the array, using the `find_area()` function.

5. If your `biggest_area` function only uses the `find_area()` function of the object, then you should be able to send it *any* object that implements a similar function. Since `Circle` objects also have a `find_area()` function, try interweaving `Rectangle` and `Circle` objects into the same area. Since they are both supposed to respond the same way, they should both be able to be treated equivalently by the `biggest_area` function.

Chapter 15

Interacting with Web Pages

In previous chapters, we have learned how objects work and how to build our own objects. However, JavaScript also comes with several existing, built-in objects for you to use. These standard objects are the gateway between your program and the rest of the system, including the HTML document, the screen, computer storage, communication facilities, and other important system features. In this chapter, we are going to use the standard `document` object to interact with the web page.

15.1 Using the JavaScript Console

In order to see these the `document` object in action, we are going to use the **JavaScript console**. The JavaScript console allows you to type JavaScript code one line at a time and see the results immediately. For information on how to access the JavaScript console on your system, see Section A.6.

Before we begin using the console, type the following web page into a file and load it into your browser:

Figure 15.1: Basic HTML File for Manipulation

```
<!DOCTYPE html>
<html>
   <head>
      <title>My Document</title>
   </head>
   <body id="mainbody">
      <h1 id="console_heading">Using the JavaScript
         Console</h1>

      <h2 id="subheading">A Heading</h2>

      <p id="first_paragraph">
         This is my first paragraph.
      </p>
   </body>
</html>
```

Now that you have your web page loaded, open up the JavaScript console as described in Section A.6. Now, just to get used to how the console works, enter 2 + 5 into the console and hit enter. What happened? It should have given 7 as the result. After each command, when you hit the enter key, the console gives you the value of what you typed.

Now type in var a = 2 + 5; and hit enter. What happened this time? It should give back undefined. Why is this? The value 7 got loaded into the variable a, but the result of the variable declaration is nothing. So, don't be surprised if, after declaring a variable, the result is undefined. That is normal.

To make sure that a received our value, just type a into a line. It should return the value 7. Now we are going to intentionally make a mistake. Type into your console a = 7 +; and hit enter. It should give you back some sort of error, such as "Syntax Error" or a similar error message. This is important to pay attention to. If you are using the console, and you get an error message, *pay attention to it* because you probably entered something wrong

somewhere. Recheck what you typed to make sure it is valid. Programming languages tend to be very picky. A miscapitalized word, an accidental space, or a misplaced semicolon will prevent your code from working.

☞ **Practice Questions**

Before moving on to manipulating the web page, you should practice with the JavaScript console.

1. Use the `alert` function to display a popup message.

2. Use the `prompt` function to get a value from the user.

3. Enter the `square_a_number` function from Chapter 10. Because the console processes each line as you type it, you will need to put the whole function on one line.

4. Now use `square_a_number` to find the squares of 3 and 6 in the JavaScript console.

15.2   Finding and Modifying Web Page Elements

Now that we have some familiarity with how the JavaScript console works, it is time to interact with our web page. JavaScript provides a special object called `document` that provides the gateway to interacting with the web page. In JavaScript, every tag on the web page is represented by its own object with its own properties and methods. Remember, a method is simply a function that is attached to an object. The list of standard object types for HTML pages, with their properties and methods, is called the **Document Object Model**, often known just as the **DOM**. We will cover some of the more common methods for these objects in this chapter.

The first thing we are going to do is to look up one of our HTML elements. Remember, an *element* is the combination of a start/end tag and all of the content in-between. Note that in the file, we added `id` attributes to several of our tags. This makes them easy to look up in JavaScript. The `document` object has a method that looks up HTML elements by their ID, called `getElementById`. It takes one parameter, which is the HTML ID to look up, and

returns the given HTML element. If it is not found, it returns the special JavaScript value `null`, which is considered an "empty" value. In your console, type in the following:

```
document.getElementById("first_paragraph")
```

This will yield an object that represents the HTML element of the first paragraph. Once we have this object, we can make modifications to it that will be reflected in the web page itself. Each browser will display this value differently in the console, but they are all the same—they are a JavaScript object that represents the HTML element we see on the screen. In any case, we don't just want to display the value, we want to manipulate it. A good first step is to store the object in a variable. Therefore, do the following:

```
var x = document.getElementById("first_paragraph");
```

Now the object representing the HTML element is stored in our variable `x`. What can we do with it? One simple thing you can do is to change out the text. HTML elements that only have text in them (i.e., they have no child elements) can have that text accessed or changed through their `textContent` property. Type out the following:

```
x.textContent
```

It should give back the value `"This is my first paragraph"`, though possibly with some extra spaces.

☞ **Errors with `textContent`**

There are a few older browsers that don't support `textContent`. If you get errors trying to use `textContent`, first double-check and make sure you typed it correctly. If you are still having errors, try using `innerHTML` instead. This is an older property that is problematic, but it should work in browsers that don't support `textContent`.

So, now that we can access the `textContent` property, we can also change it. Type the following to put new text on your paragraph:

```
x.textContent = "This is a changed paragraph.";
```

You should see your web page instantly change with the new paragraph text.

As you can see, if we attach IDs to our HTML elements, we can easily find them and manipulate them in our JavaScript programs.

☞ **Practice Questions**

Use the JavaScript console to accomplish the following tasks:

1. Look up and modify the text for our `<h1>` element.

2. Look up and modify the text for our `<h2>` element.

3. Use the `prompt` function to ask the user for a string and store that in a variable. Now set the text of the paragraph to that value.

15.3   Creating New HTML Elements

Now that we have looked up and modified an HTML element, it is time to learn how to create a new element. The `document` object has a method called `createElement` that does just this.

Enter the following code into the console:

```
var new_element = document.createElement("p");
new_element.textContent = "This is a new paragraph";
```

This creates a new element but doesn't add it to the page. It is merely floating out there, only existing in the variable. We haven't told the document where we want it to go.

We now want to put our new element as the last thing in the `<body>` element. So, first, we need to look up the body element:

```
var body_element = document.getElementById("mainbody");
```

Now we need to tell the body element to append our new element to the end of its child elements. This is done using the `appendChild` method of our body element. Type the following:

```
body_element.appendChild(new_element);
```

As soon as you type this, the new paragraph should appear!

☞ **Practice Activity**

To practice adding HTML content to web pages, we are going to create an `<ul>` tag and then, through the JavaScript console, add additional `<li>` tags to it. If you get confused on any step in here, go back through the previous sections to find out how to do each step.

1. Start out by altering the HTML file used in this section to add a `<ul>` tag in it with at least one `<li>` tag in it.

2. Give the `<ul>` tag an `id` attribute so you can find it with JavaScript in the next step.

3. Open up the JavaScript console. Use the `getElementById` method from `document` to find the `<ul>` element and put it in a variable.

4. Now use the `createElement` method from `document` to create a new `<li>` tag to put in it.

5. Now use the `textContent` property on the new tag to set it to whatever text you want.

6. Now use the `appendChild` method on your `<ul>` element to add the new `<li>` tag to the end of your list.

7. Practice by adding yet another `<li>` tag to the list.

8. See if you can create a brand new `<ul>` tag with JavaScript and add it to the bottom of the page. Then add additional `<li>` tags to your JavaScript-created `<ul>` tag. Note that if your `<ul>` tag is stored in a variable, you won't need to look

it up with `getElementById`. Instead, you can just use it directly from its existing variable.

15.4 Communicating with Input Fields

Up to now, all interaction with users has been through the `alert` and `prompt` functions. However, you might have noticed that, on the web, most interaction occurs directly within the web page itself. This is done almost exactly like the web page manipulation that we did in the previous sections. The difference is that we are going to be working with `<input>` tags. The `<input>` element object works just like the objects for other elements that we have seen, but has a special attribute called `value` that represents the text in the field.

To get a feel for how these input fields work, enter the HTML from Figure 15.2 into a file and load it into your browser.

One thing to notice—*be sure to include* the `type="button"` attribute on your button. Otherwise, clicking on the button can cause the page to reload which will cause you to lose all of your variables that you have created.

Figure 15.2: HTML File With Input Fields

```
<!DOCTYPE html>
<html>
    <head>
        <title>Input Fields Example</title>
    </head>
    <body>
        <h1>Input Fields Example</h1>
        <form>
            <p>
                Input Field 1:
                <input type="text" id="field1" />
            </p>

            <p>
                Input Field 2:
                <input type="text" id="field2" />
            </p>
            <button type="button" id="my_button">Click
                Me</button>
            <p>
                Results:
                <span id="results"></span>
            </p>
            <p id="another_paragraph">
                Another paragraph
            </p>
        </form>
    </body>
</html>
```

Now, open the JavaScript console. The first thing we need to do is look up the two <input> elements and store them into variables. To do this, enter in the following:

```
var fld1 = document.getElementById("field1");
var fld2 = document.getElementById("field2");
```

Now type **fld1** on a line by itself to make sure that it gives back an HTML element as a value. If it doesn't, you mistyped something. Do the same to check **fld2**.

Now type in the following:

```
fld1.value = "Hello";
```

As soon as you type this, the text "Hello" should appear in the first field. Go into the second field and type in the text "Goodbye" into the web page. Now type this into the JavaScript console:

```
fld2.value
```

It should now print onto the console the value that you typed (**"Goodbye"** if you followed directions). Now we know how to set and read values from <input> elements!

Now look up the <span> tag. Remember, the <span> tag is used for specifying a region of text. In our case, we are specifying the location where we want to write the result. In any case, do the following to look up the <span> tag so we are ready to write to that location in the page:

```
var results_span = document.getElementById("results");
```

Now type in **results_span** on a line by itself so that you can see if you correctly retrieved the <span> element.

What we are going to do is read a number from each input field, multiply them together, and write the result into the <span> element.

Start out by typing in two numbers, one in each input field. For this example, let's assume that you type in "5" in the first field and "7" in the second field. Now, remember, since this is typed from the keyboard, it is treated as a string, not a number. Therefore, **fld1.value** will be the string **"5"** not the number 5 and **fld2.value** will be the string **"7"** and not the

number 7. What we need to do, then, is use our `parseInt` function to convert these strings into numbers.

Type the following in the JavaScript console to read the values of the fields and store them into variables:

```
var val1 = parseInt(fld1.value);
var val2 = parseInt(fld2.value);
```

Now, `val1` and `val2` should have the numbers that you entered in them. You can verify this by typing the variable name in the console on a line by itself, and making sure it gives you back the correct value.

Now, we need to multiply the two numbers together. Type in the following to accomplish this:

```
var result = val1 * val2;
```

`result` now has the result (35) in it.

Now we just need to write the value in `result` back into the page. We will use the `textContent` property of `results_span` to do this. JavaScript will automatically convert the number to a string before it displays it. Here is the code to do this:

```
results_span.textContent = result;
```

☞ **Practice Activity**

Practice your skills by using the JavaScript console to change the text of the final paragraph in the HTML file to the value typed into one of the `<input>` elements.

15.5 Adding Functionality to Buttons

So far, we have been able to manually perform some JavaScript processing on input fields within a document. But this is not how web pages usually work. Usually, the user tells

the computer to complete a function by clicking a button. Therefore, we have to attach the functionality we want to the button.

So, to start with, we are going to create a function that performs the tasks that we did in the previous section. For readability, I am going to write it out in several lines. However, because the JavaScript console interprets one line at a time, you *must* type out the whole function on a single line. Don't worry, the JavaScript language works exactly the same whether it is one line or many—that is why it uses the semicolon to separate statements. So, as long as you type everything correctly, it will work just fine on one line. Here is the function:

Figure 15.3: A Function to Multiply Two Text Fields

```
var multiply_fields = function() {
    var fld1 = document.getElementById("field1");
    var fld2 = document.getElementById("field2");
    var val1 = parseInt(fld1.value);
    var val2 = parseInt(fld2.value);
    var result = val1 * val2;
    var results_span = document.getElementById("results");
    results_span.textContent = result;
};
```

Notice that it uses the **document** object. This works because **document** is a global variable. Also note that the function takes no parameters. It simply works from the **document** global variable.

Once you have typed the function (all in one line) into the console, calling the function should perform all of the tasks. To test it out, put two different numbers in the input fields, and then, in the JavaScript console, write:

```
multiply_fields();
```

This should multiply the two numbers and write the result in the **results <span>** tag. If it did not work, recheck your function.

Now, we want this function to run whenever a user clicks on our button. This is actually very easy to do. `<button>` tags have a property called `onclick`. If you set `onclick` to a function, it will call that function whenever it is clicked! For right now, you should only use functions that take no parameters.

So, to get this set, we need to look up the `<button>` on the page and then set its `onclick` property. Here is the code:

```
var btn = document.getElementById("my_button");
btn.onclick = multiply_fields;
```

Note that we are not *calling* the function `multiply_fields` here. We are *storing* the function itself in the `onclick` property for later use. Remember, JavaScript functions are themselves values and are stored in variables and properties just like any other value. Therefore, we are storing the function in the `btn` object, and the `btn` object will call the function when it is time.

To try it out, put in two values and click the button. If everything was set up right, it should display the results in the proper place.

15.6   Putting It All Together

Now, what we really want is to have all of this functionality load with the web page. To do that, we are going to need to put all of our code into a JavaScript file. Create a text file called `multiply.js` in the same directory as your HTML file.

Enter the following code into `multiply.js`:

Figure 15.4: Full Code for Multiplying Two Fields

```
var multiply_fields = function() {
    var fld1 = document.getElementById("field1");
    var fld2 = document.getElementById("field2");
    var val1 = parseInt(fld1.value);
    var val2 = parseInt(fld2.value);
    var result = val1 * val2;
    var results_span = document.getElementById("results");
    results_span.textContent = result;
};
var btn = document.getElementById("my_button");
btn.onclick = multiply_fields;
```

Now we need to attach it to the HTML file. To do this, add the following tag to the HTML file within the `<head>` element:

```
<script type="text/javascript" src="multiply.js" defer="defer">
</script>
```

Notice the new attribute we added—`defer="defer"`. This attribute changes *when* the JavaScript is loaded and run. Normally, JavaScript is loaded and run at precisely the point where the tag is included. In our case, that would mean that only the `<head>` element was present, since the tag occurs before the rest of the page. This would not work, because `document.getElementById("my_button")` would return `null` (i.e., no value), because it is not yet part of the page. The attribute `defer="defer"` tells your browser to wait until after the whole page is loaded before running the JavaScript code.

Now, after you have added your `<script>` tag to the HTML file and have saved everything, reload your page. After you type in two numbers and hit the button, it should give you your answer.

☞ **Practice Activity**

Now that you know how to add functionality to a web page, this project will have you
add a second function to the same page.

1. Start with the completed file from this section.

2. Next, create a new function in your JavaScript file that will add the two numbers
   rather than multiply them. Call the function `add_fields`. *Do not* remove the
   existing `multiply_fields` code. Just add a new function.

3. Now add a second button to the page. Be sure to give it a distinct ID so you can
   find it. Do not remove the existing button.

4. Now add code to your JavaScript file so that it will find the new button and attach
   your `add_fields` function to the button.

5. Test out your new page. Be sure that both buttons do the appropriate operations.

15.7   A Broader View

This chapter introduced you to the Document Object Model (DOM). You may wonder
how you know what objects, properties, and functions are available to you. It might seem
mysterious or even arbitrary that if you stick a function in the `onclick` property it magically
calls that function when a button is clicked. When programmers create systems such as
JavaScript and the DOM, they have to make choices about how things are represented and
interacted with—what the objects and properties are called and how they are used. The
names of these objects, functions, and properties are essentially arbitrary—they are whatever
the programmer decided to name them. Hopefully the names make sense and can help you
learn how to use them, but sometimes, either through sloppiness or history, things wind up
with weird names that don't make sense. This is fairly normal in programming.

The list of standard objects, properties, and functions that a system supports is called
its **Application Programming Interface**, or, more commonly, its **API**. How do you
know what objects, properties, and functions are available in an API? Usually, this is done

by programmers writing them down and sharing them through **documentation**. Most programming systems have a reference which lists all of the available functions. However, these are usually pretty lengthy since system developers try to think of all of the things that you might want to do and provide functions for each of them. Usually, though, most APIs are focused around just a few concepts, and once you learn those, the rest are details that you can look up later.

Review

In this chapter we practiced interacting with web pages using JavaScript. We have learned:

- JavaScript comes with built-in objects that allow us to interact with the rest of the system and the network.

- The `document` object is the gateway that allows us to interact with the current web page.

- The DOM is the list of objects and properties that can be used when interacting with an HTML page and its elements.

- The `id` attribute of an HTML tag can be used to find the element from JavaScript for manipulation.

- The `getElementById` method of the `document` object allows us to use the `id` attribute to get objects which represent HTML elements in our page and store them in variables to inspect them and manipulate them.

- The `textContent` property of an HTML element's object allows us to retrieve and set the text content of an HTML element.

- Elements can be created using `document`'s `createElement` method.

- Newly-created elements can be added into a page using an element's `appendChild` method. This adds the element as the last child, or sub-element, of the given element object.

- The `<input>` tag can be used to allow a user to enter in data for processing.

- The `value` property of the `<input>` tag's object can be used for reading or setting the value of the text field.

- The `<button>` tag can be used to initiate processing. Be sure to set the `type="button"` property so it will work correctly.

- Setting a `<button>` element object's `onclick` value to a function will cause that function to run when the button is clicked.

- Setting the `defer="defer"` attribute on `<script>` tags will cause it to wait for the document to be fully loaded before executing the JavaScript. This should be added to all `<script>` tags from here on out.

- An API is the list of standard objects, properties, and functions available to a programmer from the system.

- An API's documentation is the description of what objects, properties, and functions are available and the details of how they work.

Apply What You Have Learned

1. Now that you know how to get input from a user from an HTML page and how to write output to the HTML page, rewrite a program from the previous chapters to use `<input>` tags instead of the `prompt` function.

2. Create an HTML page that just has an empty `<body>` tag with just an `id` attribute. Write JavaScript to build a page with a heading, a paragraph, and a `<ul>` list with two items in it using only JavaScript code.

3. Create an HTML page that has an empty `<ul>` tag with just an `id` attribute. Write JavaScript that uses an array and a `for` loop to populate the `<ul>` element with `<li>` elements. Use the array `["One", "Two", "Three"]` and have your code loop through each element of the array to add a new `<li>` element for each member of the array.

Chapter 16

Conclusion

Congratulations—you have taken the first steps into the wide world of programming. This book introduced you to the basics of computers, the Internet, web pages, CSS, and JavaScript. However, this book certainly didn't teach you all there is to know about any of these subjects.

Hopefully now you have a basic feel for what it is like to write and run a program and the kind of thought-work required to make a program run successfully. Where you go from here is up to you. If you like websites, then you should dig deeper into the topics covered here—HTML, CSS, and JavaScript. Learning a JavaScript **framework** like JQuery might also be a good idea. Other than that, there are all sorts of specialized tools, languages, and techniques for programming different devices and applications. There are tools and languages for database systems, phone apps, e-commerce apps, games, microcontroller systems (tiny devices with small chips), and desktop applications. Each of these have their own specialized tools and languages.

Your first language, however, is usually the hardest. Once you get used to the idea of statements, loops, variables, and functions, then, even if different languages do things differently, you have already trained your mind to think in these terms. Learning JavaScript may have been challenging, but it should make your next language much easier.

Keep in mind that software development is very dynamic. A programmer spends much of his or her life staying on top of new languages, tools, and techniques that are continually changing.

In order to continue on your journey learning to program, you should check out the other books in the *Programmer's Toolbox* series at `http://www.npshbook.com/site/otherbooks`. You can also visit the `npshbook.com` website and forum to ask questions and learn new techniques from me and from other readers.

You've got a good start. Now build on it.

Chapter 17

Glossary

Below are the definitions of the bolded glossary terms used throughout the book, plus additional terms you are likely to run into when reading about programming. When a term has more than one usage, the context for the term is distinguished in parentheses.

absolute path An absolute path is a relative URL that starts with a slash. The slash indicates that the relative URL should ignore the path component of the base URL and just use the given path instead. For instance, if the base URL is `http://www.npshbook.com/example/example.html`, an absolute path of `/test.html` indicates the URL `http://www.npshbook.com/test.html`. See also *URL*, *fully-qualified URL*, *base URL*, *relative URL*.

absolute URL See *fully-qualified URL*.

accessor In object-oriented programming, an accessor is a method that accesses an object's internal properties. In object-oriented programming, it is usually recommended that code outside of the object's own code should not directly access an object's internal properties but use methods (called accessors) to retrieve the data. This allows object programmers to modify the way that their object's internal properties are stored in future versions of the object without adversely affecting other code. See also *mutator*.

anchor In a URL, the anchor is a piece of extra data that is passed to the web page through the URL. It is located at the end of the URL, even after the query string if there is one. The anchor starts with a hash symbol (#), and everything after the hash symbol is part of the anchor. Hashes were originally intended to reference a section within a page to

allow browsers to open up not just to a specific page, but also to automatically scroll to a specific section within the page indicated by the has, and marked in the HTML with `<a name="hashname"></a>`. Now it is also used as a generic means of passing in data, much like the query string. In JavaScript, the anchor is retrieved through `window.location.hash`. See also *URL*.

anonymous function An anonymous function is a function that is not given a name but is just used as a parameter in a higher-order function. See also *function, higher-order function.*

API See *Application Programming Interface.*

application layer The application layer is the seventh layer of a networking system according to the OSI model. The application layer is defined by each individual application such as email, web browsing, or file transfer. The application layer is for the main purpose of the communication, with the other layers mostly just supporting this layer. See also *OSI model.*

Application Programming Interface An Application Programming Interface (API) is a set of records, objects, functions, and classes which define the way that a programmer should interact with an existing system. An API is primarily a set of documentation of existing or new functionality and how a programmer can gain access to it. See also *documentation.*

argument See *parameter.*

arithmetic and logic unit The arithmetic and logic unit is the part of the Central Processing Unit that performs math and logic functions. See also *Central Processing Unit.*

array An array is a sequence of data values or records, usually all of similar types of data. Each element of an array is referenced by its position in the array, called the index, with zero referring to the first element. See also *data format, zero-based indexing.*

ALU See *arithmetic and logic unit.*

ASCII ASCII (the American Standard Code for Information Interchange) is a way of representing letters, digits, punctuation, and processing codes using numbers. Because computers only process numbers, ASCII allows a number to represent a letter or other mark on the screen. In ASCII, each letter is represented by exactly one byte. While ASCII has been largely superceded by UTF-8, UTF-8 is, for the most part, backwards compatible with ASCII. To the extent that it is covered, ASCII is covered in this

book because it is by far the simpler of the two systems, and ASCII is almost entirely compatible with UTF-8. See also *data format, Unicode, UTF-8.*

assignment statement An assignment statement is a JavaScript statement that is specified by an equal sign (=). An assignment statement has an expression that yields a value on the right-hand side of the equal sign and a location to store the value on the left-hand side of the equal sign. An example assignment statement is `myvar = myothervar * 2;` See also *expression, syntax, right-hand side, left-hand side.*

attribute (HTML) In HTML and XML, an attribute is a setting used to modify or add additional information to a tag. While attributes have many purposes, one of the most common reasons for adding attributes is to add a `class` or `id` attribute that can be used for specialized styling using CSS. In the following markup, the `<p>` tag has the `class` attribute set to `important`: `<p class="important">Important text here</p>` See also *HyperText Markup Language, Extensible Markup Language, tag.*

attribute (object) In object-oriented programming, an attribute is a piece of data tied to an object. For instance, if an object represents a car, that object might have attributes for where it is located on the map, how much gas it has left, and what direction it is going.

base case In recursive programming, the base case is the condition that stops the recursion and returns a simple answer. Recursive functions are usually setup to reduce the problem to a simpler and simpler problem until an answer can be provided directly. This place/condition where an answer can be provided directly is the base case. Without a base case, a recursive function would never be able to stop and would generate an infinite loop. See also *recursive function, inductive case, infinite loop.*

base URL The base URL is the starting point for relative URLs. The base URL is usually set to the URL of the current document being viewed, but in HTML this can be adjusted using the `<base>` tag. See also *URL, fully-qualified URL, relative URL.*

BBS See *bulletin-board system.*

binary The binary numbering system is a system that only uses 1s and 0s. The first few numbers of binary (starting with zero) are 0 (zero), 1 (one), 10 (two), 11(three), and 100 (four). See also *decimal, octal, hexadecimal.*

binary digit See *bit.*

binary file A binary file, as opposed to a text document, is a file which is not readable in a text editor, but requires a more specialized program in order to read and manipulate the file. See also *text document*.

bit A bit is a binary digit—either a 1 or a 0. In the binary number system, 1 and 0 are the only digits. Computers are able to work more easily with binary digits because they can be implemented using the presence or absence of electrical current. See also *byte*, *binary*.

block A block is a grouped sequence of statements. In JavaScript, blocks are indicated with opening and closing braces ({ and }). Blocks are used to designate the body of a function, a branch of an `if` statement, or the body of a loop. See also *control structure*, *function*.

bug A bug is an error in the program.

built-in function A built-in function is a function that is a part of the programming system and doesn't need to be added by the programmer. A common built-in function used in this book is the JavaScript `alert` function, which displays messages to the user. See also *function*.

bulletin-board system A bulletin-board systems was a popular method of computer communication in the days before the Internet. Basically, a computer would call a main computer over the phone lines, and the user would directly interact with the main computer on the other side. The user could leave messages and files for other users to pick up when they dialed in.

byte A byte is a sequence of 8 bits, and therefore has the ability to hold a number between 0 and 255. While individual bytes are rarely used in computer programs anymore, most quantities on computers are given in terms of bytes, such as the size of computer memory chips and hard drives. See also *bit*, *binary*.

Cascading Style Sheets Cascading Style Sheets is a text file format which specifies how HTML (or even XML) should be displayed to a user. It uses property lists to define what style should be used to lay out a block of text, and then it uses selectors to specify which tags go with which property lists.

Central Processing Unit The Central Processing Unit (CPU) is the core of a computer which actually performs all of the data processing.

chip See *integrated circuit*.

class In object-oriented programming, a class is very similar to a type and is often used interchangeably. Types usually refer to single-values, while classes refer to whole objects. Types are typically predefined by the programming language, and classes are generally defined by the programmer (with the exception of a few built-in classes). A class describes what properties are available on the *instances* of the class and what methods can be called on them. In JavaScript, objects don't really have classes, but they do have constructors, which serve a similar purpose of defining the attributes and valid functions of an object. See also *constructor, instance, object.*

CLI See *Command Line Interface*

client A client is a computer or software program which accesses the services of another computer across the network, called the server. See also *server.*

Command Line Interface A Command Line Interface (CLI) is a user-interface that allows users to interact with the computer by directly typing commands and getting textual output on the screen. Most command line interfaces have at least some amount of programmability, allowing users an almost unlimited flexibility in running system programs. See also *Graphical User Interface.*

command prompt In a Command Line Interface, the command prompt is the text that sits to the left of the blinking cursor. What the prompt actually says varies based on your computer's settings, but usually it has things like the name of the current directory, the name of the computer, the name of the current user, and then special character that indicates that you should start typing (typically either #, $, or >). See also *Command Line Interface.*

comment In computer programming, a comment is a section of text within the program that is used entirely for information for another human being reading the program. A comment is ignored by the programming language itself. For instance, if you had a piece of code that is complicated, you might include a comment to tell other programs (or yourself at a later date) why the code is so complicated and what you are trying to accomplish.

compression Compression is a process which reduces the size of a value (usually a string), usually by removing redundant information or finding simple patterns within the value.

computer A computer is a piece of hardware that uses programs called software to process data. It is called a computer because its operation primarily consists of computation. See also *general-purpose computer, special-purpose computer.*

concatenation Concatenation means combining by appending to the end and usually refers to sticking two strings together. For example, concatenating `"hello"` and `"world"` would get you `"helloworld"`.

conditional expression A conditional expression is an expression which yields a true or false value. Conditional expressions are often used in control structures to determine which branch of code to follow, or to serve as a control for a loop. See also *expression*.

console A console is a program that allows direct interaction with the programming environment. A console allows you to directly enter statements, and the console will evaluate and execute the statements immediately, yielding back the return value for you on the screen.

constructor In object-oriented programming, a constructor is a function that builds a new object instance of a specific class. In JavaScript, since there are no classes, the constructor itself fills the role of the class by setting up the properties and functions that a variable should have. See also *instance, object, class, object-oriented programming*.

content When thinking about a document, the content usually refers to the actual data that a person sees, as opposed to how it is displayed. For instance, the content would include the text on a page, but would not include the font that the text is in, the line spacing, or any background images. See also *presentation*.

content type A content type (also called a MIME type) is the format that a given piece of data is in. It is like a filename extension, but it is used for any stream of data, not just files. Content types are often used for data streams with multiple different types of data embedded in them, such as emails that contain attachments. Content types are specified with a general type and a more specific subtype, such as `image/png`, which means that it is an image (general type) and is specifically formatted as PNG image (the subtype). Webpages are of type `text/html`.

control structure A control structure is a statement or combination of statements that affect the sequencing of program statements. Control structures include function calls (which transfer the control sequence to the function), return statements (which transfer the control sequence back to the calling function), looping operations such as `while` and `for` (which repeat a given set of statements until a condition is reached), and branching operations such as `if` (which choose which path to operate based on a condition). There are other control structures, as well, which have more complicated functionality. See also *flow control statement, loop, function, syntax*.

control unit The control unit is the part of the Central Processing Unit that interprets instructions and directs the other parts of the CPU. See also *Central Processing Unit.*

CPU See *Central Processing Unit.*

CSS See *Cascading Style Sheets.*

currying Currying refers to the process of generating a function by specifying one or more parameters of another function. See also *higher-order function.*

data bus The data bus is a piece of hardware that manages communication between system components. For example, a data bus connects the Central Processing Unit to the computer memory. See also *Central Processing Unit, memory.*

data format A data format is a way to structure data so that other computer programs can read it. Since data is only a sequence of numbers, a data format defines the meanings of those numbers so that they can be used to convey information. See also *file format.*

data transformation A data transformation is a process of converting data from one data format to another. Often times there is more than one data format available for the same type of data. A data transformation converts between these different formats. Data transformations can also manipulate and summarize data into more usable forms. See also *data format, file format.*

data link layer The data link layer is the second layer of a networking system according to the OSI model. The data link layer deals with how the data on the physical layer will be divided and interpreted. It usually has a methodology for naming each local device (often called a MAC address). See also *OSI model, MAC address.*

data structure A data structure is a conceptual way of storing information. It is similar to a record, but a data structure can also refer to an entire set of different types of records that work together to accomplish a goal. See also *record.*

decimal Decimal is the numbering system that most people are used to using. It uses the digits 0–9 to make numbers. See also *binary, octal, hexadecimal.*

declaration A declaration is an instruction in a programming language that gives the language information about how to interpret other parts of a program. For instance, the declaration `var x;` is a declaration that tells the programming language that `x` will now refer to a variable. Other sorts of declarations can include what version of JavaScript is being used, or, in HTML, which set of tags are being used. See also *doctype declaration.*

directory A directory (also called a folder) is a container for files or other directories usually used to keep files on a computer organized. In a URL, directories are indicated by slashes. For example, in the URL `http://www.npshbook.com/example/test.html`, the path is `/example/test.html`. This path refers to the `test.html` document in the `example` directory. See also *URL*, *fully-qualified URL*.

DNS See *Domain Name System*.

doctype declaration In HTML and XML, the doctype declaration specifies what type of document (i.e., what set of tags) is being processed. An HTML doctype declaration looks like this: `<!DOCTYPE html>` See also *HyperText Markup Language*, *Extensible Markup Language*.

Document Object Model The Document Object Model is an API (a set of objects, functions, and object classes) that describes how a programmer should interact with an HTML page. The Document Object Model was built to simplify and standardize this interaction not just within JavaScript, but across multiple languages. That way, once you learn how to interact with web pages in JavaScript, your API knowledge can also be used in other languages that manipulate HTML. See also *API*, *class*.

documentation Documentation is any written documents or program comments that help navigate other programmers through a piece of code or a system. Documentation is important because most code will be handled by more than one person, so any information future programmers may need to update programs should be documented somewhere. Things that are especially important to document are the purpose of functions, the parameters used in a function, any global variables, and any surprise "gotcha" encountered while building the program, or that may be encountered using the code or the program.

DOM See *Document Object Model*.

Domain Name System The Domain Name System (DNS) is a system that allows people to use friendlier names for computers on the Internet. Normally, each computer on the Internet is assigned an IP address, which is just a sequence of numbers. Not only are numbers hard to memorize, but these numbers can change if a computer is moved to another network. The domain name system allows user-friendly names such as *www.npshbook.com* to be used instead of the numeric IP address. The domain name system works behind the scenes to translate the hostname into an IP address for the computer to connect to.

domain-specific language A domain-specific language is a programming language that is geared toward a particular application (domain). Such programming languages often limit the programmer to a very few set of operations, and only some of them attempt to be Universal. A configuration file can be considered a domain-specific language of sorts. However, sometimes a domain-specific language is simply a general-purpose language with domain-specific features tacked on. See also *general-purpose computer*, *special-purpose computer*, *Universal programming language*.

DSL See *domain-specific language*

element In HTML, an element consists of a start tag, an end tag, and all of the content and tags in-between them. See also *tag, start tag, end tag, markup language, HyperText Markup Language*.

encapsulation Encapsulation is a programming methodology in which access to read and manipulate data fields is only granted through functions or methods, never (or rarely) by direct access. The goal of encapsulation is to (a) make sure that fields are synchronized with each other, (b) make sure that all business and domain rules are appropriately followed concerning the data, and (c) make sure that the interface (the functions or methods) do not have to change even when the underlying data fields may change. For instance, a bank account might be encapsulated by giving the programmer no direct access to the account balance but giving methods to check the balance, deposit money, and withdraw money. In this way, it can ensure that if the programmer calls the functions to withdraw money, for example, all overdraft rules are appropriately applied rather than relying on the programmer to always remember to apply them. This also allows the implementation of these functions to change without drastically impacting other parts of the program.

encryption Encryption is a process that allows two parties to communicate without a third party listening in. It can also refer to a method of digitally signing a message to prove the identity of the sender.

end tag In HTML, an end tag marks the end of a block of content that is used for a specific purpose. An end tag looks just like a start tag but begins with a slash. So, if the start tag was <p>, then the end tag will be </p>. See also *tag, start tag, markup language, HyperText Markup Language*.

entity In HTML and XML, an entity is a named character, symbol, or sequence of characters. Entities are specified by starting with an ampersand (&) and ending with a semicolon (;). For instance, © is an entity that refers to the copyright symbol.

Ethernet Ethernet is the most prominent means of physically connecting two devices on a local area network. See also *data link layer, network, local area network.*

expression An expression is a combination of variables, literals, operators, and functions that yield a value in a single statement. For example, 2 + 3 * 5 is an expression, as is (myvar * 2) - myothervar and myfunc(myvar + 1). Individual literals and variables also count as expressions, too. Anything that can exist on the right-hand side of an assignment statement is considered an expression. See also *variable, literal, operator, function, assignment statement, right-hand side, syntax.*

Extensible Markup Language The Extensible Markup Language (usually referred to as XML) is a text-based markup language that is very similar to HTML with the primary difference being that there is not a predefined set of tags to use. Programs utilizing XML get to make up their own tags to match the type of data they are trying to convey. XML has the benefit of being more flexible than HTML, at a cost of needing different programs to be customized to understand each others' sets of tags. Many file formats today are simply predefined sets of XML tags. XML has stricter rules than standard HTML as far as how tags are formed, which makes it easier and faster to process. For example, there are cases where HTML allows start tags without corresponding end tags, while XML always requires end tags. HTML written according to these standards is sometimes called XHTML. All HTML in this book is also XHTML. See also *markup language, text document, HyperText Markup Language.*

extension See *filename extension.*

file format A file format is a way of structuring data on-disk so that the data can be read back by a computer program. A file format defines the types of data that can be stored within a file and how it is structured so that it can be read back. Since a file is only a sequence of numbers, there is no way to tell what the numbers are supposed to mean apart from the file format, which tells the program (actually, the programmer) how the sequence of numbers should be interpreted. See also *protocol, data format.*

filename extension A filename extension is a short code placed at the end of a filename which tells the computer what format the given file is in, and, in some cases, what program should be used to open the file. The filename extension is separated from the main filename by a period. For instance, the filename mydocument.rtf has a filename extension of rtf, which means that the file is in Rich Text Format. Other common filename extensions include docx for word processing documents, jpg or png for image files, and html for web pages. See also *content type.*

firewall A firewall is a device or a program that restricts access to network resources, either on a single computer or across a network of computers. The firewall is meant to separate "outside" from "inside" communication, so as to limit what resources an outside network can access. Firewalls provide an additional layer of safety and security to computers on the "inside" of the firewall.

fixed-point number A fixed-point number is a computer-stored decimal number. It is called a "fixed point" because of the way it stores the number—it has a fixed number of positions to the right and left of the decimal that it can store. This makes the range of numbers it can cover smaller than that of floating-point numbers, but makes the calculations more exact for the range that it covers. Fixed-point numbers are often used to store money amounts for that reason. See also *floating-point number*.

Flash Memory Modern computers phased out Read-Only Memory (ROM) for flash memory. Flash memory is like ROM in that it is not erased when the computer turns off, but like RAM in that it can be altered. Flash memory is often used for computer bootup instructions as well as USB-based thumb drives. See also *Random-Access Memory, Read-Only Memory, Universal Serial Bus*.

floating-point number A floating-point number is a computer-stored decimal number. It is called a "floating point" because of the way it stores the number—the digits of the number are stored separately from the location of the decimal point. This allows it to store numbers that are very large or very small but sacrifices some amount of precision. See also *fixed-point number*.

flow control statement See *control structure*.

folder See *directory*.

for loop A for loop is a type of loop that includes some amount of loop initialization and control management. In JavaScript, it takes the form, `for(initialization; loop condition; loop control) { loop body }`.
It is basically a while loop that gives a specific area for loop control statements. An example for loop should illustrate the point: `for(var i = 0; i < 10; i = i + 1) { alert(i); }`. This code will display each number from one through nine. The initialization creates the control variable and sets the value. The loop condition checks to see if the value is less than ten before executing the code. Finally, the loop control increases the control variable to go to the next number. You can put any statements you want for the initialization, condition, and control statements, but the ones in the example are fairly typical. See also *loop, loop condition, loop body, loop control variable*.

fully-qualified URL A fully-qualified URL (also called an absolute URL) is a URL that contains all of the information needed to access a remote document or service. As opposed to absolute URLs and relative URLs, fully-qualified URLs rely on no contextual information whatsoever in order to connect. A fully-qualified URL usually includes the protocol, the server, and the document path. For example, `http://www.npshbook.com/example/example.html` uses HTTP as the protocol, connects to the server `www.npshbook.com`, and accesses the document at the path `/example/example.html`. When people discuss URLs, they are usually talking about fully-qualified URLs. See also *URL, relative URL, network path.*

function A function is a sequence of steps that a computer can perform that is encapsulated as a single unit. Functions usually consist of a list of parameters, which serve as input to the function, a sequence of instructions, and a return value, which is usually where the result of the function is given. Functions are used for several purposes, including specifying a piece of code that can be run multiple times from different parts of a program and separating a program out into logically distinct components. See also *parameter, return value.*

function scope Function scope is the scope created by a function definition. Within a function, all variables declared using the **var** keyword get put in the function's scope as well as all of the function's parameters. These variables cannot be accessed by name anywhere outside of the function body. For more advanced programmers, if a function is declared *within* another function, it can access all of the variables in the enclosing function. Function scopes are actually created when the function starts executing. Therefore, if a function calls itself, each execution of the function gets its own unique copy of the scope. This will cause a separate copy of each variable to exist for each active function. See also *function, variable, variable scope, recursive function.*

general-purpose computer A general-purpose computer is a computer that can be loaded with software that can perform any possible calculation (within practical limits). See also *special-purpose computer, Universal programming language.*

global scope The global scope is a scope that is always visible to every function. See also *variable scope, global variable.*

global variable A global variable is a variable that is defined in the global scope, and thus visible within every function, unless that function has a local variable of the same name. See also *variable scope, global scope, variable.*

Graphical User Interface A Graphical User Interface (GUI, pronounced like gooey) is the typical type of interface we see on modern computers—heavy uses of icons, media,

windows, and screen management, with interactions taking place primarily through an interactive device like a mouse. See also *command line interface*.

groupware Groupware is a set of software applications that allow a user to interact with a group. Groupware usually includes scheduling and messaging applications that work together.

GUI See *Graphical User Interface*

hexadecimal Hexadecimal is a numbering system that consists of the digits 0–9 as well as the letters a–f for an expanded list of 16 total digits. Hexadecimal is often used in computer programming because every two hexadecimal numbers represents a single byte. See also *decimal, binary, octal, byte*.

higher-order function A higher-order function is a function that either takes a function as a parameter or generates and returns new functions as a result. Higher-order functions are often difficult to grasp but, once understood, can greatly simplify many programming tasks.

hostname The hostname is the name of a computer or group of computers on the Internet. For instance, in the URL *http://www.npshbook.com/*, *http* is the protocol, *www.npshbook.com* is the hostname, and / is the path. This means that the URL will transmit to the computer or group of computers named by *www.npshbook.com* using the HTTP protocol, and ask for the document /.

HTML See *HyperText Markup Language*.

HTTP See *HyperText Transfer Protocol*.

HTTP verb The HTTP protocol has several commands, called verbs, that it can receive. The two main verbs are GET, which is usually used to retrieve documents, and POST, which is usually used to transmit a form to the server.

hyperlink A hyperlink is a short piece of text in a digital document, which, when clicked, takes the viewer to another, related document.

HyperText Markup Language HyperText Markup Language (usually known simply as HTML) is a specialized markup language used for displaying documents on the web. It uses tags to mark different pieces of content for different purposes. See also *markup language, tag, text document*.

HyperText Transfer Protocol The HyperText Transfer Protocol (HTTP) is the application layer protocol used on the Internet for transferring web content (web pages, images, etc.). When the data transfer is encrypted using SSL or TLS, the protocol is referred to as HTTPS. See *application layer, Transport Layer Security.*

identifier An identifier is a programmer-chosen name for a value. Most identifiers in programming languages refer to variable names, function names, or property names. Identifiers differ from keywords and operators, which are fixed, pre-specified words that have a specific meaning in a language. Programming languages have rules for what makes a valid identifier, but usually any group of characters without spaces or special characters that start with a letter can be used an identifier. See also *variable, operator, keyword, syntax.*

IMAP IMAP (the Internet Message Access Protocol) is one of the application layer protocols used to retrieve email from an email server. See also *application layer, SMTP, POP.*

index An index is a number used in arrays and character strings to specify which item of the array or string you want to access. See also *array, string, zero-based indexing.*

inductive case In recursive programming the programmer usually tries to redefine the problem into simpler and simpler problems with the same form as the original. For instance, in the `factorial` function, the factorial is represented in terms of the factorial of smaller numbers. The conditions that cause a recursive program to call itself with a simplified version of the problem is called the inductive case. See also *recursive function, base case.*

infinite loop An infinite loop is a loop in which the loop condition is improperly written, such that the loop body never stops executing. See also *loop, loop condition, loop body.*

information architecture For websites, information architecture refers to how web pages are organized and how users can navigate through the website. For computer programs, information architecture refers to how data is divided into data structures such as objects and arrays.

inheritance See *subclass*

initialization Initialization is a term that refers to the beginning steps of a loop, program, or function, in which the programmer sets initial values to variables. JavaScript does not require that initialization happen at the beginning of a program or function, but it is usually good programming practice to do so. See also *loop initialization.*

input In computer hardware, input is anything that comes into a program from outside of the computer. Keyboards, mice, and hard drives are all examples of input systems. In computer programming, input can refer to anything that comes into a section of a program, even if it does not come from outside the computer. For instance, the input of a function can refer to external input (such as keyboards) as well as the function's parameters and global variables. See also *input/output system*, *output*.

input/output system An input/output system is a set of hardware specifications for allowing devices to be added to computers. One popular input/output system is the Universal Serial Bus (USB). See also *USB*.

instance In object-oriented programming, an instance is an object of a particular class. For example, I might have a class of `Car` that describes the basic potential features of a car and then thousands of `Car` object instances that are used to model traffic. Each instance of the `Car` class has the properties and methods that the `Car` class describes. JavaScript does not have classes, but a similar concept is built through constructors. See also *object*, *class*, *constructor*.

instruction pointer In machine language, the instruction pointer contains the memory address of the next instruction to fetch and execute. See also *machine language*, *memory address*.

integer An integer is a counting number—a number with no decimal points.

integrated circuit An integrated circuit is a piece of silicon with numerous transistors and other miniaturized semiconductors packed into a small area. Integrated circuits may be as simple as a few transistors wired together to make a timer or a few billion transistors wired together to make a modern computer microprocessor.

interface In object-oriented programming, an interface (also called a protocol) is a list of related methods that an object or class may implement that contribute toward a similar function in non-similar objects. For instance, beds and cars have very little in common, but they might both have a function called `getLocation()` and `setLocation()`. If they both implemented equivalently-named functions to accomplish similar goals, then you could regard that as an interface. Defining interfaces allows people to write general code that allows the code to be used in a variety of circumstances with different kinds of objects so long as the objects each implement the same interface.

Internet The Internet is the worldwide conglomeration of networks operating under a standard set of protocols for locating and communicating with each other. See also *network*.

Internet Protocol The Internet Protocol (IP) is the network layer protocol used on the Internet for addressing devices and routing data to them. See also *network layer, Internet, TCP/IP, IP Address.*

IP See *Internet Protocol.*

IP Address An IP address is how a computer is identified on the Internet. The Internet Protocol uses the IP address to ensure that data arrives at the proper destination. See also *Internet Protocol, network layer.*

JavaScript JavaScript is a programming language that is widely used today to make web pages more interactive.

JavaScript console See *console*

keyword A keyword is a word that looks like an identifier but has a specific meaning in the given programming language. See also *identifier, syntax.*

L-value See *left-hand side.*

LAN See *local area network.*

left-hand side In an assignment statement, the left-hand side refers to the code on the left-hand side of the equal sign (=). The goal of the left-hand side is to yield a storage location that can hold the value given in the right-hand side. Therefore, the left-hand side is interpreted differently than the right-hand side. On the right-hand side, `myarray[0]` refers to the *value* that is held in the first element of `myarray`. On the left-hand side, `myarray[0]` refers to the *storage location* that is the first element of `myarray`. Storage locations specified by the left-hand side of assignment statements are often called L-values. See also *assignment statement, right-hand side.*

library A library is a set of pre-built functions, objects, and/or other programming tools that assists a programmer to accomplish specific tasks. For instance, many websites offer JavaScript libraries that provide functions that a programmer can call to retrieve data from their website.

link See *hyperlink.*

literal A literal refers to a value that is entered directly in a programming language as opposed to one that is given as input or calculated from other values. For instance, the statement `var myvar = 0;`, the 0 in the program refers to the number 0 itself. Any value that is written directly into a program is considered a literal.

local area network A local area network (LAN) is a network of computers within a modest physical proximity that are all managed under a single administration. Most home and office networks are local area networks. See also *wide area network*.

local variable A local variable is a variable with a non-global scope. In JavaScript, local variables have function scope. See also *variable, global scope, function scope*.

loop A loop is a sequence of statements that are repeated. Loops generally consists of two logical components—the loop condition and the loop body. The loop body is the sequence of statements to be executed repeatedly, and the loop condition is a conditional expression that controls whether or not the loop continues repeating or is finished. See also *conditional expression, loop condition, loop body, loop control variable, for loop, while loop*.

loop body In a loop, the loop body is a sequence of statements that gets executed over and over again. In most types of loops, the sequence of statements executes until the loop condition evaluates to false. See also *loop, loop condition*.

loop condition The loop condition is a conditional expression that controls whether or not the loop body is executed. See also *conditional expression, loop, loop body*.

loop control variable A loop control variable is a variable that is used to gauge the progress of a loop and determine whether or not it is finished. A loop does not have to have a single loop control variable—sometimes a loop condition is controlled by a variety of conditions of several variables. However, most loops make use of a single variable to determine whether or not it should keep executing. Therefore, in order to avoid an infinite loop, it is important to make sure your loop control variable is modified properly in the loop body (or in the loop control in a for loop). See also *loop, loop condition, loop body, for loop*.

loop initialization Loop initialization is a term that refers to setting up the variables in order to execute a loop. In some forms of loops (such as the `while` loop), loop initialization is done manually while in other loops (such as the `for` loop), at least part of the initialization is part of the loop syntax itself. See also *loop, while loop, for loop*

MAC address The MAC (media access control) address is how a computer is identified on a local network (at the data link layer level). This is different than the IP address, which is how a computer is identified across a larger network such as the Internet. Computers on the Internet typically have both a MAC address and an IP address. The MAC address allows a network card to quickly identify which packets of data

belong to that network card without the complexities of understanding the Internet Protocol. See also *IP address, internet protocol, data link layer, packet.*

machine language A machine language is the set of instructions that a computer is able to process natively. The three most common machine languages are the x86 platform (used by most desktop computers), the PowerPC platform (used by many gaming systems), and the ARM platform (used by many smartphones). Most programmers do not use machine language but, instead, use other programming languages that make the task of programming easier. See also *programming language.*

markup language A markup language is a text document that has certain codes written into it that tell a person or a computer program how to interpret each piece of text. Common markup languages are XML and HTML. See also *HyperText Markup Language, Extensible Markup Language.*

memory The memory of a computer refers to the data that is held in a computer. The memory is a sequence of storage locations, each of which holds 8 bits (one byte) of data. It usually refers to Random-Access Memory, which goes away when the computer is switched off. See also *Random-Access Memory, bit byte, memory address.*

memory address The computer memory is simply a very large sequence of bytes. Each byte is given a number that refers to its position in the sequence of bytes. This number is known as a memory address. See also *memory, byte.*

message Another term used for *method*. It has a slightly different technical meaning, but they are usually used interchangeably.

method A method is a function that is attached to an object. In JavaScript, this is done by setting a property of an object to a function. When a method is called, the object that the function is attached to is passed as an implicit parameter to the function. In JavaScript, this is done by setting the special variable `this` to the object. See also *function, object.*

microchip See *integrated circuit.*

MIME type See *content type.*

modem A modem (from the words "*mod*ulator" and "*dem*odulator") is a device that converts a digital signal to an analog signal for transmission over phone lines.

modularization Modularization refers to a practice in programming of separating out a program into simpler pieces, called modules. This helps to better organize the program,

to reduce the amount of local complexity (since the units are thought of in more holistic and unified ways), to reduce the amount of global complexity (since the interaction points between the modules are better documented and understood), and to make the program more understandable (because you can reasonably understand the program at both a local level and a global level). Without modularization, oftentimes programs would have to be understood simultaneously at a broad and local level since there was nothing that partitioned the system into parts.

mutating function See *mutator*

mutator In object-oriented programming, a mutator is a method that changes an object's internal properties. In object-oriented programming, it is usually recommended that all changes to an object's properties occur through mutators so that only the object is responsible for maintaining internal consistency. Otherwise, if an object needed two values to change together, and someone using the object only changed one of them, the object would be in an invalid state. Using mutators puts the burden of object consistency on the person who wrote the code for the object to begin with. See also *object-oriented programming, accessor*.

name clash A name clash is when a programmer accidentally uses the same name for two different things (usually variables). Depending on the programming language and the way it occurs, this can either prevent the code from running (because the language can't distinguish between the two uses of the name) or causes data corruption (because two parts of the code are using the same location for different things). See also *variable*.

network A network is a group of computers that are connected together so that they can send data to each other. See also *Ethernet, local area network*.

network layer The network layer is the third layer of a networking system according to the OSI model. The network layer deals with moving data between different physical network segments. The most common network layer protocol is the Internet Protocol. See also *OSI model, Internet Protocol*.

network path A network path is like a fully-qualified URL but without the protocol specified. It is also like a relative URL, but relative only to the protocol of the base URL. A network path is indicated by starting with two slashes (//). For instance, the URL `http://www.npshbook.com/example/example.html` has a network path of `//npshbook.com/example/example.html`. Network paths are often used when a document can be accessed by more than one protocol, and you want all of the links using the same protocol. For instance, if a document can be accessed via either HTTP or

HTTPS (using `http:` or `https:` as the protocol), using network paths for links will keep the session in the same protocol as was used to access the original document. See also *URL*, *fully-qualified URL*, *base URL*, *relative URL*.

nil See *null*.

null Null (also called nil) is often used in programming languages to represent an empty value. In JavaScript, you can set values to `null` if you don't know what the value is. It is similar to `undefined`, except `undefined` is usually assigned by the system itself when a variable has not been set to anything. In other words, `undefined` is used by the JavaScript language when it doesn't know what the value should be, and `null` is used by programmers to specify that they don't know what the value should be. `null` and `undefined` are equal when compared using == but not equal when compared using ===. Most programming languages don't have separate values for undefined and null values. In other programming languages, null is defined as the number zero. See also *undefined*.

null-terminated string A null-terminated string is a way of implementing strings such that the last value is a sentinel (usually the null value) signaling the end of the string. JavaScript strings are not null-terminated (JavaScript stores the count of the characters instead), but null-terminated strings are seen on a number of programming languages. See also *string*, *null*, *sentinel*.

object An object is a data structure that can contain both regular data and functions. In JavaScript, although every value is technically an object, objects usually refer to custom-defined objects that contain multiple values.

object-oriented programming Object-oriented programming is a method of programming where data records and related functions (called methods) are encapsulated together into units called objects. See also *class*, *subclass*, *interface*, *instance*, *object*, *accessor*, *mutator*, *constructor attribute*, *property*.

octal Octal is a numbering system that only uses the digits 0–7. It is commonly used in computers since each octal digit represents exactly three bits. See also *binary*, *decimal*.

opcode The word opcode stands for "operation code." In machine language, an opcode is part of a machine instruction. It is a number that refers to what process the CPU should perform with the instruction. The CPU uses the opcode to know what operation to perform. The opcode is combined with other operands to form a complete machine instruction.

operand An operand is a value that is operated on by an operator. In the expression 2 + 3, + is the operator, and 2 and 3 are operands. Operators are like parameters to built-in functions. See also *expression*, *operator*.

operator An operator is a symbol or keyword in a programming language that tells computes a value. For instance, + is an operator that adds two values, and == is an operator that compares two values and yields true or false based on whether they are equivalent. See also *operand*.

OSI model The OSI model is a way of thinking about the different needs of a communication system broken out into independent layers. The OSI model is what, for instance, allows wired and wireless computers to interoperate on the same network despite having very different ways of physically connecting to the network. The OSI model divides the needs of a network communication system into seven layers which can each act independently of the others. See also *physical layer*, *data link layer*, *network layer*, *transport layer*, *session layer*, *presentation layer*, *application layer*.

output In computer hardware, output is anything that goes from the computer to a device outside of the computer. Your monitor, speakers, and hard drive are all examples of output systems. In computer programming, output can refer to anything that is the result of a section of a program, especially its return value, and any global variables that it modified. See also *input/output system*, *input*, *return value*.

packet A packet is a piece of a communication sent as a unit across the network. When sending or receiving data, the operating system or network can decide to break up the transmission into pieces called packets and send each packet individually. The destination computer then reassembles the packets into their proper order before sending them on to the destination program.

parameter A parameter is a value that is given to a function for processing. In JavaScript, for instance, the function call `alert("hello there");` has one parameter—the string `"hello there"`. In JavaScript, each parameter is assigned to a local variable for the duration of the function.

parent directory On a computer, files are organized in a hierarchy of directories. If a file is in a given directory, the parent directory is the directory that the given directory is located in. For instance, if a file is in the directory `/example1/example2/myfile.html`, the directory that the file is in is `example2`, and the parent directory of `example2` is `example1`. See also *director*.

parse Parsing is converting specially-formatted text from a simple string to something easier to manipulate as data. For instance, the string "25" can be parsed into the number 25, and the string "2016-03-01" can be parsed into a date.

peripheral A peripheral is an external device attached to the computer such as a mouse, keyboard, or monitor. Most peripherals today use USB to connect. See also *Universal Serial Bus, intput/output system.*

physical layer The physical layer is the lowest layer of a networking system according to the OSI model. The physical layer deals with the physical wires between devices or, in the case of wireless communication, the necessary physical requirements of the space. See also *OSI model.*

pica In typography, a pica is a size that is $\frac{1}{6}$ of an inch. See also *typography.*

point In typography, a point is a size that is $\frac{1}{72}$ of an inch. See also *typography.*

POP POP (the Post Office Protocol) is one of the application layer protocols used to retrieve email from an email server. See also *application layer, SMTP, IMAP.*

presentation When thinking about a document, the presentation usually refers to the way that data is displayed on a page, not the content itself. The presentation refers to fonts, colors, borders, backgrounds, placements, spacing, and other visual effects that are not directly tied to the text or data being presented.

presentation layer The presentation layer is the sixth layer of a networking system according to the OSI model. The presentation layer allows for the adjustment of the message before being sent to the application. Two common uses of this are encryption and compression. The TLS protocol, for instance, is a presentation layer protocol for encryption used on many websites. However, oftentimes the presentation layer is bundled into the application layer. See also *OSI model, application layer, TLS, SSL, encryption, compression.*

program stack See *stack.*

programming language A programming language is a method of conveying instructions to a computer in a way that is easier for programmers to use than the machine's native machine language but that is still precise enough to be translated into the computer's own machine language. See also *machine language.*

property (CSS) A CSS property is a setting that can be changed, such as `font-size` or `padding-left`.

property (object) An object property is a value that is set on an object. The property name is the name that the value is referred by, and the property value is the actual value stored. For instance, if we had an object called `myobj`, then the statement `myobj.myprop = "myval";` would set a property named `myprop` on the `myobj` object to the value `"myval"`.

protocol (networking) A protocol is a system of conventions used to facilitate communication or usage. In ordinary life, a common protocol is shaking hands when greeting someone or saying "hello" and "goodbye" on the telephone. On computer systems, protocols allow components and software built by independent groups to work together by sharing the same conventions. For instance, there are a number of different web browsers available for browsing the web, but they are all able to do so successfully because they all follow a standard protocol for exchanging information with the website.

protocol (object-oriented programming) See *interface*.

query string In a URL, a query string is a set of extra data that is passed to the web page through the URL. If a URL has a question mark within the URL, everything after the question mark is considered part of the query string. Query string data is usually expressed as `key=val` pairs separated by ampersands (`&`). In JavaScript, the query string can be accessed in JavaScript through `window.location.search`. See also *URL*.

RAM See *Random-Access Memory*.

Random-Access Memory Random-Access Memory (RAM) is the typical type of computer memory. It refers to memory that can be both read from and written to. The RAM of a computer is wiped when it is turned off or rebooted. See also *memory*, *Read-Only Memory*.

Read-Only Memory Read-Only Memory (ROM) is a special type of computer memory that is usually only available for reading. For instance, the instructions that help a computer boot up used to be held in ROM-based memory. Today, flash memory is usually used for this purpose. ROM, since it is read-only, is not wiped when the computer is turned off.

record A record is a set of named, related values that are stored together. For instance, a record about a person could have their name, age, and hair color. In JavaScript, records are created using objects. See also *variable*, *object*.

recursive function A recursive function is a function that calls itself. Recursive functions are used when the method to solve a problem involves figuring out the answer from a simplified set and then expanding that set. As an example, the factorial function takes a number and multiplies it by all numbers below it until it gets to 1. This means that `factorial(5)` could just be written as `5 * factorial(4)`, and `factorial(4)` can be written as `4*factorial(3)`. Each step of the factorial simply comes up with a factorial of a smaller number until it gets to 1. The 1 is called a base case, which means that it is answered directly instead of recursively. In the factorial function, the factorial is coded to simply return the answer 1 for the base case of 1. Recursive functions are possible because each time the function is called, it gets its own stack frame—its own set of parameters, local variables, and return location. This allows each invocation of the function to have its own working scratch pad of information which doesn't interfere with the other invocations of the functions that are active at the time. See also *stack, stack frame, base case, inductive case.*

refactor In computer programming, refactoring refers to the process of rewriting how a computer program works, usually in order to make it more comprehensible, less error-prone, or more flexible for future expansion. Refactoring usually involves separating out different core components that had been previously linked together. For instance, when HTML was broken out into separate languages for content (HTML), presentation (CSS), and interaction (JavaScript), this was an instance of refactoring.

relative URL A relative URL is a partial URL that uses the current base URL as the starting point for the URL. In URLs, directories are separated by slashes (/), and the relative URL starts in the same directory as the base URL. For instance, if the base URL is `http://www.npshbook.com/example/example.html`, then a relative URL of `test.html` would refer to `http://www.npshbook.com/example/test.html`. A directory of `..` refers to the parent directory so a relative URL of `../test.html` would refer to `http://www.npshbook.com/test.html`. If a relative URL starts with a slash, it becomes an absolute path. See also *URL, fully-qualified URL, base URL, absolute path, directory.*

return value In a function, the return value is the final value yielded by the function. In JavaScript, the return value is specified in the function using the `return` keyword, which also returns control back to the code that called the function. The return value can be used as a value within an expression, assigned to a variable, or ignored. See also *function, expression, variable.*

right-hand side In an assignment statement, the right-hand side refers to the code on the right-hand side of the equal sign (=). The goal of the right-hand side is to yield a value

that can be stored to the location specified in the left-hand side. See also *assignment statement, left-hand side.*

ROM See *Read-Only Memory.*

scope See *variable scope.*

Secure Sockets Layer See *Transport Layer Security.*

sentinel A sentinel is a special value that tells a program that it has reached a special place in the data (such as the end). Oftentimes the null character (ASCII 0) will be used to mark the end of a sequence of letters. See also *data format, ASCII.*

server A server is a computer or a group of computers which provide a service to other computers on the network. Computers who connect to the server are usually called clients. See also *client.*

session layer The session layer is the fifth layer of a networking system according to the OSI model. The session layer deals with starting and stopping a conversation between computers. See also *OSI model, Transmission Control Protocol.*

SMTP SMTP (the Simple Mail Transfer Protocol) is the application layer protocol used to send email out on the Internet eventually winding up on the destination email server (it may have to be sent through more than one server to get there). This is a different protocol than the one used by a user to receive email from their email server, which is usually POP or IMAP. See also *application layer, POP, IMAP.*

special-purpose computer A special-purpose computer is a computer whose computational abilities are limited to specific types of computational operations and specific ways of combining them. See also *general-purpose computer.*

SSL The Secure Sockets Layer. See *Transport Layer Security.*

stack The stack is the part of computer memory that holds the call-specific information of all active functions. The stack usually holds things like parameters, local variables and the point in the code to return to when the function is finished. Think of it as a scratch-pad for active functions. It is called a "stack" because every time a function is called, the information for the new call (newly-created local variables, the parameter list, and the location where we left off the last function) is placed "on top of the stack." Then, when the function is finished, that information is pulled off of the top of the stack to let the previous function continue running. See also *stack frame.*

stack frame The stack holds information about all active function calls currently in progress. A stack frame is the information for a specific function call. The stack frame usually holds information like function parameters, the location in the code to return to when the function is finished, and the local variables being used by the current call of the current function. See also *recursive function.*

start tag In HTML, a start tag marks the beginning of a block of content that is used for a specific purpose. Start tags are wrapped in angled brackets so that they can be recognized by the computer as being a tag. For instance, a tag marking the start of a paragraph looks like `<p>`. See also *tag, end tag, markup language, HyperText Markup Language.*

string A string is a defined sequence of displayable characters. In JavaScript, strings are designated by enclosing them in double or single quotes (`"` or `'`). Each character in a strings is usually encoded using either ASCII or a Unicode-based system such as UTF-8 or UTF-32. See also *null-terminated string, Unicode, ASCII, UTF-8, UTF-32.*

syntax In any file format or computer programming language, the syntax of the language refers to the pieces of the language that can be included, and how they can be validly combined. For instance, in JavaScript, the syntax includes the different keywords (such as `if`, `for`, `function`, etc.), the different literals (such as numbers, strings, etc.), other parts of the language, and how they can be combined together to create a valid program. Syntax only refers to whether or not a computer can successfully understand the program. It does not refer to whether or not the computer successfully performs the function desired.

subclass In object-oriented programming, a subclass is a class whose default properties and methods are "inherited" from another class, known as the superclass. Inheritance allows specialized classes to be built quickly and easily from existing classes while allowing any functionality to be overridden as needed. See also *class, object-oriented programming.*

superclass See *subclass.*

tag In a markup language, a tag is a marker that indicates a specific usage for a piece of text. In HTML specifically, a tag is written using angled brackets with a start tag at the beginning of the content block and an end tag at the end of it. Tags indicate the start and end of pieces of content used for a specific purpose. For instance, the `<h1>` tag is used to mark level-1 headings, such as this: `<h1>This is a Level 1 Heading</h1>` See also *markup language, HyperText Markup Language, start tag, end tag.*

TCP See *Transmission Control Protocol*.

TCP/IP TCP/IP refers to the combined usage of the TCP and IP protocols as the foundation for communication on the Internet. See also *Transmission Control Protocol, Internet Protocol*.

text document A text document is a file that consists entirely of displayable characters, usually encoded in ASCII or UTF-8 (see Appendix B for more information on ASCII and UTF-8). Text documents can be edited using any standard text editor. However, text documents may also be specialized (such as HTML web pages) and have specific requirements for their format. In such cases, it is usually the user's responsibility to make sure that the document follows the proper requirements. See also *binary file*.

TLS See *Transport Layer Security*.

transport layer The transport layer is the fourth layer of a networking system according to the OSI model. The transport layer deals with breaking up data into packets, making sure that each packet is delivered appropriately, and making sure they are assembled in the right order on the other side. See also *OSI model, packet, Transmission Control Protocol*.

Transport Layer Security Transport Layer Security (TLS) is the most common presentation layer encryption method on the Internet. It is the successor to the previous Secure Sockets Layer (SSL) protocol. See also *presentation layer*.

Transmission Control Protocol The Transmission Control Protocol (TCP) is the protocol used on the Internet for the transport layer and the session layer. It is in charge of starting and stopping transmissions as well as making sure data arrives intact on each side. See also *transport layer, session layer, TCP/IP*.

Turing-complete programming language See *Universal programming language*.

type A type describes the set of valid values and available operations of a variable. Types are usually predefined by the programming language, though there are exceptions. See also *variable, class*.

typography Typography is an aspect of visual design that focuses on the way that words are laid out on a page.

undefined A variable or property is undefined if no value has been set for it. It literally means "no definition." See *null* for a fuller description.

Unicode Unicode is a system for representing all of the languages and writing of the world digitally. Unicode specifies over 100,000 characters/symbols. Unicode specifies a number for each character but does not specify how the computer represents that number. Other standards, such as UTF-8 and UTF-32, define how those numbers are represented on the computer. See also *UTF-8, UTF-32, ASCII.*

Uniform Resource Locator A Uniform Resource Locator (URL) is the standard method for identifying web content. For instance, `http://www.npshbook.com/` is the URL for accessing this book's website, and `http://www.amazon.com/exec/obidos/ASIN/0975283863` is the URL for buying a previous book of mine, *Engineering and the Ultimate.* See also *protocol, hostname, path, query string, anchor.*

Universal Serial Bus Universal Serial Bus (USB) is a specification for an interface that allows many different types of hardware to be plugged into a computer and used with minimal setup. See also *input/output system, peripheral.*

Universal programming language A Universal programming language (also called a Turing-complete language) is a programming language that can represent the entire gamut of computable functions (within practical limits of memory and time). Universal languages are *not* Universal because they have an advanced computation set—in fact, you can make a Universal language just with basic arithmetic and comparison operators. Universal languages are universal because they contain sufficient control structures (looping, function calls, if statements, etc.) to build new computable functions out of any starting set of operators. Universal languages are all equivalent in the computations that they can perform, though they may not be equivalent in other ways, such as input and output mechanisms and ease-of-use for particular applications. See also *domain-specific language, general-purpose computer, special-purpose computer, control structure.*

URL See *Uniform Resource Locator*

USB See *Universal Serial Bus.*

UTF-32 UTF-32 is another character encoding based on Unicode. This encoding uses four bytes per character.

UTF-8 UTF-8 is a popular character encoding based on Unicode. It is widely used because of its backward compatibility with ASCII. Because Unicode specifies over 100,000 characters, it takes more than one byte to record each character. However, ASCII only stores one byte per character. In order to combine these two standards, the first bit of

the byte (which is unused in standard ASCII) is set to 1 if the character needs more than one byte to hold it. This makes all ASCII files work in UTF-8 settings, but it means that it is harder to find the nth character of a string because you have to check each letter to see how many bytes it takes up. See also *data format, Unicode, ASCII, string*.

variable A variable is a named location (named by an identifier) in a computer program that is used to store a value. In JavaScript, variables are created either by declaring them as parameters in a function or by using the `var` keyword. Variables, as their name indicates, can vary by being assigned different values throughout the program. See also *syntax, identifier*.

variable scope A variable's scope refers to the places in a program that a particular variable can be accessed. Two common scopes in JavaScript are *global scope* and *function scope*. For instance, a variable in function scope cannot be directly accessed outside of the function itself. See also *global scope, function scope*.

virtual private network A virtual private network (VPN) is a system that bridges together computers and networks across the internet to act as if they were all on the local network. This is usually used for data security where the local area network allows for access to more secure resources than are available across the Internet. Therefore, it brings certain computers and networks into the local area network to share those resources.

von Neumann architecture The von Neumann architecture refers to the idea of putting both the program and the data it is operating on into the same memory. This allows for far more flexibility in the way that machines are built and used.

VPN See *virtual private network*.

WAN See *wide area network*.

whitespace Whitespace refers to any non-printing character such as regular spaces, the end-of-line character, and tabs. In HTML and XML, all whitespace is treated together as if it were a single space. This is done because the writer of HTML does not know the screen size that the document will be displayed on and cannot rely on the spacing in the output matching the spacing in the document. Therefore, document authors are supposed to use tags and stylesheets instead of whitespace to ensure proper spacing. See also *text document, HyperText Markup Language, Extensible Markup Language*.

wide area network A wide area network is a network that connects two local area networks that are geographically distant from each other. See also *local area network*.

while loop A while loop is a type of loop that takes the form `while(loop condition) { loop body }`. The loop condition is evaluated *before* each iteration of the loop body. If the loop condition is true, it executes the loop body. If the loop condition is false, the loop body is skipped and the program goes to the next statement. The loop is evaluated over and over again until the loop condition is false. See also *loop, loop condition, loop body*.

widget A widget is a generic term for a somewhat self-contained user interface element. A text field is a widget. A drop-down list is a widget.

WiFi WiFi refers to the most prominent protocol used for attaching a device to a wireless network. It is similar to Ethernet, but using radio waves. See also *Ethernet, network, local area network, data link layer*.

XHTML See *Extensible Markup Language*.

XML See *Extensible Markup Language*.

zero-based indexing Most computer programming languages (including JavaScript) start their array indexes at zero. This means that the first value of an array has an index of zero. This also means that the last value in an array has an index of one less than the length. So, for an array with four items, the first index is zero (as always) and the last index is three. This method is called zero-based indexing. This is different than mathematics, which uses the number one to refer to the first element of a set of values. See also *array, index*.

Appendix A

Operating System and Browser Specifics

JavaScript is a great programming language to learn because it can be used on any modern computer, using any browser. However, there are some minor differences between computers and operating systems so that things might look and work a little bit differently depending on which computer you use. When the main chapters reference a technique or a feature that might work differently on different computers, this appendix has the details on how to use that feature on your system.

However, there are hundreds of different systems and system configurations, and I can't possibly list them all in this book. All of the different versions of Windows (XP, 7, 8, 10, etc.), Mac (El Capitan, Yosemite, Mavericks, etc.), and Linux (Red Hat, Ubuntu, CentOS, etc.) have slightly different ways of doing things. Therefore, this appendix will cover just a few representative systems, which should give you enough background information to find the right setting on your own system. If you have questions on how to do this on your system, go to the website at **npshbook.com** and look through the FAQs and forum posts. If you are still having trouble after that, post your question on the forums and see if another developer can help you!

You will find that developers often wind up with much different settings than the average user. The reason for the difference is simple—ordinary users want all of the messy details hidden from them. Programmers, on the other hand, *use* the messy details to accomplish tasks. The average user wants to know *less* about what is going on behind the scenes but programmers need to know *more*. Therefore, the defaults, made for the average user, focus on hiding technical information. Programmers tend to adjust all of their settings to show all

Figure A.1: Finding the Location Bar

of the gritty details.

A.1   The Browser Location Bar

The location bar of your web browser is at the top of the window, usually at the center or the left (see Figure A.1. For most web browsers, the location bar also doubles as a search bar. You can use the location bar to directly type in or view a URL, or if you enter in something that doesn't look like a URL, the browser will try to use a search engine (like Google or Bing) to search for the terms you typed.

However, many locations bars have stopped actually displaying your complete location and hide several important details. Some browsers show it all, some browsers hide the protocol (i.e., `http`); some browsers hide everything but the domain name (i.e., `www.example.com`). Therefore, you should know how to get the location from the location bar if it doesn't show it automatically.

In most browsers, even if the whole URL is not displayed, if you copy and paste the URL to a different document, it will paste the *full* URL. If you want to see the full URL displayed while you browse, several browsers have options for that. In Safari, for instance, if you

go to the "Safari" menu, then click "Preferences" it will open up a dialog box. Under the "Advanced" settings, there is a checkbox that says "show full website address." If you click that, it will display much more of the URL. It still hides the protocol, but it will show you the rest.

A.2   Getting to the Command Line

The command line is a program that presents you with a screen that is similar to a pre-1980's computer screen—just lines of characters and a cursor where you can type. There is no mouse interaction and no pretty pictures—just you, your keyboard, and a bunch of text on the screen. The command line works like this: your cursor starts blinking next to a bit of text called the command prompt (it usually ends with #, $, or >). It is waiting for your command. After you type in a command, the computer runs it and spits the output to the screen. You know it has finished because you will see another command prompt as the last line of text.

Sometimes, if the command you run is interactive (such as `telnet`), the program itself will ask you or allow you to type responses or to control it in some way while it runs. You will know when it is finished because you will get another command prompt.

The command line can be a programmer's best friend. It allows a much more direct access to the computer than any other interface. Rather than wading through screen after screen of options and choices, the command line gives you instant access to the computer's resources. In addition, command line programs tend to give you more information about what is going on than their more graphical counterparts.

A lot of people are intimidated by the command line because it gives you no prompting and no help. But that is also what makes it powerful. Programmers often make their programs easy to use by limiting the user's options. In those cases, it is the program that tells the user what to do, and the program tries to prevent the user from doing anything out of the ordinary. The command line, on the other hand, obeys your commands. It doesn't tell you what to do, it doesn't even make suggestions. It just does what you say. That is a little scary, but it is also empowering.

Figure A.2: Getting to the Command Line in Windows

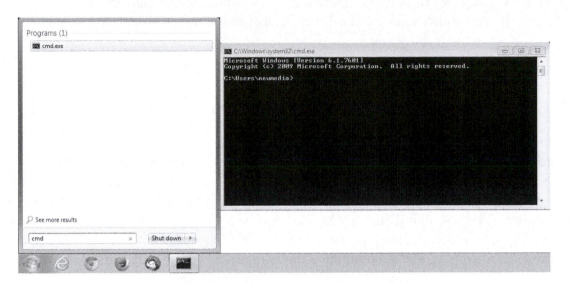

A.2.1   Getting to a Command Line in Windows

Windows is the hardest operating system in which to find a working command line. In every Windows version, Microsoft attempts to bury the command prompt a little deeper, and the command line tools are buried even further down. In Windows, the command line is a program called cmd.exe. When you hit the start button, you can usually search. Typing in cmd will usually bring up the program that you want (see Figure A.2).

However, in Windows, most of the important command line tools are missing, so you have to tell Windows to install them. In Windows 10, the process is to right-click the start button and select "Programs and Features." Then, select "Turn Windows features on or off" on the left-hand side. A list of features should open (see Figure A.3). The important one for us is "Telnet Client." Make sure that is selected, and then click "OK."

In other Windows versions, the process is very similar, but it usually is found under the "Programs" control panel.

Sometimes, the settings of the Windows telnet program are very messed up. If you are typing but can't see anything, that means that your settings are poorly set. There are two possibilities. The first possibility is that it is actually displaying what you are typing, but it moved it to the top-left of the screen instead of putting it where the cursor is. The second

Figure A.3: Activating Telnet in Windows

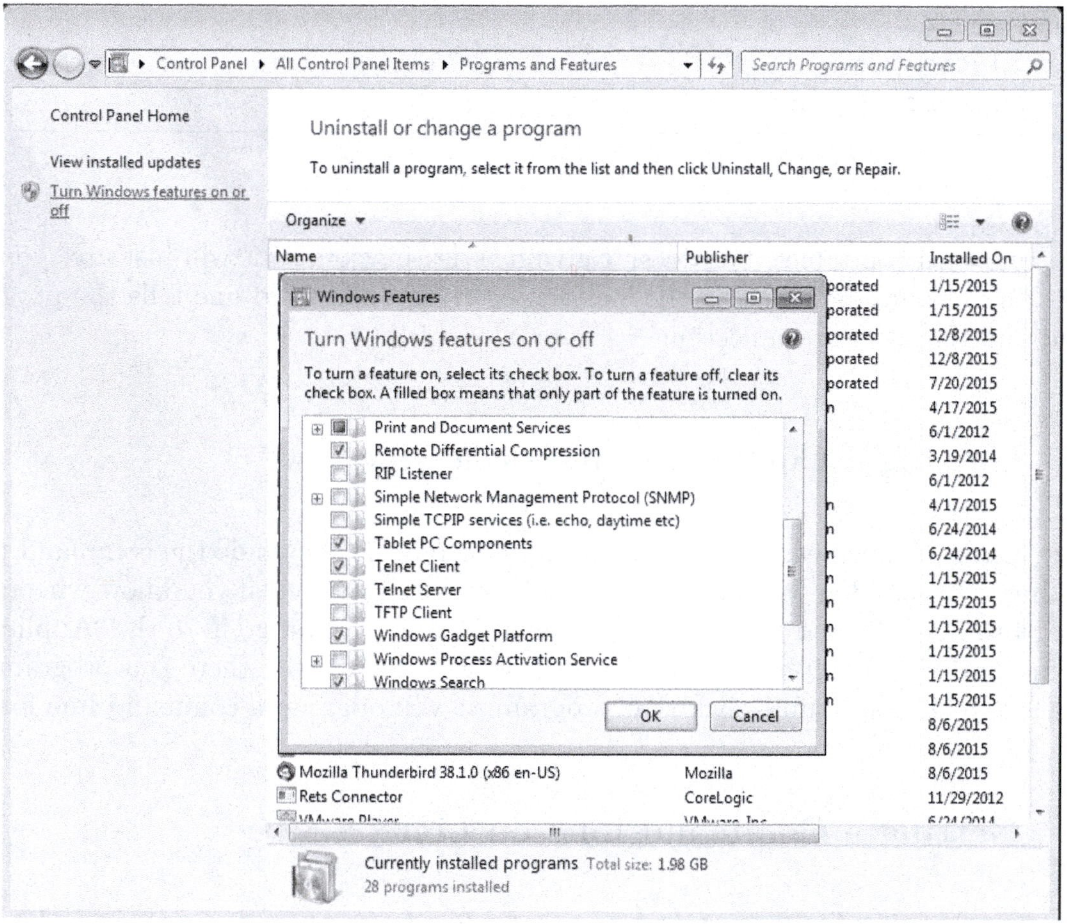

possibility is that your telnet has "localecho" set to "off." To fix that, you need to change
the way you use the `telnet` command.

If, for instance, you were going to say `telnet www.npshbook.com 80`, you would need to
type the following instead:

Figure A.4: Telnet with Turning On Local Echo

```
telnet
set localecho
open www.npshbook.com 80
```

The first line turns on telnet, but doesn't give it a destination, so it will just give you a new
prompt. The second line turns on the localecho setting. The third line tells the program to
go ahead and initiate the connection.

A.2.2   Getting a Command Line on a Mac

The Mac makes it much easier to get a command prompt. They hide the command prompt
so that unwary users don't accidentally stumble over it. However, if you know where it is, it
is not hard to find. To find it on most versions of MacOS X, first go in to the "Applications"
folder, and find the "Utilities" folder. Within the "Utilities" folder there is a program called
`Terminal.app`. If you double-click that program, it will open up a command line for you.

A.2.3   Getting a Command Line on Linux

For most people using Linux, getting a command line isn't much of a problem. Most Linux
users live on the command line. If you don't, somewhere on your desktop there is some menu
item that says "Terminal" or "Console" or "SH" or "TTY" or "Prompt." If it has an icon, it
probably looks like an old green-screen computer. That will be your command line.

A.3 Using a Text Editor

A text editor is a program that edits documents which are stored as one long string of text (for more information about text strings, see Chapter 4). A text editor *is not the same as a Word Processor*. A word processor certainly includes long strings of text, but it also includes other things, such as formatting features (underline, bold, italic, font family, font size, etc.) and non-text elements (such as images). Historically, word processing files have been binary files. This mean that the formatting functions were not described using text, but using raw numbers, since that is the normal way that computers operate on data. Because those files contained raw numbers (as opposed to text-encoded digits), they cannot be properly displayed in a text editor, which treats the entire file as one long string of characters. A **text document** is a document which *can be viewed* as simply a long string of text. Some file formats, such as HTML, include formatting instructions *as text* within the document. These files can be opened up with a text editor (which shows the bare formatting instructions themselves) as well as on a special viewer (a browser in the case of HTML), which would show the formatted version of the file.

There are numerous text editors available, each with their own advantages and disadvantages. However, one of the goals of this book is to work with the tools you already have. Therefore, we are going to focus on the text editor that shipped with your operating system. Each section below tells you how to get to your system-installed text editor.

A.3.1 Getting Windows Setup Properly

The first thing that you should do before editing text documents with Windows is to turn file extensions on. As described in Section 4.5, files use *filename extensions* to tell the user and the operating system what format the data is in. Unfortunately, in order to make it "easier" on nontechnical users, Windows often hides these extensions and just uses them internally to show the user an icon for the file format. This makes it difficult for building text files of various formats. We often need to modify the extension to tell the operating system what format we are writing in and to know precisely what the format of the file we are looking at is. Thankfully, Windows has an option to allow displaying of filename extensions. It works slightly differently in different versions of Windows, but the idea is the same.

For Windows XP and Windows 7 do the following:

1. Open up any folder on your system, such as your "Documents" folder.

2. Click on the "Tools" menu, then click on "Folder Options." For Windows 7 use the "Organize" menu in the toolbar instead.

3. Click on the "View" tab.

4. Under "Files and Folders" there is an option called "Hide extensions for known file types." Make sure this option is *not checked*.

5. Click on "Apply" and then "OK."

For more recent versions of Windows do the following:

1. Click on the Windows "Start" button.

2. Click on the "Control Panel" button.

3. Open up "Appearance and Personalization."

4. Click "Folder Options" or "File Explorer Options."

5. Click on the "View" tab.

6. Under "Advanced Settings" look for the option "Hide extensions for known file types" and make sure the checkbox is *not checked*.

7. You also might want to find the "Hidden files and folders" option and select "Show hidden files, folders, and drives." This isn't needed for this book, but I didn't ever know a programmer who didn't use that setting.

Now you will be able to see the filename extensions in Windows!

A.3.2 Using a Text Editor in Windows

The text editor that comes standard in Windows is called *Notepad*. On Windows 8 or newer, you can simply type in "notepad" on the start screen and then click the program to open

Figure A.5: Saving an HTML File with Notepad

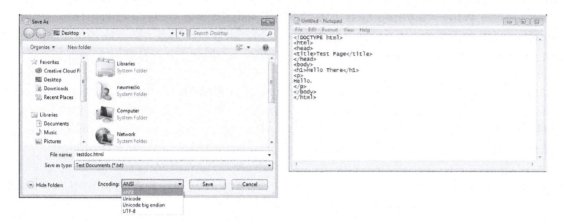

it. On earlier Windows versions, you need to click "Start," then go to "Programs," then "Accessories," and then click on "Notepad" to open it.

Once you have the program open, you can use the file menu to create, open, and save text documents. Be sure to pay special attention to the file extension you use to save documents. The operating system will use this extension to choose the program used to open the file. Generally, if you save a file with an extension other than `.txt`, you will not be able to open it back up in Notepad by double-clicking on it. Instead, you will have to open Notepad first, and then choose "Open" from Notepad's menu to load the file.

When you save files, be sure to set the file extension appropriately. Use `.html` for HTML files, `.css` For CSS files, and `.js` for JavaScript files. See Figure A.5.

A.3.3   Using a Text Editor in Mac OS

The text editor that comes standard in Mac OS is called *TextEdit*. However, TextEdit also acts as a word processor, so it is important to keep in mind which mode it is in! We will discuss how to switch modes shortly.

To open up TextEdit, you can just click on the Spotlight Search icon and type in "textedit." Clicking on the TextEdit icon will open up the application. You can also get to TextEdit through the Finder, by going to "Applications" and clicking on "TextEdit."

When TextEdit first starts, it is acting like a word processor, not a text editor. If you are in TextEdit, and it has a formatting bar (with buttons to do bold, italic, etc.), you are in the wrong mode. When opening text files with TextEdit, be sure to check the "Ignore Rich Text Commands" checkbox in order to open the file as a text file. If you get the formatting bar, you are in the wrong mode, and you must close and re-open the file.

When creating new files with TextEdit, you can easily switch from wordprocessing mode to text editing mode if it starts you in the wrong mode. Just click on the "Format" menu, and then click "Make Plain Text." Your document will now be treated as a text document. You can perform this action anytime before your first save without causing problems.

You can also set TextEdit to do text editing by default. To do that, go into the "TextEdit" menu, and then click "Preferences." Under the "New Document" tab, set the format to be "Plain Text." Under the "Open and Save" tab, check the checkbox that says "Display HTML files as HTML code instead of formatted text."

When you save files, be sure to set the file extension appropriately. Use `.html` for HTML files, `.css` For CSS files, and `.js` for JavaScript files. Also note that to open a text file, be sure to open up TextEdit first, and then open the file. Double-clicking on the file itself may open it up in some other application, such as your browser.

A.3.4   Using a Text Editor in Linux

Since there are so many different distributions of the Linux operating system, I cannot describe how each of them works, so I will cover Ubuntu. Text editing is a staple of Linux usage, so finding a text editor should not be a problem on any Linux distributions. Some popular text editors include Atom, Gedit, and Kate. If you do not already know how to use these, do not try to use Vi or Emacs if they are options. They are both powerful programs, but take a lot of time to learn to use—even just how to open and save a file!

In Ubuntu, to open up a text document, click on "Applications," then "Accessories," and then click on "Text Editor" (or it may be called "gedit"). This will open up the Gedit editor.

When you save files, be sure to set the file extension appropriately. Use `.html` for HTML files, `.css` For CSS files, and `.js` for JavaScript files. Also note that to open a text file, be sure to open up your text editor first, and then use your text editor to open the file. Double-clicking on the file itself may open it up in some other application, such as your browser.

A.3.5   Text Encoding Problems

Sometimes our text editors come up with some interesting surprises. The most common one is the text editor being set to write out using a different character encoding. Be sure, in the "Save" dialog boxes, that, if there is a character set option, that it is set to either "ASCII," "ANSI," or "UTF-8" (see Figure A.5). Also, be sure that any autocorrect features or auto-quoting/smart quoting features are turned off. In programming languages, if the language wants a double-quote character (i.e., "), the fancy curved quotes aren't going to work (i.e., "). However, some text editors will auto-replace one for the other. If that is happening to you, find the setting that is doing it, and switch it off!

To switch off smart quotes on the Mac's TextEdit program, go into the "TextEdit" menu and click "Preferences." The setting should appear under "Options." Turn off all of the smart quoting, smart dashing, and spell-correcting features.

A.4   Viewing the Source of an HTML Document

It comes as a surprise to people first learning HTML that they can easily see the HTML, CSS, and JavaScript code of any website. But, in fact, it is true, and it is true for a simple reason—in order for you to be able to *use* the web page, you have to *receive* it first. In addition, every major browser has the ability to show you the things that it downloaded.

A.4.1   Viewing the Source in Chrome

Chrome offers two different ways to view the source. The first way is to view the source *as initially downloaded*. In order to do this, once you are on a web page, first click on the "View" menu; then click on the "Developer" submenu and next click on "View Source." This will pop up a new window or tab with the source code to the page as it was downloaded.

However, JavaScript can also modify the page while you are looking at it. Therefore, Chrome also gives you a way to view the HTML of the page *as it appears now*. This tool is much more interactive and has many more features than the "View Source" menu option.

To make use of this tool, right-click (or control-click on a Mac) anywhere on the contents of the web page. This will open a context menu. Towards the bottom, click on the "Inspect"

Figure A.6: Viewing the Source Interactively on Chrome

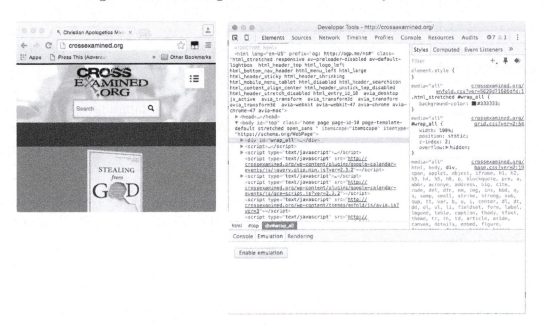

menu item. This will bring up the web page as a tree of elements (see Figure A.6). This view is the way that the browser itself thinks of the code.

A.4.2   Viewing the Source in Safari

Viewing the source in Safari is very similar, except that Safari hides the menus that programmers need by default in order to prevent them from confusing the rest of their users. Therefore, the first thing you need to do in Safari is turn on the developer tools.

To turn on the developer tools in Safari, go to the main "Safari" menu and find the "Preferences" menu under that. This will open up a dialog box with several tabs. Click on the "Advanced" tab. Towards the bottom, there will be a preference that says, "Show Develop menu in menu bar." Check that box, then close the dialog box. You will notice a new menu for Safari—the "Develop" menu.

Now, just like for Chrome, Safari will let you look at either the HTML source code as it

was originally transmitted to you, or the HTML as it presently exists after any JavaScript modifications to it. To view the source code as you downloaded it, just right-click on the contents of the web page, and click "View Source." To view the source code as it presently exists, just right-click on the contents of the web page, and click "Inspect."

A.4.3 Viewing the Source in Internet Explorer

To view the source code of a web page in Internet Explorer, simply right-click on the web page and choose "View Source" from the context menu.

A.5 Finding the URL of an Image on the Web

Finding the URL of an image on the web is actually really, really easy. In nearly every browser, all you need to do is to find the image you want to look at, right-click on it (use control-click if you are on a Mac), and there will be a menu option that allows you to copy the address of the image to your clipboard. In Chrome, the menu option is called "Copy Image Address." Note that we don't want to copy the image *itself*, just the URL (which Chrome calls its *address*).

In Internet Explorer, the process is a little different. For Internet Explorer, first right-click on the image and then choose "Properties" from the context menu. This will open up a popup window that has the URL of the image in it. You can then copy the URL from that window.

Once you copy the image URL, you can paste the address anywhere you like using control-v on Windows or command-v on a Mac.

When using Safari and Chrome, you can also open up the image in a new window or tab using the menu titled "Open Image in a New Tab." Then, you can see the image all by itself and copy the URL from the address bar of the browser.

Every once in a while, you will find images that you can't right-click on for an image URL. This is usually either because the image is a background image (this trick only works for foreground images) or because they are using a non-standard method of displaying the image. Nonetheless, there are innumerable images on the web whose URLs are available just

by right-clicking on the image.

A.6   Opening Up the JavaScript Console

The JavaScript console is a little like the command line (Section A.2), except that instead of running application programs, you can run JavaScript commands. The JavaScript console also will give you feedback about any errors that the JavaScript interpreter finds while it is trying to run your programs. Since you are new programmers, you will probably make a lot of silly mistakes (like putting in a colon when you meant to put in a semicolon), and such mistakes will break your entire program. Often, the only way to find out the problem is to open up the JavaScript console and look at the error messages.

In addition, since the JavaScript console allows you to enter in commands, it makes it easy to try out ideas. If you want to try to see if some small piece of code does what you want it to do, you can type it in the console and get immediate feedback.

To get to the console in Google Chrome or Safari, first open up a web page (even if it is one of your own). Next, right-click (or control-click on a Mac) on the page content. This will open up a context menu. Click on the "Inspect Element" menu item.

This will open the "Developer Tools" window, either at the bottom of your current screen or in a new window. In either case, the Developer Tools window will be tied to the window that you right-clicked on.

In Internet Explorer, the process is almost exactly the same, except rather than right-clicking on the page, you click the gear icon at the top right of the page, and choose "Developer Tools" (see Figure A.7). You can also get there by just pushing the F12 key.

Developer Tools is a whole suite of tools to help you analyze your HTML, CSS, and JavaScript code. When it first opens, the tab at the top labeled "Elements" is open. This is the HTML of your current page, arranged as a tree of elements. As you mouse over each bit of HTML on this tab, it will highlight the relevant portion of the web page on the main window. To the right, it lists the styles that are associated with that element and which selectors caused the style to be there.

The tab we are most interested in for this section is the "Console" tab along the top. Click on that tab to open up the JavaScript console. It should have a prompt that lets you know

Figure A.7: Getting to Developer Tools in Internet Explorer

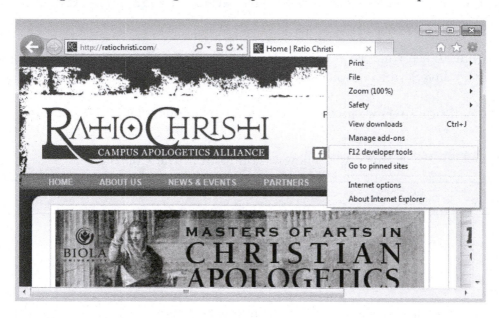

you can enter in JavaScript. If there are any red lines above the prompt, those are errors that the browser has encountered while trying to load the page and run the JavaScript code on the page.

So, the first thing to do is to click next to the prompt to make sure that the input line is active. Next, type in a single word of gibberish, like `asdfasdfasdf`, and then hit enter. It should give you back an error, which says something like `Uncaught ReferenceError: asdfasdfasdf is not defined`. This is one of the many error messages you can get. This one in particular means that it was trying to look up a variable for you (the variable `asdfasdfasdf`), and it couldn't find it.

Now, let's try defining a variable. Type in the following:

Figure A.8: Create a Variable in the Console

```
var myvar = 23;
```

After this, the console will print out `undefined`. After each line you type, the console will

print out the value of the line you typed out. In this case, assigning a variable doesn't yield a value, so it says the value is `undefined`. The variable, `myvar`, gets a value, but the whole statement doesn't return a value.

Now, if we want to see what is *in* `myvar`, we can just type `myvar` on a line by itself and hit enter. Then the JavaScript console will print out **23**.

We can even call functions with the console. Type the following in the console:

Figure A.9: Show a Popup from the Console

```
alert("Hello There!");
```

The web page will bring up an alert saying "Hello There!"

Basically, anything that is valid JavaScript can be typed into the console. In addition, we can also make use of any variables and functions that were defined by the JavaScript attached to the web page.

In addition to the JavaScript console, Google Chrome has many other tools for you to use. The "Sources" tab allows you to look at all JavaScript code that is used by the web page. The "Network" tab allows you to see any external file that the browser tries to access using HTML (with `<img>` tags, for instance) or using JavaScript. This tab gives you all of the information you need to know about where the data came from, how big it is, what the actual data is, and how long it took to download it. There are several other tabs, but these are by far the most often used.

Each browser has its own way of accessing a JavaScript console, but they are all very similar to Google Chrome's.

A.7   What to Do When a Program Doesn't Work

Every programmer has experienced it. You typed in a program, tried to run it, and then *nothing happens*. What went wrong?

I can't diagnose every problem you will have, but I can give you a short checklist of things to look for. There are some basic mistakes that are made over and over again, and I can hopefully cover them here.

If you put in a program, and the program did not work at all, or it did not work the way you wanted it to, here are some basic things to check:

1. Did you save your file as a text file with the proper extension? If your text editor has a formatting toolbar (with bold, italic, etc.), you are probably not saving your file as a text file. Convert your file to text mode and then save it (see Section A.3). Also be sure that you have file extensions turned on (see Section A.3.1). If file extensions are off, even if you specify a file extension, it will add a new, hidden file extension that you don't want.

2. Did you type in the program correctly? Computer programs are very sensitive, and *every character matters.* Changing one little character can be the difference between a successful and an unsuccessful program. Did you put in semicolons, or did you accidentally type a colon instead? Did you misspell a variable name somewhere? Did you get both the opening brace and the closing brace? Any mistake like this will cost you your entire program. Check carefully. After a while, it becomes second nature. I can now look at a page of code and spot such errors immediately. That comes with experience—for now, you have to hunt and check everything.

3. Did your text editor substitute in curly quotes for your regular quotes? Some text editors think you are typing a document and want to make your text fancy. When you type in a regular double-quote (") they will auto-substitute curly quotes ("). This causes programming languages to go bonkers because they are very definite about the characters they are looking for. If your text editor is doing this, see Section A.3.5.

4. Open up a JavaScript console (see Section A.6). Are there any error messages displayed? If there are, you can click on the filename and it will show you where in your file the error occurred. Also, you can search the Internet for the error message to get help.

5. If your program runs a little before it stops or if it runs but runs wrongly, you can often figure out what is wrong by adding in a lot of `alert()` messages in your code, so you can follow its progress. You can use `alert()` to display not only messages, but also the contents of variables. This allows you to identify exactly what is going on in the code.

6. Check your value types. One of the most common programming errors is to forget what type of value is stored in a variable. For instance, any time you get a value back from a `prompt()`, it will be a string. If you wanted a number, you need to *convert* it to a number first (using `parseInt` or a similar function).

7. Check your loops. If your program has a loop, you have to be sure that there is some way to get out of the loop. If there is not a condition that allows it to exit, then you have not properly programmed it. Also be sure that the things you want it to do *every* time are *inside* the loop body, and the things that you only want to happen once are *outside* the loop body.

8. Search engines are your friend. As a programmer, I always have a search engine open, and check the Internet to see if someone is having a similar problem.

9. Find a friend. Preferably, find a friend that has done some programming before. No matter what, you will each find mistakes that the other one didn't see. Two heads are better than one.

10. Check the forums. The website for this book, `www.npshbook.com`, has a reader forum for anyone with a question. Be sure to be as detailed as possible with your question. If you are doing an exercise from this book, be sure to say which one, and paste your code into your message. Don't worry about asking dumb questions—we've all been at the beginning.

Appendix B

Character Encoding Issues

B.1　A Short History of Character Encodings

In computer programming, the problem of how to represent character strings (i.e., lines of text) is an ever-present issue. Generally, a string of characters is represented by an array of numbers, where each number represents one character (letter, digit, punctuation mark, etc.) of text. The problem then becomes a question of which numbers represent which characters. If every program had its own way of converting numbers to characters, it would be nearly impossible for two programs to communicate. If one program used the number 6 to mean the letter F, but another program used 6 to represent a comma, trying to get those two programs to talk to each other would require code to translate the number from one system to another, which would be a lot of work. In addition, if every programmer had to solve this problem for their own program, that would take a lot of effort for every program that deals with character strings (which is basically every program).

Therefore, early on in computer programming, standards were developed for representing character strings. Not only was ASCII developed early in computing, but the standards were already in place before computers existed thanks to telegraph lines. The telegraph was a machine used in the 1800s and early 1900s for sending and receiving messages over long distances. It worked by sending short and long pulses over long wires. If you see Morse code printed out, it usually uses dots for the short pulses and dashes for the long pulses. For instance, the letter A is represented as .- in Morse code, and the letter X is represented as -..-. In Morse code, the more common letters have shorter codes, and the less common

letters have longer codes, making it easier for a telegraph operator to type messages.

In the mid-1800s, engineers developed the automated telegraph, which allowed users to type on typewriter-like machines. However, variable-length codes, which were great for manual telegraph operation, made these machines difficult to implement. Therefore, they developed a new code, called the Baudot code, which had a fixed-length character size. Eventually, the need for lowercase letters, punctuation, and other similar needs led to other codes with more expansive alphabets. In the 1960s, ASCII was developed as a further expansion and standardization for telegraph systems. Another standard, called EBCDIC, was developed for IBM mainframes based on the punch card system of early computers. However, EBCDIC has pretty much been completely superceded by ASCII and Unicode. ASCII gained wide use in computers both because it was already an international standard and because it fit nicely in the 8-bit byte that was popular in computers.

B.2   Unicode and International Character Sets

The ASCII system, however, is far from perfect. Its primary problem is that it only represents characters from the English language. As more and more countries started using computers, each of them had their own language with their own alphabet! Even more, some of the alphabets had more than 255 characters in them, and so they could not be represented by a single byte. In the beginning, some tried to accommodate for this by using extensions to ASCII, or by using a separate character set for each language. However, as the importance of multilingual documents grew, the limitations of these approaches became clear, and the need for a universal code that contained all characters from all languages became evident. Therefore, a larger list of characters had to be made in order to encompass all of the world's alphabets.

This list of characters is called **Unicode**, which currently has over 95,000 characters! Unicode assigns a number to each character for reference, but does not by itself specify how those numbers are to be encoded. For instance, the UTF-16 standard uses two bytes for every character, but the UTF-32 uses four bytes for every character. They all represent the same Unicode numbers, but they accomplish that in different ways.

When Unicode was developed, most files were still written using ASCII. A way was needed to bridge the gap between ASCII and Unicode. Therefore, developers created an encoding of Unicode, called UTF-8, which looks like ASCII and uses single bytes for common English characters, but it uses multiple bytes for non-English characters. This allowed easier migra-

tion between older programs that only understood ASCII and newer programs which wanted to support users from every country. If your document only used English characters, it was identical whether it was encoded in ASCII or UTF-8. The differences only came when you ventured into other character sets. UTF-8 is less efficient for processing, but its ability to interoperate with older programs has made it the default in many applications. JavaScript uses UTF-8 for its encodings by default.

B.3   An Abbreviated ASCII Table

Because ASCII is still popular and is the same as UTF-8 for English characters, this book provides a list of ASCII character codes below. These are also important for some of the programs in Appendix C. The list below contains ASCII codes in decimal, octal, and hexadecimal. If the meaning of an ASCII code in enclosed like `<this>`, it is a non-printable character, such as a tab, a carriage return, or a control sequence. Control sequences are used to embed extra communication information in a string of text that is not used for user display, such as a record separator, or to mark the end of a transmission. The lesser-used ASCII codes are skipped in the table below.

Decimal	Hexadecimal	Octal	Meaning
0	00	000	`<null>`
9	09	011	`<tab>`
13	0d	015	`<carriage return>`
30	1e	036	`<record separator>`
31	1f	037	`<field separator>`
32	20	040	`<space>`
33	21	041	!
34	22	042	"
35	23	043	#
36	24	044	$
37	25	045	%
38	26	046	&

Decimal	Hexadecimal	Octal	Meaning
39	27	047	'
40	28	050	(
41	29	051	)
42	2a	052	*
43	2b	053	+
44	2c	054	,
45	2d	055	–
46	2e	056	.
47	2f	057	/
48	30	060	0
49	31	061	1
50	32	062	2
51	33	063	3
52	34	064	4
53	35	065	5
54	36	066	6
55	37	067	7
56	38	070	8
57	39	071	9
58	3a	072	:
59	3b	073	;
60	3c	074	<
61	3d	075	=
62	3e	076	>
63	3f	077	?
64	40	100	@
65	41	101	A
66	42	102	B
67	43	103	C
68	44	104	D
69	45	105	E
70	46	106	F
71	47	107	G
72	48	110	H
73	49	111	I
74	4a	112	J

Decimal	Hexadecimal	Octal	Meaning
75	4b	113	K
76	4c	114	L
77	4d	115	M
78	4e	116	N
79	4f	117	O
80	50	120	P
81	51	121	Q
82	52	122	R
83	53	123	S
84	54	124	T
85	55	125	U
86	56	126	V
87	57	127	W
88	58	130	X
89	59	131	Y
90	5a	132	Z
91	5b	133	[
92	5c	134	\
93	5d	135	]
94	5e	136	^
95	5f	137	_
96	60	140	`
97	61	141	a
98	62	142	b
99	63	143	c
100	64	144	d
101	65	145	e
102	66	146	f
103	67	147	g
104	68	150	h
105	69	151	i
106	6a	152	j
107	6b	153	k
108	6c	154	l
109	6d	155	m
110	6e	156	n

Decimal	Hexadecimal	Octal	Meaning
111	6f	157	o
112	70	160	p
113	71	161	q
114	72	162	r
115	73	163	s
116	74	164	t
117	75	165	u
118	76	166	v
119	77	167	w
120	78	170	x
121	79	171	y
122	7a	172	z
123	7b	173	{
124	7c	174		
125	7d	175	}
126	7e	176	~

Appendix C

Additional Machine Language Programs

If you enjoyed the machine programs in Chapter 5, this appendix has a few others you can try. If you are really brave, you can even try to write one of your own!

C.1 Multiplying Numbers

Since this machine does not have a multiply instruction, multiplications have to happen by repeated addition. Therefore, this program will take two numbers and multiply them together by repeated addition. The numbers that are multiplied will be in memory locations 61 and 62, and the result of the multiplication will be stored in location 63.

Here is the program:

Figure C.1: Machine Language Program to Multiply Two Numbers

0 22	1 0	2 61	3 22	4 1	5 62	6 20	7 2
8 0	9 20	10 3	11 0	12 20	13 5	14 1	15 21
16 4	17 1	18 37	19 4	20 3	21 65	22 36	23 4
24 133	25 2	26 0	27 133	28 3	29 564	30 15	
31 0	32 25	33 63	34 2	35 0	36 0	37 0	38 0
39 0	40 0	41 0	42 0	43 0	44 0	45 0	46 0
47 0	48 0	49 0	50 0	51 0	52 0	53 0	54 0
55 0	56 0	57 0	58 0	59 0	60 8	61 4	62 0

This program stores the first number in register 0 and the second number in register 1. The program works by repeatedly adding the number in register 0 the number of times specified in register 1. Register 2 holds the results so far and register 3 holds the number of times we have performed the addition so far. Register 4 is used for holding comparison values. Register 5 holds the number 1 so we can add it to register 1 after each repetition.

C.2   Writing to the Screen

This program introduces a new piece of hardware—the screen. This screen will be based on really old types of screens—old-school text terminals. If you haven't seen them, they are like typewriters. No graphics, no windows, just text on the screen.

The way the screen will work is that the screen will read the last row of numbers in the Computer Memory page (memory locations 56–63) and display a single line of text based on those numbers. Each number will represent one letter to be displayed on the screen, based on the ASCII code for the letter (see Chapter 4 and Appendix B for more on ASCII codes). In addition to the standard codes, we will also treat the number 0 as a blank character. So, if the last line of of the computer memory was 72, 69, 76, 76, 79, 0, 0, 0, the screen would say HELLO. At the end of step 8, if any of these numbers have changed, the screen should update what it is displaying.

So, for our first program with displays, we will simply read the number in memory location

55. If it is greater than or equal to 100, we will write out the word Big onto the display, and if it is less than 100 we will write the word Sm to the display (I had to abbreviate "Small" to make the code fit).

Here is the program:

Figure C.2: Machine Language Program to Multiply Two Numbers

0	1	2	3	4	5	6	7
22	0	55	20	1	100	37	0
8	9	10	11	12	13	14	15
1	97	27	0	20	2	83	25
16	17	18	19	20	21	22	23
56	2	20	2	109	25	57	2
24	25	26	27	28	29	30	31
0	0	0	20	2	66	25	56
32	33	34	35	36	37	38	39
2	20	2	105	25	57	2	20
40	41	42	43	44	45	46	47
2	103	25	58	2	0	0	0
48	49	50	51	52	53	54	55
0	0	0	0	0	0	0	0
56	57	58	59	60	61	62	63
0	0	0	0	0	0	0	0

C.3   Writing a Number to the Screen

Now, in all of the arithmetic that we have done, we have ended up with a number that we have stored in memory. However, if we were to copy that number to the screen, we would get weird results because the screen would think that it was an ASCII code for some other letter. For instance, the result of the first program in this appendix was 32. If we copied the number 32 to the screen area, it would look up what the value of ASCII code 32 is, and it would find out that it was a blank space! Therefore, we would see nothing on the screen.

So, if we had a number, how would we display it on the screen? Well, look at the ASCII codes. The digits go from 48 to 57. If it was a single-digit number (i.e., less than 10), then we could simply add 48 to the number and that would be the answer. For multi-digit numbers, it is more complicated because we would have to repeatedly divide by 10 for each digit.

However, for this program, we are just going to do the single-digit case. We are going to load a single-digit number from memory location 55, convert it to its ASCII code, and write it to the screen.

Here is the code:

Figure C.3: Machine Language Program to Multiply Two Numbers

0	1	2	3	4	5	6	7
22	0	55	20	1	100	37	0
8 1	**9** 97	**10** 27	**11** 0	**12** 20	**13** 2	**14** 83	**15** 25
16 56	**17** 2	**18** 20	**19** 2	**20** 109	**21** 25	**22** 57	**23** 2
24 0	**25** 0	**26** 0	**27** 20	**28** 2	**29** 66	**30** 25	**31** 56
32 2	**33** 20	**34** 2	**35** 105	**36** 25	**37** 57	**38** 2	**39** 20
40 2	**41** 103	**42** 25	**43** 58	**44** 2	**45** 0	**46** 0	**47** 0
48 0	**49** 0	**50** 0	**51** 0	**52** 0	**53** 0	**54** 0	**55** 0
56 0	**57** 0	**58** 0	**59** 0	**60** 0	**61** 0	**62** 0	**63** 0

C.4 Going Further

Now that you know how machine language works, you might try writing your own program using this simplified system. The first thing you might try is combining the multiply program with the program to display a number and try to display the result on the screen (although it will only work if the answer is a single digit). The possibilities, though, are limitless, though your imaginations will probably require more than an 8x8 grid for memory.

If you enjoy this sort of programming, a forthcoming book in the Programmer's Toolbox series is tentatively titled *Under the Hood: Learning How Software Works at the Lowest Levels*. It is about assembly language, which is similar to machine language except that instead of writing out the numbers, you would write out the opcode itself. In addition, while the machine language we are dealing with here was invented as a learning tool, *Under the Hood* covers a real machine—the x86 family of processors.

While most programmers never need to program in machine language anymore, my hope is that doing these exercises will have accustomed your mind to the computer's way of thinking, which will help you be a better programmer in *any* programming language.

CPSIA information can be obtained
at www.ICGtesting.com
Printed in the USA
LVOW04*2249080517

533708LV00025B/706/P

Project Success
Critical Factors and Behaviours
Emanuel Camilleri
Hardback: 978-0-566-09228-2
Ebook: 978-0-566-09229-9

Strategic Project Risk Appraisal and Management
Elaine Harris
Paperback: 978-0-566-08848-3
Ebook: 978-0-7546-9211-9

Successful OSS Project Design and Implementation
Requirements, Tools, Social Designs and Reward Structures
Edited by Hind Benbya and Nassim Belbaly
Hardback: 978-0-566-08795-0
Ebook: 978-1-4094-0957-1

The Project Risk Maturity Model
Measuring and Improving Risk Management Capability
Martin Hopkinson
Hardback and CD-ROM: 978-0-566-08879-7
Ebook: 978-1-4094-2646-2

Tools for Complex Projects
Kaye Remington and Julien Pollack
Hardback: 978-0-566-08741-7
Ebook: 978-1-4094-0892-5

Visit **www.gowerpublishing.com** and

- search the entire catalogue of Gower books in print
- order titles online at 10% discount
- take advantage of special offers
- sign up for our monthly e-mail update service
- download free sample chapters from all recent titles
- download or order our catalogue